£- 16.95

CRIMINAL LITIGATION AND SENTENCING

CRIMINAL LITIGATION AND SENTENCING

Inns of Court School of Law

BLACKSTONE PRESS LIMITED

First published in Great Britain 1996 by Blackstone Press Limited,
9–15 Aldine Street, London W12 8AW. Telephone 0181-740 2277

ISBN: 1 85431 573 0

British Library Cataloguing in Publication Data
A CIP catalogue record for this book is available from the British Library.

Typeset by Style Photosetting Ltd, Mayfield, East Sussex
Printed by Ashford Colour Press, Gosport, Hants

FOREWORD

These Manuals are designed primarily to support the teaching of the Bar Vocational Course. This course was introduced at the Inns of Court School of Law in 1989, being specifically designed to equip students with practical skills and the procedural and evidential knowledge that they will need to start their legal professional careers. This course has been greeted as a major step forward in legal professional training and it has attracted substantial interest.

The Manuals have been written by teaching staff at the Inns of Court School of Law and by a range of members of the Bar. The Manuals are designed to cover all the areas of skill and knowledge which research has shown are important for the new practitioner, and the emphasis throughout is on taking a practical and professional approach. Although the Manuals are produced for a specific course their range is such that they should be of interest to all those concerned with legal training.

The whole range of Manuals has been fully revised for 1996–97. The number of Manuals has been increased to allow for additional coverage of individual skills areas and of professional conduct, and substantial parts of the materials in the Manuals have been rewritten. This has been done to reflect developments in legal skills training since the Manuals were originally written, and to reflect the experience of staff of the needs of those undergoing legal skills training.

The Manuals will continue to be revised annually, both to keep them fully up to date and to take into account the many useful comments made by practitioners, teaching staff and students. The development of legal vocational training can only be seen as an ongoing process for all those concerned in achieving and maintaining high standards. All comments are welcome, and should be addressed to the Course Director at the Inns of Court School of Law.

The enthusiasm of the staff at Blackstone Press Ltd and their efficiency in arranging the production and publication of these Manuals is much appreciated.

The Hon. Mr Justice Hooper
Chairman of the Board of Governors
of the Inns of Court School of Law
September 1996

CONTENTS

PREFACE

Criminal litigation covers the procedural rules which govern a criminal case. It spans the magistrates' and youth court as well as the Crown Court and the various appellate courts. It is crucial for anyone who may practise in the criminal courts (including all barristers, whether that is their primary intention or not) to have the more important of these rules at their fingertips. To be able to deal effectively with a criminal case means that a barrister must have a sound grasp of the main rules of criminal procedure, and must be able to apply them. It also means that where those rules are capable of different interpretations, the practitioner must be able to argue for the interpretation which favours his or her case. To do this, some understanding of the purpose behind the procedural rules is necessary. Rote learning is not enough.

This Manual deals with the rules of criminal litigation in such a way that the reader should be assisted to apply them in a practical context. The complementary subject of sentencing, which in practice is an integral part of criminal litigation, is dealt with in more detail in the second part of the Manual. Attention is devoted both to the process of sentencing and to the factors which may influence what sentence is actually passed. The Manual as a whole is firmly set in a practical context, with examples, questions and problems to help the reader apply the principles of criminal procedure and sentencing to cases as they are encountered in practice.

As a result, the Manual ought to provide assistance not only in acquiring a grasp of the relevant rules, but in performing the tasks associated with the skills of the barrister — including applying for (or opposing) bail, advising in conference on plea and sentence, delivering a plea in mitigation, and making the various procedural submissions and speeches which occur during the criminal process.

TABLE OF CASES

TABLE OF STATUTES

CRIMINAL LITIGATION

ONE

INTRODUCTION

1.1 Aims of the Course

The main intention of those responsible for designing both the Criminal Litigation element of the Vocational Course, and this Manual, has been to make the subject both real and practical. The Criminal Litigation Course should instil students with a knowledge of how the criminal justice system actually works; then give them the opportunity to demonstrate that they have assimilated such knowledge and are able to make the decisions which a barrister could find himself or herself making in practice.

1.2 Objectives of the Course

By the end of the course, and having read this Manual, you should be:

(a) Familiar with the progress of a case through the criminal courts, understanding the various stages and what each stage involves.

(b) Able to prepare for a hearing in the magistrates' court or Crown Court, knowing what the procedure will be in court and what matters will need to be covered.

(c) Capable of taking informed decisions (and, if necessary, advising your client on how to act) with regard to the various different paths that a case can take, both as to its final resolution and the intermediate hearings.

(d) Able to decide whether or not a case merits an appeal against some decision — whether it be conviction, sentence or some procedural matter.

(e) Able to prepare properly for an appeal and advise your client which is the most suitable method of appeal (where a choice exists).

1.3 The Manual

The Manual is designed primarily for use in conjunction with the Criminal Litigation classes on the Bar Vocational Course. It should prepare students to deal with a particular topic as well as supporting specific classes through the material it contains. It is also designed to stand alone as a practical and sensible guide to legal practice in the criminal courts of England and Wales. It contains most of the 'bare bones' of what anyone starting on a career in the criminal courts needs to know; it devotes rather less space to the remoter world of the Court of Appeal and the House of Lords.

Throughout the text, references will be found to other sources (see **1.6** below). These include law reports and statutes, and there are also references to relevant chapters in the two main works used by practitioners, *Archbold* and *Blackstone's Criminal Practice.* Occasional reference is also made to *Stone's Justices' Manual* (everything you need to know for the magistrates' court), the excellent book by Christopher Emmins and John Sprack, *Emmins on Criminal Procedure,* and to articles in periodicals (notably the

Criminal Law Review). These references are intended to indicate other sources of information either more eloquent, more authoritative or more detailed than this Manual. They should all promote an understanding of the subject. The Manual is a concise and, it is hoped, readable guide, both by way of introduction and as a source of practical knowledge.

1.3.1 THE STRUCTURE OF THE MANUAL

The Criminal Litigation Course starts at the beginning of the process (e.g. being charged with an offence) and works its way through to the possible endings — acquittal, conviction and sentence, appeal. This Manual reflects that pattern because this seems to be the best way of assisting students to understand the various practices and procedures that govern the passage of a case through the criminal courts. The Manual starts with preliminary matters such as powers of arrest, then the commencement of criminal proceedings against an accused person. Having dealt with the subject of bail, the Manual continues by looking at what happens when an accused person first appears in court once proceedings have started. The usual way of disposing of a case — summary trial — is next on the list, followed by a brief examination of the way that young people are treated by the criminal justice system. The focus then shifts to the Crown Court — considering first how cases are sent there (committal for trial), then the drafting of an indictment and the different pleas that might be offered by a defendant. Criminal Litigation ends with chapters on trial in the Crown Court and appeals from that court to the Court of Appeal and beyond. The Manual itself concludes with several chapters on sentencing, which is taught as a separate related subject on the Vocational Course.

1.4 Structure and Relationship of the Courts

All cases begin in the magistrates' court. A youth court is a type of magistrates' court which deals exclusively with juveniles. The vast majority of cases will be tried in the magistrates' court and will end there (unless the accused is committed to the Crown Court for sentence, or appeals to either the Crown Court or the High Court). The remaining cases will begin in the magistrates' court but be transferred for trial to the Crown Court with the possibility of an appeal to the Court of Appeal. From both the Court of Appeal and the High Court it is possible, though rare, to appeal to the House of Lords on matters of law. The interrelationship of the courts is set out in **Figure 1.1**.

1.5 The Civil Jurisdiction of the Magistrates' Court

It is appropriate at this stage to say something about the civil jurisdiction of magistrates. Although the magistrates' court is known primarily as a criminal court, it does have the power to deal with non-criminal cases. The magistrates' court is given such powers as it has by Acts of Parliament — it has no inherent jurisdiction. Numerous Acts establish the jurisdiction of the court to deal with an amazing variety of work, from excluding violent partners from the family home to granting permission to cafes to stay open after midnight. The most significant aspects for a barrister of the magistrates' jurisdiction over civil matters are, perhaps, their role in family or domestic proceedings and their power to grant licences in connection with the sale of alcohol.

1.5.1 FAMILY PROCEEDINGS

The main statute covering this area is the Domestic Proceedings and Magistrates' Courts Act 1978, but frequent reference should also be made to the Children Act 1989. Since October 1991, when dealing with matrimonial matters, magistrates sit as a 'family proceedings court', pursuant to the Children Act 1989. Such courts must be constituted in a similar way to youth courts (which deal with young offenders), in that they should usually have at least one man and one woman magistrate to hear each case. Stipendiary magistrates may sit in the family proceedings court.

Figure 1.1 Structure and Relationship of the Courts

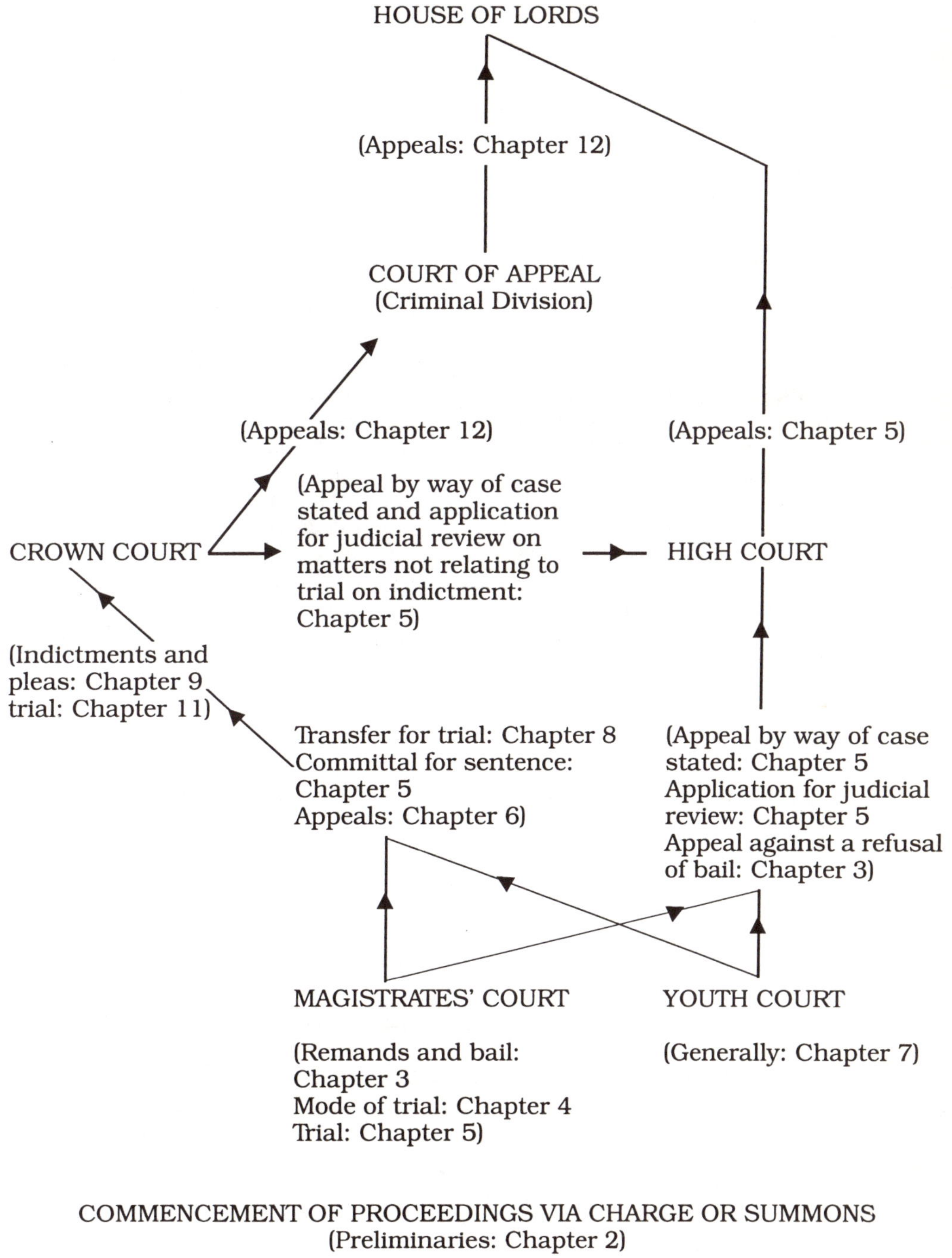

A husband or wife may apply to the family proceedings court for financial provision under the Domestic Proceedings and Magistrates' Courts Act 1978. Such provision may be for themselves or any child of the family. The family proceedings court also has power to order a party to a marriage not to use or threaten violence against their spouse or a child of the family; also, in certain circumstances, to exclude a violent partner from the matrimonial home. Applications for the adoption of children may be made to the family proceedings court, as may other applications concerning children. Following the implementation of the Children Act 1989, the jurisdiction of the family proceedings court is quite similar to that of the County Court and High Court in a number of areas. The choice of court will often depend on the need for urgency, what other proceedings are currently proceeding with regard to the same people, and the complexity or gravity of the case.

Further explanation is beyond the scope of this Manual. Readers are recommended to *Rayden and Jackson on Divorce and Family Matters*, 16th edn, especially Chapter 48.

1.5.2 LICENSING APPLICATIONS

Magistrates have the power to grant licences to those who wish to sell alcohol — either to the immediate consumer (in a public house, hotel or restaurant) or in a more indirect fashion (in a supermarket or cornershop off-licence). The main statute on this topic is the Licensing Act 1964 (as amended over the intervening years). One may find that a simple licence is sought for the sale of alcohol to be consumed off the premises — an off-licence — or perhaps a licence for alcohol to be sold with bar meals (usually giving longer hours for sale and consumption). The application may be for a single event — for example, the Church fête or a street party if alcohol is to be sold there. Generally there is little difficulty in obtaining the necessary licence so long as the requisite formalities have been observed. These usually relate to giving due notice of the application — to the police, fire brigade, in the newspapers, on the premises — and attending court with the appropriate pieces of paper (and people) to prove it. This Manual is not the proper place for a detailed examination of the licensing laws, but reference should be made (whenever necessary) to *Paterson's Licensing Acts*.

1.6 Research

Students are advised to read further about the topics covered in this course in the following books:

(a) Archbold, *Criminal Pleading, Evidence and Practice*, 1995 edn, Sweet and Maxwell.

(b) Sprack, *Emmins on Criminal Procedure*, 6th edn, Blackstone Press.

(c) *Blackstone's Criminal Practice*, 1996, Blackstone Press.

A thorough work of reference for magistrates' courts is *Stone's Justices' Manual*. Other specialist works exist and are used by practitioners, e.g. *Wilkinson on Road Traffic Offences*.

Students will find cross-reference to other publications throughout the text which follows but should also refer where necessary to the following Manuals:

(a) ***Advocacy***;

(b) ***Conference Skills***;

(c) ***Negotiation Skills***;

(d) ***Opinion Writing***;

(e) ***Drafting***;

(f) ***Evidence***;

(g) ***Case Preparation***.

Note: In some chapters of ***Criminal Litigation and Sentencing***, statistical tables are reproduced with the kind permission of the Home Office Statistics Department. Due to different recording procedures in some areas of the country and some incomplete data, the figures in these Tables should be taken only as a guide.

1.7 Abbreviations

Abbreviations are often used in the text. Some are probably familiar, e.g. *Archbold*, *Stone's*, WLR for Weekly Law Reports. Others will become familiar in time. The following list of common abbreviations should help.

BA 1976 (Bail Act 1976);

CAA 1968 (Criminal Appeal Act 1968);

CJA (Criminal Justice Act, various years but most likely are 1982, 1987, 1988, 1991 and 1993);

CJPOA 1994 (Criminal Justice and Public Order Act 1994);

CLA (Criminal Law Act, various years);

CPS (Crown Prosecution Service);

Cr App R — Criminal Appeal Reports. A specialist series, reporting cases from the Divisional Court of the Queen's Bench Division, Court of Appeal (Criminal Division), and the House of Lords;

Cr App R (S) — Criminal Appeal Reports (Sentencing). A relatively recent series, a companion to the Cr App R but concentrating on sentencing decisions;

Crim LR — Criminal Law Review. A monthly publication with brief, up-to-date reports of cases and useful articles;

CSO (Community Service Order);

CYPA 1933 or 1969 (Children and Young Persons Act, either 1933 or 1969);

JA 1974 (Juries Act 1974);

MCA 1980 (Magistrates' Courts Act 1980);

PACE 1984 (Police and Criminal Evidence Act 1984);

PCCA 1973 (Powers of Criminal Courts Act 1973);

SCA 1981 (Supreme Court Act 1981).

TWO

PRELIMINARIES

Useful article — Ian McKenzie, Rod Morgan and Robert Reiner 'Helping the police with their enquiries' [1990] Crim LR 22.

2.1 Preamble

There are essentially two methods of commencing prosecutions, namely the arrest and charge of the suspect, described at **2.2** below, and the issue of process, described at **2.3** below. Two matters may be conveniently dealt with now by way of preamble.

2.1.1 JURISDICTION AND IMMUNITY

English courts accept jurisdiction to try an accused for an offence committed in England and Wales, regardless of the nationality of the offender. In addition, English courts have jurisdiction over some offences committed abroad in certain circumstances, such as offences of murder and manslaughter where the accused is a British subject, and offences of hijacking regardless of the nationality of the accused. For a complete list of such offences, see *Archbold,* 1994 edn, para. 2–33 et seq and *Blackstone's Criminal Practice*, sections D1.71 et seq. For the limited jurisdiction of magistrates' courts, see **2.5** below.

Certain persons are entitled to immunity from prosecution. The Queen is immune, as are foreign sovereigns and heads of state, their families and personal servants. Diplomatic agents, their staff and families are also immune. For a complete list of those immune from prosecution, see *Archbold,* 1994 edn, para. 1–87 et seq.

2.1.2 THE RIGHT TO PROSECUTE

The Crown Prosecution Service (CPS) was created by the Prosecution of Offences Act 1985, and is a single, national, prosecution service, with the Director of Public Prosecutions (DPP) at its head, and under the 'superintendence' of the Attorney-General. The main duty of the CPS is to take over and conduct all criminal proceedings commenced by the police, which includes the power to discontinue proceedings or to change or amend any charges originally preferred.

The right of an individual, and of certain statutory bodies such as the Inland Revenue, to institute and conduct criminal proceedings, is expressly preserved by the Act. However, under s. 6(2), the DPP has an unfettered discretion to intervene in any proceedings, and conduct them on his or her own behalf.

2.2 Arrest and Charge

Most police powers of arrest, interviewing and charging a suspect are contained in the Police and Criminal Evidence Act 1984 (known as 'PACE') and the Codes of Practice created thereunder. In general terms, the Act provides the overall framework, and the Codes provide the fine detail. There are five Codes of Practice, namely:

Code A: Code of Practice for the Exercise by Police Officers of Statutory Powers of Stop and Search.

Code B: Code of Practice for the Searching of Premises by Police Officers and the Seizure of Property found by Police Officers on Persons and Premises.

Code C: Code of Practice for the Detention, Treatment and Questioning of Persons by Police Officers.

Code D: Code of Practice for the Identification of Persons by Police Officers.

Code E: Code of Practice on Tape Recording.

The original Codes A–D have been replaced by revised Codes which came into effect on 1 April 1991. The Codes contain detailed regulations on the exercise of police powers, and 'notes for guidance'. The notes for guidance are not provisions of the Codes, but are guidance to police officers and others about their application and interpretation.

The Codes of Practice apply to:

(a) police officers (s. 67(8) and (10)); and

(b) persons 'other than police officers who are charged with the duty of investigating offences or charging offenders' (s. 67(9)). This includes local authority officials, post office investigators and officers of the Serious Fraud Office (*R* v *Director of Serious Fraud Office, ex parte Saunders* [1988] Crim LR 837). Whether a body or person conducting an enquiry is subject to s. 67(9) is a question of fact in each case (*R* v *Seelig* [1992] 1 WLR 148).

While students should be familiar with all five codes, this Manual is mainly concerned with Code C, and any reference to 'the Code' should be understood accordingly. Students should consult the ***Evidence Manual*** and standard texts for a full discussion of this area.

2.2.1 POWERS OF ARREST WITHOUT WARRANT

A police officer has the power to arrest a suspect in any of the following circumstances:

(a) if the offence is designated by PACE 1984, s. 24, as an arrestable offence. These are:

(i) Where the sentence for the offence is fixed by law (e.g. murder).

(ii) Where the offence carries at least five years' imprisonment (e.g. theft).

(iii) Specified offences in s. 24(2), for example, taking a motor vehicle without authority or going equipped for stealing under s. 12(1) and s. 25(1) respectively of the Theft Act 1968.

(b) Under PACE 1984, s. 25, if a police officer has reasonable grounds for suspecting that an offence, not included within s. 24, has been committed or attempted, he may arrest the person he suspects of committing the offence, if one of the following conditions, known as general arrest conditions, is satisfied:

(i) That it is impossible to ascertain accurately the suspect's name and address.

(ii) That the officer has reasonable grounds for believing that arrest is necessary to prevent the suspect:

— causing physical injury to himself or herself or any other person; or

— suffering physical injury; or

— causing loss of or damage to property; or

— committing an offence against public decency; or

— causing an unlawful obstruction of the highway.

(iii) That the officer has reasonable grounds for believing that arrest is necessary to protect a child or other vulnerable person from the suspect.

(c) Schedule 2 to PACE 1984 preserves pre-existing powers of arrest created under earlier statutes, for example, where a suspect fails to provide a breath test under the Road Traffic Act 1988, s. 6(5) or is unlikely to comply with the conditions of his bail under the Bail Act 1976, s. 7 (see further **3.14**).

(d) PACE 1984, s. 46A, inserted by s. 29 of the Criminal Justice and Public Order Act 1994, provides the police with a power to arrest any person who, having been bailed by police subject to a duty to attend at a police station, fails to do so.

2.2.2 SERIOUS ARRESTABLE OFFENCES

PACE 1984 also defines certain offences as being serious arrestable offences. While these offences do not carry any greater power of arrest, the fact that the defendant is charged with a serious arrestable offence gives the police wider powers of detention (see **2.2.4** et seq.) and it is convenient to include them here. Under s. 116 and sch. 5 serious arrestable offences are:

(a) Treason.

(b) Murder.

(c) Manslaughter.

(d) Rape.

(e) Kidnapping.

(f) Incest with a girl under 13.

(g) Buggery with a boy under 16 or a person who has not consented.

(h) Indecent assault which constitutes an act of gross indecency.

(i) Causing explosions likely to endanger life or property contrary to the Explosive Substances Act 1883, s. 2.

(j) Intercourse with a girl under 13 contrary to the Sexual Offences Act 1956, s. 5.

(k) Possession of firearms with intent to injure contrary to the Firearms Act 1968, s. 16.

(l) Use of firearms and imitation firearms to resist arrest contrary to the Firearms Act 1968, s. 17.

(m) Carrying firearms with criminal intent contrary to the Firearms Act 1968, s. 18.

(n) Causing death by reckless driving contrary to the Road Traffic Act 1988, s. 1.

(o) Hostage-taking contrary to the Taking of Hostages Act 1982, s. 1.

(p) Hijacking contrary to the Aviation Security Act 1982.

(q) Offences under the Prevention of Terrorism (Temporary Provisions) Act 1989, ss. 2, 8, 9, 10 and 11 are always serious offences for the purpose of the rights contained in PACE 1984, s. 56 and s. 58.

(r) An arrestable offence is a serious arrestable offence if its commission has led to, is intended or is likely to lead to, or consists of making a threat which if carried out would lead to:

(i) Serious harm to the security of the State or to public order.

(ii) Serious interference with the administration of justice or with the investigation of offences or of a particular offence.

(iii) The death of any person.

(iv) Serious injury to any person.

(v) Substantial financial gain to any person.

(vi) Serious financial loss to any person. (Loss is serious if it is serious for the person who suffers it. See for example *R* v *McIvor* [1987] Crim LR 409.)

2.2.3 EFFECTING THE ARREST

A person is arrested by:

(a) being informed by a police officer that he or she is under arrest;

or

(b) being physically seized by a police officer, in which case he or she must be informed that he or she is under arrest as soon as is practicable after the arrest (PACE 1984, s. 28(1), and see *R* v *Brosch* [1988] Crim LR 743).

The arrested person must be told the reason for the arrest, even if it is obvious (s. 28(3) and (4)). If the reason given renders the arrest unlawful, it is irrelevant that there was a valid reason for the arrest if this was not communicated to the arrested person at the time (*Christie* v *Leachinsky* [1947] AC 573; *Abassy* v *Commissioner of Police of the Metropolis* [1990] 1 WLR 385).

If an officer arrests a person because he or she has reasonable cause to suspect that the person has committed an arrestable offence, but knows that there is no possibility of a charge being made, the arrest is unlawful, because the officer has acted on an irrelevant consideration or for an improper purpose (*Plange* v *Chief Constable of South Humberside Police, The Times*, 23 March 1992).

The arrested person must be taken immediately to a police station, unless it is reasonable to carry out other investigations first (s. 30(1) and (10), and *Dallison* v *Caffery* [1965] 1 QB 348).

In each police area, certain police stations are designated as being suitable for the detention of arrested persons (PACE 1984, s. 35(1)). If it is anticipated that the detention will exceed six hours, the arrested person must be detained in a designated police station (s. 30(2) and (3)).

2.2.4 AT THE POLICE STATION

The following (rather complicated) timetable of the detention of the arrested person (hereafter called 'suspect') is contained in PACE 1984, ss. 34–46.

Stage 1: At the police station, the suspect is taken to the custody officer. Each designated police station has one or more officers, of at least the rank of sergeant, appointed as custody officers. The custody officer is not involved in the investigation. As regards the suspect, the custody officer has several duties:

(a) To inform the suspect of his or her rights to consult a solicitor, to have someone informed, and to examine the Codes of Practice (see **2.2.8.3**).

(b) To maintain a custody record, being a complete record of the suspect's detention, including matters such as times of meals, interviews, the caution, if given, and the charge.

(c) To oversee the whole of the suspect's detention. As he or she is unconnected with the investigation the custody officer is able to take a more detached view when assessing whether the suspect should be released or detained, or whether there is sufficient evidence to charge the suspect.

(d) To order the release of the suspect, or his or her charge, unless continued detention without charge is necessary:

(i) to secure or preserve evidence relating to the offence; or

(ii) to obtain such evidence by questioning him or her.

Stage 2: If the custody officer authorises detention, periodic reviews of the detention must be made by a review officer. If the suspect has not yet been charged, the review officer must be:

(a) an officer of at least the rank of inspector; and

(b) not directly involved in the investigation.

The first review must be held within six hours of the original decision to detain.

Stage 3: A second review of the detention must be held within nine hours of the first review. Reviews must thereafter be held at not more than nine-hourly intervals.

Stage 4: After a maximum of 24 hours after arrival at the police station, the suspect must be released or charged, unless the following conditions are satisfied:

(a) the continued detention is authorised by an officer of at least the rank of superintendent; and

(b) the suspect is under arrest in connection with a serious arrestable offence; and

(c) the authorising officer has reasonable grounds for believing that the suspect's continued detention is necessary to:

(i) secure or preserve evidence relating to the offence, or

(ii) obtain such evidence by questioning the suspect; and

(d) the authorising officer has reasonable grounds for believing that the investigation is being conducted diligently and expeditiously.

Stage 5: After a maximum of 36 hours, the suspect must be released or charged unless a warrant of further detention is issued by a magistrates' court. A court may authorise detention for a further 36 hours if:

(a) the court comprises at least two magistrates; and

(b) the application for the warrant is made on oath and supported by written information which is also supplied to the suspect; and

(c) the suspect is present in court; and

(d) the suspect is detained in connection with a *serious* arrestable offence; and

(e) the court is satisfied of the matters in paras. (c) and (d) of Stage 4 above.

Stage 6: After a maximum of 72 hours the court may authorise further detention if all the conditions of Stage 5 above are satisfied. This further detention is for a maximum of 36 hours, and, in any event, the court may not authorise detention for a period of more than 96 hours.

Stage 7: No detention without charge is permitted after 96 hours. Thereafter, the suspect must be charged and/or released.

Note: These time-limits do not apply to those who are detained under the Prevention of Terrorism (Temporary Provisions) Act 1989.

2.2.5 THE CAUTION

Under para. 10 of the Code, a person who has fallen under suspicion must be cautioned before any questions about the offence are put for the purpose of obtaining evidence which may be given to a court at trial. If the answers to questions already put to him or her have given ground for that suspicion, then he or she should be cautioned at that stage.

Because a caution is required only where there are grounds to suspect the person of an offence, it need not be given where the questions are merely general, preliminary questions, to establish, for example, identity or ownership.

In addition, para. 10 provides that the caution must be given on arrest unless the suspect has already been cautioned immediately prior to arrest, or it is impracticable to administer the caution by reason of behaviour at the time.

The caution should be re-administered after a break in questioning, but see *R* v *Oni* [1992] Crim LR 183, CA, where it was held to be unnecessary after a break of only two minutes. However, the caution should always be re-administered if there is any doubt as to whether or not it is necessary.

Prior to the Criminal Justice and Public Order Act 1994, the suspect had what was referred to as a 'right to silence'. This meant essentially that no adverse inferences could be drawn from his failure to answer questions during an interview (or to testify in court). The Criminal Justice and Public Order Act 1994, s. 34 now provides that the court may 'draw such inferences from the failure as appear proper' (s. 34(2)), if evidence is given that the defendant:

> *(a) at any time before he was charged with the offence, on being questioned under caution by a constable trying to discover whether or by whom the offence had been committed, failed to mention any fact relied on in his defence in those proceedings; or*
> *(b) on being charged with the offence or officially informed that he might be prosecuted for it, failed to mention any such fact, being a fact which in the circumstances existing at the time the accused could reasonably have been expected to mention when so questioned, charged or informed, as the case may be.*

The caution is in the following terms:

> You do not have to say anything. But it may harm your defence if you do not mention, when questioned, something which you later rely on in court. Anything you do say may be given in evidence.

Provided that the sense of the caution is preserved, minor deviations from the stated form do not constitute a breach of the Code.

Students are referred to the text of the Criminal Justice and Public Order Act 1994 and the revised Codes of Practice made thereunder, for the full effect of these provisions.

Note: This is nothing to do with the use of a caution as an alternative to taking criminal proceedings against a suspect. See, e.g. **7.2**.

2.2.6 INTERVIEWS

Under paras 11 and 12 of the Code, a record must be kept of each interview that takes place, including the place of the interview, the time it began and ended, any breaks, and the names of all those present. The record should be made during the interview, unless this is impracticable, in which case it should be made as soon as practicable thereafter.

Any interview at a police station should take place in an adequately lit, heated and ventilated interview room. At the beginning of the interview the interviewing officer must identify himself or herself and any other officer present. The suspect must not be required to stand during the interview, and should be given breaks at recognised meal times. In addition, there should be short breaks for refreshment every two hours. The Code specifically provides that in any period of 24 hours, the suspect should be provided with one main and two light meals. In addition, he or she should be allowed a continuous period of eight hours' sleep without interruption, normally at night.

In the notes for guidance it is provided that the purpose of the interview is to obtain the suspect's 'explanation of the facts' and not necessarily to obtain his or her admission. Whether the questioning amounts to an interview depends on all the circumstances of the case, the arrest, the arrival at the police station, the caution and notification of rights, and the questioning itself (*R* v *Cox* (1992) 96 Cr App R 464, CA).

All interviews with persons cautioned in respect of an indictable offence or where questions are put to, or a statement of another person is shown to, a person who has been charged should be tape-recorded. Tapes need not be made if it is not reasonably practicable to do so for reasons such as the failure of the equipment, and the custody officer considers that the interview should not be delayed. For detailed provisions on tape recording and tape security, see Code E.

2.2.7 PERSONS AT RISK

Special rules apply when the police are dealing with persons at risk, that is juveniles, the mentally ill, and the mentally handicapped. The reason, according to para. 13B of the notes for guidance, is that, though capable of giving reliable evidence, they may unknowingly or without wishing to do so be prone to providing information which is unreliable, misleading or self-incriminating. Further, the investigating officers should seek corroboration of any facts admitted wherever possible.

Persons at risk should normally be interviewed in the presence of an appropriate adult. An appropriate adult is, for example, the parent or guardian of a juvenile, or the guardian of the person who is mentally ill or mentally handicapped. The appropriate adult is not expected to act simply as an observer, and should be informed of this. He or she is there to advise the person being questioned and observe whether or not the interview is being conducted fairly, and to facilitate communication with the person at risk.

In an emergency, however, a person at risk may be questioned in the absence of an appropriate adult, if Annex C to the Code applies; and it will apply if:

(a) the interview is authorised by an officer of at least the rank of superintendent; and

(b) the officer considers that delay will involve an immediate risk of harm to persons or serious loss of or damage to property.

2.2.8 THE RIGHTS OF THE SUSPECT

The suspect has three important rights in the police station.

2.2.8.1 The right to consult a solicitor

PACE 1984, s. 58(1) provides that a person who has been arrested and is being held in custody is entitled, upon request, to consult privately with a solicitor at any time. He or she must be informed of this right by the custody officer on arrival at the police station, and must sign the custody record indicating whether or not a request was made. The request must be complied with as soon as is practicable.

The right may not be denied, but may be delayed for up to 36 hours after the suspect's arrival at the police station. It may be delayed if:

(a) the suspect is detained in connection with a serious arrestable offence; and

(b) the delay is authorised by an officer of at least the rank of superintendent; and

(c) the authorising officer has reasonable grounds for believing that immediate consultation will lead to:

- (i) interference with or harm to evidence connected with a serious arrestable offence or interference with or physical injury to other persons; or
- (ii) the alerting of other persons suspected of having committed the offence but not yet arrested for it; or
- (iii) the hindrance of the recovery of any property obtained as a result of such an offence.

The suspect must be told why access to a solicitor has been delayed, and that reason must be entered on the custody record.

Wrongful denial of access to a solicitor may lead to any confession made without having taken legal advice being excluded at any subsequent trial. See for example *R* v *Samuel* [1988] 1 WLR 920; *R* v *Alladice* (1988) 87 Cr App R 380. For a full discussion of the cases where a confession has been obtained in such circumstances, students should refer to the ***Evidence Manual***.

2.2.8.2 The right to have someone informed

Under PACE 1984, s. 56(1), the suspect has the right to have a friend or relative, or some other person who is known to him or her or who is likely to take an interest in his or her welfare, told of the arrest. He or she has no right to make personal contact, it being the duty of the police to pass on the information. The request must be complied with as soon as is practicable.

The right to have someone informed may be delayed in the same circumstances as the right to consult a solicitor may be delayed.

2.2.8.3 The right to consult the Codes

The suspect has the right to consult all the Codes of Practice. This does not entitle him or her to delay unreasonably any investigation or administrative action while this is done (para. 3.1, Code C).

2.2.9 THE CHARGE

Under para. 17 of the Code, when the investigating officer considers that there is sufficient evidence upon which to prosecute the suspect, he or she must take him or her before the custody officer who will decide whether he or she should be charged. If charged, he or she should first be cautioned, and any answers made will be recorded.

Once the suspect has been charged, he or she may not be asked any further questions except where it is necessary:

(a) to prevent or minimise harm or loss to some other person or to the public; or

(b) to clear up an ambiguity in a previous answer or statement; or

(c) in the interests of justice that the suspect should have the opportunity of commenting on information that has come to light since he or she was charged.

Before any further questions are put, the suspect should first be cautioned.

After the charge the custody officer must order the suspect's release from custody under PACE 1984, s. 38(1) unless one of the situations contained in s. 38(1)(a), as amended by s. 28 of the Criminal Justice and Public Order Act 1994, applies:

(a) The suspect's name or address cannot be ascertained.

(b) The custody officer has reasonable grounds for doubting whether the name and address supplied are genuine.

(c) The custody officer has reasonable grounds for believing that:

  (i) the suspect will not surrender to bail; or

  (ii) (imprisonable offences) the detention is necessary to prevent him from committing an offence; or

  (iii) (non-imprisonable offences) the detention is necessary to prevent him from causing physical injury to any other person or loss or damage to property; or

  (iv) the detention is necessary to prevent him from interfering with the administration of justice or with the investigation of any offence or offences; or

  (v) the detention is necessary for his own protection.

If the suspect is to be released after charge, he is likely to be bailed to attend at the appropriate magistrates' court to answer to the charge on a specified day. Prior to the passing of the Criminal Justice and Public Order Act 1994, the extent to which the police could impose conditions on bail was not entirely clear. Section 27 of that Act, however, provides that s. 3 of the Bail Act 1976 (power of the court to impose conditions on bail) shall apply with certain modifications (see below) to bail granted by the police.

The bail decision is taken by the custody officer, who may not impose conditions on the grant of bail unless it appears, under s. 3A(5) of the Bail Act 1976 (inserted by s. 27 of the Criminal Justice and Public Order Act 1994) that it is necessary to do so for the purposes of preventing the bailed person from:

(a) failing to surrender to custody; or

(b) committing an offence while on bail; or

(c) interfering with witnesses or otherwise obstructing the course of justice, whether in relation to himself or any other person.

The main differences between conditions imposed by police and those imposed by the court are as follows:

(a) The court, but not the police, has the power to order that reports be compiled on the bailed person (Bail Act 1976, s. 3A(3), as inserted by the Criminal Justice and Public Order Act 1994, s. 27(3)).

(b) The court, but not the police, may require the bailed person to reside in a bail hostel (Bail Act 1976, s. 3A(2), as inserted by the Criminal Justice and Public Order Act 1994, s. 27(3)).

(c) Where the custody officer has granted bail, either he himself or another officer serving at the same police station may vary the conditions of bail, at the request of the bailed person (Bail Act 1976, s. 3A(4), inserted by the Criminal Justice and Public Order Act 1994, s. 27(3)). Further, the bailed person may apply to a magistrates' court to have conditions of bail varied, but should bear in mind that the court has the power to impose more onerous conditions (Magistrates' Courts Act 1980, s. 43B, inserted by the Criminal Justice and Public Order Act 1994, sch. 3, para. 3).

(Note that a person who is subject to investigation but has not yet been charged, may be bailed, with or without conditions, to attend at the police station on a specified date (Criminal Justice and Public Order Act 1994, s. 37(2)).)

If the suspect is detained after charge, he or she must be brought before a magistrates' court as soon as is practicable, and in any event not later than the first sitting after he or she has been charged with an offence. If no suitable court is sitting, the clerk of the court must be informed, and a special sitting will be arranged. See generally PACE 1984, s. 46.

If release is authorised, the suspect is bailed to appear before the magistrates' court on a specified day to answer the charge (see PACE 1984, s. 47).

A useful article is 'Detention in a police station and false imprisonment' by J. Mackenzie, 142 NLJ 534.

2.3 Issue of Process

The laying of an information, and the subsequent issue of a summons (known as the issue of process) is appropriate where the offence involved is not particularly serious, though in theory there is nothing to prevent all prosecutions beginning in this way. In practice, however, serious offences almost always begin with the arrest and charge of the suspect as detailed in **2.2** above.

The procedure is governed by the Magistrates' Courts Act 1980 (MCA 1980) and the Magistrates' Courts Rules 1981 (MCR 1981).

2.3.1 THE INFORMATION

The information is the formal accusation that a certain individual (the 'accused') has committed an offence, and is roughly equivalent to an indictment in the Crown Court (see **Chapter 9**).

An information will contain the following matters:

(a) The name and address of the accused.

(b) The statement of the offence. This need not be in technical language, as long as all the elements of the offence are included, and the statement gives clear information as to the nature of the charge. If the offence is created by statute, the relevant Act and section should be quoted. Each information must charge only one offence — see **Chapter 9** for the rule against duplicity.

(c) The place of the offence.

(d) The date of the offence. Magistrates may only proceed to trial of a purely summary offence if the information was laid within six months of the offence, unless the statute creating the offence provides otherwise (see MCA 1980, s. 127).

Where information is laid through a computer link between police station and magistrates' court, the information is treated as having been laid when it is fed into the computer, regardless of when the information is printed out by the court (*R* v *Pontypridd Juvenile Court, ex parte B* [1988] Crim LR 842).

Further problems as to whether the information was laid in the time arose in *Lawrence* v *MAFF* [1992] Crim LR 874, DC, and *R* v *Thames Metropolitan Stipendiary Magistrate, ex parte Hackney London Borough Council* (1993) 158 JP 305, DC.

An occasional problem arises where, the information having been laid within six months, the summons is not served promptly, due to either inefficiency or a deliberate abuse of process (for example, see *R* v *Oxford City Justices, ex parte Smith* (1982) 75 Cr App R 200). In this situation, the magistrates have a discretion to dismiss the information and acquit the accused without hearing any evidence. Inappropriate circumstances, the court may infer prejudice from the mere passage of time (*R* v *Bow Street Stipendiary Magistrate, ex parte DPP* (1989) 91 Cr App R 283). For a recent example, see *R* v *Crawley Justices, ex parte DPP* [1991] COD 365.

It is worth stressing that this is the only situation where the magistrates have such a discretion. Other than this, they may not dismiss an information without trial, for such reasons as the triviality of the charges, the seeming unfairness of the prosecution etc. This principle has recently been confirmed in *R* v *Dorchester Justices, ex parte DPP* [1990] RTR 369 and *R* v *Watford Justices, ex parte DPP* [1990] RTR 374.

(e) The signature of the prosecutor. This may be the signature either of the individual officer, or the rubber-stamped signature of a senior officer. Practices vary around the country and nothing turns on it. Note that the information must be laid in the name of an individual, and not by an unincorporated body such as 'Thames Valley Police' (see *Rubin* v *DPP* [1990] 2 QB 80). However, a technical defect of this nature is unlikely to be fatal to the proceedings.

As to where the information was signed by a person who had no authority to initiate proceedings, see *R* v *Norwich Justices, ex parte Texas Homecare* [1991] Crim LR 555.

2.3.2 LAYING THE INFORMATION

The vast majority of informations are laid in writing. Large bundles of informations and corresponding summonses are forwarded by the police to the local magistrates' court. The information is treated as having been laid as soon as it is received by the clerk's office of the magistrates' court (see *R* v *Manchester Stipendiary Magistrate, ex parte Hill* [1983] 1 AC 328).

Exceptionally, the information is laid orally. A typical example would be where there has been a dispute between neighbours in which the police do not wish to proceed. If one party goes before the magistrates and relates what happened, he or she has laid an information orally. It will be reduced into writing by the clerk of the court. As to where information is laid via a 'computer link', see *R* v *Pontypridd Juvenile Court, ex parte B* [1988] Crim LR 842. As to where it was laid by letter, see *R* v *Kennett Justices, ex parte Humphrey and Wyatt* [1993] Crim LR 787, DC.

2.3.3 ISSUING THE SUMMONS

The summons is a document issuing from the court, telling the accused that an allegation has been made against him or her and instructing him or her to attend court on a particular date to meet that allegation. The documents must contain:

(a) The name and address of the accused.

(b) The address of the court which he or she is to attend.

(c) The date and the time of the hearing.

(d) The contents of the information laid against him or her.

(e) The name and address of the informant.

The magistrate or the clerk will issue the summons on the basis of the information that has been laid. When deciding whether or not to issue a summons, the magistrate or clerk is exercising a judicial discretion. In theory, therefore, the magistrate has a discretion not to issue the summons if it appears that the prosecution is frivolous or vexatious, or where the charge is not supported by the evidence. In practice, however, the volume of business is so great that the magistrate rarely examines the information (unless it has been laid orally by a member of the public) and the issue of the summons is usually automatic.

Once the summons has been signed, everything is returned to the informant, the court retaining copies. The police will serve the summons, usually by posting it to the accused's last known or usual address.

2.3.4 JURISDICTION TO ISSUE PROCESS

The court has the power to issue process in the manner outlined above, subject to certain territorial limitations contained in MCA 1980, s. 1. These are:

(a) Where the offence is purely summary, the court may issue process if:

  (i) the offence occurred within the county; or

  (ii) the accused is already being tried for an offence by that court (whether indictable or summary). It is irrelevant in this case that the present offence did not occur within the county.

(b) Where the offence is indictable, the court may issue process if the offence was committed within the county, or the accused is believed to be or lives in the county.

(c) In either case, the court may issue process if it is necessary or expedient in the better administration of justice that the accused should be tried jointly with another person who is being proceeded against in that county.

2.3.5 TRYING TWO OR MORE INFORMATIONS

If the accused stands before the court charged with more than one offence, or if several accused stand before the court together, the question arises whether all outstanding matters can be dealt with at once.

(a) Where several accused are jointly charged with an offence, they will almost always be automatically tried together, despite any objection they may make.

(b) Where one accused stands charged with several matters, or several accused stand charged of related offences, then they may be tried together as long as no objection is made. If objection is made, the magistrates will order separate trials unless they are of the opinion that the offences are so connected that the interests of justice would be best served by a single trial. See *Chief Constable of Norfolk* v *Clayton* [1983] 2 AC 473.

If the magistrates decide against a single trial, it would seem those magistrates are debarred from hearing the case at all, as they are supposed to be unaware of any charges outstanding against an accused (see *R* v *Liverpool City Justices, ex parte*

Topping [1983] 1 WLR 119). In these circumstances, each case may have to be heard by a different bench. In *R* v *Gough* [1993] AC 646, the House of Lords held that the test in all cases of apparent bias is: Was there a real danger of bias?

2.3.6 AMENDMENT

The court has wide powers to amend the information (or indeed the summons or warrant) as originally laid. Further MCA 1980, s. 123, provides that defects in the information, or any variations between the information and the evidence subsequently adduced, are not grounds upon which objection may be taken.

It has been held that if the defect or variation was trivial, and the accused was not in fact misled, any subsequent conviction will be upheld. See, for example, *R* v *Sandwell Justices, ex parte West Midlands Passenger Transport Board* [1979] Crim LR 56. On the other hand, if the defect or variation is substantial, the prosecution should seek to amend the information. The magistrates will then consider whether the accused has been misled by the defect, and if so, offer an adjournment so that he or she can prepare for and meet the case now put forward by the prosecution. Failure either to amend, or adjourn, in these circumstances is likely to lead to any subsequent conviction being quashed. See, for example, *Wright* v *Nicholson* [1970] 1 WLR 142.

Late amendments cannot cure an information which discloses no offence known to law (*Garman* v *Plaice* [1969] 1 WLR 19).

2.3.7 DUPLICITY

An information is said to be duplicitous when two offences are charged within it. In such a situation, the prosecution may elect which charge to proceed with (Magistrates' Courts (Miscellaneous Amendments) Rules 1993 (S.I. 1993 No. 118)).

Students are referred to **Chapter 9** for a full full discussion of duplicity.

2.4 Issue of a Warrant

Instead of issuing a summons, a magistrate may issue a warrant for the arrest of the person named therein. A warrant should contain the following information:

(a) The name of the court.

(b) The name and address of the accused.

(c) The offence alleged.

(d) The signature of the magistrate (the signature of the clerk is insufficient).

(e) If the warrant is to be backed for bail, any conditions of bail imposed by the magistrate (see **3.12**).

2.4.1 CONDITIONS FOR THE ISSUE OF A WARRANT

Before the warrant can be issued the following conditions must be met:

(a) The information must be in writing and supported by sworn evidence. In practice, the police officer applying for the warrant will simply swear that all the allegations contained in the information are true, without having to detail what the allegations are.

(b) The offence must be imprisonable (or the accused is a juvenile or resides at an unknown address).

(c) The proceedings must take place before a magistrate, not a clerk.

2.4.2 WARRANTS 'BACKED FOR BAIL'

In most cases a warrant will not be necessary. Less serious offences can be commenced by the issue of a summons, and more serious offences are arrestable in any event. However, the warrant is important where the accused fails to appear in answer to the summons, or fails to surrender to bail. A warrant issued in these circumstances is often referred to as a 'bench warrant'.

If the magistrates think that the accused's absence is due to an error, they may order that the warrant be 'backed for bail', that is, the conditions of bail upon which the accused may be released once arrested are endorsed on the back of the warrant. After arrest, the accused must be released once the conditions are complied with (see also **Chapter 3**).

2.5 Jurisdiction to Try Offences

The jurisdiction of the magistrates' courts to try offences is similar to their jurisdiction to issue process, described at **2.3.4** above. More specifically:

(a) Where the offence is triable either way: magistrates have the power to try offences which are triable either way wherever they were committed, as long as the accused has consented to summary trial as described at **4.2** (MCA 1980, s. 2(3) and (4)).

(b) Where the offence is triable summarily only: magistrates have the power to try summary offences where:

(i) The offence was committed within the county for which they act (MCA 1980, s. 2(1)).

(ii) The offence was committed outside the county, but the court is already trying the accused for another offence (MCA 1980, s. 2(6)).

(iii) The offence was committed outside the county, but it is necessary or expedient in the better administration of justice that the accused should be jointly tried with another person who is being proceeded against in that county (MCA 1980, s. 1(2)(b) and s. 2(2)).

Under MCA 1980, s. 3 an offence committed within 500 yards of the county border may be dealt with by the courts in either county. This is to avoid disputes as to exactly where the offence was committed, and which court, therefore, has jurisdiction.

2.6 Legal Aid

Legal aid may be divided into two categories.

2.6.1 LEGAL ADVICE AND ASSISTANCE

This covers the initial need for legal advice at the very beginning of the criminal justice process, i.e. matters preliminary to the hearing. There are two ways in which such advice can be given:

(a) *The Green Form Scheme:* This is a quick and efficient method of obtaining legal advice and is designed to cover the initial interview between a solicitor and client. A solicitor operating the scheme will be paid out of the Legal Aid Fund in the form of a fixed fee for the interview. The Green Form will be filled in at the interview and signed by the client. Advice under the Green Form Scheme is automatically available for defendants on income support, family credit or disability working allowance. If the defendant's income or capital is above designated levels, it is not available.

(b) *The Duty Solicitor Scheme*: There is no means test for this free advice and assistance. Solicitors taking part in the duty solicitor scheme attend a magistrates' court on a regular basis and are on call day and night to attend at a police station or elsewhere where a suspect is being questioned about an offence. They are also expected to give telephone advice to a suspect who requests it. The duty solicitor who is on the rota for attending at a magistrates' court can give free advice and represent a defendant on his or her first appearance. The scheme is designed to cover matters such as bail applications and simple pleas in mitigation. Should the case be more complicated, it should be adjourned so that the defendant can apply for legal aid and give full instructions to a representative of his or her choice.

2.6.2 LEGAL AID

This is governed by the Legal Aid Act 1988 and by various regulations. The Legal Aid in Criminal and Care Proceedings (General) Regulations (S.I. 1989 No. 344) as amended, sets out the details of obtaining legal aid and the Legal Aid in Criminal and Care Proceedings (Costs) Regulations (S.I. 1989 No. 343) as amended, deals with remuneration.

Criminal legal aid is available for proceedings before a magistrates' court, the Crown Court, the Court of Appeal and the House of Lords.

In the first instance legal aid can only be granted by the court before which the proceedings are to be heard. In addition, magistrates' courts have power to grant legal aid for proceedings before the Crown Court where the defendant has been committed for trial or for sentence, or is appealing against a decision of the magistrates' court.

2.6.2.1 When legal aid must be granted

Under the Legal Aid Act 1988, s. 21(3) legal aid *must* be granted (subject to the defendant's means):

(a) Where the defendant is committed for trial on a charge of murder.

(b) Where the prosecution is seeking to appeal to the House of Lords.

(c) To enable a bail application to be made where the defendant is:

(i) unrepresented and wishes to be represented; and

(ii) appears before a magistrates' court in pursuance of a remand in custody when he was not represented; and

(iii) may be again remanded or committed in custody.

(d) Where the defendant is remanded in custody (by a magistrates' court or by the Crown Court) for the preparation of reports prior to sentencing.

2.6.2.2 When legal aid may be granted

In all other situations, legal aid may be granted if it is in the interests of justice and the defendant's resources are such that he or she requires assistance in meeting the costs which he or she may incur. Factors that the court should take into account are set out in the Legal Aid Act 1988, s. 22(2), and include the following:

(a) the offence is such that if proved the accused is likely to lose his or her liberty, livelihood or suffer serious damage to his or her reputation; or

(b) the case may involve consideration of a substantial question of law; or

(c) the accused may be unable to understand the proceedings or state his or her own case because of inadequate knowledge of English, mental illness or mental or physical disability; or

(d) the defence involves the tracing and interviewing of witnesses or expert cross-examination of prosecution witnesses; or

(e) it is in the interests of someone other than the accused that the accused be represented.

By s. 21(7) any doubts as to eligibility must be resolved in favour of the defendant.

2.6.3 MAKING THE APPLICATION

An application for legal aid will usually have been made by the instructing solicitor, but where this has not been done counsel may:

(a) make a simple oral request to the magistrates. This should be accompanied by a statement of means (i.e. details of the defendant's financial resources and commitments — on Form 5). If no such statement has yet been made, legal aid may be granted, subject to means; or

(b) help the defendant to complete Form 5 (statement of means) and Form 1 (application).

These forms are available from the court clerk or usher and the completed forms must be handed in to the bench or court clerk. The forms are reproduced at the end of this Chapter.

Legal aid may be granted or refused by the justice(s) or the clerk.

If the applicant is in receipt of social security benefits (e.g. income support), the applicant must produce evidence of receipt of the benefit. This evidence will take the form of the address of the relevant benefit office and the applicant's reference number (shown on the letter noting the award of the benefit or the payment book).

2.6.4 CHALLENGING REFUSAL OF LEGAL AID BY A MAGISTRATES' COURT

If the justices' clerk refuses legal aid otherwise than on the grounds of means, the defendant may renew the application in open court before the magistrates.

If legal aid is refused by the magistrate(s) otherwise than on the grounds of means the defendant may:

(a) Renew the application if there is a change of circumstances or new information has come to light.

(b) If the case is to be committed to the Crown Court, make a fresh application on Form 5 and Form 1 to the Crown Court. Note that the Crown Court has no power to grant legal aid in respect of summary trial or committal proceedings.

(c) Apply for judicial review of the refusal. This applies only where the grant of legal aid is obligatory under s. 21(3) (see **2.6.2.1**), or where the magistrates have acted unreasonably in exercising their discretion to grant legal aid under s. 21(2). However, the general rule where an inferior tribunal refuses to exercise its discretionary power in favour of a party to the proceedings is that the Divisional Court will intervene only if the decision was arrived at by taking into account irrelevant considerations, or ignoring relevant ones, or was manifestly unreasonable.

(d) Apply to the Area Committee of the Legal Aid Board. The decision may be reviewed if the following criteria are satisfied:

(i) the refusal was by a magistrates' court, magistrate or clerk; and

(ii) the defendant has been charged with an indictable offence or an offence triable either way; and

(iii) the application was refused on the grounds that it was not in the interests of justice (see **2.6.2.2**); and

(iv) the application for review was lodged within 14 days of the refusal; and

(v) the application was made no more than 21 days before the trial date, if that had been set.

2.6.5 CONTRIBUTION ORDER

The defendant (or an 'appropriate contributor', i.e. parent or guardian, where the defendant is under 16) may be required to pay a contribution towards the cost of representation. If the defendant receives income support, family credit or disability working allowance there can be no contribution order. For other defendants the granting of legal aid may be conditional upon the payment of such a contribution. If a contribution from income is ordered this sum must be paid on a weekly, fortnightly or monthly basis at the discretion of the court. If the contribution is from capital the defendant must pay it immediately unless the court orders payment within a time it considers reasonable. Where sums due under the contribution order have not been paid before the conclusion of the case, the court can:

(a) require payment within seven days; and

(b) if that is not complied with, invite representations as to the reasons for non-compliance.

If satisfied that the assisted person is able to pay the contribution but has failed to do so, the court can revoke the grant of legal aid. In addition, unpaid contributions can be recovered in the same way as fines where the non-payment results from a wilful refusal to comply with the contribution order.

If a legally aided defendant is acquitted, any contributions he or she has paid towards to the cost of his or her defence will be repaid to him or her and any unpaid contributions will be remitted, unless the court decides the defendant brought the prosecution on him- or herself.

2.6.6 PAYMENT OF COUNSEL

Counsel has to fill in a claim form showing the work done and the time expended in the case. This must be submitted within three months of the conclusion of the case.

2.6.6.1 Crown Court

In respect of Crown Court fees, the amount to be paid by the Legal Aid Board to solicitors and counsel is initially fixed by a determining officer at the Crown Court. This figure will be a standard figure set out in the Legal Aid in Criminal and Care Proceedings (Costs) Regulations (which are amended yearly) unless it appears to the determining officer that the standard fee would be inappropriate taking into account all the relevant circumstances of the case. If counsel is not satisfied with the fees awarded, an application for reassessment can be made to the Crown Court, with further appeals to the taxing master and the High Court.

2.6.6.2 Magistrates' court

The Legal Aid Board pays counsel for work done in the magistrates' court. Most cases will be paid on the basis of standard fees. If a solicitor intends to instruct unassigned counsel the solicitor will negotiate counsel's fees with counsel's clerk. The Legal Aid Board will pay the agreed figure to counsel and the balance of the standard fee to the solicitor. Non-standard fees will be paid when counsel is assigned by the legal aid order.

If counsel is assigned he or she will be paid at an enhanced rate. An appeal against the level of fees can be made by counsel to the Legal Aid Area Committee. An application for review must be made within 21 days of notification of assessment.

2.7 Costs

Under the Prosecution of Offences Act 1985, ss. 16–21, the court finally disposing of a case has the power to make various orders as to costs, of which the most important are set out below.

2.7.1 DEFENDANT'S COSTS ORDER

Under s. 16, a defendant who has been acquitted may have an order made in his or her favour for the payment of sums out of central funds (i.e. the Government) for expenses properly incurred by him or her in the proceedings. This may, but need not, be the full amount which the defendant claims.

2.7.2 PROSECUTION COSTS

Under s. 17 a private prosecutor (but not the CPS or other prosecuting authority) may be awarded, out of central funds, an amount which the court thinks reasonably sufficient to compensate him or her for expenses properly incurred. The prosecution does not have to be successful for such an order to be made. Again, this need not be the full amount.

2.7.3 COSTS AGAINST THE DEFENDANT

Under s. 18, if the defendant is convicted, he or she may be ordered to pay to the prosecution such a sum as is just and reasonable.

2.7.4 MAKING THE ORDER

The making of an order of costs is discretionary, but the approach the courts tend to take is that an acquitted defendant should normally expect to recover his or her costs unless:

(a) the defendant was at fault in bringing suspicion on himself or herself and allowing the prosecution to believe that their case against him or her was stronger than it actually was; or

(b) he or she was acquitted on a technicality, but the prosecution was properly brought.

See generally *Practice Direction (Costs: Acquittal of Defendant)* [1981] 1 WLR 1383.

Few guidelines have been issued on the making of an order for costs against a convicted defendant. However, it has been said that, while the costs of a trial on indictment are greater than those of a summary trial, the defendant should not be 'punished' for electing trial on indictment by an excessive order for costs (*R* v *Bushell* (1980) 2 Cr App R (S) 77). Where an order for costs is likely, the prosecution should be in a position to provide an estimate of costs, which should not be an overestimate (*R* v *Maher* (1983) 76 Cr App R 309).

Further, in *R* v *Nottingham Justices, ex parte Fohmann* (1986) 84 Cr App R 316, it was said that justices should not make an order for costs against a convicted person in such a sum that, through lack of means, he or she would be unable to pay that sum within a reasonable period of about a year. However, it has been held, in relation to the payment of fines, that a period of two years would seldom be too long, and that three years may be acceptable in appropriate cases (*R* v *Olliver and Olliver* (1989) 11 Cr App R (S) 10). See also **18.7.4** for a full discussion.

Finally, students should refer to *Practice Direction (Crime: Costs)* at [1991] 1 WLR 498 which has effect where a magistrates' court, the Crown Court, Divisional Court or the Criminal Division of the Court of Appeal is considering an award of costs in criminal proceedings in the exercise of its discretion.

Application for Legal Aid in Criminal Proceedings Magistrates' or Crown Court

Form 1
Regulations 11 and 18
(also known as
Crown Court Form 5131)

I apply for Legal Aid –

For the purpose of proceedings before the [Crown / Magistrates' / Youth Court*]

1. Personal Details *(Please use **BLOCK** letters and **BLACK** ink)*

(a) Surname [ ] *(e)* Date of birth [ ]

(b) Forenames [ ]

(c) Permanent address [ ]

(d) Present address *(if different from above)* [ ]

2. Case Details

(a) Describe briefly what it is you are accused of doing, *e.g.*, "stealing £50 from my employer", "kicking a door causing £50 damage". [ ]

(b) The following other person(s) is/are charged in this case. [ ]

(c) Give reasons why you and the other persons charged in this case, if any, should not be represented by the same solicitor. [ ]

3. Court Proceedings *(Complete section (a) or (b) whichever applies)*

(a) I am due to appear before [the Magistrates' / Youth Court* on 19 at a.m./p.m.]

or

(b) I appeared before [the Magistrates' / Youth Court* on 19 at a.m./p.m.]

and *(tick whichever applies)*

☐ my case has been transferred to the Crown Court for trial

☐ I was convicted and committed for sentence to the Crown Court

☐ I was convicted and/or sentenced and I wish to appeal against the [conviction and / or sentence*]

*Cross out whichever does not apply.

1

4. Outstanding Matters

(a) If there are any other outstanding criminal charges or cases against you, give details including the court where you are due to appear (only those cases that are not yet concluded)

5. Your Financial Position *(Tick the box which applies)*

(a) ☐ I receive Income Support, Family Credit or Disability Working Allowance, and I authorise the court to make such enquiries of the Benefits Agency as it considers necessary. I consent to the disclosure of information to confirm that I am in receipt of benefit.

(You may also tick this box if your spouse or partner receives any of these benefits and you are living together)

Give:

(i) the address of the Social Security office dealing with the benefit

(ii) National Insurance number of person receiving benefit

(iii) Type of benefit

You should produce documentary evidence that you are receiving the benefit (*e.g.*, order book). If you cannot produce evidence you should give your reasons below

(b) ☐ I have already given a statement of my means to the Court and there has been no change in my financial position. *(A new statement is required if there has been any change)*

(c) ☐ I attach a statement of my means in these proceedings *(details of your income and expenditure)*

(d) ☐ I am under 16 and I attach a statement of my parents' means. If you are unable to provide a statement of their means, give their name and address

6. Legal Representation

Note

(a) **If you do not have the name and address of a solicitor the court will select a solicitor for you.**

(b) **You must tell the solicitor that you have named him, unless he has helped you to complete this form.**

(c) **If you have been charged together with another person or persons, the court may assign a solicitor other than the solicitor of your choice.**

(a) The solicitor I wish to act for me is

(b) Give the firm's name and address (if known)

2

7. Reasons for wanting Legal Aid

- To avoid the possibility of your application being delayed or legal aid being refused because the court does not have enough information about the case, you must complete the rest of this form.
- When deciding whether to grant legal aid, the court will need to know the reasons why it is in the interests of justice for you to be represented.
- If you need help in completing this form, and especially if you have previous convictions, you should see a solicitor. He may be able to advise you free of charge or at a reduced fee.

Note: If you plead **NOT GUILTY** neither the information in this form nor that in your statement of means will be made available to the members of the court trying your case unless you are convicted or you consent. If you are acquitted, only the financial information you have given in your statement of means will be given to the court.

Tick any boxes which apply and give brief details or reasons in the space provided

	Details	Reasons for grant or refusal *(for court use only)*
(a) It is likely that I will lose my liberty *(You should consider seeing a solicitor before answering this question)* ☐		
(b) I am subject to a: suspended or partly suspended prison sentence ☐ conditional discharge ☐ probation order ☐ supervision order ☐ deferment of sentence ☐ community service order ☐ care order ☐ combination order ☐ *Give details as far as you are able, including the nature of the offence and when the order was made*		
(c) It is likely that I will lose my livelihood ☐		
(d) It is likely that I will suffer serious damage to my reputation ☐		
(e) A substantial question of law is involved *(You will need the help of a solicitor to answer this question)* ☐		

(Please give authorities to be quoted with law reports references)

3

	Details	Reasons for grant or refusal *(for court use only)*
(f) I shall be unable to understand the court proceedings or state my own case because: (i) My understanding of English is inadequate ☐ (ii) I suffer from a disability *(Give full details)* ☐		
(g) Witnesses have to be traced and/or interviewed on my behalf *(State circumstances)* ☐		
(h) The case involves expert cross examination of a prosecution witness *(Give brief details)* ☐		
(i) It is in someone else's interests that I am represented ☐		
(j) Any other reasons: *(give full particulars)* ☐		

8. Declaration

If you knowingly make a statement which is false, or knowingly withhold information, you may be prosecuted. If convicted, you may be sent to prison for up to three months, or be fined, or both *(section 39(1) Legal Aid Act 1988).*

After your application has been considered by the court, you may be asked to give further information or to clarify information or to provide further proof of the information you have given.

If you stop receiving Income Support, Family Credit, Disability Working Allowance or if your financial position changes in any way after you have submitted this form, you must tell the court. This is a requirement of the Legal Aid regulations.

I understand that the court may order me to make a contribution to the costs of Legal Aid, or to pay the whole costs if it considers that I can afford to do so and, if I am under 16, may make a similar order with respect to my parents.

Signed **Dated**

4

Multiple-Choice Questions

1. The police have reasonable grounds for suspecting that Edward has committed an armed robbery in which £500,000 was stolen. On a Monday morning Edward is arrested, cautioned and taken to the police station. He arrives at the police station at 11.30 am. The custody officer is of the opinion that there is not sufficient evidence to charge Edward. The same officer also has reasonable grounds for believing that the detention of Edward is necessary to obtain such evidence by questioning him. Edward is interrogated on a number of occasions. At 11.30 pm on the next day, Tuesday, what action should be taken?

[A] Edward should be released or charged unless his continued detention without charge for a further nine hours is properly authorised by the station superintendent.
[B] Edward should be released or charged unless his continued detention for a further 12 hours is properly authorised by the station superintendent.
[C] Edward should be released or charged unless earlier on Tuesday a magistrates' court issued a warrant of further detention authorising the keeping of Edward in police detention.
[D] Edward should be released or charged unless the police intend to apply to a magistrates' court for a warrant of further detention (authorising the keeping of Edward in police detention), in which case they may hold Edward at the police station overnight and should apply for such a warrant at the next scheduled sitting of the magistrates' court (which will be at 10 am on the following morning, Wednesday).

2. Kelvin is charged with, and acquitted of, an offence of criminal damage. He was refused legal aid on the ground of means. He now makes an application for costs which the magistrates refuse because (a) Kelvin is a man of substantial means, and (b) Kelvin was acquitted on a technicality and the prosecution was properly brought. The basis of the magistrates' decision is:

[A] Correct as regards (a) but incorrect as regards (b).
[B] Correct as regards (b) but incorrect as regards (a).
[C] Incorrect on both points.
[D] Correct on both points.

Tutorial Question

You are briefed to appear at Casterbridge Magistrates' Court on 26 May 1996 to represent Amanda, who has been charged that, on 11 May, she stole from a department store a china figure worth £50. Amanda is aged 22, single, unemployed and in receipt of social security benefits. She has one previous conviction, that also being for shoplifting. She was given a conditional discharge by the Sanditon Magistrates' Court of which she will be in breach if convicted. Amanda has made one previous court appearance in connection with the present charge, that being on 12 May when she was unrepresented and was remanded for a fortnight on unconditional bail. Your solicitors state that Amanda did not instruct them until the morning of the 22nd and that it has not been possible in that time to make an application for legal aid. They therefore ask you to take whatever steps are necessary to obtain legal aid for Amanda.

(a) Describe what you would do to comply with your instructing solicitors' request and summarise the considerations which will be taken into account in deciding whether the legal aid application should be granted or not.

(b) Assuming that the application is refused, what further steps could the defence take to obtain legal aid?

THREE

REMANDS AND BAIL

Useful articles — Neil Corre, '3 Frequent Questions on the Bail Act' [1989] Crim LR 493; Brink and Stone, 'Defendants Who Do Not Ask for Bail' [19881 Crim LR 152 and Morgan, 'Remands in Custody: Problems and Prospects' [1989] Crim LR 481; editorial on Bail Decisions [1992] Crim LR 321; Brown and Hullin, 'Contested Bail Applications: the treatment of ethnic minority and white offenders' [1993] Crim LR 107.

3.1 What is a Remand?

Put in very simple terms, a remand is another name for an adjournment of a case — the postponement of its final resolution. However, the criminal justice system knows the remand as having a particular meaning. When a case is adjourned, the court may have the power or duty to remand the accused, rather than simply adjourn the case to another day. It would be accurate to say that, while all remands are adjournments, not all adjournments are remands.

The main Acts of Parliament referred to in this Chapter are:

(a) The Magistrates' Courts Act 1980 (MCA 1980).

(b) The Bail Act 1976 (BA 1976).

(c) The Criminal Justice Act 1988 (CJA 1988).

3.1.1 REMANDS IN THE CRIMINAL JUSTICE SYSTEM

If a criminal case before a court in England and Wales is not disposed of conclusively on one day, it will have to carry over into another day. For an analysis of how many cases are concluded on first appearance in court, see **Figure 3.1**.

Examples of such 'carry over' are:

(a) A trial which is too long to finish in a single day.

(b) A trial which has finished in a single day but the court wants more information on the offender before passing sentence (e.g. getting a pre-sentence report). See **14.6**.

(c) A case which has been listed for a preliminary matter only to be determined (e.g. which court will try a defendant charged with an offence triable either way).

(d) A case which has been listed for trial but either party (or perhaps the court, if it has insufficient time that day) is unable to proceed with the case there and then.

(e) A case which has finished in one court but is going to another — on appeal or committal.

Note that, with regard to (a) above, a part-heard trial in the Crown Court continues on the next day. A part-heard case in the magistrates' court may continue the next day or may resume in several weeks' time.

3.1.2 REMAND — BAIL OR CUSTODY?

In all of these examples, the case will be adjourned to another day. Whether this adjournment is a remand depends upon whether it falls within any one of several statutory situations. Essentially, the difference between 'remanding' a defendant and simply 'adjourning' the case is that the court is under a duty when remanding a defendant to decide whether he or she should be released on bail or kept locked up in custody. If a case is simply 'adjourned', then the defendant is put on trust to return to court at the place, date and time that he or she is told to.

3.1.3 SURRENDERING TO CUSTODY

If the defendant is remanded, he or she will either:

(a) be kept in custody — i.e. stay locked up until produced by the (police or prison) authorities for the next court appearance; or

(b) be freed on bail. Being released on bail imposes a duty on a defendant to return to court at the appointed date, place and time (sometimes called 'surrendering to custody'). Failure to attend the next hearing is itself a crime (BA 1976, s. 6; see also **3.14** below).

It appears that a defendant surrenders to custody by:

(i) turning up at the court where he or she was due to appear

(ii) on the due date

(iii) at the appointed time (usually 10 am) and

(iv) reporting to the appropriate person.

See *DPP* v *Richards* [1988] QB 701.

Even though the defendant is then allowed to remain apparently at liberty, by staying in the public areas of the court building, nevertheless he or she is in custody until the case comes up in court. It follows that the defendant is under an implied obligation not to leave the building without first obtaining permission to do so. (Permission should be sought from the court or someone acting on its behalf.) If the defendant leaves without consent, the court may issue a warrant for his or her arrest. See BA 1976, s. 7(2); *DPP* v *Richards* above; confirmed in *R* v *Central Criminal Court, ex parte Guney* [1995] 1 WLR 376.

Remember that some defendants are released on police bail subject to a duty to surrender to custody, not at a court but at a police station, typically where enquiries are being pursued and the individual has not been charged with an offence.

3.2 When will a Case be Remanded?

Whenever magistrates adjourn a case, they may remand the defendant. The MCA 1980 provides several situations where, on an adjournment, a magistrates' court must remand a defendant and then consider the alternatives of bail and custody. See **Figure 3.1**.

Figure 3.1 Will the adjournment be a remand?

1. When D first appeared in the court, was he on bail or in custody?
   If YES — he must now be remanded (on bail or in custody).
   If NO —
2. Has D been remanded at any time during the proceedings for this offence?
   If YES — he must now be remanded (on bail or in custody).
   If NO —
3. The magistrates have a choice to remand or simply adjourn the case.

Figure 3.2 Defendants proceeded against at magistrates' courts — average time for criminal cases by offence type and stage of proceedings, percentage dealt with on first appearance, average number of times case listed and average length of adjournments[1]

England and Wales

Offence type	Average number of days: from offence to disposal	from offence to charge or summons	from charge or summons to first listing	from first listing to disposal	Percentage of defendants dealt with on first court appearance	Average number of times case listed in court	Average length of adjournments in days	Percentage of defendants pleading guilty[2]	Number of defendants in sample (thousands)
Indictable offences									
1985	98	38	18	41	31	2.8	23	65	20.7
1986	108	41	20	46	29	3.0	23	62	27.3
1987	114	41	22	51	26	3.3	22	59	26.7
1988	117	40	21	55	24	3.4	23	57	26.4
1989	122	40	22	61	22	3.5	24	54	24.3
1990	127	40	22	64	22	3.5	26	53	25.5
1991	128	42	22	65	21	3.6	25	51	26.3
1992	129	43	22	64	20	3.4	27	48	26.3
1993[3]	120	39	25	56	21	3.3	24	48	23.5
Summary non-motoring offences									
1985	107	61	29	17	72	1.4	38	70	7.7
1986	124	73	36	16	74	1.4	37	73	8.0
1987	123	71	35	17	74	1.5	36	71	7.6
1988	127	73	35	20	73	1.5	40	69	8.0
1989	125	66	37	22	70	1.6	39	65	9.2
1990	134	69	40	25	69	1.6	43	63	9.0
1991	135	71	39	26	66	1.6	40	56	9.7
1992	137	79	37	21	70	1.5	42	52	10.9
1993[3]	132	75	38	19	67	1.6	32	52	9.4
Summary motoring offences									
1985	129	68	39	21	69	1.5	43	76	24.6
1986	135	72	40	22	69	1.5	41	74	26.8
1987	148	75	42	31	59	1.8	39	73	17.0
1988	146	73	42	31	61	1.8	39	73	18.7
1989	155	75	42	38	57	1.9	41	73	17.9
1990	156	77	41	38	55	2.0	39	71	17.3
1991	162	76	43	43	55	2.0	41	67	18.7
1992	163	79	42	41	50	2.0	41	61	18.8
1993[3]	152	80	38	33	52	2.0	33	59	17.0

(1) Based on proceedings in sample weeks in February, June and October for indictable offences, and June only for summary offences. The 1985 figures for indictable offences are based on June and October only.
(2) Defendants pleading guilty at a summary trial, as a proportion of all those proceeded against.
(3) Changes in recording procedures have led to small discrepancies. It is estimated that the average period from first listing to completion has been reduced by 2 days for indictable offences.

3.2.1 SITUATIONS WHERE REMAND IS REQUIRED

(a) *Magistrates dealing with an offence triable either way.* If, before or during the trial of such an offence, an adjournment is needed, then usually the defendant must be remanded on bail or in custody. See **Figure 3.1**.

(b) *Magistrates determining which court will try an 'either way' offence.* If the magistrates adjourn a case while determining whether the defendant will be tried by the magistrates or a jury (MCA 1980, ss. 19–23), usually they must remand the defendant on bail or in custody (see MCA 1980, s. 18(4)). See **Figure 3.1**.

(c) *Magistrates committing an accused to the Crown Court for trial.* In this case, following a decision to send the accused to the Crown Court for trial, if the accused is currently remanded in custody the magistrates may either order that he be kept in custody pending his trial or release him on bail with a direction that he appear before the Crown Court for trial (MCA 1980, s. 8(1)).

There are two other situations to be aware of:

(d) *Magistrates dealing with a summary offence.* Prior to deciding whether a defendant is guilty or innocent in such a case, the magistrates may have to adjourn the proceedings. If they do so, they have a choice — either to remand the defendant or simply to adjourn (MCA 1980, s. 10(4)). If the defendant fails to appear at court on the next appointed date, the magistrates may proceed to try the case in the absence of the defendant or, in some circumstances, issue a warrant for arrest (MCA 1980, ss. 11 and 13). See **Chapter 5**.

(e) *Magistrates deferring sentence.* Where a magistrates' court defers sentence on a convicted defendant (for up to six months) under the Powers of Criminal Courts Act 1973, s. 1, this is not a remand, and the defendant, although released subject to a duty to return to court, is not on bail. (See the Powers of Criminal Courts Act 1973, s. 1(6A); *R* v *Ross* (1988) 86 Cr App R 337.)

3.2.2 THE USE OF REMANDS OR ADJOURNMENTS BY MAGISTRATES

For an analysis of the use of remands or adjournments by magistrates, see **Figure 3.3**.

3.3 Who Can Remand a Case?

3.3.1 REMANDS IN THE MAGISTRATES' COURT

It might seem, from what you have just read, that only magistrates can remand a criminal case. This is not the whole story. The vast majority of remands occur in the magistrates' court simply because that is where the bulk of criminal litigation takes place, particularly when you realise that almost all hearings in a case prior to trial occur in the magistrates' court.

3.3.2 REMANDS IN THE CROWN COURT

The question of a simple adjournment never seems to arise in the Crown Court. A defendant who is committed to the Crown Court (whether for trial or sentence) will be remanded either on bail or in custody. Once there, the Crown Court judge has the power to grant bail for the period before the matter is dealt with (see Supreme Court Act 1981, s. 81, as amended). In 1987 (the last year for which figures are available), about 35% of those tried at the Crown Court had been remanded to a future sitting of the court (either on bail or in custody) at some stage of their case.

Once a Crown Court trial has started, the judge will remand the accused either in custody or on bail during any lunch or overnight breaks in the trial. Whether or not to release on bail is usually regarded as a matter solely within the power and discretion of the trial judge; see the observation by Peter Gibson LJ in *R* v *Central Criminal Court, ex parte Guney* [1995] 1 WLR that from 'the commencement of a [Crown Court] trial it is for the court conducting the trial to decide whether the defendant should be in custody or on bail'.

Figure 3.3 Persons proceeded against at magistrates' courts by type of remand and outcome of proceedings

England and Wales 1993 — Thousands and percentages

	All persons charged or summonsed(1)			Total		
Outcome	Not remanded by magistrates	Bailed by magistrates	Remanded in custody by magistrates(2)	1994	1993	1992
			Number of persons (thousands)			
Acquitted or not proceeded with etc.	369.2	133.2	10.6	513.1	506.0	488.7
Convicted:						
non-custodial sentence	1,031.0	237.8	14.1	1,282.8	1,308.6	1,390.4
sentence of immediate custody	8.5	19.9	7.9	36.3	27.5	23.2
committed for sentence:						
on bail	0.4	1.6	0.2	2.1	2.7	4.7
in custody	0.3	0.3	1.5	2.1	1.9	2.7
Committed for trial:						
on bail	7.3	61.1	3.7	72.1	70.9	78.5
in custody	1.7	2.2	16.9	20.9	19.8	20.3
Failed to appear to court bail	—	50.0	1.0	51.0	46.9	36.6
Total	1,418.2	506.1	55.9	1,980.2	1,984.1	2,044.9
			Percentage of persons			
Acquitted or not proceeded with etc.	26	26	19	26	26	24
Convicted:						
non-custodial sentence	73	47	25	65	66	68
sentence of immediate custody	1	4	14	2	1	1
committed for sentence:						
on bail	—	0	0	0	0	0
in custody	—	0	3	0	0	0
Committed for trial:						
on bail	1	12	7	4	4	4
in custody	1	1	30	1	1	1
Failed to appear to court bail	—	11	2	3	2	2
Total	100.0	100.0	100.0	100.0	100.0	100.0

(1) Excluding those who failed to appear following summons or police bail.
(2) Includes those remanded for part of the time in custody and part on bail.

3.4 Duration of Remands

3.4.1 GENERAL EXAMPLES

There are various maximum periods for a remand by magistrates in different circumstances.

Before conviction

(a) Three clear days in police custody.

(b) Eight clear days in prison custody. (Exception: if an 'either way' offence is to be tried by the magistrates but they cannot convene in time, remand to whenever they can convene the court.)

(c) Twenty-eight clear days in prison custody if the defendant is legally represented in court, is not a juvenile and consents to being remanded for this length of time. (But see **3.4.2**.)

(d) Twenty-eight clear days in prison custody if the defendant has at least that long still to serve on a current custodial sentence.

(e) Any period to which both the prosecution and defence agree on bail.

After conviction

(f) Three weeks in custody for inquiries or reports for sentencing.

(g) Four weeks on bail for inquiries, etc.

Each of these periods is the maximum duration for a *single* remand. At its conclusion, the defendant will be produced before the magistrates once more. At that time, and subject to the custody time limits (see **3.6.4** below), the magistrates may again remand him or her either on bail or in custody for a further period. Once a defendant is sent to the Crown Court, either for trial or sentence to be passed, he or she is remanded on bail or in custody until such time as the case is listed for hearing (again, subject to the custody time limits).

3.4.2 EXTENSION OF THE MAXIMUM PERIOD FOR REMANDS

The proportion of the prison population which is on remand is quite large. It is a tremendous administrative and logistical burden to produce defendants from custody once a week, every week. It was to save on time, energy and costs that MCA 1980, s. 128 was amended by the CJA 1982 to allow the usual remand period of one week to be extended effectively to four weeks, if the defendant had a lawyer and consented to this extended period (see MCA, s. 128(3A)).

Clearly, this meant that if there was no defence lawyer in the case or the defendant did not consent, the defendant still had to be produced in court every week. Even if MCA 1980, s. 128(3A) could be used in a case so that the defendant did not appear at court each week, strictly speaking he or she was still being remanded every eight days in his or her absence. His or her case still had to be listed at court once a week and the magistrates had formally to announce that it (and he or she) would be remanded to the following week.

This situation was altered by CJA 1988, s. 155. This introduced an additional element to the MCA 1980, s. 128A, which allows magistrates to remand an accused person for up to 28 clear days. This time no consent is required from the defendant, nor need there be a defence lawyer at court. Basically, all that is necessary is that:

(a) the accused has been remanded in custody already in the case; and

(b) the accused is present in court when the extended remand is ordered; and

(c) the court has fixed a date when the next stage in the proceedings will take place.

3.5 What are the Alternatives to Remanding a Case?

These have been mentioned already but, in brief, the court may:

(a) *Try the case anyway.* If a case is ready for summary trial and the accused does not appear, the magistrates may go ahead and try the case in his or her absence, having entered a formal plea of not guilty. This power to try absent defendants does not exist in the Crown Court — the accused must be present at the start of a jury trial to enter a plea to the indictment personally. (See **5.1.1** and MCA 1980, s. 11(1).)

(b) *Adjourn to another date.* A case may be simply adjourned to another date and the prosecution and accused told to turn up at court. No penal sanction exists in that situation to compel attendance on the adjourned hearing. The defence may seek an adjournment in order, for example, to instruct an expert witness to appear as a witness for the defendant. (See *R* v *Sunderland Justices, ex parte Dryden, The Times*, 18 May 1994.)

(c) *Adjourn indefinitely and issue a warrant for arrest.* If the accused does not appear at court, the result will often be the issue of a warrant for his or her arrest (sometimes called a 'bench' warrant) (see MCA 1980, s. 13). Such a warrant will normally result, when executed, in the defendant staying in custody until a court hearing can be arranged but, if the magistrates suspect there may be a reasonable excuse for non-attendance, they may grant bail (known as 'backing a warrant for bail'). This has the effect that the defendant is arrested and taken to the police station but is then released on bail to attend the magistrates' court at a later date. Crown Court judges can also issue such warrants if a defendant is absent from court without permission. (See also **2.4** and **3.14**.) The warrant may be issued once the court is satisfied that the information against the accused has been supported on oath, that the accused is aware of the hearing and the offence is imprisonable. Warrants may be issued for non-imprisonable offences if the first two criteria are satisfied *and* the court proposes to impose a disqualification on the defendant.

(d) *Dismiss the case.* If the prosecution is not ready to proceed with a summary trial, it is possible that the magistrates will dismiss the charge if there has been a long delay between the commission of the alleged offence and the court hearing. See, for example, *R* v *Oxford City Justices, ex parte Smith* (1982) 75 Cr App R 200; cf. *R* v *Barnet Magistrates' Court, ex parte DPP, The Times*, 8 April 1994. See also **2.3.1**.

3.6 Bail — Practice and Procedure

3.6.1 'UNCONDITIONAL' BAIL

The question of whether to release a defendant on bail or keep him or her in custody arises whenever a case is remanded (see **3.1** above). If a defendant is granted bail, this means that he or she is released from court subject to a primary duty to attend the next court hearing in the case. This is known as the duty to surrender to custody. (See BA 1976, s. 3(1).) Failure to do so at the appointed place, time and date is itself a criminal offence leading to a fine or imprisonment (BA 1976, s. 6 — see **3.14** below).

The primary duty may be accompanied by secondary duties imposed on the defendant — for example, to keep a curfew within certain hours; to report to the local police station once a week; to surrender one's passport. These secondary duties are often described as 'conditions of bail' (see **3.12** below). A defendant who is released on bail, subject only to the primary duty to surrender to bail at the next court hearing, is often referred to by barristers as being released on 'unconditional' bail.

The text of the Bail Act 1976, s. 3(1), is as follows:

Incidents of bail in criminal proceedings

3.—(1) A person granted bail in criminal proceedings shall be under a duty to surrender to custody, and that duty is enforceable in accordance with section 6 of this Act.

Figure 3.4 Persons summonsed, released on bail by the police or remanded on bail at magistrates' courts: proportion who failed to appear by offence group

England and Wales

Thousands and percentages

Offence group	Persons summonsed					Persons bailed by the police					Persons remanded on bail at magistrates' courts				
	Total number summonsed (thousands)	Number failing to appear (thousands)	Percentage of number summonsed who failed to appear			Total number bailed (thousands)[1]	Number failing to appear (thousands)	Percentage of number bailed who failed to appear			Total number bailed (thousands)[1]	Number failing to appear (thousands)	Percentage of number bailed who failed to appear		
	1993	1993[2]	1993[2]	1992	1991	1993	1993[2]	1993[2]	1992	1991	1993	1993[2]	1993[2]	1992	1991
Indictable[3]	58.7	10.1	17.2	12.2	11.7	455.9	40.6	8.9	7.3	7.2	342.6	34.9	10.2	8.4	7.9
Summary (other than motoring)	431.8	2.9	0.7	0.6	0.7	120.0	11.6	9.6	6.6	6.1	70.2	6.0	8.5	6.0	4.9
Summary motoring	830.8	53.2	6.4	3.8	2.7	121.2	7.4	6.1	4.7	4.8	76.1	5.6	7.4	6.0	5.5
Total	1,321.3	66.2	5.0	3.3	2.7	697.1	59.6	8.5	6.8	6.6	488.9	46.5	9.5	7.7	7.0

(1) Including those also held in custody at some stage.
(2) Part of the increase in numbers failing to appear, particularly in 1993, is due to more complete recording.
(3) Including summary offences of criminal damage.

3.6.2 THE RIGHT TO BAIL

The Bail Act 1976, s. 4 gives a 'general right to bail' (sic) for defendants in criminal litigation. However, s. 4 does not apply to all defendants in the criminal justice system nor at all stages of the system (see **3.6.3** below). Furthermore, even those defendants to whom BA 1976, s. 4 applies cannot demand to be released on bail automatically. There is a presumption, but no more, that such a defendant will be released on bail if a case is remanded. Section 4(1) says that a person to whom s. 4 applies shall be granted bail (this is the 'right'), *except* as provided in BA 1976, sch. 1, when bail will be denied, and he or she will be remanded in custody (see **3.9** below). For the views of one experienced practitioner on how the right to bail works in practice and how it might be reformed, see Michael Mansfield QC, *Presumed Guilty*, Mandarin, 1993, Chapter 12.

3.6.3 WHERE THERE IS NO RIGHT TO BAIL

It is important to realise that the 'right' to bail under BA 1976 *usually* applies only prior to conviction. It also only applies when a defendant appears in court (see BA 1976, s. 4). So there is no right to bail in the following situations:

(a) When being arrested.

(b) When being charged with an offence.

(c) When a warrant for the arrest of an accused person is issued.

(d) After conviction for the offence **unless:**

(i) the case is being adjourned so that inquiries or reports can be made to assist in passing sentence; or

(ii) the defendant is brought before a magistrates' court to be dealt with for breach of probation or a community service order (BA 1976, s. 4(3) and (4)).

In situations where there is no right to bail, it should not generally be thought that the defendant cannot be released on bail. The court, if it remands such a case, usually has a *discretion* to grant bail. This discretion is unfettered by the need to satisfy BA 1976, sch. 1, if bail is to be refused — in other words, the court has more freedom to refuse bail in such circumstances. On the grant of bail at the police station following charge, see PACE 1984, s. 38 (see **2.2.9**).

There are two further exceptions to the general right to bail that we must note; they are created by the Criminal Justice and Public Order Act 1994 (CJPOA 1994). First, if a defendant is charged with murder, manslaughter or rape (or an attempt, where appropriate) and he has a previous conviction for one of those offences, then he shall be refused bail (see CJPOA 1994, s. 25). In a case where the previous conviction was for manslaughter, the prohibition only applies if the defendant received a custodial sentence for that offence. Secondly, where a defendant appears in court charged with an offence triable either way and it appears to the court that he was already on bail at the time of the present offence, he need not be granted bail; that is, bail is simply a matter for the discretion of the court (see CJPOA 1994, s. 26, inserting paragraph 2A into BA 1976, part I, sch. 1).

3.6.4 CUSTODY TIME LIMITS

Certain limits have been introduced on the length of time that a defendant can be kept on remand in custody, under the Prosecution of Offences Act 1985. These limits do not apply to summary offences or treason. See the Prosecution of Offences (Custody Time Limits) Regulations 1987 (S.I. 1987 No. 299), as amended.

The regulations state definite periods within which a specified stage of the proceedings must be reached (e.g. the defendant must be sent for trial within 70 days of his first appearance in court, if he is then remanded in custody). If these limits are exceeded, the defendant *must* be released on bail (or in certain circumstances, acquitted). The prosecution can apply for an extension of the period; it needs to show (on a balance of probabilities) good and sufficient cause for an extension; and that it has acted with all due expedition.

In a magistrates' court the maximum length of time that a defendant should spend in custody is 70 days. This period should be calculated as follows:

(a) 70 days from first court appearance to the start of summary trial (for either way offences);

(b) 70 days from first court appearance to a decision on committal for trial (for either way offences and offences which must be tried on indictment).

Note that, in (a) above, if the magistrates take a decision to proceed to summary trial within 56 days of the defendant's first court appearance, the custody time limit becomes 56 (not 70) days. Note further that, in (b) above, if the committal proceedings are held pursuant to MCA 1980, s. 6(1) (i.e. with consideration of the evidence), then the 70-day limit is satisfied if the magistrates start to hear the prosecution's evidence within that period: they need not reach a decision on whether to commit the accused for trial within that period.

In the Crown Court, the maximum length of time that a defendant should spend in custody prior to his or her trial is 112 days, beginning with the date that he or she was sent for trial by the magistrates and expiring with the date of his or her arraignment (i.e. being asked in Crown Court to plead either guilty or not guilty). This period can be extended, but any use of a 'sham' arraignment simply to defeat the purpose of the custody time limit will be struck down. See, for example, *R* v *Maidstone Crown Court, ex parte Hollstein, The Times*, 4 November 1994 — H was sent for trial on 24 March 1994, his custody time limit should have expired on 14 July 1994 but was extended to 22 July 1994. He should then have been released on bail but was kept in custody and produced in court on 27 July 1994 when he was arraigned on the indictment and further remanded in custody. He was still remanded in custody on 13 October 1994 (some three months after the expiry of the original time limit) when the Queen's Bench Divisional Court granted his application to quash the decision of 27 July 1994 to remand him in custody — no date for his trial had been fixed and the arraignement was an artificially created situation. Finally, one should note that the 112-day limit does not apply to certain defendants who are awaiting trial for offences of homicide and rape (see BA 1976, s. 4(8) (as amended), pursuant to CJPOA 1994, s. 25). When a defendant is freed on bail due to the expiry of a custody time limit, his bail should only have conditions attached to it that the defendant can comply with *after* his release (e.g. reporting to a police station or a condition to reside at a specified address). Conditions which must be complied with *prior* to release (e.g. providing a financial surety) cannot be imposed. The significance of this can be seen in *Re Ofili* [1995] Crim LR 880, where O was originally granted bail, subject to providing a surety of £4,000. O could find no one to stand surety in that sum, so he remained in custody. On the expiry of the custody time limit, he was entitled to be freed on bail, subject only to reporting or residence conditions.

See Archbold, 1995 edn, paras. 1–303, 3–55; *Blackstone's Criminal Practice*, 1996, D5.20 and D9.4.

3.6.5 BAIL ACT 1976, s. 4

Bail for accused persons and others

4.—(1) A person to whom this section applies shall be granted bail except as provided in Schedule 1 to this Act.

(2) This section applies to a person who is accused of an offence when—

(a) he appears or is brought before a magistrates' court or the Crown Court in the course of or in connection with proceedings for the offence, or

(b) he applies to a court for bail in connection with the proceedings.

This subsection does not apply as respects proceedings on or against a person's conviction of the offence or proceedings against a fugitive offender for the offence.

(3) This section also applies to a person who, having been convicted of an offence, appears or is brought before a magistrates' court to be dealt with under Part II of Schedule 2 to the Criminal Justice Act 1991 (breach of requirement of probation, community service, combination or curfew order).

(4) This section also applies to a person who has been convicted of an offence and whose case is adjourned by the court for the purpose of enabling inquiries or a report to be made to assist the court in dealing with him for the offence.

3.7 Taking a Decision on Bail — When and How

3.7.1 WHEN IS THE DECISION TAKEN?

Usually, the question of bail or custody is decided at the end of each day's proceedings in the case, immediately prior to remanding it to another day. (If a case is being heard in court in the morning, and will continue in the afternoon, the court should determine whether the accused will take lunch in the cells (custody) or in the restaurant of his or her choice (bail), immediately before breaking for lunch.) A typical example of this is in committal proceedings in the magistrates' court — the court will determine whether the defendant is to be sent for trial to the Crown Court first, then determine the witness orders for trial, give an alibi warning if needed and, finally, consider the twin issues of bail and legal aid. Sometimes, though, the question of bail is the sole reason for a case appearing in court. Examples are:

(a) The defendant, committed in custody to the Crown Court for trial or sentence, who applies to the Crown Court for bail pending the anticipated appearance in the Crown Court.

(b) The defendant who has been refused bail by magistrates and appeals to a Crown Court judge (see **3.16.1** below).

(c) The defendant who has been refused bail by magistrates and/or a Crown Court judge and appeals to a High Court judge (see **3.16.2** below).

3.7.2 HOW IS THE DECISION TAKEN?

The court must decide for itself whether or not to grant bail. It may be addressed by representatives of both prosecution and defence if the grant of bail is opposed, but the decision is one for the court. Lay magistrates will often retire briefly to consider whether to grant bail if release on bail is opposed by the prosecution. Stipendiary magistrates and Crown Court judges will normally decide in court, straight after counsel have finished their submissions. If the release of the defendant on bail is unopposed by the prosecution (and especially if the defendant is already on bail in the current proceedings), the decision to grant bail is usually a formality.

3.7.3 RECORDS, REASONS, CERTIFICATES AND RIGHTS

3.7.3.1 Records

There are two common situations when a record must be kept of a decision on bail. Pursuant to BA 1976, s. 5(1), these are:

(a) whenever bail is granted (either by the police or a court);

(b) whenever a defendant with the right to bail under BA 1976, s. 4 is remanded in custody by a court.

Also, if an application is made to a court either:

(i) to attach conditions to a grant of bail which was hitherto unconditional; or

(ii) to vary any extant conditions of bail,

the court must make a record of its decision. Examples of such records can be seen in *Stone's Justices' Manual*, vol. 3, part IX, Forms 149–153.

If the defendant asks for a copy of the record, he or she must be given one (BA 1976, s. 5). In some of the situations set out below, the defendant must be given a copy of the record even if one is not requested.

3.7.3.2 Reasons

1. *For refusing to grant bail, etc.*

If a defendant has a right to bail under BA 1976, s. 4, then if a court:

(a) refuses to grant bail; or

(b) grants bail subject to conditions; or

(c) on application for the purpose, imposes or varies conditions in respect of bail,

the court shall give reasons for its decision (BA 1976, s. 5(3)).

These reasons shall be entered on the s. 5 record and a copy must be given to the defendant (s. 5(4)). However, if the decision is taken by the Crown Court, the defendant is legally represented in court, and the representative does not request a copy, a copy need not be given (BA 1976, s. 5(5)). The purpose of giving reasons in these situations is to enable the defendant to make an informed decision about applying to another court about bail.

2. *For granting bail*

If a defendant is charged with any one of five specific offences, then, if a court grants bail notwithstanding that the prosecution have made certain representations, the court must state its reasons for granting bail, and these should be entered on the s. 5 record. The offences are: murder (including attempts); manslaughter; and rape (including attempts).

The prosecution must have made representations that, if the defendant was granted bail, he or she would either fail to surrender to custody, or commit an offence whilst on bail; or interfere with witnesses or otherwise obstruct the course of justice.

The requirement to state reasons in this situation is imposed on the court by BA 1976, sch. 1, part I, para. 9A (inserted by CJA 1988, s. 153).

3.7.3.3 Certificates

Under BA 1976, s. 5(6A), if magistrates withhold bail after hearing a fully argued application for bail, they must issue a certificate stating that they heard full argument. After two unsuccessful bail applications in a case, if the magistrates allow the defendant a third application (which is unsuccessful), they should issue a certificate indicating the change in circumstances or new consideration that persuaded them to hear the third application. See BA 1976, s. 5(6A) and (6B); also BA 1976, sch. 1, part IIA (inserted by CJA 1988, s. 154). See further **3.15** and **3.16** below.

3.7.3.4 Rights

If a magistrates' court withholds bail from an unrepresented defendant, it must inform the defendant of his or her right to apply to a judge of the High Court to be granted bail. If the magistrates are committing the defendant to the Crown Court for trial, or have issued a certificate under BA 1976, s. 5(6A), they must also tell the defendant that he or she may apply to a Crown Court judge for bail. (See BA 1976, s. 5(6).)

3.8 Applying for Bail— What Happens in Court?

The procedure for determining whether a defendant is to be released on bail or not does not really vary from court to court, either between courts on the same level of the court system or between courts on different levels. Although some defendants have a right to bail under BA 1976, s. 4, while others can only seek the exercise of the court's discretion in their favour, in practice it is incumbent on the defendant to apply for bail. See [1988] Crim LR 397 for a contrary view.

3.8.1 THE BAIL APPLICATION WHICH IS OPPOSED

When a court hearing is adjourned and the defendant is to be remanded, the defendant (or defence counsel) is asked whether he or she seeks release on bail. If the answer is yes, the prosecution will be asked if there are any objections to bail (see **3.9** below). If there are, these will now be given to the court, usually by the prosecutor (note that the strict rules of evidence do not apply to bail applications).

If no agreement can be reached between defence and prosecution prior to coming into court (see **3.8.3**), after the objections have been set before the court, defence counsel makes oral submissions dealing with the objections to bail. Counsel may suggest that the objections are groundless and/or propose any conditions which might be attached to bail to overcome the objections (see further **3.11** and **3.12.4** below). The defence may call potential sureties into the witness box to help persuade the court that the defendant is unlikely to abscond. Finally, the court takes its decision to remand either on bail or in custody.

(See further **Chapter 34** in the ***Advocacy Manual*** for a checklist and flow chart on bail applications.)

3.8.2 THE UNOPPOSED APPLICATION FOR BAIL

In this situation, the defence having indicated that bail is sought, the prosecution offer no objection. Although the court could try to investigate whether there are reasons why it should withhold bail from the accused, it is unlikely to do so — largely because its normal source of information critical of the accused is the prosecution. If prosecuting counsel sees no reason to object, the court is unlikely to discover such a reason from that source for itself.

3.8.3 DEALING WITH THE OPPOSITION

Often, defence counsel will seek out the prosecution before the case is called into court and ask whether there are any objections to bail. If not, the application will be unopposed and is likely to succeed (see **3.8.2**). If there are objections, defence counsel may ask what these are and then think about what bail conditions might overcome them. If defence counsel can get the defendant's agreement to such conditions, the approval of the prosecution may then be sought. If this is obtained, the defence can apply to the court for bail and offer the 'agreed' terms. As the application is now unopposed in effect, success (with the agreed conditions) is likely.

3.9 Objections to a Release on Bail

As mentioned above, the prosecution may object to the defendant being freed on bail. In practice, any objections will correspond to one or more of the reasons for refusing bail to a 's. 4' defendant, found in BA 1976, sch. 1. These will be substantiated with information by the prosecutor. Examples are:

(a) 'The accused is likely to fail to surrender to bail': he failed to turn up last time and we had to get a warrant; he has three convictions for this sort of thing already and faces a long spell in prison; he has no permanent address.

(b) 'The accused is likely to commit offences if freed': he was already on bail for an offence when he was arrested for this lot; he's done it in the past; he makes his living from crime.

(c) 'The accused must be remanded in custody for his own protection': he is on 12 charges of burglary, all from houses on the estate where he lives. Some of the residents have told the police that he's a dead man if he shows his face round there.

3.10 Refusing to Release a Defendant on Bail

3.10.1 CIRCUMSTANCES WHEN THIS CAN HAPPEN

If a defendant has the right to bail under BA 1976, s. 4, and asks to be released, then the court can only withhold bail where the offence is imprisonable if one (or more) of the following criteria is present in the case:

(a) The court is satisfied that there are substantial grounds to believe that the defendant would:

- (i) fail to surrender to custody;
- (ii) commit an offence whilst on bail;
- (iii) interfere with witnesses or otherwise obstruct the course of justice.

(b) The court is satisfied that the accused must be kept in custody for his or her own protection (or welfare, if the accused is a child or young person — see **Chapter 7** for definition of these terms).

(c) The accused is currently serving a custodial sentence imposed for a previous offence.

(d) If this is the first time that the case has been in the court and the court is satisfied it has not been practicable to obtain all the information necessary for a proper decision on bail to be made.

(e) If the accused has already failed to surrender to bail in the current case (or has broken the conditions attached to the grant of bail) and has been arrested for this.

(See BA 1976, sch. 1, part 1.)

3.10.2 CONSIDERATIONS FOR THE COURT

Schedule 1 to the Bail Act 1976 (at part I, para. 9) says that when a court is considering whether one of the reasons for refusing bail referred to in (a) (in **3.10.1**) exists, it should take account of:

(a) The nature and seriousness of the offence (and probable sentence).

(b) The character, antecedents, associations and community ties of the accused.

(c) His or her record of fulfilling bail requirements in the past.

(d) The strength of the case against the accused (unless adjourning for reports or inquiries before passing sentence).

(e) Any other considerations as appear relevant.

With regard to (b), the disclosure of D's *antecedents* means that the magistrates learn of his or her criminal record, if any. There are several points to note about this:

(i) evidence of any criminal record should be tendered in writing, not orally (*R v Dyson* (1944) 29 Cr App R104);

(ii) the press *should not* report any convictions which are publicised, at that time (*R* v *Fletcher* (1949) 113 JP 365) (NB there is no direct power to coerce the media, although note Contempt of Court Act 1981, s. 4(2));

(iii) any magistrate who sits on a bail application hearing and learns of previous convictions is disqualified from subsequently trying D's guilt/ innocence (MCA 1980, s. 42).

Also on 'associations and community ties', see the suggestions in *Stones' Justices' Manual* (1995) at 1–433. The phrase covers:

(i) name, age, nationality and (if applicable) length of residence in the UK;

(ii) family circumstances (married? dependent children? does he live with wife/parents/other relatives?);

(iii) residence (type of accommodation; recent addresses and length of stay);

(iv) employment (recent record; present job — location and income);

(v) possible sureties, any relative, friend, employer in court . . .;

(vi) anything else that the defendant wants to put forward, e.g. medical problems, difficulties with job or home if remanded in custody.

Remember, if a court withholds bail from a 's. 4' defendant, it must give its *reasons* in open court and on the record (BA 1976, s. 5(3); see **3.7.3** above).

3.10.3 BAIL FOR NON-IMPRISONABLE CRIMES

The grounds for refusing bail set out in **3.10.1** are applied only to defendants charged with crimes for which they can be sent to prison, if convicted. The Bail Act 1976, sch. 1 also covers bail for non-imprisonable offences and is more liberal in allowing bail. The grounds for withholding bail now are:

(a) For the protection of the defendant.

(b) Where the defendant is already serving a custodial sentence.

(c) Where the defendant has been arrested for a bail offence in connection with this case (see **3.14** below).

(d) Where the defendant has previously failed to surrender to bail and, in the light of that failure, the court is satisfied he or she would not surrender to bail if released now.

The detailed provisions which govern the imposition of bail conditions are to be found in BA 1976, sch. 1, part I, para. 8. Part I applies to defendants 'accused or convicted of *imprisonable* offences' (emphasis added). There is no corresponding text in sch. 1, part II, which deals with *non-imprisonable* offences. It might be thought, then, that the BA 1976 makes no provision for attaching conditions to a grant of bail where a defendant is accused or convicted of a non-imprisonable offence. In fact, it has been decided that the basic power to attach conditions to a grant of bail (BA 1976, s. 3) applies to both imprisonable and non-imprisonable offences (see *R* v *Bournemouth Magistrates' Court, ex parte Cross* (1989) 89 Cr App R 90).

This decision can produce a rather odd result by virtue of the different criteria which now apply to non-imprisonable offences when (i) refusing bail and (ii) imposing conditions. BA 1976, s. 3(6) and sch. 1, part I, para. 8 both allow a court to attach conditions to a grant of bail if it appears necessary to do so in order to ensure that the defendant surrenders to custody; but sch. 1, part II, does not allow a court to withhold bail on the grounds that it believes the defendant will not surrender to custody. So if the court fears that a defendant will abscond, it may attach conditions to his bail but if there are no conditions that will allay such fears, they must release on bail anyway.

3.11 Overcoming Objections to Bail — The Power of Imagination

It was mentioned earlier (in **3.8.1** above) that if the prosecution is objecting to the release of the defendant on bail, defence counsel can suggest that certain conditions be attached to the grant of bail. These suggestions can be made to the prosecutor before going into court or once the prosecutor states the objections in court. Additionally, defence counsel can make (or repeat) these suggestions in his or her final submissions to the court. Apart from some qualifications on the power of the courts to attach conditions to a grant of bail, the conditions which can be used to overcome the fears of the prosecution or court are almost limitless.

3.11.1 KEEPING ONE'S IMAGINATION WITHIN REASONABLE BOUNDS

There are some very common conditions (see **3.12** below) which will be suggested by the defence almost as an automatic reaction to certain objections. Nevertheless, one should not be afraid to put forward novel solutions to allay any objections, subject only to two observations. First, that one should always get the defendant's consent before putting a suggestion forward. Apart from the ethical problem of arguing a case with no instructions from the lay client to do so, there is a practical problem — to get your client released on bail, subject to conditions which he or she will not or cannot accept, is effectively not getting bail. Secondly, remember that the everyday bail conditions are used so often because they are workable and answer a particular objection sensibly. Do not invent new ones which fail to satisfy those criteria. One should seek only to improve the commonplace conditions to deal with novel situations when they arise.

3.12 Attaching Conditions to Release on Bail

In **3.6.1** above it was said that any grant of bail was subject to a primary duty — to surrender to bail at the appointed time, date and place — but also, in some circumstances, that secondary duties (known as 'conditions of bail') could be imposed on a defendant. The Bail Act 1976 specifies two forms of condition and the circumstances in which they may be used — the surety and security (see BA 1976, s. 3(3) and (4)). Originally, the police were limited to just these two conditions when releasing a defendant on bail from a police station. Conversely, courts could impose any conditions that they thought necessary to secure certain objectives — e.g. that the defendant would surrender to custody, not offend whilst on bail and not interfere with witnesses (see BA 1976, s. 3(6) below).

The 1993 Royal Commission on Criminal Justice, chaired by Lord Runciman, recommended that the police should have the power to release a suspect on bail subject to conditions (see para. 5.22 and recommendation 94 of the report). There was concern that people who could properly have been released on bail, if conditions were attached to their bail, were instead being kept in custody. This often led to defendants being brought from custody to a magistrates' court where they would apply for bail and have it granted subject, perhaps, to those conditions that the police were prepared to impose but lacked the power to do so. The Runciman Commission's recommendation was taken up by the Government, and the police now have far greater powers to attach conditions to a grant of bail. Section 47 of PACE 1984 has been amended so that now the 'normal powers to impose conditions of bail' shall be available to a custody officer (PACE 1984, s. 47(1A)). Section 3(6) of the Bail Act 1976 has also been amended so that the police are now almost as free as the courts to impose conditions on a grant of bail (see CJPOA 1994, s. 27).

The main restrictions that the police are subject to now are that the condition(s) must appear to be necessary to ensure that a defendant surrenders to custody, or does not offend whilst on bail, or does not interfere with witnesses or otherwise obstruct the course of justice (see BA 1976, s. 3A(5)). In addition, police cannot make it a condition of bail that the accused resides in a bail hostel (BA 1976, s. 3A(2)), nor do the special provisions on obtaining medical reports relating to defendants facing a charge of murder apply to police bail (BA 1976, s. 3A(3)).

As regards a person granted bail, BA 1976, s. 3, provides that:

> *(2) No recognizance for his surrender to custody shall be taken from him.*
> *(3) Except as provided by this section—*
> *(a) no security for his surrender to custody shall be taken from him,*
> *(b) he shall not be required to provide a surety or sureties for his surrender to custody, and*
> *(c) no other requirement shall be imposed on him as a condition of bail.*
> *(4) He may be required, before release on bail, to provide a surety or sureties to secure his surrender to custody.*
> *(5) If it appears that he is unlikely to remain in Great Britain until the time appointed for him to surrender to custody, he may be required, before release on bail, to give security for his surrender to custody.*
> *The security may be given by him or on his behalf.*
> *(6) He may be required to comply, before release on bail or later, with such requirements as appear to the court to be necessary to secure that—*
> *(a) he surrenders to custody,*
> *(b) he does not commit an offence while on bail,*
> *(c) he does not interfere with witnesses or otherwise obstruct the course of justice whether in relation to himself or any other person,*
> *(d) he makes himself available for the purpose of enabling inquiries or a report to be made to assist the court in dealing with him for the offence, and, in any Act, 'the normal powers to impose conditions of bail' means the powers to impose conditions under paragraph (a), (b) or (c) above.*

3.12.1 THE SURETY

If the court (or police, following an arrest or charge) considers it is necessary to ensure that the defendant surrenders to custody, the defendant may be required to provide sureties to guarantee his or her surrender (BA 1976, s. 8). If no sureties are forthcoming, the defendant stays in custody, although technically bail has been granted. A surety is a person — usually a friend, relative or employer — who agrees to ensure that the defendant attends court at the next hearing. The surety acknowledges that, should the defendant fail to surrender, the surety is liable to forfeit a specified sum of money to the court. See also **3.14.3** below on forfeiture. A person may stand as a surety either in court or in any of the situations covered by BA 1976, s. 8(4) (for example, at the police station after being charged; by the gaoler at court if the surety arrived too late to appear in court; at the prison holding the defendant).

3.12.2 THE SURETY IN COURT

Before starting the final submissions to the court, defence counsel should call any proposed sureties into the witness box. The 'surety' will take an oath and defence counsel should then explain the obligation to ensure the defendant's surrender to bail and the possibility of the surety losing money should this not happen. He or she should then be asked if he or she is still willing to be a surety. If so, counsel will enquire what sum of money he or she is prepared to run the risk of forfeiting and how this will be paid if required by the court to do so. The court will examine the surety's financial resources, character and any criminal record, and relationship to the defendant (kinship, geographical, etc.). (See also ***Advocacy Manual***.)

3.12.3 SECURITY

If it appears that a defendant is unlikely to remain in Great Britain until the time for surrender, the defendant may be required to provide security for his or her surrender (BA 1976, s. 3(5)). This may take the form of money or other valuables (BA 1976, s. 5(9)) and may be demanded from the defendant personally, unlike a surety. It will be deposited with the court and, if the defendant fails to surrender to custody, it may be forfeited by court order, either totally or in part.

3.12.4 OTHER BAIL CONDITIONS

A court can impose any conditions it (or defence counsel) can think of, but they must be considered to be necessary to ensure that the defendant either:

(a) surrenders to custody; or

(b) does not commit offences while on bail; or

(c) does not interfere with witnesses; or

(d) does not obstruct the course of justice; or

(e) is available for inquiries or reports to be completed.

(See BA 1976, s. 3(6).)

See *Stone's Justices' Manual* (1995) at 1–435. Remember also that the police have considerable flexibility now in attaching conditions to a grant of bail (BA 1976, s. 3(6), as amended), but are unlikely to be influenced by representations from defence counsel since counsel will not be in attendance at the police station. The ability of a defendant's solicitor to suggest or influence bail conditions remains to be explored.

3.12.5 COMMON CONDITIONS

3.12.5.1 Reporting to a police station

A defendant may be ordered to do this in order to ensure that he or she stays within the vicinity. This may be strictly enforced — for example, 'daily at 7 am and 7 pm' — or be a quite loose check — for example, 'every Thursday'. The purpose of this is to ensure the defendant is around to surrender to custody on the appointed date.

Now that the police are able to be more creative in attaching conditions to bail, there is room for confusion here. The police could always release a suspect on bail, subject to a requirement that he attend subsequently at the police station for further inquiries — that was not conditional bail as the attendance was a primary obligation on the accused. Nowadays, the police may also require a suspect to report to the police station if they are concerned that he may abscond — this would be a secondary obligation (he is not being required to surrender to custody) and if the suspect failed to report as required he would only be in breach of a bail condition; he would not have committed an offence under BA 1976, s. 6 (see **3.14.1** below).

3.12.5.2 Keeping curfew

Originally a medieval rule requiring fires to be extinguished at a certain hour at night, this now means the obligation to stay indoors between certain hours (usually at night). This condition is often used where a number of crimes have allegedly occurred at roughly the same time of day — for example, five houses have been burgled in the early hours of the morning: curfew to be kept between 11 pm and 6 am. It is commonly used for juvenile defendants.

3.12.5.3 Staying out of/in a certain area

These are separate conditions. The first aims to separate the accused from temptation — the woman who has been charged with shoplifting from four West End stores in London may be ordered not to go within a two mile radius of Oxford Circus. (As precise measurement of this is virtually impossible for the average citizen, it is wiser not to tempt fate!) The second condition is intended to prevent the defendant either absconding or, occasionally, from contacting prosecution witnesses. Compliance with both conditions may be very difficult to check but, if a breach does come to the attention of a police officer, the defendant may be re-arrested. In a novel twist on this common condition, it was reported in the press in May 1994 that the Marquis of Blandford had a bail condition that he must not use taxi-cabs unless accompanied by his solicitor; at the time, he was charged with, *inter alia*, using taxis and dishonestly not paying the fares.

3.13 Changing Bail Conditions

If circumstances change, so that the original conditions are no longer appropriate, the defence can apply to the court to alter or remove them. In exceptional situations, the prosecution can apply for existing conditions to be altered (presumably to strengthen them), or for conditions to be attached to an unconditional grant of bail.

Such application is made under BA 1976, s. 3(8), either to the magistrates' court which is dealing with the case or, if the case has been sent to the Crown Court, to a Crown Court judge. Where a defendant has been sent to Crown Court for trial but has not yet been required to surrender to custody at the Crown Court, then the magistrates' court which sent him for trial has concurrent jurisdiction with the Crown Court to hear any application for variation of bail conditions (see *R* v *Lincoln Magistrates' Court, ex parte Mawer* [1995] Crim LR 878). Once the defendant has surrendered to custody at the Crown Court, the magistrates cease to have any jurisdiction over the matter. See also BA 1976, s. 3(8A) — this extends the Crown Court's jurisdiction to cover applications made in serious fraud cases which go to Crown Court on a notice of transfer. (For notices of transfer, see **Chapter 8**.) See *Archbold*, 1995 edn, at para. 3–13; also at para. 3–186b and c, and para. 3–178 for the relevant Crown Court Rules (rr. 19 and 20) and the procedure for Crown Court applications.

It should be noted that if a defendant is released by the police on conditional bail, he or she may apply to a custody officer to vary those conditions (see BA 1976, s. 3A(4)). The custody officer may impose different conditions and may even make them more onerous than before. Counsel is very unlikely to be involved in such an application. However the defendant may choose to apply to the magistrates' court and counsel may then be briefed (see MCA 1980, s. 43B).

3.14 What Happens if the Defendant Disobeys?

3.14.1 THE PENALTY FOR FAILURE TO SURRENDER TO CUSTODY

Under BA 1976, s. 6, it is an offence for a defendant to fail to surrender to custody at the appointed time and place. The crime is usually referred to by the court (and by counsel when in court) as 'absconding'. It is otherwise commonly referred to, particularly by defendants, as 'doing a runner'. It is punishable, following summary conviction or as a contempt of court, by a fine and/or imprisonment. Any securities or sureties will be liable to forfeiture by court order.

The absconder should always be given the chance to explain such absence, and his or her counsel should be invited to address the court, if appropriate (see *R* v *Davis (Seaton Roy)* (1986) 8 Cr App R (S) 64); *R* v *Boyle* [1993] Crim LR 40; *R* v *How* [1993] Crim LR

201). The punishment may be severe if it is thought necessary to deter others. See, e.g., *R* v *Neve* (1986) 8 Cr App R (S) 270, where a defendant (who had been acquitted at a trial) was nevertheless sentenced to six months' imprisonment and ordered to forfeit £10,000 for going to Spain in an attempt to avoid his trial.

The court will usually issue a warrant for the arrest of the accused (unless, perhaps, defence counsel is able to offer an explanation for the absence). When the warrant is executed and the accused is brought before the court, the court is very likely to remand the accused in custody; if the accused originally had the right to bail (BA 1976, s. 4), he or she has not got it now (BA 1976, sch. 1). No offence is committed if the accused can show he or she had reasonable cause for failing to surrender to custody as required. See also *Murphy* v *DPP* [1990] 1 WLR 601.

It seems that around 5–7% of all defendants who are remanded on bail by magistrates subsequently fail to surrender to custody. The proportion does not vary much whether one looks at indictable offences or summary offences; see **Figure 3.4**.

3.14.2 NON-COMPLIANCE WITH OTHER CONDITIONS

No separate offence is committed in this situation but the accused is at risk of arrest (without warrant) by a police officer who has reasonable grounds to believe that a bail condition has been broken. Indeed, a police officer can arrest a defendant when he or she has reasonable grounds to believe that the defendant is likely to break a bail condition (see BA 1976, s. 7(3)). Once arrested, the accused must be produced in court within 24 hours, when the question of remand on bail or in custody will be considered afresh.

When the defendant is produced in court, a magistrate (*not* a Crown Court judge) has to form an opinion whether the defendant is unlikely to surrender to custody or has broken (or is likely to break) any condition of his bail (BA 1976, s. 7(5)). This hearing is quite informal — usually a police officer will attend the court to state the grounds for his belief that a bail condition either has been or is likely to be broken. This may involve hearsay evidence being tendered to the court. The defendant should be given an opportunity to respond. If the magistrate forms the requisite opinion, then the defendant may be remanded in custody or released on conditional bail (the conditions may be the same as the original ones). See *R* v *Liverpool City Magistrates' Court, ex parte Director of Public Prosecutions* (1992) 95 Cr App R 222.

3.14.3 FORFEITURE OF A SURETY

If a defendant was granted bail subject to providing a surety, then a failure by the defendant to surrender to custody puts the surety in jeopardy of losing the sum which he or she guaranteed by his or her oath to the court.

The basic assumption made on a hearing for forfeiture is that the whole sum becomes payable, unless it is fair and just to forfeit a lesser sum or nothing at all. There is a heavy onus on the surety to prove why he or she should not forfeit the full amount. This should be done either by showing a lack of means to meet the forfeiture or by establishing that he or she acted responsibly. The surety has a duty to maintain contact with the defendant and to keep him- or herself informed as to the conditions of bail in order to ensure the defendant's surrender to custody. It has recently been pointed out by the Court of Appeal that any reduction in the amount ordered to be forfeit, following a defendant absconding, 'must be the exception not the rule and be granted only in really deserving cases'. Hoffmann LJ observed that 'in one sense the system has unfairness built into it. It may result in persons entirely innocent having to suffer on account of the wrongdoing of another'. Lack of culpability by a surety is a factor to consider but in *R* v *Maidstone Crown Court, ex parte Lever* [1995] 1 WLR 928, two sureties who were found to be blameless for the absconding nevertheless were ordered to forfeit 85% of their total surety of £59,000.

Usually, the obligation of a surety will end when the defendant is arraigned on the charges as this is when trial normally commences. At this moment, the defendant is understood to have surrendered to the custody of the court and the surety has done all that the court required of him or her. This is subject to exceptions, though, and a surety should remain well-informed as to the exact status of the defendant and the view of the court as to whether the surety's obligation is at an end or continues. The penalty for being ill-informed is seen in *R* v *Central Criminal Court, ex parte Guney* [1994] 1 WLR 438, where a surety for Asil Nadir was ordered to forfeit £650,000 following Mr Nadir's departure to Northern Cyprus. It could have been worse, as originally he stood surety for £1 million; in fact, it got even better for Mr Guney, as the Court of Appeal later quashed the forfeiture completely (see [1995] 1 WLR 376).

See also MCA 1980, s. 120; *Archbold*, 1995 edn, para. 3–147/150; *Blackstone's Criminal Practice*, 1996, D5.48.

3.14.4 PROCEDURE FOR BA 1976, s. 6

The Bail Act 1976, s. 6(1) creates a single offence — failure to surrender to custody. The following distinctions may be made.

Police bail: must be dealt with (by magistrates) as a summary offence in such circumstances. It is irrelevant whether the duty to surrender is to a police station or magistrates' court. The prosecution must either charge the defendant or lay an information. A six-month time limit (MCA 1980, s. 127) applies. There is a maximum penalty of three months' imprisonment and/or a £5,000 fine for absconding while on police bail.

Magistrates' bail: if bail was granted by the magistrates and the duty is to surrender to the *magistrates' court*, it is not necessary or desirable to lay an information. There is no time limit. Magistrates should initiate proceedings of their own motion *but* only on the express invitation of the prosecutor (compare *France* v *Dewsbury Magistrates' Court*, below).

It seems that the magistrates are then dealing with the offence as if it were a contempt of court. The result is that the maximum punishment is 12 months' imprisonment and/or an unlimited fine under s. 6(7), although in practice this is restricted by MCA 1980, s. 31, i.e. to six months' imprisonment rather than 12 months. It seems unnecessary to conclude whether magistrates have the power to treat a failure to surrender to custody at the magistrates' court as a contempt of court or must regard it as a summary offence: *Schiavo* v *Anderton* [1987] QB 20 and the *Practice Direction (Bail: Failure to Surrender)* [1987] 1 WLR 79 favour contempt; *Harbax Singh* [1979] QB 319 and BA 1976, s. 6(7) favour a summary offence (according to Parker LJ in *Murphy* v *DPP* [1990] 1 WLR 601). The matter was expressly left by the Court of Appeal in *Murphy* for decision in a more relevant case.

Crown Court bail: when bailed to attend Crown Court either by magistrates or by the Crown Court itself. Failure here will usually be dealt with as if it were a contempt of court. No time limit applies. The Crown Court's powers are to imprison for up to 12 months and/or an unlimited fine.

Note: in *France* v *Dewsbury Magistrates' Court* [1988] Crim LR 295 the Divisional Court warned justices against tying the hands of the prosecution over an absconding charge — magistrates should not fetter the Crown Prosecution Service by expressing a view (of leniency) at an interim hearing in the case. It is for the accused to show that he or she had reasonable cause for not surrendering (BA 1976, s. 6(3)). The standard of proof is on a balance of probabilities.

3.15 Renewing an Application for Bail

(or 'If at first you don't succeed, try again — but only once!')

See BA 1976, sch. 1, part IIA.

1. If the court decides not to grant the defendant bail, it is the court's duty to consider, at each subsequent hearing while the defendant is a person to whom s. 4 above applies and remains in custody, whether he ought to be granted bail.

2. At the first hearing after that at which the court decided not to grant the defendant bail, he may support an application for bail with any argument as to fact or law that he desires (whether or not advanced previously).

3. At subsequent hearings the court need not hear arguments as to fact or law which it has heard previously.

3.15.1 OBLIGATION TO CONSIDER BAIL

According to BA 1976, sch. 1, part IIA (inserted by CJA 1988, s. 154), at every hearing of a case (when the defendant is in custody) the magistrates' court is obliged to consider whether he or she should be released on bail. The defence is allowed to make up to two applications for bail at which the same arguments may be used. If the accused is still in custody after this, the court may consider the matter of bail no longer open to argument from the defence.

Although the court is under a duty (CJA 1988, s. 154) to consider bail at subsequent hearings in the case, these will be formalities. The defence may only reopen the issue of bail by raising fresh circumstances or arguments. Section 154 represents the statutory embodiment of a common law rule which was first reported in *R* v *Nottingham Justices, ex parte Davies* [1981] QB 38.

There have been several cases involving decisions as to what constitutes a 'change in circumstances'. It seems to be a question of fact in each case, although the Queen's Bench Divisional Court has stated that the change need not be major. *R* v *Blyth Juvenile Court, ex parte G* [1991] Crim LR 693 offers an illustration. Where there has been no application for bail by a defendant on the first appearance of a case at court and he has been remanded in custody, it seems that he has a right to apply for bail at a later hearing of the case (see *R* v *Dover and East Kent Justices, ex parte Dean* [1992] Crim LR 33).

3.15.2 THE MAGISTRATES' CERTIFICATE

Under BA 1976, s. 5(6A), if magistrates withhold bail after hearing a fully argued application for bail, they must issue a certificate stating that they heard full argument. After two unsuccessful bail applications in a case, if the magistrates allow the defendant a third application (which is unsuccessful), they should issue a certificate indicating the change in circumstances or new consideration that persuaded them to hear that third application. See BA 1976, s. 5(6A) and (6B); also BA 1976, sch. 1, part IIA (inserted by CJA 1988, s. 154); Form 151A, *Stone's Justices' Manual*, vol. 3 (1995).

3.16 Appealing Against a Refusal to Release a Defendant on Bail

3.16.1 APPLY TO A CROWN COURT JUDGE

A defendant can apply to a Crown Court judge for bail in the following situations (contained in the Supreme Court Act 1981, s. 81, as amended by CJA 1982).

(a) Where a magistrates' court has committed the defendant to the Crown Court in custody (either for trial or sentence).

(b) Where the case is proceeding in the magistrates' court but magistrates have heard a fully argued application for bail and refused bail (proved by producing a BA 1976, s. 5(6A) certificate — see **3.15.2** and **3.7.3** above).

(c) Where the defendant has been convicted by magistrates, given a custodial sentence, and refused bail pending an appeal to the Crown Court.

The appeal is heard either by the Crown Court to which the case has been committed or by the nearest Crown Court dealing with Class 4 (low-grade) crime. The appeal is usually heard by a judge sitting 'in chambers' — this means that counsel need not wear a wig and gown, even though the appeal often takes place in a court room. Unless the appeal is made by the prosecution (rare), the accused will not be present at the appeal unless the Crown Court grants permission for this (also rare).

3.16.2 APPLY TO A HIGH COURT JUDGE

Under RSC, O. 79, r. 9, a High Court judge may grant bail in the following situations:

(a) Where a magistrates' court has refused to grant bail.

(b) Where a defendant who is in custody applies to the Divisional Court (QBD) for *certiorari* to quash a decision of the magistrates.

(c) Where a defendant in custody appeals by way of case stated to the High Court against a decision of the Crown Court (or applies for *certiorari* to quash a Crown Court decision).

(d) Where bail has been granted and variations in the conditions are proposed.

The application is made by summons, supported by an affidavit. The summons is served on one's opponent at least 24 hours before the hearing. The summons will be heard by a High Court judge, sitting in chambers. In the Royal Courts of Justice, the judge in chambers (as he is known) sits in Room 92. One should also note the possibility of seeking the issue of a writ of *habeas corpus* under RSC, O. 54. This application is made to the Divisonal Court (QBD). See also SCA 1981, s. 81.

3.16.3 DEFENDANT'S CHOICE

A defendant may apply to either a Crown Court judge or a High Court judge, assuming they both have jurisdiction to hear the application. The defendant may try first one, and, if unsuccessful, the other. In such circumstances the second judge should be told of the earlier, unsuccessful attempt.

What a defendant should *not* do is apply for judicial review under RSC, O. 53. This method of challenging bail decisions was criticised by the Queen's Bench Divisional Court in *R* v *Blyth Juvenile Court, ex parte G* [1991] Crim LR 693. The case involved a decision by magistrates not to hear an application for bail on the grounds that the defendant could not demonstrate a change in circumstances. She was advised that she could demonstrate this and sought to challenge the decision by judicial review. The Divisional Court allowed the application (and directed the justices to hear the application for bail) but stated that the appropriate means to challenge an improper refusal to grant bail was through an application to the judge in chambers under RSC, O. 79, r. 9. It is not thought that this judgment affects the choice between High Court or Crown Court judge, where it is available.

3.16.4 APPEALS BY THE CROWN PROSECUTION SERVICE

A limited right of appeal *against* the grant of bail has been conferred on the prosecution by the Bail (Amendment) Act 1993. It is confined to cases where the magistrates grant bail to a person who has been charged with (or convicted of) either:

(a) an offence punishable with imprisonment for five or more years; or

(b) an offence of taking a conveyance without authority; or

(c) an offence of aggravated vehicle taking.

If such a person was granted bail despite objections from the prosecution, and the prosecution is being conducted by the Crown Prosecution Service, an appeal may be made. If the Crown Prosecution Service decides to appeal, it must say so (give oral notice of appeal) before the defendant is released from custody. Written notice of appeal must follow, within two hours, and be served on the court and the defendant. The defendant will be kept in custody until the appeal is determined by the Crown Court — the appeal must be heard within 48 hours (excluding bank holidays and weekends). The Crown Court judge will decide the application on its merits and may remand the defendant in custody or release him or her on bail. The judge may attach conditions to a grant of bail if it is thought appropriate to do so.

The prosecution now has a limited ability to ask for 'reconsideration' of a decision to release a defendant on bail. The Bail Act 1976, s. 5B, enables a prosecutor to apply to a magistrates' court to reconsider such a decision, whether it was originally taken by the court or by a custody officer. Having reconsidered, the magistrates may attach conditions to unconditional bail, vary the current conditions, or withhold bail (BA 1976, s. 5B(1)) or, presumably, preserve the status quo. Reconsiderations may only be sought where the defendant is on bail for an offence which must or may be tried on indictment; the application must be based upon information which was not available to the magistrates (or custody officer) when the original decision was taken.

3.17 Legal Aid for Bail Applications

3.17.1 APPLICATIONS IN THE MAGISTRATES' COURT

A defendant who has legal aid in the magistrates' court will find that this covers all applications for bail to magistrates and to the Crown Court on appeal. Even if a defendant is not in receipt of legal aid for a case in the magistrates' court, he or she must be given legal aid to apply for bail in the following situation: if the defendant has been remanded in custody by the court on an earlier occasion; was not legally represented then; is in danger of being remanded in custody again (or committed to the Crown Court in custody) now; and wishes to be legally represented; then (subject to his or her financial resources), the defendant must be granted legal aid for representation on the question of bail. See Legal Aid Act 1988, s. 21(3)(c).

3.17.2 CASES IN THE CROWN COURT AND APPEALS TO THE HIGH COURT

Once a case has been committed to the Crown Court (or has gone there on appeal against conviction/sentence), if the accused is legally aided then bail applications are covered by his or her legal aid order. No criminal legal aid is available for appeals to a High Court judge. If a defendant cannot afford to appeal to a High Court judge on his or her own resources, he or she can ask that the Official Solicitor be appointed to represent him or her for the appeal. If this is done, the Official Solicitor prepares the papers but does not attend the hearing, so this is not a popular method of appeal with defendants, and is rarely successful. It appears to be the case that a defendant may be granted legal aid to be represented on an application to the High Court, on an *ad hoc* basis, by applying for emergency legal aid in **civil** proceedings.

3.18 Remands, Bail and Juveniles

The provisions of BA 1976 apply to juveniles in basically the same manner as they do to adult defendants. That is, juveniles may be remanded on bail or in custody. If a young person is not remanded on bail, he or she should be committed into local authority care. (The position is the same for children charged with homicide.) Local authority accommodation may be required to be 'secure' for juveniles aged 12–16 but such places are currently very limited in number; if no secure local authority accommodation is available, the juvenile may be held in police detention (see CJPOA 1994).

See further *Archbold*, 1995 edn, 3–72 to 3–79; CYPA 1969, s. 23 as substituted by the Children Act 1989, and Home Office Circular 91/1977.

3.19 Final Note

Any question of bail being granted which is not governed by s. 4 of BA 1976 is at the discretion of the court.

Multiple-choice Questions

1. Andrew has been convicted in the magistrates' court of criminal damage to a bus shelter. The value of the damage done was £800. The magistrates decide to adjourn prior to sentencing, to enable a medical examination and report to be made. A fully argued bail application is made on Andrew's behalf but he is remanded in custody. Which of the following possibilities most accurately describes what Andrew may now do with a view to obtaining bail?

[A] He may only apply for bail in the Crown Court.
[B] He may apply for bail in the Crown Court and if unsuccessful may then apply for bail to a judge in chambers in the High Court.
[C] He may apply for bail to a judge in chambers in the High Court and if unsuccessful may then apply for bail in the Crown Court.
[D] He may apply for bail in the way described in [B] or in the way described in [C], the choice being his.

2. The Bail Act 1976, s. 4 provides that a person to whom it applies 'shall be granted bail except as provided in Schedule 1'. In which one of the following situations does s. 4 apply?

[A] When a person is convicted on indictment and his case is adjourned for reports prior to sentencing.
[B] When a person, convicted and sentenced by magistrates, is appealing against sentence.
[C] When a person, convicted and sentenced by magistrates, is appealing against conviction.
[D] When a person, convicted by magistrates, is committed by them to the Crown Court for sentence.

Tutorial Questions

Aim: To consider what to suggest the court ought to do (from the range of legitimate options) when a defendant does not attend court for his or her case.

In each of the following situations, you are defence counsel appearing in the magistrates' court. Note that you are alone, that is there is no representative from instructing solicitors present. You can, of course, telephone the solicitor's office.

(a) Your client is due to appear for the first time on a charge of assault occasioning actual bodily harm. The court clerk informs you that he has sent a medical certificate, dated five days previously, which states that he is 'unfit to work for two weeks'. What application can you make? Do you anticipate any problems?

(b) Your client is due to appear for the second time on a shoplifting charge. In your instructions, it is stated that he has two other shoplifting charges outstanding. Court begins at 10.00 am. By 10.30 am he has not appeared. What should you do?

(c) Your client is charged with burglary of a shop. This is the second appearance. On the first appearance two weeks ago, he was granted bail unconditionally. He is jointly charged with his brother, whom you also represent, who tells you, 'He's done a runner'. You have telephoned your solicitor, who knows nothing of his whereabouts. What is likely to happen? What can you do about it?

(d) Your client is charged with shoplifting (two tins of baked beans). The date is 13 April. In your instructions you are told that she is also due to appear on a charge of possessing cannabis on 13 May. She has no previous convictions. The prosecutor tells you that the CPS wishes to adjourn the shoplifting charge, to review the matter and decide whether to proceed. Your client was bailed to attend court at 9.45 am and has not arrived by 10.15 am. Your solicitor has received no message and the client is not on the telephone. What should you say to the court?

(e) Your client is charged with burglary of a dwelling house. He was bailed to attend court at 10.00 am. He did not appear in court by 11.40 am, when the court issued a warrant for his arrest, not backed for bail. At 11.45 am, as you are about to leave, an usher informs you that your client has just arrived. What should you do?

Now go through those situations again and think about how you, as prosecuting counsel, might respond to a submission by the defence in each of them.

R* v *Bruce

Aim: This case will be used in a Criminal Litigation class to illustrate the context and some of the issues involved in an application for bail. The accused is in custody, the case is to be remanded today by the magistrates, and the accused wishes to apply for bail.

Before the class, it will help if you look at **Chapter 34** in the ***Advocacy Manual***. Consider the order in which people will do things and what those things are. What ought to happen if the question of bail arises? Plan what you should do as counsel, basing your plan upon the brief either for the prosecution or defence (you will be told before the class which party you represent; remember the opponent's instructions are confidential). Also, you may be called on to play any one of the roles in the hearing — perhaps a barrister, court clerk, or the accused. The more you have thought about how the hearing as a whole should be conducted and what everyone's part will be in it, the easier the class should be.

After the 'hearing' has taken place, there will be a class discussion on how the hearing went — maybe you would have decided the question of bail differently from the 'court', or you had different suggestions that could have been made in the application.

IN THE BLACKHEATH MAGISTRATES' COURT

R

— v —

Barry Bruce Defendant

Instructions to Counsel for the Defence

Counsel has herewith:

1. Summary of the charges
2. Proof of evidence from the Defendant
3. Letter from the Defendant's father
4. Defendant's antecedents

Counsel is instructed to represent Mr Bruce at the next hearing of the case. He faces 2 charges — one of theft, the other handling stolen goods, both contrary to the Theft Act 1968. He will plead Not Guilty to both charges. His Proof of Evidence will fill in the details of the defence case.

He is currently on remand in custody, having elected summary trial, and counsel is requested to make an application for bail at the next appearance, next Thursday at 10.00 am. Counsel is advised that the court refused bail on the only other application, made last week by Instructing Solicitors, on the ground that Mr Bruce might interfere with the main Prosecution witness — Ashley Arthur — who is known to him.

Mr Bruce lives quite near to Mr Arthur in Blackheath. However, Mr Bruce's parents live in Ealing, some considerable distance away, and if he went to live there, there could be little chance of contact with the witness in the ordinary course of events.

Also, Mr Bruce (currently unemployed) now has the offer of a job from his uncle, Charlie Campbell, doing painting and decorating. It is unlikely that Mr Campbell will be able to attend the hearing as this is a busy time of year for him. Mr Bruce's father is in hospital but has given Instructing Solicitors a written assurance that his son may live with him, pending the outcome of these proceedings.

Counsel is asked to use his best endeavours in the circumstances and make a strong application. Mr Bruce is a regular client of Instructing Solicitors — our experience indicates that he 'does not suffer fools (or timidity) gladly'!

Copy of letter from Mr Bruce's father:

364B Buttermelt Tower,
Ealing, West London.

1st of September 1996

To whom it may concern,

I know that my son is in trouble with the law again. I am going into hospital on the 1st of October for an operation and will be in for about 2 weeks. Barry can come and stay but only until his trial comes up. He's always been a handful and as his mother and I get older, we can't control him. If he does not behave this time, he'll have to go back inside as we don't want the aggravation at our age. Still, he is our son and this will always be his home.

Yours faithfully,

(signed) J. Bruce

Details of charges (taken by Instructing Solicitors from charge sheet)

Charge 1: On a day unknown between the 3rd August 1996 and 10th August 1996, Barry Bruce dishonestly received stolen goods, namely a Sanyo hi-fi stereo music system, knowing or believing them to be stolen.

Charge 2: On the 9th of August 1996 Barry Bruce stole a video cassette, the property of AA Newsagents Limited.

Proof of Evidence

Mr Barry Bruce of 255, Hazlitt Gardens, Blackheath, who will say —

I have been falsely accused of two crimes. They are both supposed to have occurred when I was in the local newsagent's shop. The owner, Ashley Arthur, is someone I know from my local pub, The Red Herring. Occasionally, I have sold him some stuff that I had got from other friends — boxes of video tapes, jewellery and the like. It's all been no questions asked and went smoothly till the last time. I was promised by a friend that he was due to take delivery of some top quality hi-fi equipment. It was going to cost me a monkey but I managed to persuade Arthur to buy it from me (unseen) for a straight £1,000.

Unfortunately, after he took delivery of it Arthur's place got raided by the police. I think he was clean except for the hi-fi, which he persuaded them he come by innocently. The police took the hi-fi away and I think Arthur blamed me for tipping them off (which I did not do). Anyway, the next time I went into Arthur's shop we had a bit of a barney about the raid and his hi-fi. At one point he disappeared out the back of the shop for a couple of minutes. That must be when he rung the police because they turned up about 5 minutes later. The police came in the shop and spoke to Arthur. He said something like 'That's the man'. One of the police then grabbed hold of me and arrested me for handling.

At the police station, I was searched and they found a video tape. This was from a batch that I had sold on to Arthur a couple of weeks previous but I had kept about 12 for myself. I know Arthur has been knocking them out in his shop but there is no way that mine came from there. They already had price labels on when I got them. I got a bit violent in the shop and started swearing but this was because I had been fitted up. I said to Arthur that I would tear his head off and spit down his throat but it was in the heat of the moment. I have had time to reflect on matters in custody and am quite content to see that justice is done in the court.

I have spoken to my father on the telephone and understand I can live with him until my trial. Also, my mum told me on a visit that my uncle, Charlie Campbell, is holding a job open for me with his firm. Although the job is based in Blackheath, I won't be there much as we will be doing jobs all over London.

I badly want bail as I am very worried about leaving my girlfriend alone in the last few months of her pregnancy.

I can remember my last three convictions. Two were in Ealing Magistrates' Court in 1994 for burglary (I got Community Service, about 150 hours) and one in 1995 at Blackheath Magistrates. That was for a fight in a pub — I was done for simple GBH and got a 3-month suspended sentence.

Metropolitan Police

Antecedents of: Barry BRUCE

Address: 255, Hazlitt Gardens, Blackheath, London

Age: 22

Date of Birth: 31.3.74

Place of Birth: Paddington, West London

Date of 1st entry into UK: N/A

Occupation: Unemployed

Education: He attended Boyson Comprehensive School, leaving aged 16, with 3 GCSEs in English, General Studies and Art.

Main employments during last 5 years
Has had several jobs of short duration since leaving school. These include casual labour for market stallholders and delivering community (free) newspapers.

Home conditions and domestic circumstances
Lives with his girlfriend (who is expecting their child) in a 1 bedroom flat. Is not claiming Social Security as such, although the rent for the flat is paid by the DSS. No regular commitments. Girlfriend's parents sometimes help with shopping bills.

Outstanding matters
If convicted, will be in breach of a 3-month suspended sentence imposed by Blackheath Magistrates' Court on 2.12.95.

List of previous convictions attached: Yes/No
Date of arrest: 9.8.96 —/In custody

Officer in case: D. C. Duncan
Station: Blackheath East
Telephone number: Date: 6.9.96
Supervising Officer:

Convictions Recorded Against: Barry BRUCE — CRO No. 34567/91
Charged in name of Barry BRUCE — Date of Birth 31.3.74

Date	Court	Offences	Sentence Release Date
Total number of convictions 6. Has not previously served a custodial sentence.			
5.7.91	B'heath M/C	Theft	Fine £30
15.9.91	Greenwich M/C	1. Handling 2. Handling	Con. Dis. 1 year
1.5.94	Ealing M/C	1. Burglary 2. Burglary	Comm. Serv. 150 hours
2.12.95	B'heath M/C	Causing GBH	3 months' imprisonment suspended for 1 year

IN THE BLACKHEATH MAGISTRATES' COURT

R

— v —

Barry Bruce (Defendant)

Instructions to Prosecute

Herewith:

1. The charges against the accused
2. List of objections to bail
3. Antecedents/CRO form
4. Case summary

This case is due in court again next Thursday. The accused has elected summary trial and a date is likely to be fixed by the court at the next hearing. There are two civilian witnesses and two police officers. The time estimate is — half a day.

The accused is currently remanded in custody. On the last occasion that bail was actively considered by the court, it was denied due to possible interference with the chief prosecution witness, Mr Ashley ARTHUR.

Charges:—

1: On a day unknown between the 3rd August 1996 and 10th August 1996, Barry Bruce dishonestly received stolen goods, namely a Sanyo hi-fi stereo music system, knowing or believing them to be stolen.

2: On the 9th of August 1996 Barry Bruce stole a video cassette, the property of AA Newsagents Limited.

Objections to bail:—

1. Likely interference with prosecution witness — the accused knows him and lives nearby.

2. Likely to commit further offences — has a record of similar crimes in his record. No apparent income. See antecedents.

3. May abscond. If convicted of either charge, the accused will be in breach of a suspended sentence. See antecedents.

Case summary:—
In late July 1996, ARTHUR was offered by BRUCE (and agreed to buy) an expensive hi-fi system. On the 4th August, a Mr Smollett was the victim of a burglary at his flat. Among items taken was an expensive hi-fi. This was later sold by BRUCE to ARTHUR; it was recovered from ARTHUR on the 7th and identified by SMOLLETT as his.
ARTHUR owns a shop in Blackheath. On 9th August, BRUCE went in and ARTHUR called the police.
BRUCE was arrested in the shop and became very aggressive and abusive towards ARTHUR, threatening him with serious injury.
A video cassette was later found on BRUCE at the police station. This was identified by ARTHUR as coming from his shop. BRUCE had not bought it.
At the station, BRUCE made a full confession of both offences to D. C. Duncan and P. C. Ewart.

[Note: Antecedents and CRO form are not copied — see the Defence brief.]

FOUR
MODE OF TRIAL

4.1 Classification of Offences

All offences fall into one of the following categories:

(a) Summary offences, i.e. those which must be tried in the magistrates' court.

(b) Offences triable only on indictment, i.e. those which must be tried in the Crown Court.

(c) Offences which are triable either way, i.e. those which may be tried in either the magistrates' court or the Crown Court.

4.1.1 SUMMARY OFFENCES

Summary trial, i.e. trial by magistrates, is a creature of statute, and all summary offences, similarly, are created by statute. The statute usually does this by providing a maximum penalty for summary conviction, with no alternative penalty for conviction on indictment. A huge number of offences are summary. See **Figure 4.1** for examples.

4.1.2 OFFENCES TRIABLE ONLY ON INDICTMENT

All common law offences are triable only on indictment, i.e. by a judge and jury in the Crown Court, such as murder and manslaughter. Other offences in this category are created by statute which provides for a maximum penalty for conviction on indictment, with no alternative penalty on summary conviction. See **Figure 4.1** for examples.

4.1.3 OFFENCES WHICH ARE TRIABLE EITHER WAY

Offences which are triable either way are technically indictable but may be tried in the magistrates' court if both the magistrates and the defendant agree. See **4.2** below for details. Offences are shown to be triable either way by either:

(a) the statute which created them providing for alternative penalties on summary conviction or conviction on indictment;

or

(b) re-classification by statute, in particular the Magistrates' Courts Act 1980 (MCA 1980), s. 17, which downgrades to triable either way many offences which were formerly triable only on indictment: see the list in sch. 1 to the Act.

4.2 Procedure for Determining the Mode of Trial

Where the offence is triable either way, and may be tried in *either* the magistrates' court or the Crown Court, it must first be determined which court should try the case.

Figure 4.1 Classification of Offences

Type of Offence	Triable only on Indictment	Triable Either Way	Triable only Summarily
1. Offences against the person	Murder Manslaughter Attempt to procure an abortion Causing grievous bodily harm with intent	Inflicting grievous bodily harm Unlawful wounding Assault occasioning actual bodily harm Assault with intent to resist arrest	Common assault Assault on a police constable in the execution of his duty
2. Sexual offences	Rape: Intercourse with a girl under 13 Buggery Incest	Unlawful sexual intercourse with a girl under 16 Indecent assault Living on the earnings of a prostitute	Soliciting
3. Theft Act offences	Robbery Aggravated burglary Blackmail Assault with intent to rob Burglary comprising commision of, or intention to commit, an offence only triable on indictment Burglary of a dwelling with threats to occupants	All Theft Act offences not being in the other two categories	Taking a motor vehicle without consent Taking a pedal cycle without consent
4. Criminal damage	Damage or arson with intent to endanger life	Damage where the value involved is over £5,000	Damage where the value involved is £5,000 or less
5. Road traffic	Causing death by dangerous driving	Dangerous driving	Most other traffic offences, e.g.: Speeding Failing to report an accident Driving while disqualified Driving without insurance Drunk in charge of a motor vehicle Failing to stop at a red traffic light
6. Miscellaneous	Perjury Attempt to pervert the course of justice Possessing a firearm with intent to endanger life Using a firearm to resist arrest Carrying a firearm to commit an indictable offence Collecting, communicating, etc. information intended to be useful to an enemy Riot	Making false statements on oath not being in judical proceedings Carrying a loaded firearm in a public place Shortening a shot gun Having an offensive weapon in a public place Using, communicating, etc. information entrusted in confidence to a person holding office under the Crown Violent disorder Affray Stirring up racial hatred All offences under the Forgery & Counterfeiting Act 1981 Offences under the Misuse of Drugs Act 1971	Interference with vehicles Being drunk and disorderly Obstructing police Using threatening words or behaviour Dropping litter Failure to pay TV licence All offences under the Factories Act 1961

4.2.1 PRESENCE OF DEFENDANT

The defendant will usually be present in court, but the court may proceed in his or her absence, in the following situations:

(a) Where, by reason of the defendant's disorderly conduct, the court considers it impracticable to continue the proceedings in his or her presence (MCA 1980, s. 18(3)).

(b) Where the defendant is legally represented, and consents to the case continuing in his or her absence (such consent being indicated by the representative), and the court is satisfied that there is a 'good reason' (such as illness) for that absence (MCA 1980, s. 23(1)(a) and (b)).

4.2.2 THE PROCEDURE

The procedure may be followed before a lay justice sitting alone, under MCA 1980, s. 18(5), though it is far more usual to have two or more.

The following steps, contained in MCA 1980, ss. 19–21 are followed:

(a) The charge is written down and read to the accused. He or she is not asked to plead, as the purpose of the proceedings is not to determine guilt or innocence.

(b) The accused is asked if he or she is aware of his right to advance information of the prosecution case. See **4.6** below.

(c) The prosecution and defence (in that order) have the opportunity of making representations to the court as to the more appropriate forum. The preference of the prosecution is not conclusive unless the prosecution is being carried on by the Attorney General, Solicitor General or Director of Public Prosecutions. If one of these applies for trial on indictment, the court must comply.

(d) The court decides which mode of trial is suitable, taking into account:

   (i) the nature of the case;

   (ii) whether the circumstances make the case one of a serious character;

   (iii) whether the penalties available in the magistrates' court are likely to be adequate;

   (iv) any other circumstances which indicate that one mode of trial could be more suitable than the other;

   (v) any representations made by the prosecution or defence.

Note: Where magistrates consider their sentencing powers inadequate, they should take this into account at this stage and commit for trial, rather than for sentencing at a later stage (*R* v *Manchester Magistrates' Court, ex parte Kaymanesh* (1994) 158 JP 401, DC).

Until relatively recently, little judicial guidance was given to magistrates in making an appropriate mode of trial decision. However, in October 1990, the Queen's Bench Divisional Court produced the National Mode of Trial Guidelines (see *Practice Note* [1990] 1 WLR 1439). In March 1995, these were revised and updated by the Secretariat of the Criminal Justice Consultative Council.

The guidelines are intended to assist magistrates in making an appropriate mode of trial decision, and are not intended as directions. They begin by making a number of general observations about mode of trial, and then set out features which would render trial on indictment appropriate for the following offences: burglary, criminal damage, dangerous driving, drugs offences, fraud, handling, indecent assault, Public Order Act offences, social security frauds, theft, unlawful sexual intercourse, violence (including domestic violence) and violence to and neglect of children. See **4.7** below for details of the general observations and features of some offences by way of example.

(e) If the court decides on summary trial, the court must explain to the defendant in ordinary language that:

(i) summary trial is more appropriate, but that the final choice belongs to the defendant, who can consent to summary trial, or elect trial on indictment; and

(ii) if he or she is tried summarily, he or she may still be committed to the Crown Court for sentence under MCA 1980, s. 38. See **5.3**.

(f) The defendant is then asked if he or she consents to summary trial, or wishes to be tried by jury. The choice is only that of the defendant, who should respond personally. He or she may either:

(i) consent to summary trial. If he or she consents, the court will proceed to trial, though an adjournment may be necessary, for example, if there is insufficient court time;

or

(ii) elect trial on indictment, in which case the court will commence committal proceedings. Again, an adjournment may be necessary.

(g) If, as an alternative to (e) above, the court decides that *the case is more suitable for trial on indictment*, nothing is explained to, or asked of, the defendant as in (e) and (f) above. The court will simply tell the defendant of its decision. His or her consent is not required. The court will commence committal proceedings, after adjournment if necessary,

Note: The fact that the prosecution prefers an additional charge in order to secure a trial on indictment is not an abuse of process as long as such a course is appropriate on the facts (*R* v *Redbridge Justices, ex parte Whitehouse* (1992) 94 Cr App R 332); but the facts may be such as to make it an abuse of process: *R* v *Brooks* [1985] Crim LR 385.

Similarly, should the defendant elect trial on indictment, there is nothing to prevent the prosecution adding a further charge which is triable only summarily, and offering no evidence on the triable either way charge (*R* v *Canterbury and St Augustine Justices, ex parte Klisiak* [1982] QB 398; and see *R* v *Barking Magistrates, ex parte DPP* [1993] COD 108). The CPS must however be careful to act within the Code for Crown Prosecution (see para. 7.3 of the Code).

4.2.3 FAILURE TO COMPLY WITH THE PROCEDURE

The procedure outlined in **4.2.2** is obligatory. Any deviation from it is likely to render the whole proceedings null and void. The defendant then has the option of applying for judicial review to quash any eventual conviction. For example, in *R* v *Kent Justices, ex parte Machin* [1952] 2 QB 355, the magistrates failed to tell the defendant of the possibility of a committal for sentence, and the conviction and subsequent committal were quashed.

It is open to the prosecution to seek judicial review of the magistrates' decision, although such proceedings are rare, and are unlikely to be successful. However, for a case where the Divisional Court did overrule the magistrates, see *R* v *Northampton Magistrates' Court, ex parte CCE* [1994] Crim LR 598.

4.2.4 CHANGING THE MODE OF TRIAL

Either the defendant or the magistrates may alter their decision as to the mode of trial in the following circumstances:

4.2.4.1 The defendant

The defendant may change his or her election from summary trial to trial on indictment, or vice versa, if the magistrates consent. The typical situation is that the defendant has elected summary trial without taking proper advice and then sought legal representation for the purposes of trial or sentence. In these circumstances the magistrates are likely to allow the change, but it is a matter within their discretion. The test is whether the defendant understood the nature and significance of the choice which he or she was being asked to make (*R* v *Birmingham Justices, ex parte Hodgson* [1985] QB 1131).

According to *R* v *Bourne Justices, ex parte Cope, The Times*, 12 November 1988, the essential issue is whether the defendant realised that by his or her election he or she was depriving himself or herself of the right to a jury. The fact that the prosecution witnesses were present and ready to give evidence, and that it would not be desirable to delay the case further was not relevant to the defendant's understanding. However, once it was established that he or she did understand the decision he or she was being asked to make, these matters were ones which the justices could take into account in exercising their discretion to allow a change of election.

If the magistrates allow a change of election, they should also allow a change of plea, if one has been given, as the plea is a major influence on where the defendant should be tried (*R* v *Birmingham Justices, ex parte Hodgson* [1985] QB 1131).

4.2.4.2 The magistrates

The magistrates may themselves change their decision from summary trial and vice versa:

(a) *From summary trial to trial on indictment.* Under MCA 1980, s. 25(2), the magistrates may make the change at any stage before the close of the prosecution case. Thus they will have the opportunity of examining the prosecution evidence and, if it appears that the case is more serious than they first thought, may proceed with a view to committal for trial. If the defendant elects summary trial and pleads guilty, then the court cannot change from summary trial because there has been no trial as such, and no prosecution evidence within the meaning of s. 25(2) (*Re Gillard* [1986] AC 442). On a similar point see *R* v *Telford Justices, ex parte Darlington* (1988) 87 Cr App R 194 and *R* v *Birmingham Stipendiary Magistrates, ex parte Webb* (1992) 95 Cr App R 75.

The power of the magistrate does not arise under s. 25(2) until he has 'begun to try the information summarily'. These words should be given a narrow interpretation (*R* v *Birmingham Stipendiary Magistrate, ex parte Webb* (1992) 95 Cr App R 75). The entering of a not guilty plea initiates the trial process, but is not sufficient of itself to begin a trial within the meaning of s. 25(2) so as to permit the magistrates to redetermine the mode of trial. However, the trial process not only begins with the giving of evidence, but there are a number of other circumstances where the court could begin a trial, for example where the court makes a preliminary ruling on a point of law. See generally *R* v *Horseferry Road Magistrates' Court ex parte, K, The Times*, 22 February 1996.

(b) *From trial on indictment to summary trial.* Under MCA 1980, s. 25(3) magistrates may change from committal proceedings to summary trial at any stage of the proceedings, but:

(i) both prosecution and defendant must be asked if they have any representations to make; and

(ii) the possibility of a committal for sentence must be explained to the defendant; and

(iii) the defendant must consent.

4.3 Criminal Damage

Under MCA 1980, s. 22, where the defendant is charged with criminal damage (other than where the damage was caused by fire) the magistrates must proceed as if the offence were summary only, when the value of the damage is less than £5,000. The court is only proceeding *as if* the offence is summary, but it is not summary for all purposes (*R* v *Considine* (1980) 70 Cr App R 239).

4.3.1 SPECIAL PROCEDURE IN CRIMINAL DAMAGE CASES

Under s. 22, before embarking on the normal procedure for determining the mode of trial as set out in **4.2.2** above, the procedure set out below must be followed:

(a) The court shall, having regard to any representations made by the prosecution or defence, consider the value of the thing involved. There is no appeal on the basis that the value was mistaken (s. 22(8)).

(b) If the value is:

   (i) £5,000 or less, the court proceeds to summary trial. The defendant has no right to trial on indictment, nor may he or she be committed for sentence under s. 38. The maximum penalty is three months' imprisonment or a £2,500 fine;

   (ii) more than £5,000, the offence is triable either way, and the court follows the procedure to determine the mode of trial set out in **4.2.2** above. If the offence is tried summarily the maximum penalty is six months' imprisonment and a £5,000 fine;

   (iii) uncertain, the court will ask the defendant if he or she consents to summary trial, after the lower penalty and absence of any power to commit for sentence have been explained. If consent is given then the court proceeds to summary trial. If not, the court will follow the procedure for determining the mode of trial set out in **4.2.2** above. See s. 22(4)–(6).

4.3.2 A SERIES OF OFFENCES

If the defendant is charged with two or more offences which appear to the court to be a series of offences of the same or a similar character, then the court has regard to the aggregate value in determining the mode of trial. Thus, if the value of all items damaged totals £5,000 or less, then the magistrates proceed as if the offences are all summary, regardless of the number of offences. See s. 22(11), inserted by CJA 1988, s. 38. For an example of the operation of s. 22(11) see *R* v *Braden* (1988) 87 Cr App R 289.

Students are referred to Home Office Research Study No. 125, entitled *Magistrates' Courts or the Crown Court? Mode of Trial Decisions and Sentencing*, London: HMSO, 1992.

4.4 Linked Summary and Indictable Offences

The Criminal Justice Act 1988, ss. 40 and 41 introduced two exceptions to the otherwise inflexible rule that summary offences are only triable summarily. The two sections are similar, but contain important distinctions, and should be analysed with care.

Note: If the defendant is dealt with by the Crown Court under either section, the powers of the Crown Court with regard to sentence are limited to those of the magistrates.

4.4.1 TRIAL OF A SUMMARY OFFENCE ON INDICTMENT: s. 40

If the defendant has been committed for trial in respect of an indictable offence, then the prosecution may include in the indictment a count for a summary offence if:

(a) the summary offence is common assault, taking a motor vehicle without consent, driving whilst disqualified, or criminal damage within MCA 1980, s. 22, or is punishable by imprisonment or disqualification and is specified by the Home Secretary as being suitable for inclusion;

and

(b) the summary offence is either founded on the same facts as the indictable offence or is, or forms part of, a series of offences of the same or similar character;

and

(c) the evidence before the committing court discloses a summary offence.

The magistrates simply commit for trial on the indictable offence. The initiative for including the summary offence must come from the prosecution. Once the summary offence is included in the indictment, then, if the defendant pleads not guilty to both the indictable and summary offences, or even just the summary offence, the defendant will be tried by jury, following the procedure set out in **Chapter 11**. If he or she is convicted the Crown Court powers of sentence in respect of the summary offence are limited to those of the magistrates.

The effect of s. 40, taken together with CLA 1967, s. 6(3), is that if a person is indicted on a count charging assault occasioning actual bodily harm, he or she can only be found guilty of common assault if that offence is specifically included in the indictment. This also applies to other offences included in s. 40 (*R* v *Mearns* (1990) 91 Cr App R 312). See also **Chapter 11** for CLA 1967, s. 6(3).

In *R* v *Lewis* (1991) 95 Cr App R 31, the Court of Appeal decided that if a count was incorrectly joined under s. 40, then, following *R* v *Newland* [1988] QB 402 (see **9.6**), the whole indictment was defective, as was everything that flowed from it. *R* v *Callaghan* (1991) 94 Cr App R 226 held that, since summary offences are essentially parasitic, the misjoinder of a summary offence does not render the counts alleging indictable offences invalid. The latest case on this point, *R* v *Simon* [1992] Crim LR 444 preferred *Callaghan*, but did not finally decide the point.

4.4.2 COMMITTAL FOR PLEA: s. 41

Where magistrates commit for trial on an either way offence, they may also commit the defendant for any summary offence, punishable with imprisonment or disqualification, that arises out of circumstances which are the same as, or connected with, the either way matter.

The summary offence need not be disclosed by the evidence. The prosecution merely indicates that, in the course of committing the either way offence, he or she also committed the summary offence. The offence itself is not included in the indictment, and the magistrates do not commit for trial, but only for a plea to be taken.

Under s. 41, the offence for which the defendant is committed to the Crown Court *must* be an offence which is triable either way. If the committed offence is triable only on indictment, the committal under s. 41 is null and void (*R* v *Miall* [1992] QB 836).

Where a summary offence is committed to the Crown Court under s. 41, it is *not* committed for a not guilty plea to be taken followed by a trial, as would be appropriate under s. 40. Under s. 41, assuming the defendant has been convicted of the triable either way offence, he or she will plead guilty to the summary offence, and the court will proceed to sentence. If he or she does not wish to plead guilty to the summary offence, or is acquitted of the triable either way offence, the case is remitted to the magistrates' court to be dealt with summarily.

The correct approach when dealing with committals under s. 41 was described in *R* v *Foote* (1992) 94 Cr App R 82, CA:

(a) The court must first deal with the indictable offence or offences.

(b) Only if the court convicts on one indictable offence does it then go on to consider whether s. 41 applies to the summary offence.

(c) If s. 41 does apply, a plea may be taken.

(d) Only if the accused pleads guilty to the summary offence can the Crown Court deal with it, and then only with the powers of the magistrates.

(e) If the accused is acquitted of the indictable offence, the Crown Court powers cease. The case goes back to the magistrates who are deemed merely to have adjourned it unless the Crown Court dismisses it.

4.4.3 DIFFERENCES BETWEEN s. 40 and s. 41

Sections 40 and 41 are easy to confuse. The following table, containing the points described above, is intended to highlight the differences between the two sections.

	Committal for trial: s. 40	**Committal for plea: s. 41**
1.	The summary offence must be common assault, taking a motor vehicle without consent, driving whilst disqualified, criminal damage or assaulting a prison custody officer or secure training centre officer.	The summary offence must be one which is punishable by imprisonment or disqualification, but is not otherwise specified.
2.	The magistrates play no part in including the summary offence in the indictment. It is a matter for the prosecution.	The magistrates must commit for a plea to be taken.
3.	The offence must be disclosed by the evidence.	The offence need not be disclosed by the evidence. The prosecution merely indicates that a summary offence has been committed.
4.	The summary offence must be founded on the same facts or form or be part of a series of offences of the same or a similar character as the main offence.	The summary offence must arise out of the same or connected circumstances as the main offence.
5.	The main offence may be triable either way or triable only on indictment.	The main offence must be triable either way.
6.	The defendant is *tried* in the Crown Court for the summary offence, following a plea of not guilty.	The defendant is *sentenced* in the Crown Court, following a plea of guilty, and assuming that a conviction on the either way offence has been recorded.

4.5 Advantages and Disadvantages of Each Mode of Trial

There are many matters to be taken into account in advising on the most appropriate forum:

(a) *Speed* Whether a case in the magistrates' court is likely to be heard more quickly than if it had been listed for hearing in the Crown Court depends on local waiting lists. However, the case itself is likely to take less time in the magistrates' court.

(b) *Expense* Proceedings in the magistrates' court are much less expensive than in the Crown Court — a very important consideration if the defendant is not legally aided.

(c) *Informality* Proceedings in the magistrates' court are much more informal than in the Crown Court, as fewer people are involved, and counsel do not wear wig and gown. The Crown Court can be daunting to someone who has little experience of criminal courts.

(d) *Sentence* The magistrates' powers of sentence are very much less than those of the Crown Court, though they do have the power to commit to the Crown Court for sentence. However, if the defendant intends to plead guilty, he or she is likely to opt for a hearing in the magistrates' court in the hope that they do not commit him or her to Crown Court for sentence. See **Chapters 15–24** for details of the magistrates' powers of sentence.

(e) *Division between the tribunals of fact and law* In the magistrates' court, the tribunals of fact and law are the same, so that they will first have to hear evidence before deciding on any question of admissibility, and then, if inadmissible, endeavour to forget it. In the Crown Court this problem simply does not arise. The judge alone will decide on admissibility, and evidence will only go before the jury if it is admissible.

(f) *Legal submissions* Despite the fact that lay magistrates are advised by a clerk, nevertheless any submissions on the law are made to laymen. (The case may be heard by a stipendiary magistrate, but this would not be known when determining the mode of trial.) In the Crown Court, the same submission would be made to a professional lawyer.

(g) *Advance information* The defendant, on a trial on indictment, will have full knowledge of the prosecution case against him or her because he or she will have a copy of all the committal documents. The defendant is not entitled to full disclosure of the prosecution case if the offence is to be tried summarily. As to what he or she is entitled to, see **4.6** below.

(h) *Appeals* Appeals from magistrates may be made without leave, see **Chapter 8**. Appeals from the Crown Court usually require leave, and the procedure generally is much more complicated. See **Chapter 12**.

(i) *The benefit of the doubt* It is generally assumed that a jury is more likely to give the defendant the benefit of the doubt than magistrates. In any event, if the case involves a substantial attack on the police evidence, the defendant is likely to find a jury more sympathetic than magistrates.

4.6 Advance Information

The degree to which the defence will have advance information of the prosecution case will depend on the mode of trial, and the type of offence.

(a) *Trial on indictment* Whether the offence is triable either way or triable only on indictment, the defence will have full knowledge of the prosecution case through committal proceedings.

(b) *Triable either way offences* Under the Magistrates' Courts (Advance Information) Rules 1985, r. 4, (SI 1985/601) the prosecution must provide the defence with copies of its witness statements, *or* a summary of the evidence upon which it proposes to rely, on receiving a request for such information. In very many cases, the CPS provides the defence with copies of the witness statements, so that the defendant has full knowledge of the case against him or her, but is not *entitled* to the statements — only to the statements *or* a summary. The practice of the CPS as to how much information is given tends to vary from area to area.

The prosecution is entitled to refuse a request, but, under r. 5, only where it thinks that compliance would lead to the intimidation of witnesses or some other interference with the course of justice. Failure to comply for any other reason will lead to an adjournment, unless the court considers that the defendant has not been prejudiced. See generally r. 7.

The request for information should be made *before* mode of trial proceedings have been held, and the information should be provided as soon as practicable. Thus, the defendant is able to make his or her decision as to the mode of trial with full knowledge of all the circumstances. It is the duty of the court, under r. 6, to satisfy itself that the defendant is aware of his or her right to advance information.

The purpose of obtaining advance information is to facilitate a mode of trial decision. The request should therefore be made before the mode of trial hearing, and the information should be provided as soon as practicable. Practice again varies and sometimes the information will be ready to be served on the defendant at court on the first appearance. Indeed in some areas this will inevitably be the case.

Obtaining advance information is now very common, but the defence may decide against a request if clearly one mode of trial is preferable. However, it is the duty of the court under r. 6 to satisfy itself that the defendant is aware of his or her rights.

Note that the magistrates have no power to *order* disclosure under these rules (*R* v *Dunmow Justices, ex parte Nash* (1993) 157 JP 1153, DC).

(c) *Summary offences* The Magistrates' Courts (Advance Information) Rules 1985 apply only to offences triable either way, so if the defendant is charged with a purely summary offence he or she has no right to know the case against him or her. In very many cases, however, the CPS will provide the defendant with full information, but the practice varies from area to area, so the defendant may have copies of all witness statements, or nothing at all. This does not affect the duty of the prosecution to make available to the defence a witness whom it does not intend to call, but who may be able to supply material evidence. See *R* v *Leyland Justices, ex parte Hawthorn* [1979] QB 283.

4.7 National Mode of Trial Guidelines

The guidelines are intended as assistance and not as directions, and are not intended to impinge on the magistrates' duty to consider each case individually and on its own special facts. They begin by making the following general observations about the mode of trial decision:

(a) The court should never make its decision on the grounds of convenience or expedition.

(b) The court should assume for the purpose of deciding mode of trial that the prosecution version is correct.

(c) The fact that the offences are alleged to be specimens is a relevant consideration; the fact that the defendant will be asking for other offences to be taken into consideration, if convicted, is not.

(d) Where cases involve complex questions of fact or difficult questions of law, including difficult issues of disclosure of sensitive material, the court should consider committal for trial.

(e) Where two or more defendants are jointly charged with an offence, each has an individual right to elect his mode of trial.

Note that the original guidelines stated that where two or more defendants were jointly charged, and the court decided that the case was more suitable for summary trial, and one defendant elects trial on indictment, then the court *must* proceed as examining justices. However, in *R* v *Brentwood Justices, ex parte Nicholls* [1992] 1 AC 1 applied in *R* v *Ipswich Justices, ex parte Callaghan, The Times*, 3 April 1995, it was held that where only one of a number of defendants elects trial on indictment, and the rest do not, the magistrates are *not* bound to commit all the defendants for trial on indictment. The right of election in s. 20 is given to each defendant individually, and is unaffected by any different decision made by a co-defendant. The new guideline follows their decision.

The prosecution should not attempt to persuade the magistrates to exercise their discretion under s. 25(2) (discontinuing the summary trial and proceeding with committal proceedings, see **4.2.4.2** above) in order to get round the decision in *ex parte Nicholls*, even if they thought it was unfortunate that the defendants should not be tried together. See *R* v *West Norfolk Justices, ex parte McMullen* [1993] COD 25.]

(f) In general, except where otherwise stated, either way offences should be tried summarily unless the court considers that the particular case has one or more of the features set out as follows *and* that its sentencing powers are insufficient. (It should be noted that this observation is repeated in relation to almost all the offences dealt with by the guidelines.)

(g) The court should also consider its powers to commit an offender for sentence, under MCA 1980, s. 38, as amended by CJA 1991, s. 25, if information emerges during the course of the hearing which leads it to conclude that the offence is so serious, or that the offender is such a risk to the public, that its powers to sentence him or her are inadequate. This amendment means that the committal for sentence is no longer determined by reference to the character and antecedents of the defendant.

Case law prior to the guidelines decided that the magistrates should not take into account any previous convictions that may be recorded against the defendant and should proceed on the basis that he was a man of good character. See *R* v *Colchester Justices, ex parte North East Essex Building Co. Ltd* [1977] 1 WLR 1109. Further, the original Mode of Trial Guidelines provided that the antecedents and personal mitigating circumstances of the defendant were irrelevant in determining the mode of trial. However, this guideline has now been removed, reflecting the provisions of CJA 1991, s. 29. Under s. 29, the defendant's antecedents may aggravate the matter, and his or her personal mitigating circumstances may be such as to reduce the seriousness of the offence, so that the matter may properly be dealt with by the magistrates.

Where reference is made to property or damage of 'high value' it means a figure equal to at least twice the amount of the limit (currently £5,000) imposed by statute on a magistrates' court when making a compensation order.

The following offences included in the guidelines are included here by way of illustration.

4.7.1 OFFENCES UNDER THE GUIDELINES

4.7.1.1 Burglary

1. *Dwelling house*

(a) Entry in the daytime when the occupier (or another) is present.

(b) Entry at night of a house which is normally occupied, whether or not the occupier (or another) is present.

(c) The offence is alleged to be one of a series of similar offences.

(d) The offence has professional hallmarks.

(e) The unrecovered property is of high value (see **4.7** for definition of high value).

Note: Attention is drawn to para. 28(c) of sch. 1 to the Magistrates' Courts Act 1980, by which offences of burglary in a dwelling *cannot* be tried summarily if any person in the dwelling was subjected to violence or the threat of violence.

2. *Non-dwellings*

(a) Entry of a pharmacy or doctor's surgery.

(b) Fear caused or violence done to anyone lawfully on the premises (e.g. night-watchman, security guard).

(c) The offence has professional hallmarks.

(d) Vandalism on a substantial scale.

(e) The unrecovered property is of high value (see **4.7** for definition of high value).

4.7.1.2 Theft and fraud

(a) Breach of trust by a person in a position of substantial authority, or in whom a high degree of trust is placed.

(b) Theft or fraud which has been committed or disguised in a sophisticated manner.

(c) Theft or fraud committed by an organised gang.

(d) The victim is particularly vulnerable to theft or fraud, e.g. the elderly or infirm.

(e) The unrecovered property is of high value (see **4.7** for definition of high value).

4.7.1.3 Handling

(a) Dishonest handling of stolen property by a receiver who has commissioned the theft.

(b) The offence has professional hallmarks.

(c) The property is of high value (see **4.7** for definition of high value).

4.7.1.4 Dangerous driving

(a) Alcohol or drugs contributing to dangerousness.

(b) Grossly excessive speed.

(c) Racing.

(d) Prolonged course of dangerous driving.

(e) Degree of injury or damage sustained.

(f) Other related offences.

4.7.1.5 Indecent assault

(a) Substantial disparity in age between victim and defendant, and the assault is more than trivial.

(b) Violence or threats of violence.

(c) Relationship of trust or responsibility between defendant and victim.

(d) Several similar offences, and the assaults are more than trivial.

(e) The victim is particularly vulnerable.

(f) Serious nature of the assault.

Multiple-choice Questions

1. Colin is charged with criminal damage to David's Rolls Royce motor car. The value of the damage has been estimated by a Rolls Royce approved dealer at £5,579.86. Colin asks you about the appropriate court of trial. Which ONE of the following statements about this situation is correct?

[A] He must be tried summarily.
[B] He may be tried summarily but only if both he and the magistrates agree.
[C] He may only be tried on indictment if both he and the magistrates agree.
[D] He must be tried on indictment.

2. Brian is charged with theft. He appears before the magistrates to determine the mode of trial. Which of the following propositions is **false**?

[A] He may be tried on indictment if he so elects, despite the wishes of the magistrates.
[B] He must be tried on indictment if the magistrates so decide whatever his wishes are.
[C] He may only be tried summarily if both he and the magistrates agree.
[D] He may only be tried on indictment if the prosecution is brought by the DPP, Attorney General or Solicitor General.

Tutorial Questions

MODE OF TRIAL

Questions 1 to 3 deal with the procedure for determining the court in which the defendant will be tried.

1. Edward appears before Muggleton Magistrates' Court charged with:

(a) dangerous driving;

(b) taking a motor vehicle without the owner's consent; and

(c) driving while disqualified.

The prosecution case is that officers in a marked police vehicle saw Edward driving a car on a public road. Knowing him to be disqualified, they signalled to him to stop but he accelerated, driving at speeds of 70 mph in a built-up area, going onto the wrong side of the road, causing oncoming traffic to brake sharply, and eventually crashing the car into a lamppost. He then escaped on foot but was later arrested at his home address. Enquiries reveal that the car Edward was allegedly driving was taken without the owner's consent earlier that day. It is expected that Edward will plead not guilty to all charges and allege mistaken identification on the part of the police. Dangerous driving is an offence triable either way; driving while disqualified and taking a vehicle without the owner's consent are summary offences.

(a) Describe the procedure by which the mode of trial for the dangerous driving charge will be determined.

(b) Advise Edward of the extent to which he is entitled to know the nature of the prosecution case in advance of trial (i) if he is tried on indictment and (ii) if he is tried summarily.

(c) Advise the prosecution on whether, if the dangerous driving charge is committed for trial, it will be possible for the other two charges to be tried on indictment also.

2. David appears before Kingsport Magistrates' Court charged with two offences of criminal damage. The first charge alleges that, on 1 September, he intentionally damaged a motor vehicle; the second alleges that, on 3 September, he intentionally damaged a window. The prosecution case as regards the first offence is that, following an argument with a relative, he threw a stone at the windscreen of the relative's car as he was driving away from David's house. As regards the second offence, the case is that, after being told to leave a public house because he was the worse for drink, he threw a brick through a window of the pub. The value of the damage involved in the first charge was £50; the value of the damage in the second was £100. David wishes to be tried on indictment.

Advise him as to whether he has a right to be so tried.

3. Sid appears before Muggleton Magistrates' Court charged with assault occasioning actual bodily harm (an offence triable either way). Describe the procedure which will be followed in order to determine whether he will be tried summarily or on indictment.

ELECTION

Questions 4 to 8 deal with the defendant's decision whether to elect Crown Court trial

In each of these situations, you are defence counsel in the magistrates' court. Today the court will determine the mode of trial for the defendant. He or she may be asked to choose whether he or she wishes to be tried in the magistrates' court or Crown Court. The defendant is likely to want your advice on this matter. Consider what you could say.

4. Arnold (aged 32) appears at the magistrates' court on two charges. The first (theft) alleges that he stole two loaves of bread and a pint of milk from a milk float in the street. The second (making off without payment) alleges that, having ordered and consumed a fried breakfast, Arnold tried to leave a cafe without paying for his meal. According to prosecution witnesses, he was caught 'red-handed' on both occasions.

Arnold has no fixed address, staying in hostels when he can afford to do so. His employment record consists largely of casual jobs which were menial and low-paid. He has seven convictions, covering the last ten years. Offences involve dishonesty (of a minor nature) or violence/breaches of the peace. If convicted of either of the two latest offences, he will be in breach of a conditional discharge imposed five months ago by another court.

Instructions from the client: Arnold is in custody and would like to stay there for the winter months. He intends to plead Not Guilty, insisting he is innocent, but he has no witnesses. He says the prosecution eye witnesses are lying and have grudges against him.

5. Bertie has been charged with theft from his employer. The allegation is that he took stock (electrical components) from his employer's warehouse over a period of several months, with a total value of £4,300. No property has been recovered.

There are two main prosecution witnesses, the works supervisor and another colleague from Bertie's former place of work. Both say they saw him walk out of the warehouse with items, place them in the boot of his car in the car park and eventually drive home with the items at the end of his shift. Bertie made no admissions to police officers, and refused to be interviewed without his solicitor being present.

Bertie is aged 26 and has no previous convictions. He is married with two young children.

Instructions from the client: Bertie says he can call his ex-employer to testify that he was being considered for promotion at the time of his arrest. He says that he suspected the two prosecution witnesses of stealing the stock that he is charged with stealing.

6. Craig is aged 34. He is charged with stealing a car. The car was recovered from a multi-storey car park attached to a block of flats some 200 metres from Craig's house. Police arrested Craig inside the car. He has four previous convictions for theft (not of cars) and has been in prison on two occasions. He is alleged to have made a full confession on the way to the police station. There are no eye witnesses to the theft.

Instructions from the client: Craig will plead Not Guilty. He says that the car had been in the car park for three days before his arrest and that he thought it had been abandoned. He was thinking about using it for spares for his own car. He denies making the confession, saying that he has always maintained his innocence.

7. Dennis is charged with assault occasioning actual bodily harm. The incident occurred at a nightclub when an argument developed over who was going to drive a young lady home. The victim (and main prosecution witness) suffered a broken nose and lost two teeth. Dennis (aged 18) is a promising amateur boxer and was not marked.

The victim (aged 24) has several previous convictions for offences of violence. Dennis has no previous convictions. At the police station, Dennis expressed contrition for his part in the incident.

Instructions from the client: Dennis will plead Not Guilty, relying on self-defence. He has no witnesses. He says his 'admission' was an expression of regret for losing his self-control but was not meant to be an acceptance of guilt.

8. As in (7) above, but this time Dennis already has a case pending in the Crown Court. The indictment alleges that he took part in an affray at a local football match, where about 75 youths were involved. He will plead Not Guilty to this too.

Now go through those situations again and think about how you, as prosecuting counsel, might address the court on the suitable location for the case to be dealt with. (Remember you should liaise with the staff of the Crown Prosecution Service if this is a CPS prosecution.)

FIVE

SUMMARY TRIAL

5.1 Procedure at Trial

Some 96% of all criminal cases are tried in magistrates' courts. The procedure is the same, whether the offence is triable only summarily, or triable either way, though if the offence is triable either way, the magistrates must first determine the mode of trial (see **Chapter 4**).

See generally *Stone's Justices' Manual* (1995) at 1–410 *et seq* and *Blackstone's Criminal Practice* at D17 and D18.

5.1.1 THE ABSENCE OF THE DEFENDANT

Although the defendant will in fact often be present in court for the hearing, the magistrates have the power to proceed in his absence. There are three situations in which this may arise:

5.1.1.1 Where the defendant fails to attend

Under MCA 1980, s. 11(1), the magistrates have a discretion to hear the case in the defendant's absence if he or she fails to attend court in answer to a summons. If the offence is triable either way, the prosecution must first establish that the defendant actually knew of the summons, for example, through attending an earlier hearing.

If the offence is triable only summarily, then the prosecution may prove that the summons was served simply by establishing that, for example, it was sent by registered post to the defendant's last known address, but the prosecution does not have to prove that the defendant received it.

Once service of the summons has been proved, a plea of not guilty will be entered on the defendant's behalf and the prosecution evidence will be called. Such hearings often end in the conviction of the defendant, as none of the prosecution evidence will have been tested by cross-examination, and the magistrates will not have heard the defence case.

If the defendant did not, in fact, know of the proceedings, he or she may make a 'statutory declaration' of this under MCA 1980, s. 14, within 21 days of finding out about them. If the declaration is made, the summons, trial and conviction are rendered void. However, the information remains valid, so that the prosecution can start again.

The discretion to proceed in the absence of the defendant should be exercised judicially. This includes giving the defendant a fair opportunity to be present, and to give or call evidence. See *R* v *Bolton Magistrates' Court, ex parte Merna* [1991] Crim LR 848, where the court proceeded in the absence of the defendant, despite a letter from his doctor saying that he was unfit to attend court.

Whether the defendant's absence should lead to a rehearing of the case was a matter within the justices' discretion, and as long as this was based on facts the justices were entitled to find, the divisional court would not overturn it (*R* v *North Shields Justices, ex parte Darroll* [1991] COD 317).

The s. 11 procedure tends to be used only for the less serious offences. In any event, if the defendant is charged with a triable either way offence, the defendant normally has to be present during mode of trial proceedings.

5.1.1.2 Pleading guilty by post

Under MCA 1980, s. 12 as substituted by sch. 5 to the Criminal Justice and Public Order Act 1994, a defendant may plead guilty by sending a letter to court. This can be done if:

(a) the offence is summary;

(b) the maximum penalty is not more than three months' imprisonment; and

(c) proceedings have been started by the service of a summons.

In such circumstances the procedure is as follows:

(a) The prosecution serves on the defendant:

  (i) the summons;

  (ii) a brief statement of the facts upon which the prosecution proposes to rely; and

  (iii) a notice explaining the procedure.

(b) If he or she wishes to plead guilty, the defendant notifies the court and may enclose a statement of his or her mitigation. Subsequently, the defendant may withdraw this plea, and the case then proceeds as if it were a not guilty plea.

(c) Neither the prosecution nor the defence is represented or appears at court, and the court proceeds on the basis of the statements which are read out in court. Failure to do so will lead to the conviction being quashed, as in *R* v *Epping and Ongar Justices, ex parte Breach* [1987] RTR 233 where the defendant's statement in mitigation was not read out. The magistrates may refuse to accept the plea of guilty if the statement in mitigation discloses information which amounts to a defence.

(d) The magistrates, if content to accept the plea, may sentence, or adjourn for the accused to be present. The magistrates may only sentence the defendant in his or her absence if he or she is to be fined, absolutely discharged, or have his or her driving licence endorsed.

Note that the court ought to be reluctant to try, in his absence, an offender who is young, has not been placed on bail and/or has no record of failing to appear (*R* v *Dewsbury Magistrates' Court, ex parte K*, *The Times*, 16 March 1994).

Section 12A of the MCA 1980 deals with the situation where the defendant actually appears in court. Two situations may occur:

(a) The defendant has informed the court that he or she wishes the case to proceed under s. 12, but he nevertheless appears in court at the appointed time. The court may proceed to deal with the matter as if he or she were absent, if he consents to such a course: s. 12A(1).

(b) The defendant has not notified the court that he or she wishes the case to proceed under s. 12, and appears at the appointed time. If he or she indicates that he or she wishes to plead guilty, and consents, the court may proceed to deal with the matter as if he or she were absent: s. 12(A)2.

In either case, the court must afford the defendant an opportunity to make oral submissions with a view to mitigation of sentence (s. 12(5)(c)).

5.1.1.3 The disorderly defendant

If the defendant's behaviour is so disruptive that the proceedings cannot continue, he or she may be removed, and the court may proceed in his or her absence under MCA 1980, s. 11.

Note: If the defendant is represented, he or she is deemed to be present unless his or her presence is expressly required by statute (MCA 1980, s. 122(2)).

5.1.2 ABSENCE OF THE PROSECUTION

Under MCA 1980, s. 15, if the prosecution fails to appear at the time and place fixed for the summary trial, the magistrates may adjourn the case or dismiss the information. Where the magistrates act unreasonably in dismissing a case, their decision is a nullity, and the mandamus would issue (*R* v *Hendon Justices, ex parte DPP* [1994] QB 167, DC).

If the case is adjourned part-heard, then the magistrates may proceed in the absence of the prosecution, the evidence given on the earlier occasion being treated as the entirety of the prosecution case. In these circumstances, the defendant will not face cross-examination of his or her evidence by the prosecution.

5.1.3 REPRESENTATIONS IN PRIVATE

A decision to hear representations in private is within the magistrates' discretion, but careful consideration should always be given to whether such a step is appropriate, given the magistrates' role as fact-finder. In order to guard against injustice, steps must be taken to ensure that all parties are notified of the hearing and are represented, with a contemporaneous note being taken, normally by the clerk (see *R* v *Nottingham Justices, ex parte Furnell, The Times*, 18 December 1995).

5.1.4 TAKING THE PLEA

The defendant must plead unequivocally guilty or not guilty. In practice, this often throws up two separate problems:

(a) *The defendant who wishes to change his plea* The court may consider an application made by a defendant who has unequivocally pleaded guilty to change his or her plea, at any time before sentence (see *S (an infant)* v *Recorder of Manchester* [1971] AC 481). Whether he or she will be allowed to change the plea is entirely within the discretion of the magistrates. If they take the view that the defendant understood the charge, the consequence of his or her plea, and had intended to make it, they will be unlikely to allow a change. See generally *R* v *McNally* [1954] 1 WLR 933.

Where the magistrates have allowed the defendant to change his plea from guilty to not guilty, they should also allow him to reconsider his consent to summary trial (*R* v *Bow Street Magistrates' Court, ex parte Welcome* (1992) 156 JP 609).

Where the defendant has pleaded not guilty, and wishes to change his or her plea to guilty, he or she may do so with leave of the court (which for obvious reasons is likely to be granted) any time before the court retires to consider the verdict.

(b) *The defendant's plea is equivocal* This covers three situations:

(i) The defendant, when pleading guilty, explains his or her plea in words amounting to a defence. See *R* v *Emery* (1943) 29 Cr App R 47, where the defendant said 'Plead guilty in self-defence'. The magistrates should then explain the law and the defendant is asked to plead again. If the plea is still equivocal, the magistrates must record a plea of not guilty and proceed to trial. If they make no enquiry into the plea, the defendant may later challenge the validity of the plea on appeal.

(ii) The defendant unequivocally pleads guilty, but the plea is rendered equivocal by information given to the magistrates before sentence (see *R* v *Durham Justices, ex parte Virgo* [1952] 2 QB 1 contrasted with *R* v *Birmingham Crown Court, ex parte Sharma* [1988] Crim LR 741). In *P. Foster (Haulage) Ltd* v *Roberts* [1978] 2 All ER 751, it was said that this should not be termed an equivocal plea, and is merely a situation in which the magistrates have a discretion to allow a change of plea.

(iii) The defendant unequivocally pleads guilty and no further information is given to the court casting doubt on the correctness of the plea. However, if the defendant argues that the plea was made under duress, the Crown Court may treat it as an equivocal plea. See *R* v *Huntingdon Crown Court, ex parte Jordan* [1981] QB 857.

In any event, the magistrates should always ensure that the defendant, particularly an unrepresented defendant, understands the offence, the consequences of the plea, and intends to make that plea. The proper forum for any dispute is the Crown Court, which may review the case, and, if it decides that the plea was equivocal, it should remit it to the magistrates with an order that they enter a plea of not guilty and proceed to trial. Before making any such order, the Crown Court should read affidavits from the magistrates and the clerk as to what happened, and magistrates and clerks should cooperate by swearing such affidavits. See *R* v *Plymouth Justices, ex parte Hart* [1986] QB 950.

5.1.5 THE PROSECUTION OPENING SPEECH

Magistrates will be familiar with the cases that frequently come before them, so that, although the prosecution has the right to an opening speech, it is usually brief and is often not made.

5.1.6 THE PROSECUTION EVIDENCE

The prosecution calls the evidence upon which it relies. This will take the form of witnesses and written statements, if admissible and appropriate. See **11.5.2** and ***Evidence Manual***.

As to the defence knowledge of the prosecution case, see **4.6**.

5.1.7 THE SUBMISSION OF NO CASE TO ANSWER

At the end of the prosecution evidence, the defence may make a submission of no case to answer. According to Lord Parker CJ, in *Practice Direction (Submission of No Case)* [1962] 1 WLR 227, a submission that there is no case to answer may properly be made and upheld:

(a) when there has been no evidence to prove an essential element in the alleged offence;

or

(b) when the evidence adduced by the prosecution has been so discredited as a result of cross-examination or is so manifestly unreliable that no reasonable tribunal could safely convict on it.

The magistrates have to decide, not whether they would convict, but whether a reasonable tribunal might convict on the evidence of the prosecution witnesses, and if not, they should dismiss the case. (See further **Chapter 21** of ***Advocacy Manual*** for how to make, or respond to, a submission of no case to answer.)

5.1.8 THE DEFENCE CASE

Assuming no submission of no case to answer is made, or is made and fails, the defence may present its case. The right of the defence to make an opening speech is rarely exercised (see **5.1.9**) and the defence usually begins to call its evidence straight away. The defendant should give evidence before any other witnesses he intends to call (PACE 1984, s. 79).

5.1.9 CLOSING SPEECHES

The defence has the right to either an opening or a closing speech, and invariably elects a closing speech, thus having the benefit of the last word.

If either party wishes to make a second speech, it may do so with the leave of the court; but if the court is going to allow one party to make a second speech, it must allow the other party a second speech also. If both parties are allowed a second speech, the prosecution must go first, thus allowing the defence the benefit of the last word.

5.1.10 THE VERDICT

Lay magistrates usually retire to consider their verdict, and no one must retire with them as this may create the impression that they have somehow influenced the decision. As to the position of the clerk to the justices, see **5.2** below. The verdict is a majority decision, and the chairman has no casting vote. Therefore, if an evenly numbered court is equally divided, it must adjourn for a fresh hearing before a new bench (*R* v *Redbridge Justices, ex parte Ram* [1992] QB 384).

Stipendiary magistrates rarely retire, and usually announce their decision immediately after the defence's closing speech.

Magistrates should not, and do not, give reasons for their decisions.

It should be noted that the provisions of CLA 1967, s. 6(3), do not apply in magistrates' courts. Thus the magistrates have no power to find the defendant guilty of a lesser offence not specifically charged (except under s. 24(3) and (4) of the Road Traffic Offenders Act 1988, under which a defendant charged with reckless driving or reckless cycling may be found guilty of careless driving or careless cycling). See generally *Lawrence* v *Same* [1968] 2 QB 93. However, it would be open to the magistrates to ask for a summons for the lesser offence to be preferred immediately and proceed to deal with it at once. As to where the magistrates convict on a more serious charge and dismiss others because further convictions would be oppressive, see *DPP* v *Gane* [1991] Crim LR 711, DC.

For a discussion of CLA 1967, s. 6(3) see **Chapter 11**.

5.1.11 SENTENCE

If the magistrates find the case proved, they will proceed to sentence, after an adjournment if necessary. A detailed analysis of the procedure prior to sentence is found in **Chapter 14**, but in brief is as follows:

(a) The prosecution gives details of the defendant's character and antecedents.

(b) Any pre-sentence or other reports are placed before the court.

(c) The defence enters a plea in mitigation.

(d) The court passes sentence.

The magistrates' sentencing powers are discussed in full in **Chapters 15** to **24**. However, in brief, the magistrates may sentence a person over the age of 21 to a maximum period of six months' imprisonment on each offence, or the statutory maximum, whichever is the less. Where the person is convicted of two or more offences, triable either way, the sentences may be made to run consecutively to a maximum of 12 months. The jurisdiction to exceed a total of six months' imprisonment only arises where the defendant is convicted of two or more offences which are triable either way. If the defendant is convicted of, say, theft (maximum sentence in magistrates' court six months) and assaulting a police officer (a summary offence carrying a maximum sentence of three months), the magistrates cannot exceed an aggregate sentence of six months.

The same rules apply where the court is sentencing a person between the ages of 17–20 inclusive to detention in a young offender institution. In addition the magistrates may fine an offender up to £5,000 per offence. See generally MCA 1980, ss. 31, 32 and 133.

5.1.12 POWER TO RECTIFY MISTAKES

Under MCA 1980, s. 142 as amended by the Criminal Appeal Act 1995, a Magistrates' court may vary or rescind a sentence or other order imposed or made by it, if it appears to the court to be in the interests of justice to do so. The purpose of this provision is to prevent the judicial review of proceedings which clearly should be re-heard.

The following points should be noted:

(a) The magistrates may reopen the case regardless of whether the defendant pleaded guilty or not guilty.

(b) There is no time limit to the re-opening of the case.

(c) The magistrates reopening the case need not be the same magistrates who dealt with the case originally.

These three points were introduced by the Criminal Appeal Act 1995, and considerably widen the magistrates powers under s. 142. It may be that many matters which could previously only have been dealt with by way of appeal may now be dealt with under s. 142. For this reason, students should always consider s. 142 when dealing with any error made by the magistrates.

Two further points should be made:

(a) When a person is convicted by a magistrates' court, and it appears in the interest of justice that the case should be re-heard by a different bench, the court may so direct (s. 142(2), as amended). In this situation the case is treated as if it had simply been adjourned.

(b) The court's right to exercise its powers under s. 142 are lost after the case has been appealed to the Crown Court or the High Court by way of case stated, and the court has determined the appeal (s. 142(1A) and (2A) inserted by the Criminal Appeal Act 1995, s. 2b(3) and (5)).

The amendments to s. 142 came into force on 1 January 1996.

5.2 The Clerk to the Justices

The clerk to the justices is a barrister or solicitor of at least five years' standing. He or she is usually supported by assistant clerks who often are, but need not be, legally qualified.

The clerk has a wide administrative function. This derives from the magistrates' jurisdiction over both domestic and licensing matters in addition to their criminal jurisdiction. Here the clerk is involved in a number of areas, such as the taking of informations, the issue of summonses, and the grant of legal aid.

During a trial, the clerk has several duties. The most important are:

(a) To speak on behalf of the court, if required to do so. This includes reading the charge to the defendant, putting the election as to the mode of trial to him or her, and taking the plea.

(b) To advise the justices on any question of law and procedure. This advice should be given in open court, so that all parties know the advice given, and the basis upon which the magistrates made their decision.

Where the justices wish their clerk to advise them on matters of law, it is essential that the clerk is present in court during the submissions of the parties (*R v Chichester Magistrates' Court, ex parte DPP* (1993) 157 JP 1049). The clerk should give his or her advice in open court, so that all parties know the advice given, and the basis on which the magistrates made their decision. For example, where the clerk wishes to refer the justices to an authority not previously cited, the advocates in the case should be informed and given the opportunity to comment (*W* v *W*, *The Times*, 4 June 1993).

The clerk plays no part in deciding either the facts or the defendant's guilt, but may advise the justices on the law, after they have retired to consider their verdict, and should accompany them only if specifically requested to do so. As soon as he or she has given the advice the clerk should withdraw, unless the case is so complex that his or her advice is required throughout the decision-making process. (See *R* v *Consett Justices, ex parte Postal Bingo Ltd* [1967] 2 QB 9.) For recent examples of where the decision-making process was interfered with, see *R* v *Eccles Justices, ex parte Farrelly* (1992) 157 JP 77 and *R* v *Birmingham Justices Court, ex parte Ahmed* [1994] COD 461.

(c) To take a note of the evidence. The clerk may refresh the magistrates' memories, and draw their attention to any issues involved in the matters before the court.

(d) To intervene in the case to assist the course of justice when the court is dealing with an unrepresented defendant. But it should be noted that the clerk is there to assist the court by ensuring that the parties present their case clearly and unambiguously, and that he or she is not there to assist one party as against the other.

(e) To advise the magistrates on the range of sentences available. As reaching a decision on sentence can be a very involved process, it is rarely done in open court, to avoid an unseemly debate as to the appropriate sentence taking place in front of the defendant.

5.3 Committal to the Crown Court for Sentence

In certain circumstances, the magistrates, having found the defendant guilty of an offence or if the defendant pleads guilty may commit him or her to the Crown Court for sentence. The most important powers of committal are as follows:

5.3.1 COMMITTAL UNDER MAGISTRATES' COURTS ACT 1980, s. 38

When magistrates accept the summary trial of an offence triable either way, they do so on the basis that the defendant is a person of good character, and that they have sufficient powers to deal with him or her. However, having heard all the evidence in the case, the court may form the opinion that it does not, in fact, have sufficient powers. In these circumstances, the magistrates may wish to commit the defendant to the Crown Court, so that the Crown Court, using its greater powers, may impose an appropriate sentence. Under MCA 1980, s. 38, as substituted by CJA 1991, s. 25, the magistrates may commit for sentence *only* in view of either the seriousness of the offence or the nature of the offence, as explained below.

(a) *The seriousness of the offence* Under MCA 1980, s. 38(2)(a), in order to commit for sentence, the court must be of the opinion that the offence, or the combination of the offence and other associated offences, is so serious that greater punishment should be inflicted than the court has power to impose. The associated offences are those offences of which the defendant has been convicted or sentenced at the same time as the main offence, or is an offence which he or she is asking the court to take into consideration on sentencing (CJA 1991, s. 31(2)(a)). In order to commit under MCA 1980, s. 38(2)(a), the court must be dealing with a person of not less than 18 years old (s. 38(1)).

The following matters may also render the offence 'serious' and justify a committal under s. 38:

(i) Where the defendant has previous convictions (CJA 1991, s. 29(1), as amended by CJA 1993, s. 66(6)).

(ii) Where new information has come to light since the decision to try summarily was made. However, there is nothing in MCA 1980, s. 38, as amended, to suggest that a magistrates' court which accepted jurisdiction initially could not change its mind at a later stage in the proceedings. To that extent, the discretion of the magistrates is unfettered (*R* v *Sheffield Crown Court, ex parte DPP* (1994) 15 Cr App R (S) 768; *R* v *Dover Justices, ex parte Pamment* (1994) 15 Cr App R (S) 778; *R* v *North Sefton Magistrates' Court, ex parte Marsh* (1994) 159 JP 1).

It should be said, however, that in most cases where the magistrates commit for sentence on this basis, they do so because new information arises during the trial, and students are referred to the following cases by way of example, *R* v *King's Lynn Justices, ex parte Carter* [1969] 1 QB 488; *R* v *Lymm Justices ex parte Brown* [1973] 1 WLR 1039; and *R* v *Tower Bridge Magistrates, ex parte Osman* [1971] 1 WLR 1109. Further, in *R* v *Manchester Magistrates Court, ex parte Kaymanesh* [1994] COD 380, it was stressed that the new sentencing policy of the CJA 1991 did not entitle the magistrates to ignore the principles established by earlier cases, which still remain applicable. These principles make it clear that if magistrates consider their sentencing powers inadequate, this should be dealt with at the time of deciding the mode of trial. Further, both *ex parte Pamment* and *ex parte Marsh* stressed the importance of the magistrates' initial decision, on the basis that the defendant is entitled to expect that he would not be committed for sentence on the same facts upon which the magistrates accepted jurisdiction.

(iii) Where the defendant asks for other offences to be taken into consideration (see **12.9**).

(b) *The protection of the public* Under s. 38(2)(b), in order to commit for sentence, the court must be of the opinion, in the case of a violent or sexual offence, that a sentence of imprisonment for a term longer than the court has power to impose is necessary to protect the public from serious harm from the offender.

Students should refer to CJA 1991, s. 31(1), for a full definition of the terms 'sexual offence' and 'violent offence', and should consult the sentencing section of this Manual. The reference to protecting the public from harm means protecting them from death or serious injury, whether physical or psychological, occasioned by further such offences committed by the defendant (CJA 1991, s. 31(3)).

The committal may be in custody or on bail (s. 38(2)). However, traditionally the committal has almost invariably been in custody, as the defendant is likely to be sentenced to a reasonably long period of imprisonment. See *R* v *Coe* (1969) 53 Cr App R 66.

At the Crown Court, the case is heard by a judge (usually a circuit judge or recorder) sitting with two lay magistrates. The defendant is asked if he or she admits the conviction and committal, which in most cases he or she does. If the defendant does not admit them, then they must be formally proved against him or her. The court will then sentence, the procedure being similar to that on a plea of guilty, detailed in **Chapter 14**, and in brief is as follows:

(a) The prosecution outlines the brief facts of the offence.

(b) The prosecution supplies the court with the defendant's character and antecedents.

(c) Any pre-sentence or other reports are placed before the court.

(d) The defence enters a plea of mitigation.

(e) The court proceeds to sentence.

The Crown Court may sentence the defendant, under the PCCA 1973, s. 42, as if he or she had just been convicted on indictment before it. Thus, the court can exercise any of its usual sentencing powers and impose any sentence, including a sentence which had been available to the magistrates, if it takes a less serious view of the matter than did the magistrates. However, in many cases the Crown Court takes an equally serious view of the matter and usually imposes a fairly heavy sentence.

The Crown Court may remit the case to the magistrates, but only where the committal order was bad on its face (*R* v *Sheffield Crown Court, ex parte DPP* (1994) 15 Cr App R (S) 768).

5.3.2 BREACH OF CROWN COURT ORDER

Where the defendant is convicted of an offence which constitutes a breach of a Crown Court order, the magistrates may commit the offender to the Crown Court (see **19.10** for further details). The most important orders are:

(a) A suspended sentence. If the defendant is convicted of an imprisonable offence committed while subject to a suspended sentence, the magistrates may either commit for sentence or simply notify the Crown Court of the breach (PCCA 1973, s. 24).

(b) A probation order or conditional discharge. If the defendant is in breach of either order the magistrates may commit him or her in custody or on bail or deal with him or her themselves. If it is a breach of a conditional discharge, the committal is likely to be on bail.

5.3.3 COMMITTAL UNDER CRIMINAL JUSTICE ACT 1967, s. 56

Section 56 provides that where the magistrates are committing a defendant to the Crown Court in any of the circumstances outlined in **5.3.1** or **5.3.2**, they may also commit for any other offences of which the defendant has been convicted.

The effect is that the magistrates may commit to the Crown Court summary offences which could not otherwise be committed. Thus, a single court can deal with the defendant for all outstanding offences, and this avoids the otherwise inconvenient result of the magistrates' court dealing with the summary offences and the Crown Court dealing with everything else.

The purpose of the section is convenience, and to ensure consistency of sentencing. In these circumstances it would be unfair to the defendant if he or she incurred any greater penalty as regards the summary offences, and therefore the powers of the Crown Court when dealing with a defendant on a committal under s. 56 are limited to those of the magistrates. For a recent example, see *R* v *Whitlock* (1992) 13 Cr App R (S) 157, CA.

5.3.4 COMMITTAL UNDER MAGISTRATES' COURTS ACT 1980, s. 37

An adult magistrates' court may impose a maximum of six months' detention in a young offender institution on an offender aged 18–20 inclusive; and a youth court may impose a maximum of six months' detention on an offender aged 15–17. (These maxima are increased to 12 months in the case of an offender being sentenced for two or more triable either way offences.) If the court takes the view that six months is inadequate, the adult magistrates' court may commit under s. 38, and the youth court may commit under s. 37.

The two forms of committal are very similar, but there are two important differences:

(a) Under s. 38, the Crown Court has at its disposal all its usual sentencing powers. Under s. 37, the court may impose a maximum of 24 months' detention in a young offender institution but is otherwise limited to the powers of the youth court.

(b) The magistrates may commit under s. 38 only in view of either the seriousness of the offence or to protect the public (see **5.3.1**). Under s. 37, the magistrates may commit if they consider six months' detention inadequate for whatever reason.

5.3.5 APPEALS

If the defendant wishes to appeal against committal, he or she must apply for judicial review (see **8.3**). He or she cannot appeal to the Crown Court as a committal is neither a conviction nor a sentence (see **8.1**). Nor can he or she appeal by way of case stated as the case has not yet finished (see **8.2.1**).

SIX

COMMITTAL PROCEEDINGS

The vast majority of cases which are dealt with by the Crown Court, are dealt with initially by the magistrates. This being so, a mechanism is required to remove the matter from the magistrates' court and place it before the Crown Court. This mechanism is in the form of committal proceedings.

Committal proceedings are not used in every case which is transferred to the Crown Court. The exceptional situations are serious fraud cases, cases involving children, and voluntary bills of indictment. They are dealt with after committal is considered.

6.1 Committal Proceedings

There are two types of committal proceedings, *viz.* the full, oral type and the short type.

A full, oral, or 'old-style', committal under MCA 1980, s. 6(1), involves consideration of the evidence of the case. Such a committal will be held if the defence wishes to cross-examine the prosecution witnesses, make a submission of no case to answer, or call evidence on its own behalf.

This form of committal has the advantage that if the submission succeeds, the case will be thrown out and the accused discharged, saving the trouble and distress of a trial. It should be noted that the standard of proof at committal is very low, and such discharges are not common. In any event, a discharge does not rank as an acquittal, and the prosecution may seek to commit the accused for trial a second time, or apply for a voluntary bill of indictment. See **6.3.3**.

An additional feature is that the defence case may be revealed in whole or in part, and the accused may lose the element of surprise, giving the prosecution witnesses a chance to rehearse their evidence.

Note that when the Criminal Procedure and Investigations Act 1996 comes into force, full committal proceedings will be abolished. The prosecution case will be on the basis of documentary evidence only and there will be no opportunity for the defendants to give or call evidence. However, the defence will still be able to make a submission of no case to answer.

A short committal under MCA 1980, s. 6(2) does not involve the consideration of evidence, and will be held if the defence accepts that there is a case to answer, or wishes to reserve its position until trial. This form of committal is often referred to as a 'six-two' or a 'paper' committal.

It is usually the defence which decides which type of committal should be adopted, although in exceptional cases the prosecution may wish to hold full committal proceedings in order to test the strength of its own case.

In general terms, the defence will adopt full committal proceedings in the following situations:

(a) if the statements of the prosecution witnesses do not reveal a case to answer;

(b) the statements of the prosecution witnesses reveal a case to answer, but the defence thinks that the witnesses can be discredited by cross-examination;

(c) where identification is in issue — Guidelines issued by the Attorney-General in written answers to the House of Commons on 27 May 1976 and 25 July 1979, state that full committal proceedings should always be held, unless both counsel and the examining justices agree to proceed by way of a s. 6(2) committal. Full committal proceedings enable witnesses to be cross-examined on the identification at a relatively early stage of the proceedings.

Under MCA 1980, s. 4(3), the accused must be present throughout committal proceedings. However, evidence may be given in the accused's absence, under s. 4(4), if:

(a) his or her conduct before the justices is so disorderly that it is not practicable for the evidence to be given in his or her presence; or

(b) he or she cannot be present for reasons of health, but is represented and consents to evidence being given in his or her absence.

Committal proceedings are open to the public, although the justices have a discretion to sit *in camera* (MCA 1980, s. 4(2)). The press may also attend, but is restricted in what it may report.

6.1.1 FULL COMMITTAL PROCEEDINGS

The procedure for committal with consideration of the evidence, governed by MCA 1980, s. 6(1) and MCR 1981, r. 7, is as set out below. Remember that at any stage the examining justices may change the proceedings from committal to summary trial, as set out in **4.2.4.2**.

(a) *The charge.* The charge is written down by the clerk of the court (if it has not been written down already) and read to the accused. He or she is not asked to plead, as the purpose of the proceedings is not to determine guilt or innocence.

(b) *Reporting restrictions.* See **6.2.1**.

(c) The prosecution makes an *opening speech*, outlining the case to the examining justices and relating the evidence to the charge.

(d) *The prosecution calls its evidence*, either in the form of oral testimony or written statements or a combination of the two.

(i) *Oral testimony*: the evidence-in-chief of each witness may be subject to cross-examination, and re-examination if appropriate, and recorded in the form of a *deposition*. The taking of a deposition has four elements:

— the evidence of the witness is reduced into writing by the clerk of the court; and

— the writing is read back to the witness by the clerk who asks if the witness wishes to add, alter or amend anything (any alterations are also recorded by the clerk); and

— the writing is then signed by the witness; and

— the signature is then authenticated by a certificate from the examining justices.

This procedure is mandatory, and any deviation from the rules is likely to be fatal. The committal itself, and the resultant indictment, trial and any conviction, are all likely to be held null and void.

Where a witness is (a) too ill to attend court and is unlikely to recover, or (b) is a child in a sexual case, a deposition may be taken from him or her prior to the committal proceedings (MCA 1980, ss. 103 and 105).

(ii) *Written statements*: there will often be witnesses whose evidence the defence does not wish to challenge at committal, either because their evidence is non-contentious, or because the defence wishes to reserve its cross-examination until trial. In these circumstances, the evidence of such a witness may be tendered in the form of a written statement under MCA 1980, s. 102.

In order to comply with s. 102:

- the statement must be signed by the person who made it; and
- the statement must contain a declaration as to its truth; and
- a copy must be served on all parties; and
- none of the parties must object to the statements being tendered in evidence.

The advantage of a statement being tendered under s. 102 is that it saves time and money and is convenient for witnesses. However, the defence does not have the opportunity to cross-examine the maker of the statement and, for the purposes of the committal, accepts that the statement is accurate.

The prosecution need not call all its evidence, as long as the evidence it does call is sufficient to establish a prima facie case, and provided that he or she informs the defence that certain evidence has been omitted. Note, however, that the prosecution may not take the defence by surprise at trial, and if it did not rely on the evidence at committal, a Notice of Additional Evidence must be served before the witness may be called at trial.

If the prosecution seeks to rely on a confession which is challenged in the ways outlined by PACE 1984, s. 76(2), then the court is under a duty, at committal proceedings as well as at trial, to hold the enquiry contemplated by the subsection (*R* v *Oxford City Justices, ex parte Berry* [1988] QB 507). However, the discretion to exclude evidence under PACE 1984, s. 78 should only be used in the most clear-cut case, and in exceptional circumstances (*R* v *King's Lynn Justices, ex parte Holland* [1993] 1 WLR 324).

(e) *Submission of no case to answer.* At the end of the prosecution case, the defence may submit that the prosecution has failed to establish a prime facie case. In order to decide whether the prosecution has established a prima facie case, the justices apply either the test contained in the *Practice Direction (Submission of No Case)* [1962] 1 WLR 227 (see **5.1.7**) or the test set out in *R* v *Galbraith* [1981] 1 WLR 1039 (see **11.6**).

If the submission *succeeds*, the accused is discharged. See (i) below for the effect of the discharge.

If the submission *fails*, the court will continue with the procedure set out below, although it should be noted that it is very rare for the defence to call evidence at this stage.

Where the justices find a case to answer, the accused is informed and, if he or she does not wish to call evidence, is committed on that basis. The accused is also asked if he or she wishes to say anything in answer to the charges. It is rare for the accused to say anything of substance, but if he or she does, this is recorded by the clerk of the court.

(f) *The alibi warning.* See **6.2.2**.

(g) *The defence case.* The accused may now call evidence on his or her own behalf. It is very rare to do so, as in most cases any defence will be reserved for the trial. If evidence is called, it will be recorded in the form of a deposition, as above.

(h) *Second submission of no case to answer.* The defence has the opportunity of making a second submission, this time on the whole of the evidence before the court.

(i) *Committal or discharge.* If, after hearing the whole of the evidence the justices consider that there is sufficient evidence to put the accused on trial, they must commit. The accused is informed of the charges upon which he or she is being committed. Again, these need not be the charges with which the accused was originally charged. The justices may commit on alternative charges which emerge from the evidence tendered at committal.

If there is insufficient evidence to put the accused on trial, the justices must discharge him or her. If the justices decide not to commit the accused for trial, he or she is discharged, but it should be noted that a discharge does not rank as an acquittal, and the prosecution may bring further committal proceedings (*R* v *Manchester City Stipendiary Magistrate, ex parte Snelson* [1977] 1 WLR 911). Alternatively, the prosecution may apply for a voluntary bill of indictment (see **6.3.3**).

6.1.2 COMMITTALS WITHOUT CONSIDERATION OF THE EVIDENCE

Under MCA 1980, s. 6(2) and MCR 1981, r. 6, a committal may be made without consideration of the evidence if the following conditions are satisfied:

(a) all the accused must be represented, although, under CJA 1982, s. 61, the representative need not be present in court during the hearing. However, the representative often will be present in order to deal with any bail application (see **6.2.3**); and

(b) all the evidence must be in the form of written statements under MCA 1980, s. 102; and

(c) none of the accused wishes to make a submission, give evidence, or call witnesses.

If these conditions are satisfied, the justices formally commit the accused to the Crown Court, following the procedure set out below. It should be noted that the vast majority of committals follow this route.

(a) The charge is read to the accused by the clerk of the court. No plea is taken.

(b) The clerk asks the accused whether he or she wishes to ask any questions, call any evidence or make a submission of no case to answer. The accused, usually through his representative, declines to do so.

(c) The prosecution hands to the justices the s. 102 statements. No witnesses are called and no submissions are made.

(d) The alibi warning is given, if appropriate.

(e) The justices formally commit the accused for trial.

6.2 Common Considerations

The following matters are common to both types of committal.

6.2.1 REPORTING RESTRICTIONS

At committal proceedings, the reporting restrictions are explained to the accused, and any application to lift them is made. Under MCA 1980, s. 8, only the technical details of the case, as opposed to the evidence, may be reported. This is to prevent any potential jury forming a view as to the accused's guilt before the case comes to trial.

Under s. 8(4) the media may report:

(a) the identity of the court; and

(b) the names of the examining justices, counsel and solicitors; and

(c) the names, addresses, ages and occupations of the parties and the witnesses; and

(d) the charges against the accused, and those on which he or she is committed for trial; and

(e) decisions as to bail and legal aid.

Note: Magistrates should be slow to impose restrictions on reporting over and above those contained in MCA 1980 (*R* v *Beaconsfield Magistrates' Court, ex parte Westminster Press* (1994) 158 JP 1055).

By s. 8(A) it is an offence to publish material other than that permitted. A person is liable to a fine not exceeding level 5 on the standard scale, upon summary conviction.

Reporting restrictions will be lifted in committal proceedings if the accused charged alone applies. An accused may wish restrictions to be lifted in the hope, for example, that publicity will attract the attention of potentially helpful witnesses who may then come forward.

If one of several defendants applies for the restrictions to be lifted, and the others object, restrictions will be lifted only if the justices consider it necessary in the interests of justice (see MCA 1980, s. 8(2A)). The onus is on the accused who wishes the restrictions to be lifted to show that his or her chances of a fair trial will be prejudiced in the absence of publicity (*R* v *Leeds Justices, ex parte Sykes*) [1983] 1 WLR 132), but the court must give all the accused a chance to make representations (*R* v *Wirral District Magistrates' Court, ex parte Meikle* (1990) 154 JP 1035).

Once restrictions have been lifted, MCA 1980, s. 8 will not operate to re-impose them. However, if it is appropriate to do so, the justices may make an order under s. 4(2) of the Contempt of Court Act 1981. Such an order postpones the reporting of all or part of a case if contemporaneous reporting would involve a 'substantial risk of prejudice to the administration of justice'. In deciding whether to make such an order, the magistrates have a discretionary power to hear representations from the press (*R* v *Clerkenwell Metropolitan Stipendiary Magistrate, ex parte The Telegraph plc* [1993] QB 462).

6.2.2 NOTICE OF ALIBI

Under CJA 1967, s. 11 the accused, on a trial on indictment, may not, without leave of the court, adduce evidence in support of an alibi unless he gives notice of the alibi at committal, or within seven days thereof. The accused must therefore be warned, at the committal stage, of the consequences of failing to give notice. If the warning is *not* given, the trial court *must* allow the accused to call evidence of the alibi (s. 11(4)). If the warning *is* given, but the accused fails to give notice of alibi, then whether the evidence may be given is entirely a matter for the trial judge.

Where the accused is the only witness as to the alibi, the warning and the notice should still be given (*R* v *Jackson* [1973] Crim LR 356).

Clearly, not every accused relies on the defence of alibi, and the alibi warning need not be given in every case. The usual course is for the clerk of the court to ask the defence representative whether the alibi warning is appropriate, and only to give the warning if the answer is in the affirmative. The notice is usually served *after*, and not at, the committal proceedings.

Under the Criminal Procedure and Investigations Act 1996, the position relating to alibi evidence will change, so that it will be similar to defence disclosure generally (see **10.2.3**).

6.2.3 BAIL

Committal proceedings are often an appropriate time to review bail, although such review is not automatic.

6.2.4 LEGAL AID

At committal proceedings, the court has power to extend legal aid to cover the Crown Court proceedings. This is likely to be granted if the accused's resources are unchanged from the time the legal aid was originally granted.

6.2.5 WITNESS ORDERS

At committal proceedings, the justices will make orders for each witness, requiring them to attend at the trial and give evidence under s. 1 of the Criminal Procedure (Attendance of Witnesses) Act 1965. The orders may be 'full' or 'conditional'. A fully bound witness, subject to a 'full witness order', *must* attend at the Crown Court. A conditionally bound witness, subject to a 'conditional witness order', need not attend unless he or she is subsequently notified that his or her presence is required. A witness who is conditionally bound often gives evidence which is essential to the prosecution case but which is not in dispute.

6.3 Avoiding Committal Proceedings

In exceptional circumstances, cases may reach the Crown Court without first going through committal proceedings.

6.3.1 SERIOUS FRAUD CASES

Under CJA 1987, s. 4 the prosecution may serve notice transferring a case of serious fraud to the Crown Court if the following conditions are satisfied:

(a) a person has been charged with an indictable offence; and

(b) in the opinion of the prosecuting authority:

  (i) there is sufficient evidence for the person charged to be committed for trial; and

  (ii) the charge reveals a case of fraud of such seriousness or complexity that it is appropriate that the management of the case should, without delay, be taken over by the Crown Court; and

(c) the magistrates' court has not yet begun to inquire into the case as examining justices.

The prosecuting authorities in serious fraud cases are the Director of Public Prosecutions, the Director of the Serious Fraud Office, the Commissioners of Inland Revenue and Customs and Excise, and the Secretary of State.

The notice of transfer must specify the charges against the accused, and the appropriate Crown Court, and must be accompanied by written statements of the evidence. Once the case has been transferred to the Crown Court, a preparatory hearing will normally take place at which the judge may rule that the written statements do not reveal a case to answer. Note that this matter is dealt with by a judge, and not by a magistrates' court. See generally CJA 1987, ss. 3 to 10.

6.3.2 CASES INVOLVING CHILDREN

Under CJA 1991, s. 53, if a person is charged with one of the offences listed below, the Director of Public Prosecutions (or someone acting on her behalf) may serve notice transferring the case to the Crown Court, if she is of the opinion:

(a) that the evidence is sufficient for the person charged to be committed for trial;

(b) that a child will be called as a witness who is alleged:

  (i) to be a person against whom the offence was committed; or

  (ii) to have witnessed the commission of the offence; and

(c) that for the purpose of avoiding any prejudice to the welfare of the child, the case should be taken over, and proceeded with by the Crown Court without delay.

Such a notice should be served before the magistrates begin to sit as examining justices (s. 53(2)).

The decision to transfer the proceedings is not appealable in any court (s. 53(4)). However, the accused can apply to a judge of the Crown Court for the case to be dismissed (sch. 6, para. 5) but the child in question may not be called as a witness on that application (sch. 6, para. 5(5)).

Notices of transfer in this situation apply:

(a) to an offence which involves an assault on, or injury or threat of injury to, a person;

(b) to an offence under CYPA 1933, s. 1 (cruelty to persons under 16);

(c) to an offence under the Sexual Offences Act 1956, Indecency with Children Act 1960, Sexual Offences Act 1967, Criminal Law Act 1977, s. 54, and the Protection of Children Act 1978; and

(d) to an offence which consists of attempting or conspiring to commit, or aiding and abetting, counselling, procuring or inciting the commission of an offence.

For the purpose of notices of transfer, a child is a person under the age of 14, in relation to the offences mentioned in (a) and (b) above and 17 in relation to the offences in (c) above. Note that if the child's evidence is given by way of a video recording, made while the child was under 14 or under 17 respectively, then the relevant ages of the child are 15 and 18 respectively.

The purpose of transferring the proceedings by notice is to protect child victims and child witnesses, by sparing them the stress of court appearances (e.g. at committal proceedings) and by getting the case tried expeditiously.

For the detailed provisions of the procedure, students should consult CJA 1991, sch. 6.

6.3.3 VOLUNTARY BILLS OF INDICTMENT

Under the Administration of Justice (Miscellaneous Provisions) Act 1933, s. 2, a High Court judge has the power to prefer a voluntary bill of indictment, that is, he or she may order that the accused be tried on indictment. In making such an order, committal proceedings or transfer for trial proceedings are avoided.

The voluntary bill procedure may not be used wholesale, however, to avoid committal. In the *Practice Direction (Crime: Voluntary Bills)* [1990] 1 WLR 1633, it was stated that voluntary bills should only be granted where 'the interests of justice, rather than considerations of administrative convenience' require it.

Traditionally, voluntary bills have been sought in two situations:

(a) where committal proceedings have resulted in the discharge of an accused, and the prosecution does not wish to hold a second set of committal proceedings — although the prosecution should be slow to reject the views of the magistrates; or

(b) where the prosecution case is that an offence was committed jointly by two or more persons, and at least one of them has already been committed for trial, and an indictment signed against him or her. In these circumstances, the prosecution will wish to try all the accused together, but may only do so if a second indictment is signed against all the accused. A voluntary bill of indictment will achieve the desired result.

Under para. 2 of the *Practice Direction*, applications for a voluntary bill must be accompanied by:

(a) a copy of any charges on which the defendant has been committed for trial;

(b) a copy of any charges on which his committal for trial was refused by the magistrates' court;

(c) a copy of any existing indictment which has been preferred in consequence of his committal;

(d) a summary of the evidence or other document which:

  (i) identifies the counts in the proposed indictment on which he has been committed for trial (or which are substantially the same as charges on which he has been so committed); and

  (ii) in relation to each other count in the proposed indictment, identifies the pages in the accompanying statements and exhibits where the essential evidence said to support that count is to be found;

(e) marginal markings of the relevant passages on the pages of the statements and exhibits identified under (d) (ii) above.

The defence has no right to attend or make representations, although the judge has a discretion to receive any written representations that the defence may wish to make (*R* v *Raymond* [1981] QB 910, and see *Practice Direction* [1990] 1 WLR 1633).

A High Court judge's decision to issue a voluntary bill is subject to review, according to *R* v *IRC, ex parte Dhesi, The Independent*, 14 August 1995, despite other authority to the contrary (*R* v *Manchester Crown Court, ex parte Williams* (1990) 154 JP 589). However, given the nature of the voluntary bill, where the application is made *ex parte* and therefore against the rules of natural justice, the courts' jurisdiction in respect of judicial review is limited and could only be exercised in the case of alleged malice on the part of the prosecutor.

Note: Once the bill of indictment has been preferred, it is an indictment like any other, and capable of amendment under the Indictments Act 1915, s. 5 (*R* v *Wells* (1995) 159 JP 243).

Tutorial Questions

COMMITTALS FOR SENTENCE

1. (See Question 3, p. 78.) The case is heard summarily. The information is put to Sid and he pleads guilty. The prosecuting solicitor tells the magistrates that Sid is a police officer who committed the offence when off duty, as a result of the victim provoking him deliberately by making offensive remarks about the police. The magistrates were not previously aware that Sid was a police officer. Antecedent evidence shows Sid to have no previous convictions. No other offences are taken into consideration. Can the magistrates properly commit Sid to the Crown Court to be sentenced under s. 38 of the Magistrates' Courts Act 1980?

2. Howard, aged 21, appears at the Barchester Crown Court and is convicted of theft. He is sentenced to 180 hours' community service. He completes 50 hours and then fails to attend on the next four occasions when required to do so. He is summoned to appear before the Blackacre Magistrates' Court and is found to be in breach of the community service order. What options are open to the magistrates in dealing with Howard?

3. Lorna appears at Whiteacre Magistrates' Court and pleads guilty to an offence of criminal damage. She is in breach of a sentence of three months' imprisonment, suspended for two years, imposed by another magistrates' court. What action can be taken in respect of the suspended sentence?

4. Martin, aged 22, appears in Barchester Magistrates' Court charged with obtaining property by deception, contrary to s. 15 of the Theft Act 1968. The magistrates accept the matter is suitable for summary trial; Martin elects to be tried summarily and pleads guilty. Martin is further charged with having (on another occasion) interfered with a motor vehicle, contrary to s. 9 of the Criminal Attempts Act 1981. This is a summary offence punishable with a maximum of three months' imprisonment. Martin again pleads guilty. He has previous convictions for dishonesty.

What powers to commit for sentence do the magistrates possess in respect of Martin and what powers of sentence will the Crown Court possess in the event of such committal?

SEVEN

JUVENILES AND THE COURTS

7.1 Why Distinguish the Juvenile from Other Defendants?

7.1.1 DIFFERENT COURT, DIFFERENT SYSTEM

For most people charged with a criminal offence, there are only two courts to worry about. These are the magistrates' court and Crown Court. (Although remember that cases can go *on appeal* to the Divisional Court or Court of Appeal and then to the House of Lords.)

For juveniles there is another, separate court — the youth court. This court is a special type of magistrates' court (see **7.3** below). For the avoidance of confusion, the ordinary magistrates' court will be referred to in this chapter as the *adult* magistrates' court.

The usual method of classifying offences (i.e. in terms of which court can or must try the offence; see **4.1**) does not apply to juveniles. Apart from homicide offences, there are no offences for which a juvenile *must* be tried on indictment. The concept of offences triable either way is inapplicable to juveniles — the mode of trial procedure set out in MCA 1980, ss. 18–21 is not used and juveniles cannot elect trial by jury. (See further **7.5.1** below.) The general principle is that juveniles should be tried summarily and that such trials will usually be in the youth court.

7.1.2 WHAT DO WE MEAN BY 'JUVENILE'?

A juvenile is basically anyone under the age of 18 (CJA 1991, s. 68). Once an individual has reached his or her eighteenth birthday, he or she must be treated like any other adult defendant. This could lead to problems if the defendant's eighteenth birthday occurs while a case is pending at court (see **7.6** below). Thus, while for the layman the term 'juvenile' generally means a youth or young person, for the criminal justice system one's youth ends on the eighteenth birthday.

(For sentencing purposes, it is also necessary to divide those 'adult' defendants aged 18–20 inclusive from defendants aged 21 and over. See **Sentencing** at **Chapter 13** et seq.)

7.1.3 TWO SUB-CATEGORIES: 'CHILDREN' AND 'YOUNG PERSONS'

Juveniles between the ages of 10 and 13 inclusive are often described in criminal law statutes as 'children', but this is not a universal usage. Those aged between 14 and 17 years inclusive are usually described as 'young persons'. (See Criminal Justice Act 1991, s. 68; sch. 8.) There are two reasons for distinguishing between these groups — sentencing powers and the presumption of innocence.

7.1.3.1 Sentencing powers for 'children' and 'young persons'

These are dealt with at length in the Sentencing part of this Manual. For now it is sufficient to note that the sentencing powers of the courts are quite different when they have to deal with children or young persons, rather than adult offenders. There are significant differences in terms of both the types of sentence available to the courts and the maximum severity of such sentences. However, it should be observed that there are moves in the direction of 'toughening up' on juvenile offenders, and the area of sentencing is one obvious way to do so. For example, prior to the Criminal Justice and Public Order Act 1994, the only way that a child would receive a custodial sentence would be if found guilty of a homicide. Now, the Crown Court has power to sentence a 10 to 13 year-old to long-term detention for certain grave offences other than homicide, for example burglary of a house, certain types of arson and criminal damage and robbery. In theory, such detention may be for as long as an adult offender might be sent to prison for — perhaps as long as 14 years (see CJPOA 1994, s. 16).

Secondly, the maximum period of detention for less serious crimes has been increased for offenders aged 15–17; the Crown Court can now order these offenders to be incarcerated for a maximum of two years (this was previously one year; see CJPOA 1994, s. 17). Thirdly, in certain circumstances, an offender aged 12–14 may now be sent to a secure training centre for a period of up to one year (see CJPOA 1994, s. 1). Whilst these changes are symptomatic of a change of approach to juvenile crime (compare, for example, the recent call by Northumbria Police for a 'fast-track' legal system to deal with persistent juvenile offenders: *Legal Action*, February 1996), nonetheless they do show that different maxima and different types of sentence and order are applied to juvenile offenders. This is also borne out by the non-custodial sentences for juveniles — the range is smaller than for adult offenders. For example, no-one under the age of 16 is in jeopardy of a community sentence, although 16- and 17-year-olds may receive a community sentence just like adult offenders (see CJA 1991, s. 6); and the maximum levels of fine are lower following a summary conviction — for children, £250, for young persons, £1,000, and for adults, £5,000 (see CJA 1991, s. 17).

7.1.3.2 The presumption of innocence for 'children'

This group of juveniles has the benefit of a presumption that they do not know right from wrong and cannot, therefore, form the *mens rea* necessary to be guilty of a crime. This presumption must be overcome in order to obtain a finding from the court that the child is guilty of the offence charged. The test is usually expressed as — did the child know that what he or she was doing was *seriously wrong*? (See, e.g., *J. M. (a minor)* v *Runeckles* (1984) 79 Cr App R 255.) The burden of proof is on the prosecutor; the standard of proof is beyond a reasonable doubt.

The presumption is sometimes called the *doli incapax* rule, or the obligation to prove a 'mischievous discretion' on the part of the child. It is often possible to effect proof simply by reference to the facts of the offence then being tried (see e.g. *T* v *DPP* [1989] Crim LR 498). Where the crime charged alleges dishonesty, proof of this may also suffice to prove mischievous discretion. Courts have considered the following matters relevant:

(a) Age of the child (the nearer to 10, the stronger the evidence required).

(b) Has the child been brought up in a bad home? (although this may be highly prejudicial on other issues in the case, in such a home he or she is likely to be brought up without knowledge of right and wrong: *F* v *Padwick* [1959] Crim LR 439).

(c) Has the child been brought up in a good home? (evidence that he or she comes from a respectable family, has been properly brought up and is generally well-behaved is admissible and may be sufficient to rebut the presumption: *B* v *R* (1958) 44 Cr App R 1).

(d) Does the child admit knowing what the crime alleged against him or her means? (*ex parte N* [1959] Crim LR 523); see *T* v DPP — 'it ain't nothing to do with me, I didn't steal it'.

(e) What about running away? In *T* v *DPP*, the act of climbing over the wall and denying theft was enough to show that the child knew that what he was doing was wrong. In *A* v *Sharples* [1992] Crim LR 34, the Queen's Bench Divisional Court said that merely running away did not displace the presumption. The court emphasised that the child (here aged 11) had to be shown to know what he was doing was seriously wrong, not just naughty.

Sometimes, a prosecutor may decide to produce evidence of the child's previous criminal record in order to rebut the presumption. This is permissible, although it clearly ought to be avoided if possible as it must be difficult to avoid the impression that the court is swayed more by the revelation of previous crimes than by evidence of present guilt. (This practice was approved by the House of Lords in *R* v *B* [1979] 1 WLR 1185; *Archbold* 1–97.)

In 1994, an attempt was made by the Queen's Bench Divisional Court to terminate the notion of *doli incapax*. Laws J described it as 'unreal and contrary to common sense' and 'in principle objectionable' (see *C (A Minor)* v *DPP* [1994] 3 WLR 888). The Court considered three reasons why the presumption ought to stay and dismissed them all. It also disliked the distinction which the presumption maintained between 'children from what used to be called good homes' and others. The matter was resolved after a fashion by the House of Lords, which gave a stay of execution to the presumption, holding that the presumption was a rule of the common law and could only be abrogated by statute. The House went on to say that the topic was ripe for investigation by Parliament, with possible legislative change thereafter. In the meantime, the House restated that the presumption may be rebutted only by clear positive evidence that the child knew his or her act to be seriously wrong, and that such evidence was not to be found simply in the evidence of the 'criminal' acts themselves 'however horrifying or obviously wrong' those acts may be. See further *C (A Minor)* v *DPP* [1995] 2 WLR 383.

The topic has since been revisited by the Divisional Court, in *CC (A Minor)* v *DPP* [1996] 1 Cr App R 375. Here, Mitchell J noted that a court, when faced with the question 'Has the presumption been rebutted?', could not apply a second presumption, the 'presumption of normality':

> That presumption is to this effect: any normal boy of his age in society, as it is today, must have known that what he was doing was seriously wrong. Such an approach as that reverses the relevant presumption of *doli incapax*.

On the facts of *CC (A Minor)* v *DPP*, the juvenile, aged 12 at the time, had handed over a lock-knife to his partner, who had the victim around the neck. The magistrates further found that the juvenile realised that any money handed over by the victim would not be his (i.e. CC's), and that the money would not have been handed over voluntarily. Finally, after the demand for money had been made, CC told his partner to 'Cut his nose to make sure'. The magistrates found that CC came from a reasonable home, his mother was in court supporting him and that the instruction he gave to his confederate showed 'a remarkable degree of criminality . . . a design and ferocity which in itself satisfied us beyond reasonable doubt that [CC] knew what he was doing was seriously wrong'. Mitchell J said that magistrates had confused evidence which is capable of rebutting the presumption (which was not before them) with evidence which was before them as to age and conduct which, in combination, would determine how readily the presumption was rebuttable by *other* evidence. Mitchell J went on to state that:

> Proof of mental normality has in practice been largely accepted as proof that the child can distinguish right from wrong and form a criminal intent and it will be recalled that Lord Lowry concluded [in *C (A Minor)*]: 'Very little evidence is needed but it must be adduced as part of the prosecution's case, or else there will be no case to answer'.

7.1.4 WHAT ABOUT THE UNDER-10's?

In the technical sense mentioned above, 'children' are a sub-category consisting of those aged between 10 and 13 years. What about children (in the every day sense) who are under 10 years of age? Children below the age of 10 years are *conclusively presumed to be incapable* of committing a crime and therefore do not fall within the criminal jurisdiction of any court.

The use of such children by others to commit crimes on their behalf (a situation similar to that of Fagin and Oliver Twist) may nevertheless result in the conviction of the 'manipulator', usually as the principal offender (the child being regarded as an innocent agent or tool of the other). (See *Archbold*, 1–95; 18–2.)

7.2 Juveniles Who Could be Prosecuted But are Not

7.2.1 THE CAUTION

It is felt that juveniles may be damaged by contact with the criminal justice system. An alternative method has developed of giving the juvenile a caution instead of prosecuting him or her. The effect may be less traumatic as no court appearance is necessary.

The current version of the Code for Crown Prosecutors states:

> 6.8 Crown Prosecutors must consider the interests of a youth when deciding whether it is in the public interest to prosecute. The stigma of a conviction can cause very serious harm to the prospects of a youth offender or young adult. Young offenders can sometimes be dealt with without going to court. But Crown Prosecutors should not avoid prosecuting simply because of the defendant's age. The seriousness of the offence or the offender's past behaviour may make prosecution necessary.

7.2.2 WHO GIVES THE CAUTION?

The caution is given by a senior police officer, who will usually emphasise the likelihood of a court appearance should the juvenile reoffend, how fortunate the juvenile is to escape with a caution, and the shame which must have been suffered by his or her parents, together with a reminder of any damage caused by the juvenile.

7.2.3 WHEN CAN A CAUTION BE USED?

A juvenile may be cautioned only when certain criteria are satisfied. First, only the guilty should be given a caution. This is established by checking whether there is sufficient evidence to prosecute and, if so, asking the juvenile whether he or she admits that he or she committed the offence. Secondly, the parents of the juvenile must give their consent to the matter being disposed of by the use of a caution. If one of these conditions is not fulfilled, then a caution may not be used — the options are then to prosecute (if the evidence is strong enough) or drop the matter. The application of the cautioning criteria by the police and Crown Prosecution Service is open to judicial review. See *Ex parte L; Ex parte B* [1991] Crim LR 841 where the Queen's Bench Divisional Court stated that a decision to continue with a prosecution, rather than use a caution, was susceptible to judicial review, *but* would succeed only rarely. It must be shown that the decision was made regardless of, or clearly contrary to, settled policy or guidelines.

7.2.4 THE EFFECT OF A CAUTION

The caution is given at a police station. A form is filled in with the details of the juvenile and the offence. This form is signed by the officer who gives the caution and the juvenile's parents. The form is kept by the police for at least three years and may be referred to if a court needs subsequently to know about the juvenile's character.

For further information on caution see: *Emmins on Criminal Procedure*, 3.2.1; Gelsthorpe and Giller, 'More Justice for Juveniles' [1990] Crim LR 153; Wilkinson and Evans, 'Police Cautioning of Juveniles' [1990] Crim LR 165; Ball, 'Young Offenders and the Youth Court' [1990] Crim LR 277; Westwood, 'The effects of Home Office Guidelines on the cautioning of offenders' [1991] Crim LR 591; Home Office Circulars 59/1990, 18/1994; Evans, 'Cautioning: Counting the Cost of Retrenchment' [1994] Crim LR 566.

7.3 Who Will Be in Court?

7.3.1 WHO WILL TRY THE CASE?

When a youth court hearing is held, the court will usually consist of three lay magistrates. They will be selected from a panel of magistrates who are thought to be well-suited to dealing with juveniles and who have had some special training in this. There should be at least one male and one female magistrate in court for the hearing. If all three magistrates are of the same sex, they may hear cases only if this arrangement could not have been foreseen and they do not think it is expedient to adjourn proceedings. (The same result will occur if two magistrates are sitting and both are of the same sex.)

7.3.2 STIPENDIARY MAGISTRATES

These professional magistrates may deal with cases in the youth court but should be accompanied by a lay magistrate. A stipendiary should hear cases alone only if no lay magistrates are available to sit with the stipendiary *and* it is thought not to be expedient to adjourn proceedings. Stipendiary magistrates will not appear often in youth court proceedings.

7.3.3 THE PARENTS OF THE JUVENILE

It is quite understandable that the parents of a juvenile may want to attend court to support their child when he or she is appearing in court. This is not always the case, however, and the trial courts possess the power to compel the parents' attendance at court. If the juvenile is aged 15 or under, the court must order the attendance of a parent, unless it would be unreasonable to do so. If the juvenile is aged 16 or 17, the court may make such an order. (See CYPA 1933, s. 34A, inserted by CJA 1991, s. 56.) When they attend, the parents sit next to their child in the court.

7.3.4 PUBLIC ACCESS TO THE YOUTH COURT

The youth court operates differently from other courts with regard to public access. There is no general right to enter a youth court — in fact, only certain groups are entitled to enter the youth courtroom. In addition to the juvenile, his or her parents, the parties' legal representatives and the magistrates, there will usually be:

(a) Court officers (clerk, ushers).

(b) Reporters from the media (but not photographers).

(c) Probation officers and social workers.

(d) Witnesses both during and after testimony.

(e) Anyone else directly concerned in the case being heard.

(f) Anyone whom the magistrates permit to be present in exceptional circumstances (law students studying the youth court system, for example).

These restrictions are usually enforced strictly.

There are three points to make about the restricted categories. First, a barrister whose case is listed in a youth court may find it difficult to liaise with court officers on the day of the hearing as the barrister will not be allowed into the courtroom while another case is being heard. Secondly, reporters often have a dual function — to report for the media and to photograph (or film). The purpose of the restriction is to prevent photographs, etc. being taken which could enable the public to identify the juvenile. Indeed, reporters are subject to similar restrictions, affecting what they can report about the proceedings. See **7.3.5**. Finally, probation officers and social workers often seem to remain in the courtroom, regardless of whether they are involved in the case then being dealt with.

7.3.5 ACCESS TO ADULT MAGISTRATES' COURTS AND CROWN COURTS DEALING WITH JUVENILES

The adult magistrates' court and the Crown Court both operate their usual policy of being open to the general public when hearing a case, whether or not the case involves a juvenile either as witness or defendant. These courts have a power to order the court to be cleared if a juvenile witness is to testify in a trial involving offences of indecency or immorality. Further, under CYPA 1933, s. 39, any court may direct that no newspaper report of proceedings shall reveal the name, address, school or any particular calculated to lead to the identification of a child or young person in the proceedings, whether involved as accused, witness or victim. Similar powers exist to censor sound, television and cable broadcasts.

An example of the Crown Court using its power under s. 39 was the 'Jamie Bulger' murder trial at Preston Crown Court in November 1993, where the trial judge ordered that the two accused be known simply as 'child A' and 'child B'. The fact that the identities of these children became public knowledge is an illustration of the fact that such a ban may be only temporary. Typically, it will last initially until the end of the trial itself; if the juvenile is acquitted, it will continue in force but if the juvenile is convicted, it may be removed. Although the age of the offender and the potential damage that a young person may suffer by being publicly identified as a criminal must be considered, there may be a public interest to be served in naming the offender. See further *R* v *Lee (Anthony William) (A Minor)* [1993] 1 WLR 103; *R* v *Inner London Crown Court, ex parte Barnes (Anthony), The Times*, 7 August 1995.

7.3.6 JUVENILES AND EVIDENCE BY LIVE TELEVISION LINK

Since 1 May 1989, if a juvenile aged 14 or under is to testify as a witness (not as defendant), he or she may do so via a live television link if the court gives permission. Under CJA 1988, s. 32 the offence must *either*:

(a) involve an assault on, or injury or a threat of injury to a person (not necessarily the witness or another juvenile); *or*

(b) be one of several specified offences involving cruelty to, or sexual misconduct with, juveniles (not necessarily the witness).

Section 32 has been supplemented by a new Crown Court Rule, r. 23A, which specifies the procedure to be used when applying to the Crown Court to use a live television link (see S.I. 1988 No. 2160; *Archbold*, 8–53a). The witness should be accompanied, during testimony, by one other person — someone 'acceptable to a judge of the Crown Court' (CCR 1981, r. 23A(10)).

CJA 1988, s. 32 originally applied only to Crown Court trials, but its scope has been extended to appeals to the Court of Appeal, references by the Home Secretary to the Court of Appeal, proceedings in youth courts and appeals from youth courts to the Crown Court (see CJA 1991, s. 55).

Courts are also now able to receive children's evidence in the form of an interview prerecorded on video between an adult and the child witness (see CJA 1988, s. 32A, inserted by CJA 1991, s. 54). Leave must be sought from the court for the evidence to be tendered in this form and the child should be made available for cross-examination. CJA 1988, s. 32A applies to the same offences and in the same proceedings as CJA 1988, s. 32, above (except that in certain circumstances, the 'child' may be 15 or even 16 at the time of recording the interview).

Note: In cases using CJA 1988, ss. 32 or 32A, the defendant is not permitted to cross-examine in person the child witness — see CJA 1988, s. 34A, inserted by CJA 1991, s. 55.

It has been suggested (Glaser and Spencer, cited below) that a prerecorded interview may be less upsetting and more accurate than the more traditional forms of examining a witness in child abuse cases. It remains to be seen who will conduct the interview with the child — CJA 1988, s. 32A refers simply to 'an adult'. It may be that videos made by professionals outside the criminal justice system (for example, a child psychologist), in the early stages of an offence coming to light, and which were not intended to be used as evidence in court could be sought by the Crown Prosecution Service to be so tendered in evidence. See also, Jenny McEwan, 'In the Box or on the Box? The Pigot Report and Child Witnesses' [1990] Crim LR 363; Glaser and Spencer, 'Sentencing, Children's Evidence and Children's Trauma' [1990] Crim LR 371; Birch, 'Children's Evidence' [1992] Crim LR 262.

7.4 How Will the Youth Court Work?

7.4.1 WHERE WILL THE YOUTH COURT BE?

Youth courts often sit in the same buildings and rooms used by the local adult magistrates' court. In order to minimise the amount of contact that juvenile defendants have with adult offenders, the youth court must hear its cases at a time when the adult court is shut. At least one hour must pass between the adult court stopping and the youth court starting to hear cases (CYPA 1933, s. 47). In some places, mainly inner city areas where the number of juvenile proceedings justifies the cost, special youth courts have been built to deal with the workload (e.g. in London at Balham and Seymour Place, Marylebone). Adult defendants never appear in these courts.

7.4.2 WHERE DOES EVERYONE SIT?

The general public cannot enter the youth court room, so that every seat is usually allocated to a particular person — the juvenile, a lawyer, the clerk, for example. The magistrates do not sit up on a raised platform, but often are on ordinary chairs behind plain tables. Since the court clerk, the lawyers, probation officers and social workers also sit on ordinary chairs behind desks, it is not as obvious as in other courtrooms where one should sit.

As a rule of thumb, the chairs in the centre of the room will be reserved for the juvenile(s) and parents. These chairs will face the desk where the magistrates sit. (The Royal Coat of Arms may be on the wall behind the magistrates.) The clerk's desk will be at the side of the one used by the magistrates and, usually, the lawyers' seats and desks will be on the same side of the room as the clerk's. No dock is ever used in youth court hearings — usually there will not be one in the courtroom but, if the room is also used for adult hearings, it may contain a dock (if so, the juvenile sits in front of the dock).

7.4.3 PROCEDURE AT THE HEARING

As the youth court is a special type of magistrates' court, most of what happens in a hearing is the same as for adults in the adult magistrates' court. In particular, a juvenile can be tried summarily, sentenced if found guilty and remanded if a case is adjourned for any reason by the youth court. The youth court can issue a warrant for the arrest of a juvenile defendant who fails to attend the hearing (see BA 1976, s. 7; MCA 1980, s. 13). There are some differences, however, which are largely semantic. See **Figure 7.1**.

Note the special protection given to juveniles in the Code of Practice C on detention and questioning and, in particular, the need for an 'appropriate adult' to be present during an interview with the juvenile. If the rules are not adhered to, admissions may be excluded at trial under either PACE 1984, s. 76 or s. 78.

Figure 7.1

Name Juveniles (both defendants and witnesses) are addressed by their first names. Oath Juveniles promise to tell the truth. The usual form of oath requires a witness to swear to do so. (Those aged under 14 give evidence *unsworn*: CJA 1988, s. 33A.) Guilt A juvenile is never 'convicted' of an offence, the court will simply record a finding of guilt. The difference is largely cosmetic, presumably to avoid the trauma of conviction. Sentence A juvenile is not sentenced to a punishment after the case has been proved, rather the court makes an order upon a finding of guilt. Again, the distinction is semantic.

7.4.4 KEEPING IDENTITY A SECRET

Efforts are made at court to minimise the fact that the juvenile is passing through a part of the criminal justice system (different terminology, different rooms, for example). A further effort is made to allow the juvenile to lead as normal a life as possible after the court proceedings are over. To minimise public knowledge about the fact that the juvenile has been taken to court, there is a ban on reportage by the media of any details which may identify any juvenile involved in the case (whether as defendant or witness) (CYPA 1933, s. 49). This ban may be lifted, on application by either the defence or the prosecution. For the defence, publicity must be appropriate for the avoidance of injustice to the juvenile accused (often where it needs to publicise details of the incident to attract the attention of potential defence witnesses). For the prosecution, publicity may be sought where the offence is serious (punishable with 14 or more years' imprisonment in the case of an adult offender), is a violent or sexual offence (see CJA 1991, s. 31) and the juvenile defendant is 'unlawfully at large'; here, publicity is intended to aid in recapturing the juvenile. The ban which usually applies to reporting proceedings is reinforced by excluding the general public from the youth court room.

The position is reversed if a juvenile appears in the adult courts (see **7.3.5** above and CYPA 1933, s. 39).

7.5 Which Courts Can a Juvenile Defendant Appear in?

7.5.1 THE USUAL SYSTEM FOR CLASSIFICATION OF OFFENCES DOES NOT APPLY TO JUVENILES

A juvenile *never* has the right to elect trial in the Crown Court, and the usual distinction between offences which must be tried summarily, those which must be tried on indictment, and those which are triable either way has no relevance when determining where a juvenile will be tried.

7.5.2 THE USUAL FORUM — YOUTH COURT

By a combination of statutory provisions, the court in which the juvenile makes his or her first appearance when being prosecuted for any offence is normally the youth court (CYPA 1933, s. 46; CYPA 1963, s. 18). The juvenile may be the sole defendant or may be charged with others. If the juvenile is charged alone or with other juveniles, then he or she will appear in the youth court. This court will hear all the proceedings in the case, from the first occasion when the juvenile comes before a court up to the final disposal of the case. There is only one exception to this — if the youth court decides that the juvenile should be sent to the Crown Court. This can happen for three different reasons and is considered below at **7.5.6**.

7.5.3 WHEN WILL A JUVENILE APPEAR IN AN ADULT MAGISTRATES' COURT?

Exceptionally, a juvenile defendant may make his or her first court appearance, after being charged, in an adult magistrates' court. This will occur in any of the following four situations:

(a) the juvenile is on a joint charge with an adult defendant;

(b) the court mistakenly believes the juvenile to be aged 18 or over;

(c) the juvenile is charged with aiding and abetting an adult to commit a crime (or vice versa);

(d) the juvenile is charged with a crime which arises out of circumstances which are the same as, connected with, those which resulted in a charge against an adult defendant.

It should be noted that in three of these situations the appearance of the juvenile in an adult magistrates' court is the consequence of being allegedly involved with an adult defendant. (See **Figure 7.2**.)

7.5.4 A JUVENILE CHARGED JOINTLY WITH AN ADULT DEFENDANT

Here, a juvenile and adult defendant will be produced in an adult magistrates' court together. What will happen next is governed by the classification of the offence.

(a) If the offence is *summary*, the procedure is governed by MCA 1980, s. 29 (see **7.5.4.2**).

(b) If the offence is *triable on indictment*, then MCA 1980, s. 24(1)(b) applies. It is necessary first to see which court will try the adult defendant.

If the offence must be tried on indictment (e.g. robbery), there will have to be proceedings to transfer the adult to the Crown Court for trial (see **7.5.4.1**). If the offence is triable either way (e.g. theft), the adult magistrates' court must follow the mode of trial procedure in MCA 1980, ss. 19–21 for the adult. This will result in a decision for either transfer for trial proceedings (see **7.5.4.1**) or summary trial. If the decision is for summary trial, the procedure thereafter is the same as that for a summary offence (see **7.5.4.2**).

7.5.4.1 Adult defendant to be tried in the Crown Court

If the adult is to be transferred to the Crown Court for trial, the magistrates must decide whether it is necessary, in the interests of justice, to transfer the juvenile there as well. If that is their decision, the case against both defendants will be transferred to the Crown Court for trial, with one exception. The defendants have the right to apply to the magistrates to dismiss the charge against them if there is no prima facie case. Clearly, if the juvenile makes such an application and succeeds, he or she will not be transferred for trial. If he or she fails, or does not apply at all, but the adult defendant succeeds in having the charge dismissed, MCA 1980, s. 24 ceases to apply. In that situation, the juvenile will not be transferred for trial but will have a summary trial and be asked to enter a plea to the charge.

If the plea is guilty, the adult magistrates' court may pass a limited range of sentences on the juvenile, but they are more likely to exercise their discretion to send him or her to the youth court for sentence to be passed. If the plea is not guilty, the juvenile may (and usually would) be sent to the youth court for summary trial there.

Figure 7.2 Juvenile Appears with an Adult Defendant in the Adult Magistrates' Court

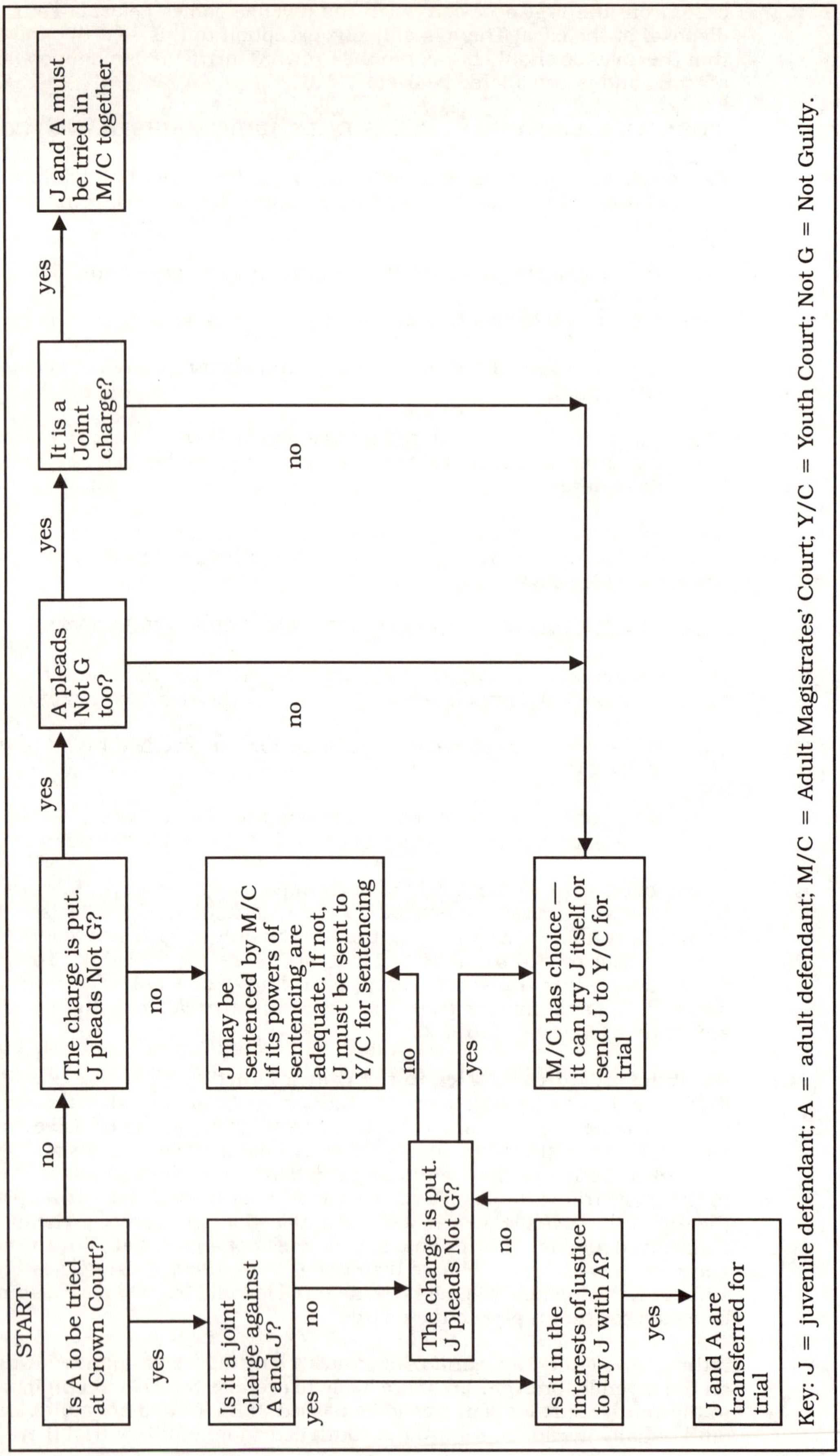

Key: J = juvenile defendant; A = adult defendant; M/C = Adult Magistrates' Court; Y/C = Youth Court; Not G = Not Guilty.

7.5.4.2 Adult defendant to be tried in the magistrates' court

If the adult is not to be transferred to the Crown Court for trial (*either* after mode of trial procedure or because the joint charge alleges a *summary offence*), both adult and juvenile defendants are asked whether they plead guilty or not guilty to the charge.

(a) *Juvenile pleads not guilty:* If juvenile and adult both plead not guilty, they *must* be tried together in the adult magistrates' court. If the juvenile pleads not guilty but the adult pleads guilty, the magistrates may try the juvenile but have a discretion (which would almost certainly be used) to send the juvenile to the youth court for the trial. (See MCA 1980, s. 29(2)(a).)

(b) *Juvenile pleads guilty:* If the juvenile pleads guilty, the adult's plea is irrelevant. The adult magistrates' court can now proceed to pass sentence on the juvenile, but their sentencing powers are limited. They may only impose a fine or a conditional/absolute discharge or require a recognisance from his or her parents to ensure future good behaviour (and make ancillary orders, e.g. disqualification from driving). If none of these sentences is suitable, they must send the juvenile to the youth court for sentence (CYPA 1969, s. 7(8)).

Note: The adult magistrates' court cannot pass a custodial sentence on a juvenile; nor can it commit a juvenile to the Crown Court for sentence either under MCA 1980, s. 37 (this power may only be used by a youth court) or MCA 1980, s. 38 (the juvenile is too young for this section to be used).

7.5.5 THE JUVENILE WHO DOES NOT FACE A JOINT CHARGE

If one of the two other situations in **7.5.3** occurs where the juvenile appears with an adult defendant, the adult magistrates' court has a discretion to try both juvenile and adult together or send the juvenile to the youth court for trial. As above, if the adult pleads guilty and the juvenile not guilty, it is very likely that the juvenile will be sent to the youth court for trial.

If an adult magistrates' court starts to deal with a single defendant, *mistakenly* thinking him or her to be an adult, it can continue to hear the case or remit it to the youth court for further proceedings, whichever seems to be more appropriate. See CYPA 1933, s. 46(1).

7.5.6 WHEN WILL A YOUTH COURT SEND A JUVENILE TO THE CROWN COURT?

The normal principle for juveniles is that they should be tried summarily (at magistrates' court level), and that such trial should normally be in the youth court. It is only in exceptional cases that a juvenile will be sent for trial to the Crown Court. As we saw in **7.5.4.1**, if the juvenile is charged with an adult, then the juvenile may be sent to the Crown Court for trial if the adult is to be tried by Crown Court (see **Figure 7.2**). The other way for a juvenile to be tried in the Crown Court is if he is sent there by the youth court.

The youth court *must* deal with any case where a juvenile appears in that court, except as set out below. It cannot send the juvenile to the adult magistrates' court at all. The youth court can send a juvenile to the Crown Court in only three situations, two of which result in the trial of the juvenile taking place in the Crown Court, the third resulting in him or her being sentenced there (see **Figure 7.3**). It follows that decisions in the first two situations must be taken before the juvenile is asked to plead to the charge. In the third situation, a decision becomes necessary only if the juvenile is found guilty.

(On sentencing juveniles to periods of detention either under MCA 1980, s. 37 (detention up to one year) or CYPA 1933, s. 53(2) (detention longer than one year) see **Chapter 24**. On committal hearings, see generally **Chapter 5**. On indictable offences, see **4.1**.)

7.5.7 MCA 1980, s. 24(1)(a)

A youth court can only pass a maximum custodial sentence of six months for a single offence. If a youth court committed a juvenile to the Crown Court for sentence under MCA 1980, s. 37, the Crown Court could only pass a maximum custodial sentence of 24 months. The only situation where a court can pass a longer custodial sentence on a juvenile is in the Crown Court and then only if it can use CYPA 1933, s. 53(2) (or the offence involves homicide).

CYPA 1933, s. 53(2), can be used in the situation set out in **Figure 7.3**, item 2 — serious offences, i.e., following a trial in the Crown Court. A youth court can send a juvenile to the Crown Court for trial, using MCA 1980, s. 24(1)(a).

The Court of Appeal has stated that (because a sentence under CYPA 1933, s. 53(2) is not available following a committal for sentence under MCA 1980, s. 37) youth courts should not hesitate to use their power to commit for trial under MCA 1980, s. 24(1)(a), if 24 months' detention might not be an adequate sentence for that offence, following conviction. See *R* v *Corcoran* [1986] Crim LR 568; *R* v *Learmouth* [1988] Crim LR 774. See also *R* v *Fairhurst* [1986] 1 WLR 1374, CA.

Figure 7.3 When can a youth court send a juvenile to the Crown Court

1. **Homicide** The youth court has no power to deal with such crimes and the case against the juvenile must be transferred to the Crown Court for further proceedings.

2. **Detention of 15/16/17-year-olds** If the juvenile is aged 15, 16 or 17 *and* is convicted by the youth court of any indictable offence, *and* if that court feels that the juvenile should be sentenced to more than six months' detention in a young offender institution for that offence, it may commit the juvenile to the Crown Court for sentence (where the maximum will be 24 months' detention). See MCA 1980, s. 37.

3. **Serious offences** If the youth court considers that, if he or she is found guilty of an offence, a juvenile should be sentenced to a long period of detention due to the exceptional seriousness of the offence, it may transfer him or her to the Crown Court for trial. See MCA 1980, s. 24(1)(a). This applies only to certain serious offences as follows:

(a) any offence which is punishable with 14 or more years' imprisonment for adult offenders (not being an offence which has a sentence fixed by law);

(b) indecent assault on a woman (max. 10 years' imprisonment for adult offenders);

(c) causing death by dangerous driving (max. 10 years' imprisonment for adult offenders);

(d) causing death by careless driving while under the influence of drink or drugs (max. 10 years' imprisonment for adult offenders).

Items (a) and (b) apply to all juvenile defendants, from age 10 to 17; items (c) and (d) apply only to young persons, aged 14–17. Following transfer for trial, the case will be tried by a judge and jury (as usual in the Crown Court) and if the juvenile is found guilty (or pleads guilty), he may be ordered to be detained 'in such place and on such conditions . . . as the Secretary of State may direct . . . or arrange . . .'. See CYPA 1933, s. 53(2).

When considering the possible application of s. 24(1)(a), magistrates should hear representations from both prosecution and defence lawyers about the seriousness of the offence but should not consider any evidence (*R* v *South Hackney Juvenile Court, ex parte R. B. and C. B.* (1983) 77 Cr App R 294). Further, the magistrates should not be told about the accused's previous criminal record (*R* v *Hammersmith Juvenile Court, ex parte O* (1988) 86 Cr App R 343). It seems that it is only the gravity of the offence then charged which is decisive of the operation of s. 24(1)(a).

7.6 Can the Youth Court Deal with an Adult Defendant?

7.6.1 DEFENDANTS AGED 18 OR OVER AT THE START OF PROCEEDINGS

The youth court has no jurisdiction over such defendants. If a defendant was aged under 18 when charged with an offence, but is 18 when the case first comes to court, he or she should appear in the adult magistrates' court. Parents may be charged with offences such as not sending their child to school. This will be a matter for an adult magistrates' court to hear and to determine the appropriate steps to take to ensure the well-being of the juvenile.

7.6.2 DEFENDANTS WHO REACH THEIR EIGHTEENTH BIRTHDAY AFTER THEIR CASE HAS BEGUN IN THE YOUTH COURT

When a youth court decides to hear the case against a juvenile (that is, none of the situations in **Figure 7.3** exist), then the juvenile will be asked to plead guilty or not guilty to the offence with which he or she is charged.

(a) *Under 18 at time of plea:* At this moment, if the juvenile has not attained his or her eighteenth birthday (even though this may happen before the case is finally disposed of), the youth court has the power to hear the case and impose a sentence. If the defendant's eighteenth birthday falls after the plea and before final disposal of the case, the youth court may nevertheless sentence the defendant as if he or she was still a juvenile (CYPA 1963, s. 29).

(b) *18 at the time of plea:* If the juvenile has reached age 18 by the time he or she is asked to enter a plea to the offence, the court must treat him or her as an adult (see *R* v *Islington North Juvenile Court, ex parte Daley* [1983] AC 347; followed in *R* v *Nottingham Justices, ex parte Taylor* [1992] QB 557). The result is that offences which are triable only on indictment must undergo proceedings for transfer for trial as a preliminary to Crown Court trial, whilst the court must turn to the mode of trial process used by the adult magistrates' court for any offences which are triable either way. Any proceedings pending transfer for Crown Court trial should be sent to the adult magistrates' court to follow the normal process. Any summary trial will take place in the adult magistrates' court.

Multiple-choice Questions

1. Which of the following groups is not allowed into a youth court room during a hearing?

[A] Probation officers concerned in the hearing.
[B] Journalists reporting the hearing.
[C] Witnesses, after they have testified in the hearing.
[D] Barristers waiting for their case to start.

2. Portia (aged 16) appeared with Quentin (aged 20) in the adult magistrates' court on a joint charge of theft. Quentin elected to be tried on indictment. The magistrates felt that it was not necessary in the interests of justice to commit Portia to the Crown Court for trial. Portia has now been tried and convicted by the adult magistrates' court. Which one of the following statements is correct?

[A] Portia must be sent to the youth court to be dealt with.
[B] Portia must be sent to the youth court to be dealt with if the magistrates do not think a custodial sentence is called for.
[C] Portia may be committed to the Crown Court for sentence if the magistrates think that a custodial sentence is called for.
[D] Portia may be dealt with in the magistrates' court or, if none of that court's sentences is appropriate, sent to the youth court to be dealt with.

Tutorial Questions

1. Fiona (aged 16), Gillian (aged 14) and her twin brother, George, are all found guilty in the youth court of three offences of burglary and one of inflicting grievous bodily harm. On each occasion, they went to a house where an elderly person lived alone, tricked their way in by asking to use the lavatory, after which two of them would search the premises while the third kept the victim occupied in conversation. Pension money, savings and jewellery were stolen to a total value of approximately £1,000. On the third occasion, the victim became suspicious and tried to stop them leaving. They knocked her to the ground, causing bruising and a head wound which required 20 stitches. Reports reveal that Gillian and George have a difficult background. Their mother admits that she cannot keep control of them. Moreover, their father and older siblings all have criminal records. George has previous findings of guilt for shoplifting and stealing a car radio, but Gillian has not been in trouble before. Fiona is also of previous good character. She comes from an excellent home, and the report can give no explanation for her involvement in the offences other than 'a desire for thrills'. She apparently met Gillian and George at a youth club where together they planned the offences.

(a) What are the magistrates' maximum custodial sentencing powers?

(b) What are their powers, if any, to commit for sentence?

(c) Was this an appropriate case to be tried in the youth court?

2. *R* v *Barley*

Aim: To familiarise yourself with both the procedure at a summary trial and the special rules relating to juveniles.

This is a simple case of theft in the youth court. You should prepare this as you would for any summary trial. There will not be role-play in the class but you should be ready to discuss all issues relevant to the case.

IN THE BLACKHEATH MAGISTRATES' COURT

R

v

Billy Barley

Instructions to Prosecute

Billy Barley is charged with theft. He is alleged to have stolen a leather jacket, the property of Newtrend Limited, on 3rd August 1996. He was stopped by a store detective, employed by the company, a short distance from their shop after a chase. The jacket was recovered from him. Police were called and Constable Field attended the scene. No admissions were made.

Both witnesses — the store detective, Ellis Farmer, and Constable Field — have been warned to attend court on the next hearing.

Billy Barley is in receipt of legal aid and has instructed Messrs Planter and Reaper of 22 Harvest Street, WC5.

Barley's date of birth is 1st of February 1983.

STATEMENT OF WITNESS

Statement of: Ellis FARMER
Age of witness: 25 (d.o.b. 1.1.71)
Occupation of witness: Store detective

[Usual declaration omitted]

Signed: E. Farmer
Signature witnessed by: Drew Field, PC 202Y

I am employed as a store detective by Newtrend Limited. I have held this position for 3 years. For the last 6 months I have been at the Oxford Street Branch.

On the 3rd August 1996, I was on duty on the ground floor of the shop when my attention was caught by a youth who I now know to be Billy BARLEY. He was standing by a mirror and was wearing one of our new leather jackets. He seemed to be more interested in watching what was going on around him than looking in the mirror.

I moved to a different position, keeping him under observation the whole time. After I had been observing him for about thirty seconds, he suddenly ran towards the exit, still wearing the jacket. I was unable to stop him before he left as several customers were between us.

When I got outside, I saw him running through the mall and gave chase. I caught him just around the corner in Orchard Street, some 300 metres from the shop. He had taken the jacket off and appeared to be about to hide it. I took him by the arm and said, 'You're coming with me. The police will have to come. You've stolen this jacket and it's store policy always to prosecute.' He said, 'I don't know what you're talking about. A boy just gave this to me.' I replied, 'We'll let the police sort this out. Come with me'.

We returned to the shop where I called the police and eventually repeated my story to Constable Field in the presence of Billy Barley. The jacket was recovered intact and there is no claim for compensation.

Dated 4.8.96

Signed: E. Farmer
Signature witnessed by: D. Field

STATEMENT OF WITNESS

Statement of: Drew FIELD
Age of witness: Over 21
Occupation of witness: Police Constable 202Y

[Usual declaration omitted]

Signed: D. Field
Signature witnessed by: G. Fallow P. Sgt 545Z

On the 3rd August 1996 at 4.25 pm I was on duty in Oxford Street when, as a result of information received, I attended the premises of Newtrend Limited at 755 Oxford Street. There I spoke to an employee of the store, Ellis FARMER, and then I asked a youth, who I know to be Billy BARLEY, 'The store detective says you were seen trying the jacket on and then you ran out of the store without paying for it. What have you got to say?' He replied, 'It's a mistake. I was waiting for my bus when a boy came running around the corner, threw the coat down and kept running. I went to pick it up when this person came up and arrested me.'

The store detective said, 'I got a good look at him in the shop. I know it was him.' I said to BARLEY, 'I am not satisfied with your answer. I am arresting you for theft of this leather jacket from Newtrend.' I then cautioned BARLEY and he said 'Can I ring my Mum?' We then went to Paddington Green Police Station where, at 7.45 pm and in the presence of his parents, he was charged with theft of the jacket, cautioned and made no reply.

Dated 10.8.96

Signed: D. Field
Signature witnessed by: G. Fallow

Extract from Record of previous Findings of Guilt:

Billy BARLEY (d.o.b. 1.02.83) has 2 findings of guilt recorded against him, both in the Westminster Youth Court. Both offences were for burglary of dwelling houses. The first finding of guilt, recorded on 13.05.95, resulted in an order that there be a fine of £50. The second, dated 10.02.96, resulted in an order that he be conditionally discharged for 1 year.

WESTMINSTER YOUTH COURT

Sitting at Seymour Place, W1

R v Billy Barley

Instructions to Counsel for the Defence

Counsel is instructed to represent Billy Barley at Seymour Place Youth Court on his trial. He is charged with shoplifting — taking a leather jacket from a Newtrend shop in Oxford Street. No one else is alleged to be involved. He will plead *Not Guilty*.

Instructing solicitors understand that there are 2 Prosecution witnesses, a store detective and arresting officer.

The evidence seems quite weak, in the opinion of instructing solicitors, with the case turning on identification. Counsel is, of course, familiar with the guidelines for such cases, laid down by the Court of Appeal in *R* v *Turnbull* [1977] QB 224. Billy Barley was found in possession of the jacket, a fact which he does not deny, but he has an explanation which he told the arresting officer.

There are no defence witnesses, apart from Billy, although his parents have been told by instructing solicitors to attend Court with him. Counsel is asked to use his best endeavours to secure an acquittal.

Proof of Evidence

Billy Barley of 65 Plough Lane, London W9, who will say:

On the day in August when I was supposed to have stolen the jacket, I was in Oxford Street, looking around the shops. I had arrived there at about 2 p.m. and saw all that I wanted to by about 4.30. Then I went to catch the bus home. This is a number 85 which stops in Orchard Street, just off of Oxford Street.

I had just got to the stop when a boy came running around the corner from Oxford Street. He was running hard so I watched to see why. He had something in his hand and threw it to the ground as he went past the bus stop. He kept going, up towards Baker Street.

I was curious about what he had thrown away so I went and picked it up. It was a leather jacket, brand new. I saw it still had the price ticket in and was just looking to see the size when this person came up and told me I was under arrest for shoplifting. I said I did not know anything about it but I was taken to a shop, Newtrend, in Oxford Street.

I did not know what to do but eventually the police came. The store detective said that I had been under observation in the shop and had run out with the jacket. When the police officer asked me if that was true, I denied it and told them what happened. No one believed me and I was taken to the police station.

My Mum and Dad were called down to the station and got me. I have never admitted to stealing the jacket. I would not recognise the boy who had the jacket. I did not know him. There were some other people at the bus stop who must have seen it all but there is no way I could trace them.

I think the jacket is a size 40-inch chest. That is too big for me.

EIGHT

APPEALS FROM DECISIONS OF MAGISTRATES

There are three ways of appealing against the decision of the magistrates:

(a) Appeal to the Crown Court.

(b) Appeal to the High Court by way of case stated.

(c) Application for judicial review.

Students should also be aware of the power of the magistrates to rectify mistakes under MCA 1980, s. 142, discussed at para. **5.1.12**. This may often prove to be a quick and simple way to correct an error.

8.1 Appeal to the Crown Court

The defendant may appeal against conviction and/or sentence to the Crown Court, except that, if he or she has pleaded guilty, he or she may only appeal against sentence (MCA 1980, s. 108). If the defendant has pleaded guilty, in order to appeal against the conviction he or she must argue that the plea is equivocal (see **5.1.2**).

8.1.1 PROCEDURE FOR APPEALING

(a) Notice of appeal is given in writing to the clerk of the magistrates' court and to the prosecution within 21 days of sentence. The 21 days run from the date of sentence, even if the appeal is against conviction and the appellant was convicted and sentenced on different days.

(b) The notice of appeal must state whether the appeal is against conviction, sentence or both, but the grounds of appeal need not be given.

(c) All documents are forwarded to the Crown Court, where the listing officer will place the appeal on the list, and send notice of the time and place to the appellant, the prosecution and the magistrates' court.

(d) The appellant may appeal out of time by applying for leave in writing from the Crown Court. Leave is not otherwise required.

8.1.2 BAIL

If the appellant is in custody and gives notice of appeal, the magistrates may grant him or her bail, with a duty to appear at the hearing of the appeal (MCA 1980, s. 113). If bail is refused, or unacceptable conditions are imposed, the appellant may appeal against the decision to the Crown Court under the SCA 1981, s. 81 or to a judge of the High Court in chambers under the CJA 1967, s. 22. (See further **3.16**.)

The appellant does not have the right to bail, but bail may well be granted if the sentence is likely to have been served before the appeal is heard.

8.1.3 THE HEARING

At the hearing, the judge (usually a circuit judge or recorder) sits usually with two lay magistrates who have not been concerned with the case in the magistrates' court.

Where the appeal is an appeal against conviction, the hearing itself is a complete re-hearing of the whole case. It is not a review of what happened before the magistrates. Thus, either party may call evidence not called before the magistrates, or omit evidence that was called before the magistrates.

The lay magistrates must accept the law from the judge, but the decision on the appeal itself is a majority decision. Thus, the lay magistrates may outvote the judge. However, if an evenly numbered court is equally divided, the judge has a casting vote.

A Crown Court judge giving the decision of the court must give reasons for its decision, and a refusal to do so might amount to a breach of natural justice. The reasoning required would depend on the circumstances of each case, but should be enough to demonstrate that the court had identified the main contentious issues, and how it had resolved them. An appellant is entitled to know the basis upon which the prosecution case had been accepted by the court. See *R* v *Harrow Crown Court, ex parte Dave* [1994] 1 WLR 98, DC.

8.1.4 POWERS OF THE CROWN COURT

Under the SCA 1981, s. 48, as amended by the CJA 1988, s. 156, the Crown Court may:

(a) Confirm, reverse or vary any part of the decision appealed against. Thus, if the defendant has appealed against only part of the magistrates' decision, the Crown Court is not restricted to reviewing just that part, but may review the whole decision.

(b) Remit the case to the magistrates with its opinion. This will usually be a direction to enter a plea of not guilty and hear the case, if it thinks the plea was equivocal.

(c) Make any such order as it thinks just. This includes a power to increase sentence up to the maximum sentence which was available to the magistrates. This power is rarely exercised, but its existence is a means of discouraging frivolous appeals, bearing in mind that no leave to appeal is required.

8.1.5 APPEAL AGAINST SENTENCE

The appropriate court to deal with an appeal against sentence is normally the Crown Court, where the case may be appealed by way of re-hearing (see **8.2.1(d)**).

8.2 Appeals to the High Court by Way of Case Stated

Under MCA 1980, s. 111, either party to the proceedings, or any person aggrieved by the decision of the magistrates, may question that decision on the ground that it was wrong in law or in excess of jurisdiction by asking the magistrates to state a case for the opinion of the High Court.

8.2.1 SUBSIDIARY POINTS ON APPEALS BY WAY OF CASE STATED

(a) The magistrates have no power to state a case until they have reached a final determination on the matter. Thus, they have no power to state a case during the hearing and must wait until the end. Similarly, it is not an appropriate method of challenging a committal for sentence (see **5.3.5**).

(b) Both the defence and the prosecution have the right to apply for a case to be stated, and so may a third party whose legal rights have been affected. This means that effectively the prosecution can appeal against the defendant's acquittal, and if it is successful the acquittal will be reversed.

(c) The appellant must show that the decision of the magistrates was either wrong in law or in excess of jurisdiction. Questions raised will therefore be questions of jurisdiction, admissibility of evidence and so on. If the appeal is based on the facts of the case, then generally speaking it will be refused, unless the magistrates have made a finding of fact which is totally unsupported by the evidence, or is one which no reasonable tribunal, properly directing itself, could have reached, in which case the High Court may treat it as an error of law. As to where the magistrates are entitled to draw inferences from facts, see *Plowden* v *DPP* [1991] Crim LR 850.

(d) An appeal against sentence by way of case stated should only proceed in the most exceptional of circumstances (*R* v *St Albans Crown Court, ex parte Cinnamond* [1981] QB 480 applied in *Tucker* v *DPP* [1992] 4 All ER 901 and *R* v *Ealing Justices, ex parte Scrafield, The Times*, 29 March 1993, DC). The Divisional Court can only interfere where the magistrates have passed a sentence they have no power to pass, or where the sentence they have passed is so harsh as to be in excess of jurisdiction.

(e) Once an application to state a case to the High Court is made, the right to appeal to the Crown Court is lost (MCA 1980, s. 111(4)).

(f) If the same point arises in several cases on the same day, the appellants may apply for a collective case to be stated.

8.2.2 PROCEDURE

(a) The application must be made in writing within 21 days of the sentence, and should state the point of law upon which the opinion of the High Court is sought.

(b) The application is sent to the clerk of the convicting magistrates' court.

(c) The magistrates may refuse to state a case, but this decision is reviewable by the High Court on an application for judicial review. For a recent example of such an application see *R* v *Huntingdon Magistrates' Court, ex parte Percy* [1994] COD 323. Magistrates may legitimately refuse to state a case in two situations:

   (i) If they consider that the application is frivolous. The magistrates must give the appellant a certificate to that effect, enabling him or her to seek judicial review of the decision not to state a case. It is doubtful whether the justices are required to give any reason, beyond that the application was frivolous (*R* v *Carlisle Crown Court, ex parte Jackson* [1991] COD 273).

   (ii) They may refuse to state the case unless the appellant enters into a recognisance to prosecute the appeal without delay, and to pay such costs as the High Court may award. Such a condition would be imposed if the magistrates think the appellant is likely to abandon the appeal halfway through, having incurred expense and wasted time.

(d) The statement itself is usually drafted by the clerk of the magistrates' court, though exceptionally it may be drafted by either the appellant or the magistrates. The draft must be prepared within 21 days.

Note: It is a part of the procedure for stating a case that if a properly drafted question was to be altered, the party which framed the original question must be allowed to comment on the changes (*Waldie* v *DPP, The Times*, 18 April 1995).

(e) The draft statement is submitted to the parties for their comments, which must be lodged with the court within 21 days. The statement may be adjusted in response. Where it is adjusted, the court will consider only the final statement, and not any earlier variations.

(f) The contents of the statement are:

  (i) The names of the parties and of the court.

  (ii) The charges.

  (iii) The findings of fact, but not the evidence upon which those findings were made, unless the appellant's argument is that, on that evidence, the magistrates could not have come to the conclusion that they did (see *Crompton and Crompton* v *North Tyneside Metropolitan Borough Council* [1991] COD 52).

  (iv) The points of law involved, and the authorities relied on. This should include the arguments heard by the justices (*DPP* v *Kirk, The Times*, 4 December 1992).

  (v) The decision of the magistrates.

  (vi) A request for the opinion of the High Court, posing the question which the appellant wishes the High Court to answer.

(g) Once the final draft is completed, the magistrates sign it and send it to the appellant.

(h) The appellant then has ten days in which to lodge the statement at the Crown Office of the High Court, and a further four days to serve notice on the respondent.

Note: All the time limits set out above may be extended except the first limit of 21 days, which is statutory and cannot be varied (see s. 111(2) and *Michael* v *Gowland* [1977] 1 WLR 296. And see *Reid* v *DPP* [1993] COD 111, DC, where 'pressure of work' on the part of the solicitor was insufficient reason for extending time).

8.2.3 BAIL

Under MCA 1980, s. 113, the appellant may be granted bail pending the outcome of the hearing in the High Court. Bail will be granted on the basis that the appellant returns to the magistrates' court within ten days of the High Court hearing, unless the conviction is quashed.

8.2.4 THE HEARING

Under the SCA 1981, s. 66(3), the court must consist of at least two judges, though there are usually three. The court acts entirely on the basis of the facts as set out in the case, and no new evidence is adduced. The hearing therefore consists solely of legal argument by counsel.

If only two judges are sitting, and cannot agree, the decision of the judge who agrees with the court below prevails, and thus the appeal will fail.

Note: In considering the matter, the judge should not act as prosecutor in the absence of the prosecution advocate. This amounts to a procedural irregularity, as the judge is not sufficiently removed from the proceedings to meet the requirement of justice (*R* v *Wood Green Crown Court, ex parte Taylor, The Times*, 25 May 1995).

8.2.5 POWERS OF THE HIGH COURT

Under the Summary Jurisdiction Act 1857, s. 6, the High Court may affirm, reverse or vary the decision of the court below, make any other order it thinks fit, or remit it back to the original court with its opinion. The High Court decision is enforced as if it were the decision of the court below. Thus, if the High Court thinks that the acquittal is incorrect, it can remit it back to the magistrates with a direction to convict and sentence. Generally speaking, the High Court does not deal with sentence itself, taking the view that it is not the appropriate forum. However, it may deal with sentence if it is obvious what the sentence should be.

The power of the High Court under s. 6 includes a power to order a rehearing of the case before the same or a different bench of justices whenever such a course is appropriate (see *Griffith* v *Jenkins* [1992] AC 76); *R* v *Farrand and Galland* [1989] Crim LR 573).

8.2.6 CASE STATED FROM THE CROWN COURT

Appeal lies to the High Court from the Crown Court on matters not related to a trial on indictment, by way of case stated. Thus, if the defendant has appealed to the Crown Court against conviction or has been committed to the Crown Court for sentence, either party may appeal to the High Court by way of case stated, under the SCA 1981, s. 28, on the basis that the final decision was wrong in law or in excess of jurisdiction.

The procedure is much the same as for applications from the magistrates' court, except that it is usually the appellant who drafts the statement. The respondent also has the right to submit a draft. The judge, who was the judge at the hearing of the appeal or the committal, will read the drafts submitted to him and state a case on that basis.

For a recent example, see *R* v *Crown Court at Portsmouth, ex parte Thomas* [1994] COD 373.

A useful article is, 'Rights of appeal by way of case stated — should it be satisfied?', J Backhouse, 156 JPN 310.

8.3 Application for Judicial Review

Judicial review is the method by which the High Court controls the activities of inferior tribunals, that is, magistrates' courts and the Crown Court in matters not relating to trial on indictment.

8.3.1 PREROGATIVE ORDERS

The High Court exercises its control by the use of prerogative orders, namely *certiorari, mandamus* and prohibition.

(1) *Certiorari. Certiorari* has the effect of quashing the decision appealed against. In addition, the High Court may:

(a) Remit the case to the court concerned with a direction to reconsider it and reach a decision in accordance with the finding of the High Court (SCA 1981, s. 31(5)).

(b) Substitute for an unlawful sentence one which the court had the power to pass (SCA 1981, s. 43(1)).

It is usually said that *certiorari* 'will go' (i.e. be issued) in three situations:

(a) Where there is an error on the face of the record. However in a magistrates' court, the record is brief, and in any event magistrates rarely give reasons for their decisions. If the magistrates in fact give reasons, or include them in any affidavit that they are swearing for consideration of the High Court, the High Court will treat them as part of the record.

(b) Where the court acts in excess of jurisdiction. See, for example, *R* v *Tunbridge Wells Justices, ex parte Tunbridge Wells Borough Council* (unreported) 1 May 1994, where the justices adjourned the case, part heard, after a submission of no case to answer was made. The High Court set aside the decision to accept the submission, which was subsequently pronounced in open court by a different bench of magistrates, as being *ultra vires*. See also *R* v *Parker and the Barnet Magistrates' Court, ex parte DPP* (1994)158 JP 1061. The High Court may also set aside a sentence if it is one which the magistrates have no power to pass, but such an error is rare. However, in very limited circumstances, the High Court will treat a sentence which is so harsh and oppressive that no reasonable tribunal could have passed it, as being in excess of jurisdiction, and quash it accordingly, even though it was in fact within the court's powers (see *R* v *St Albans Crown Court, ex parte Cinnamond* [1981] QB 480). But such a course is exceptional, and should only be followed when an appeal against sentence to the Crown Court has failed (*R* v *Battle Justices, ex parte Shepherd* (1983) 5 Cr App R (S) 124). But see also on this point *R* v *Bradford Justices, ex parte Wilkinson* [1990] 1 WLR 692.

(c) Where the court acts in breach of the rules of natural justice. The court is under a duty to act fairly, there being two aspects of this duty:

(i) No person may be a judge in his or her own cause. See, for example, *Dimes* v *Grand Junction Canal* (1852) 3 HLC 759 and *R* v *Altrincham Justices, ex parte Pennington* [1975] 1 QB 549.

(ii) The court must hear both sides of the case. This rule will be relied on where there has been some procedural irregularity which has prejudiced the appellant, and the court must now employ the test laid down by the House of Lords in *R* v *Gough* [1993] AC 646, and ask: Was there a real danger that the appellant did not receive a fair trial? There are many and varied examples of the application of this principle to be found in the law reports and the following are included merely by way of example:

— *R* v *Thames Magistrates' Court, ex parte Polemis* [1974] 1 WLR 1371 (where the defendant was not given sufficient time to prepare his case);

— *R* v *Marylebone Justices, ex parte Farrag* [1981] Crim LR 182 (where a verdict of guilty was announced before defence counsel's closing speech);

— *R* v *Romsey Justices, ex parte Gale* [1992] Crim LR 451 (where one of the magistrates, during the prosecution case, prepared a note of what he proposed the bench should say if it were to convict);

— *R* v *Ely Justices, ex parte Burgess* [1992] Crim LR 888 (where the justices travelled to view the *locus in quo* with the prosecutor, and did not allow the defendant to be present — either or both of these factors would allow the conviction to be quashed);

— *R* v *Hendon Justices, ex parte DPP* [1994] QB 167 (where the magistrates announced an acquittal without hearing prosecution evidence and without having a good reason to refuse to hear witnesses);

- *Vincent* v *The Queen* [1993] 1 WLR 862, PC (where the fact that the defendant, following normal practice, was not given detailed notice of the evidence against him was not sufficient to establish that he had been denied a fair hearing);

- *R* v *Newbury Justices, ex parte Drake* [1993] COD 24 (where the allegedly partisan demeanour of the clerk was held not to have affected the magistrates' decision);

- *R* v *Nottingham Justices, ex parte Fraser, The Times*, 13 May 1995 (where the magistrates took into account the adequacy of the defendant's representation).

Note: An order of *certiorari* to quash an acquittal on the ground that it had been procured by fraud or perjury should seldom if ever be made (*R* v *Portsmouth Crown Court, ex parte DPP* [1994] COD 13, DC).

(2) *Mandamus*. An order of *mandamus* compels an inferior tribunal to carry out its duties. It will be ordered when the court refuses to act when it should; not when it has acted and made a mistake. The appropriate remedy in the latter case would be *certiorari*. See, for example *R* v *Hendon Justices, ex parte DPP* [1994] QB 167, CA.

(3) *Prohibition*. Prohibition will be ordered to stop the court acting in excess of its powers. Parties do not have to wait for the final outcome of the hearing, and if there is genuine doubt as to the court's powers, the court will adjourn, so that the opinion of the High Court can be sought.

8.3.2 DISCRETION

The power to award any of the prerogative orders is entirely discretionary, and even though the appellant has established a prima facie case, the order may still be refused. See, again, *R* v *Battle Justices, ex parte Shepherd* (1983) 5 Cr App R (S) 124.

8.3.3 PROCEDURE

Under the SCA 1981, s. 31, and the Rules of the Supreme Court, O. 53, the procedure is as follows:

(a) Within three months of the decision, the applicant must file an application for leave to apply for judicial review, setting out his or her name and address and that of his or her solicitor, the relief sought and the grounds. This application must be supported by affidavit evidence.

(b) The application for leave is heard *ex parte* (i.e. in the absence of the other side), usually without a hearing. If there is no hearing, the judge will simply read the papers in chambers. If the applicant specifically applies for a hearing, one may be held, and this may be in court.

(c) If leave is refused, the applicant has ten days in which to renew his or her application before the Divisional Court.

(d) If leave is granted, the application is made by originating motion. Notice of motion must be served on the other side, and on the court below.

(e) The hearing itself consists of affidavit evidence and argument from counsel. Evidence is not usually called, though it may be necessary to establish the error of the court below.

(f) The court will reach a decision, and make any appropriate orders.

8.3.4 BAIL

Magistrates have no power to grant bail for an application for judicial review. The application for bail must be made to the High Court judge in chambers under the CJA 1967, s. 22. However, if the application is from the Crown Court on a matter not relating to trial on indictment, the Crown Court may grant bail.

8.3.5 CASE STATED AND JUDICIAL REVIEW COMPARED

In many situations, the appellant could apply for either a case to be stated or judicial review, and in some respects the two are similar. However, by appealing by way of case stated, the appellant is challenging the actual decision of the court, alleging, for example, that a statute has been misapplied. In some circumstances this may be said of judicial review, but judicial review tends to be directed, not at the decision itself, but more at the decision-making process. It is the legality of the process which is under review, not whether the decision is right or wrong.

If both remedies do apply, the appellant should appeal by way of case stated, as all the facts can then be placed before the High Court (*R* v *Ipswich Crown Court, ex parte Baldwin* [1981] 1 All ER 596 and *R* v *Oldbury Justices, ex parte Smith* (1995) 7 Admin LR 315). See also *R* v *Ipswich Justices, ex parte D* (unreported) 5 December 1994.

8.4 Appeal to the House of Lords

A decision of the High Court in a criminal cause or matter is appealed directly to the House of Lords, and there is no right of appeal to the Court of Appeal (Administration of Justice Act 1960, s. 1). The appeal will lie if the following conditions are satisfied:

(a) the High Court certifies that the case involves a point of law of general public importance; and

(b) leave is granted by either the High Court or the House of Lords.

Multiple-choice Questions

1. Alphonse is convicted in the magistrates' court of theft. He wishes to appeal to the Crown Court against his conviction. Which of the following is the appropriate procedure:

[A] Alphonse notifies the magistrates' court and the prosecution of his intention to appeal.
[B] Alphonse notifies the magistrates and the prosecution of his intention to appeal, and sets out his full grounds of appeal.
[C] Alphonse applies to the magistrates for leave to appeal to the Crown Court.
[D] Alphonse applies to the Crown Court for leave to appeal to that court, stating brief grounds of appeal.

2. Graham is convicted of two offences of handling stolen goods in the magistrates' court, and sentenced to two months' imprisonment on each offence, to run consecutively. He wishes to appeal against sentence. In dealing with Graham the Crown Court may:

[A] Pass any sentence that it could have passed following a trial on indictment.
[B] Pass any sentence that the magistrates could have passed.
[C] Pass any sentence which is not greater than the sentence that the magistrates actually passed.
[D] Treat the case as if Graham had been committed to them for sentence.

Tutorial Questions

APPEALS FROM THE MAGISTRATES' COURT

1. Fiona is charged with driving without due care and attention, contrary to the Road Traffic Act 1991. She pleads not guilty. At the close of the prosecution case, her solicitor makes a submission of no case to answer. The chairman of the magistrates, upholding the submission and acquitting Fiona, says:

We take the view that your driving clearly fell below the standards of a reasonable prudent driver. However, we put that down to inexperience on your part. There is nothing in the prosecution evidence to suggest that you were not doing your best to drive properly. You did not mean to be careless. For that reason we find that there is no case to answer.

Advise the prosecution on whether, and if so, how, it can appeal againt the magistrates' decision.

2. (See Question 3, p. 78.) Assume that Sid is committed for sentence to the Crown Court. Describe the procedure by which Sid can apply to the High Court to have the committal quashed.

3. Christine is charged with stealing from Harridges, a large department store, an expensive box of chocolates. She is jointly charged with her husband, Harold. She agrees to summary trial. Christine pleads guilty and Harold not guilty. In view of her plea, the prosecution offers no evidence against Harold. Having learnt that Christine has previous convictions for shoplifting and considered a pre-sentence report, the magistrates pass a sentence of three months' imprisonment. When the defence solicitor goes to see Christine in the cells, she tells him for the first time that Harold made her steal the chocolates by threatening her with violence if she did not do so. Also, on the morning of her first appearance before the magistrates, he had said to her, 'You'd better not tell them I made you do it or it will be the worse for you when I get you home'.

Is it possible for Christine to appeal to the Crown Court against conviction? If so, how do you think the Crown Court would deal with the case?

4. Ben, aged 23, is charged with wounding Claude. The offence is alleged to have taken place in a public house shortly after a football match between 'United' and 'City'. Ben is a 'United' supporter whereas Claude supports 'City'. Ben intends to plead not guilty — he says he was acting in self-defence and that he was attacked by Claude and other 'City' supporters. Ben has two previous convictions for offences of violence. He appears at the Whitehaven Magistrates' Court and elects summary trial. Ben does not give evidence at his trial. After hearing all the evidence the magistrates convict Ben and sentence him to three months' imprisonment.

A week after the hearing Ben's solicitors discover that the police had taken a statement from Desmond, a witness whose evidence supported Ben's account. Neither Ben nor his solicitors knew about Desmond. Ben wishes to appeal against both conviction and sentence. Advise Ben as to his rights of appeal.

5. Francis appears at Blackacre Magistrates' Court charged with theft. The magistrates find the matter is suitable for summary trial and Francis elects summary trial. At the end of the prosecution evidence, his solicitor makes a submission that there is no case to answer. The magistrates retire to consider and when they retum the chairman announces that they find Francis guilty. What steps can be taken to quash the conviction? Describe in brief outline the appropriate procedure.

6. Barry is charged with being found drunk in a public place. The prosecution alleges that he was found in the garden of a block of flats. Barry admits that he was drunk but says that the gardens are not a public place. He is convicted. Describe the procedure on an appeal against conviction by way of case stated to the High Court.

NINE

INDICTMENT AND PLEAS

9.1 What is an Indictment?

The indictment is the factual document on which a Crown Court trial is based. It contains a list of the counts (i.e. offences) to which the defendant must plead before the trial begins.

9.1.1 WHAT DOES AN INDICTMENT CONTAIN?

(a) The heading or commencement contains the word 'Indictment', the venue of the trial and the name of the case. After the names(s) of the defendant(s) come the words 'charged as follows'.

(b) Then there follows the count or counts with which the defendant is charged.

See **Figure 9.1**.

9.1.2 WHAT DOES A COUNT CONTAIN?

There may be only one count in the indictment (as in **Figure 9.1**) or there may be several. Each count must contain:

(a) The statement of the offence. This will consist of the name of the offence (e.g. 'attempted burglary') and, where appropriate, the statute and the section contravened (e.g. 'contrary to Section 1(1) of the Criminal Attempts Act 1981').
(b) The particulars of the offence. This will give reasonable information about the nature of the charge, usually including the essential elements of the offence.

9.1.3 EXAMPLES

Examples of counts for some of the more common indictable offences follow. Note that you need only say where the offence occurred if it is material, e.g. 'a building' for burglary — see Specimen Count (3).

The drafting of indictments is dealt with in more detail, with further examples, in the chapter entitled 'Indictments' in the ***Drafting Manual***.

Figure 9.1 Example indictment

INDICTMENT No. 960316

The Crown Court at Greenbridge

The Queen v PAUL MARTIN

PAUL MARTIN is charged as follows

Statement of Offence

ATTEMPTED BURGLARY contrary to Section 1(1) of the Criminal Attempts Act 1981

Particulars of Offence

PAUL MARTIN on the 1st day of January 1996, attempted to enter as a trespasser a building known as 12 Coleridge Crescent, Greenbridge, with intent to steal therein.

Date: 10th April 1996 D Thomas

An Officer of the Crown Court

Example Counts

(1) **Theft**

Statement of Offence

Theft, contrary to Section 1(1) of the Theft Act 1968.

Particulars of Offence

Alan Adamson, on the 2nd day of February 1996, stole a wallet belonging to Arthur Archer.

(2) **Robbery**

Statement of Offence

Robbery, contrary to Section 8(1) of the Theft Act 1968.

Particulars of Offence

Bronwen Beale, on the 3rd day of March 1996, robbed Basil Brush of a gold chain and £56 in money.

(3) **Burglary**

Statement of Offence

Burglary, contrary to Section 9(1)(a) of the Theft Act 1968.

Particulars of Offence

Charles Craddock, on the 4th day of April 1996, entered as a trespasser a building known as 83 Lower Marsh Avenue, Ambridge, with intent to steal therein.

Statement of Offence

Burglary, contrary to Section 9(1)(b) of the Theft Act 1968.

Particulars of Offence

Charles Craddock, on the 4th day of April 1996, having entered as a trespasser a building known as 83 Lower Marsh Avenue, stole therein a television set and a video recorder.

(4) **Deception**

Statement of Offence

Obtaining property by deception, contrary to Section 15(1) of the Theft Act 1968.

Particulars of Offence

Desmond Deacon, on the 5th day of May 1996, dishonestly obtained from David Dawson the sum of £500 with the intention of permanently depriving David Dawson thereof by deception, namely, by falsely representing that he, Desmond Deacon, was entitled to the sum of £500 in payment for goods delivered to the employee of David Dawson.

(5) **Handling**

Statement of Offence

Handling stolen goods, contrary to Section 22(1) of the Theft Act 1968.

Particulars of Offence

Eleanor Etheridge, on the 6th day of June 1996, dishonestly received certain stolen goods, namely a cheque card and cheque book belonging to Ethel Elden, knowing or believing the same to be stolen goods.

or

Statement of Offence

Handling stolen goods, contrary to Section 22(1) of the Theft Act 1968.

Particulars of Offence

Eleanor Etheridge, on the 6th day of June 1996, dishonestly undertook or assisted in the retention, removal, disposal or realisation of certain stolen goods, namely a cheque card and cheque book belonging to Ethel Elden, by or for the benefit of another, or dishonestly arranged so to do, knowing or believing the same to be stolen goods.

(6) **Criminal Damage**

Statement of Offence

Damaging property, contrary to Section 1(1) of the Criminal Damage Act 1971.

Particulars of Offence

Frederick Fraser, on the 7th day of July 1996, without lawful excuse, damaged a motor car belonging to Felicity Falstaff, intending to damage such property or being reckless as to whether such property would be damaged.

(7) **Arson**

Statement of Offence

Arson, contrary to Section 1(1) and (3) of the Criminal Damage Act 1971.

Particulars of Offence

Gerald Goodman, on the 8th day of August 1996, without lawful excuse damaged by fire a boat belonging to George Gladstone, intending to damage such property or being reckless as to whether such property would be damaged.

(8) **Assault ABH**

Statement of Offence

Assault occasioning actual bodily harm, contrary to Section 47 of the Offences Against the Person Act 1861.

Particulars of Offence

Harold Hewitt, on the 9th day of September 1996, assaulted Henry Howard, thereby occasioning him actual bodily harm.

(9) **Wounding**

Statement of Offence

Unlawful wounding, contrary to Section 20 of the Offences Against the Person Act 1861.

Particulars of Offence

Ian Inglis, on the 10th day of October 1996, unlawfully and maliciously wounded Ingrid Inman.

(10) **Wounding with Intent**

Statement of Offence

Wounding with intent, contrary to Section 18 of the Offences Against the Person Act 1861.

Particulars of Offence

James Jarvis, on the 11th day of November 1996, unlawfully wounded John Jameson with intent to do him grievous bodily harm.

(11) **GBH with Intent**

Statement of Offence

Causing grievous bodily harm with intent, contrary to Section 18 of the Offences Against the Person Act 1861.

Particulars of Offence

Kevin Killick, on the 12th day of December 1996, unlawfully caused grievous bodily harm to Keith Kitson, with intent to do him grievous bodily harm.

(12) **Possession of Drugs**

Statement of Offence

Possessing a controlled drug, contrary to Section 5(2) of the Misuse of Drugs Act 1971.

Particulars of Offence

Laura Lyle, on the 13th day of January 1996, had in her possession a controlled drug, namely cannabis resin.

9.1.4 WHO DRAWS UP THE INDICTMENT?

Usually, an employee of the Crown Prosecution Service drafts the indictment and sends it to the Crown Court with the committal papers. Where the case is sufficiently complex, counsel may be instructed to advise on the indictment. In any event, it is checked by an officer of the Crown Court to ensure that there has been a committal for trial, a notice of transfer or a voluntary bill of indictment. Provided that the defendant is properly in the charge of the Crown Court by one of these routes, the appropriate officer is obliged to sign. Until he or she does so, the document is, strictly speaking, a 'bill of indictment'. After signature by the Crown Court officer, it is an indictment.

Once counsel is instructed in the case (either to draft the indictment or, in due course, for trial), it is his or her responsibility to ensure that the indictment is correct (*R* v *Moss* [1995] Crim LR 828).

The bill of indictment should be preferred (i.e. delivered to an appropriate officer of the Crown Court) within 28 days of committal. The period may be extended by an appropriate officer for 28 days, or by a Crown Court judge for any period.

9.1.5 WHAT COUNTS CAN BE INCLUDED?

The person drafting the bill of indictment will read the evidence from the committal proceedings, decide what indictable offences are disclosed, and draft the indictment on that basis. Crucially, the indictment is *not* limited to the offences upon which the defendant was committed. Even if the magistrates dismissed a particular charge, it can be included in the indictment. Of course, that will only be done rarely, and must be based on the evidence.

By proviso (i) to s. 2(2) of the Administration of Justice (Miscellaneous Provisions) Act 1933, any charge upon which the accused was not committed can only form part of the indictment if it is 'in substitution for or in addition to' a count upon which he was committed. Further, any such extra counts must be of a kind that can lawfully be joined in that indictment, e.g. such joinder must be in accordance with r. 9 of the Indictment Rules (see **9.2.1** and *R* v *Lombardi* [1989] 1 WLR 73 below.

9.1.6 CHECKLISTS

In order to identify the offences disclosed by a particular set of facts, it is vital to know the elements of the common offences. A series of checklists of the elements necessary for some of the more common indictable offences follows:

Checklists of Elements

(**Note:** These are a rough guide only, and should be compared with the precise wording of the statute.)

(1) **Theft** The elements (see Theft Act 1968, s. 1):

(a) dishonestly

(b) appropriates

(c) property

(d) belonging to another

(e) with intention of permanently depriving.

(2) **Robbery** The elements (see Theft Act 1968, s. 8):

(a) theft (see '**Theft**' above) and

(b) immediately before or at the time of the theft

(c) uses or threatens force in order to commit the theft

(d) on any person.

(3) **Burglary** The elements (see Theft Act 1968, s. 9), **either** (s. 9(1)(a)):

(a) entry

(b) to any (part of a) building

(c) as a trespasser

(d) with intent to

(i) steal (see **'Theft'** above) or

(ii) inflict grievous bodily harm (see below) or

(iii) rape or

(iv) do unlawful damage to the building or its contents.

or (s. 9(1)(b))

(a) having entered

(b) any (part of a) building

(c) as a trespasser

(d) (i) (attempts to) steal any contents (see **'Theft'** above) or

(ii) (attempts to) inflict grevious bodily harm (see below).

(4) **Deception** The elements (see Theft Act 1968, s. 15):

(a) by

(b) deception

(c) dishonestly

(d) obtains

(e) property

(f) belonging to another

(g) with intention of permanently depriving.

(5) **Handling** The elements (Theft Act 1968, s. 22), **either** Receiving

(a) otherwise than in the course of stealing

(b) dishonestly

(c) receives

(d) stolen goods

(e) (i) knowing or

(ii) believing them to be stolen.

or Handling

(a) otherwise than in the course of stealing

(b) dishonestly

(c) (i) undertakes or arranges to undertake or

(ii) assists or arranges to assist in

(d) (i) retention

(ii) removal

(iii) disposal or

(iv) realisation

(e) of stolen goods

(f) (i) knowing or

(ii) believing them to be stolen

(g) by or for the benefit of another.

(6) **Criminal damage** The elements (see Criminal Damage Act 1971, s. 1):

(a) without lawful excuse

(b) (i) destroys or

(ii) damages

(c) property

(d) belonging to another

(e) (i) intentionally or

(ii) recklessly.

(7) **Offensive weapon** The elements (see Prevention of Crime Act 1953, s. 1):

(a) without

(i) lawful authority or

(ii) reasonable excuse

(b) has with him

(c) in any public place

(d) any article

(i) made or

(ii) adapted or

(iii) intended by him to cause injury to the person.

(**Note**: In (a) the legal burden of proof is on the accused.)

(8) **Assault occasioning actual bodily harm** The elements (see Offences against the Person Act 1861, s. 47):

(a) does an act

(b) (i) intentionally or

(ii) recklessly

(c) which applies to another

(d) unlawful force

(e) thereby

(f) occasioning

(g) that other

(h) actual bodily harm.

(9) **Wounding, etc.** The elements (see Offences against the Person Act 1861, s. 20):

(a) unlawfully and maliciously

(b) (i) wounds or

(ii) inflicts grievous bodily harm

(c) (on) any other person

(10) **Section 18 wounding, etc. with intent** The elements (see Offences against the Person Act 1861, s. 18):

(a) unlawfully and maliciously

(b) (i) wounds or

(ii) causes grievous bodily harm

(c) (to) any other person

(d) with intent to

(i) cause GBH or

(ii) resist arrest/detention or

(iii) prevent arrest/detention of anyone.

9.2 Joinder of Offences and Defendants

An indictment may contain one count only (as in our examples so far) or it may contain several. Where a defendant is alleged to have committed more than one offence, it may be very important to decide whether the offences are tried together on one indictment, or separately, by different juries, on different indictments. Frequently, the defence is anxious to avoid a joint trial so that the jury does not know about the other matters alleged against the defendant. On the other hand, a single trial of several offences can save a lot of court time and minimise inconvenience to witnesses.

There are two separate but related issues:

(a) When can different offences be joined in one indictment?

(b) When can two or more defendants be joined in one indictment?

9.2.1 WHEN CAN OFFENCES BE JOINED IN A SINGLE INDICTMENT?

Under the Indictment Rules 1971, r. 9, the rule is that separate counts can be included in an indictment if:

(a) They are founded on the same facts (e.g. the defendant is alleged to have taken someone's car without permission, driven it dangerously, and stolen the radio-cassette on leaving the car. The indictment would usually include counts of theft, dangerous driving, and taking a motor vehicle without consent — the last count being added by virtue of s. 40 of the Criminal Justice Act 1988).

(b) They are part of a series of offences of the same or similar character (e.g. the defendant is alleged to have been involved in a 'shoplifting expedition' from a number of shops on the same afternoon).

As far as (b) is concerned, the courts have given a wide interpretation to the phrase 'series of offences of the same or similar character'. In *Ludlow* v *MPC* (1970) 54 Cr App R 233, HL, L was charged with attempted theft from a public house in Acton and robbery at a different public house in Acton. The second offence occurred 16 days after the first. The House of Lords held:

(i) that two offences can constitute a 'series' for the purposes of r. 9 of the Indictment Rules;

(ii) that in deciding whether the offences are similar in character, both the law and the facts should be taken into account. For the offences to be similar, there must be a nexus between them;

(iii) that in this case, the offences were similar in law and fact. Both had the same ingredient of actual or attempted theft. They involved public houses in the same neighbourhood. The time interval was only 16 days.

Although r. 9 is widely interpreted, its requirements must be carried out. For example in *R* v *Hudson* (1952) 36 Cr App R 94, the indictment contained counts for:

(a) breaking and entering (now burglary);

(b) receiving; and

(c) criminal damage.

It was held wrong to include the count for criminal damage, which was unconnected, on the facts, with any breaking and entering.

Even if the counts all fit one or other of these two rules for joinder, the judge has a discretion to 'sever' (under Indictments Act 1915, s. 5) and order separate trials if the defendant would be embarrassed or prejudiced by a joint trial. If the counts are tried together, the judge will in any event explain to the jury that it must come to a separate decision on each count, and exclude from its mind evidence relevant only to another count.

9.2.2 JOINDER OF DEFENDANTS

When can two or more defendants be indicted jointly? There are two different situations:

(a) A single count in the indictment charges two or more defendants with committing a single offence. This can be done when they were parties to the offence in question. It does not matter whether each was a principal offender. A defendant who aided, abetted, counselled or procured the commission of the offence can be charged in the same count with the principal offender(s). In fact, by s. 8 of the Accessories and Abettors Act 1861, a secondary party is liable to be 'tried, indicted and punished as a principal offender'. Hence, if A acted as lookout while B and C burgled the premises, all three can be jointly charged in a single count alleging that 'A, B and C, having entered a building . . . as trespassers, stole therein'. Whilst A did not actually enter the building, the prosecution case is that he or she is guilty on the basis of joint enterprise.

(b) The defendants may be charged in separate counts, but in the same indictment, provided that there is a linking factor between the counts. Assume, for example, in the burglary dealt with above, D handles the proceeds of the burglary. He or she must be charged in a separate count, since the offence is different. But the offence is linked to the burglary, so A, B, C, and D may be charged in the same indictment.

Again, the trial judge has a discretion to sever the trials. This is more likely to happen in situation (b) above than in situation (a).

9.2.3 ALTERNATIVE COUNTS

Sometimes the facts alleged by the prosecution will be open to two or more conclusions, each of which would be consistent with finding the defendant guilty, but of an offence which is more serious or less serious, e.g. D assaults P, injuring her. The extent of the injury, and D's intention, is in dispute. He or she can be charged in a single indictment with counts alleging:

(a) Causing grievous bodily harm with intent to cause grievous bodily harm (Offences against the Person Act 1861, s. 18).

(b) Inflicting grievous bodily harm (s. 20).

(c) Assault occasioning actual bodily harm (s. 47).

These offences are in decreasing order of gravity. When summing up, the judge will direct the jury to consider count (a). If that is proved to the necessary standard, the jury can disregard counts (b) and (c). If it is not, it should then consider (b). Again, if the jury is satisfied so that it is sure about (b) that ends the matter. If not, it must consider (c).

It is also possible that the indictment may contain alternative counts of roughly equal gravity. A common example is the pairing of theft and handling, e.g. where D is found in possession of stolen goods and may or may not be the original thief. The jury should then be asked to convict on one or the other. It may not convict on both, since theft and handling are mutually contradictory (s. 22 of the Theft Act 1968 lays down that handling must be otherwise than in the course of theft). The two alternative forms of handling are also commonly paired in an indictment (see Specimen Count (5) in **9.1.3** above).

9.2.4 DUPLICITY

Each count must, on its face, allege one offence only. If two or more offences are wrapped up in a single count, then that count is 'duplicitous' or 'bad for duplicity'. The defence can bring a motion to quash that count, which should not be put to the defendant in that form. For example, a count alleging that 'Oliver Oakland assaulted Oswald Oxley on the 16th day of April 1995, and Otis Osprey on the 17th day of April 1995, thereby occasioning them actual bodity harm' is bad for duplicity and should be quashed. The reason is simple. How should Oliver plead if he committed one assault but not the other? Even if Oliver denies both assaults, what verdict should the jury return if it is sure he committed one but not the other? To proceed with a count such as this would be a recipe for confusion.

But note that several different acts can together constitute one offence, in certain circumstances. For example, in *R* v *Wilson* (1979) 69 Cr App R 83, the indictment contained two counts for theft. The first alleged that W stole from Debenhams, on 10 August 1977, three jumpers, a pair of shorts, two pairs of trousers, four dimmer switches and a cassette tape. The second alleged that on the same day he stole from Boots eight records and a bottle of aftershave lotion. At the close of the prosecution case, the defence submitted that the evidence called showed that the stolen goods had come from different departments of the stores in question. The counts were, it was argued, bad for duplicity, and there should be a separate count in relation to the goods stolen from each department. The submission was rejected by the trial judge, W appealed, and his appeal failed. He had 'entirely failed to satisfy' the court that either of the counts complained of disclosed more than one offence. Browne LJ concluded that 'Whether there is one or more offence disclosed is really a question of fact and degree'.

9.2.5 OVERLOADING THE INDICTMENT

There are two main situations in which the prosecution may be said to be 'overloading the indictment':

(a) A number of different defendants and/or offences may be included so that an unnecessarily long and complicated trial ensues. In *R* v *Novac and Others* (1977) 65 Cr App R 107 the Court of Appeal said that it was convinced that nothing short of the criterion of absolute necessity could justify the imposition of a very long trial upon the court. It considered that the trial should have been split into five separate trials.

(b) What the defendant did may make him or her guilty of a number of different offences, as a matter of strict law. The prosecution should nevertheless consider carefully what the 'real' offence(s) were, and confine the counts in the indictment accordingly. Only if there is uncertainty should alternative counts be included (*R* v *Staton* [1983] Crim LR 190).

The Court of Appeal has perceived a particular problem in relation to counts of conspiracy, where the indictment charges conspiracy in addition to the substantive offence. This offends against the principles outlined in both (a) and (b) above, since it may lead to an inordinately long trial (as it did in *Novac*), and may also mean that the defendant is charged with two offences where one would be appropriate to deal with the wrongdoing. As a result, the following Practice Direction was issued:

***Practice Direction (Crime: Conspiracy)* [1977] 1 WLR 537**

1. In any case where an indictment contains substantive counts and a related conspiracy count, the judge should require the prosecution to justify the joinder, or,

> *failing justification, to elect whether to proceed on the substantive or on the conspiracy counts.*
> *2. A joinder is justified for this purpose if the judge considers that the interests of justice demand it.*

It follows that the prosecution will have to justify the inclusion of a substantive count and a related conspiracy count. If they are not justified, then the prosecution must elect one on which to proceed (see *R* v *Watts*, *The Times*, 14 April 1995).

9.3 Voluntary Bills of Indictment

So far, we have been dealing with an indictment drafted on the basis of committal proceedings. There are two other routes by which indictable offences can come to the Crown Court for trial. One is by preferment of a voluntary bill of indictment (see **6.4.3**). The other is by notice of transfer (see **6.2**). The rules about duplicity, joinder, etc., apply equally to indictments which arise in either of these ways.

9.4 Amending the Indictment

The court's power to amend the indictment is governed by s. 5 of the Indictments Act 1915, which reads in part:

> **5**(1) *Where, before trial, or at any stage of a trial, it appears to the court that the indictment is defective, the court shall make such order for the amendment of the indictment as the court thinks necessary to meet the circumstances of the case, unless, having regard to the merits of the case, the required amendments cannot be made without injustice . . .*

Prior to amendment, it is usual for the judge to invite the views of counsel on the proposed amendment.

The power to amend is a wide-ranging one, subject to the court being satisfied that there is no injustice occasioned thereby. It includes, for example, the substitution of a different offence for that originally charged in the indictment, or even the inclusion of an additional count for an offence not previously charged. Amendment can be made at any stage of the trial, although the longer the interval between arraignment and amendment the less likely it is that the amendment can be made without injustice (*R* v *Johal and Ram* (1972) 56 Cr App R 346).

The crucial point is whether the amendment might result in injustice. Contrast:

(a) *R* v *Harris* (1976) 62 Cr App R 28, CA. After the Crown had closed its case and a submission of no case had been rejected, the trial judge directed amendment of the indictment. The count in question alleged an express false representation ('. . . he had sufficient funds to pay the debt. . .'). It was amended to allege a false representation by conduct ('. . . he intended to pay the said sum . . .'). The Court of Appeal held that no injustice could have resulted.

(b) *R* v *Thomas* [1983] Crim LR 619, CA. At the end of the prosecution case, a count of receiving was added to an indictment alleging theft. The facts disclosed recent possession of stolen property. The Court of Appeal quashed the conviction. It was not possible to say that the conduct of the defence up to the close of the prosecution case could not have been hampered in some way by the fact that the indictment did not include the second count. Injustice may have been caused.

One way in which injustice may be caused by late amendment of the indictment is that defence counsel's cross-examination may have been made on the wrong basis.

9.5 Quashing the Indictment

The indictment (or a count in it) can be quashed if, for example, the bill has been preferred without authority, or if the count is bad on its face for duplicity. Where the indictment includes a count on which the justices did not commit for trial, that is not in itself objectionable (see **9.1.5**). But if the evidence upon which the prosecution applied for committal does not disclose a case to answer on that count, the defendant may apply for the count to be quashed. The judge will read the papers in order to decide whether there is a case to answer. If there is not, then that count will be quashed.

This is an exception to the general rule that the trial judge at the Crown Court may not go behind the result of the committal proceedings to decide whether the indictment is correct.

As far as the defence is concerned, a motion to quash is unlikely to be of much practical use. The prosecution is often able to prevent the indictment from being quashed by amending it, e.g., splitting in two a count which appears to be bad for duplicity. In any event, a successful motion will result, not in acquittal, but merely in the accused being discharged. Nevertheless, a successful motion to quash at least has the merit of ensuring that the issues to be decided are clear.

9.6 Effect of Invalid Indictment

Assume that the indictment is invalid because it joins two sets of counts contrary to r. 9 of the Indictment Rules. One way of proceeding is for the court to amend the indictment by exercise of its power under s. 5(1) of the Indictments Act 1915 to delete the counts which have no nexus. There can then be a trial on the remaining counts. A separate trial of the deleted counts will not be possible, however, without a voluntary bill of indictment. This cannot be ordered by the trial judge unless he or she is a High Court judge and acts under the appropriate procedure. (See *R* v *Newland* [1988] QB 402.)

Provided that the original indictment is stayed rather than quashed, however, the trial judge (whether a High Court judge or not) may give leave to the Crown to prefer two or more fresh indictments out of time, provided that each complies with r. 9 of the Indictment Rules, and is based upon the depositions and statements at committal proceedings (*R* v *Follett* [1989] QB 338).

9.7 The Arraignment

At the start of a trial on indictment, the defendant is arraigned. The indictment is read over to the defendant by the clerk. After each count, the clerk will ask the defendant whether the plea is 'guilty' or 'not guilty'. (See **11.2**.)

The defendant must be present for the arraignment, and a bench warrant for arrest will be issued by the judge if he or she has failed to surrender to bail.

9.8 Fitness to Plead

Occasionally the question arises whether the defendant is fit to plead. A defendant is not unfit merely because he or she is mentally disturbed, or suffering from amnesia and hence unable to remember the incident. The question is: Can the defendant comprehend the proceedings of the trial so as to be able to make a defence against the charge? Crucial in determining this will be a decision as to whether the defendant is able to understand the evidence and instruct legal representatives. If the issue is raised, a jury will be specially empanelled to make this decision. The court is permitted to postpone the consideration of whether the defendant is fit to plead until any time up to the opening of the defence case, if it is in the defendant's interests to do so (Criminal Procedure (Insanity) Act 1964, s. 4(2)).

Where the jury has determined that the defendant is unfit to plead, then the question that must be decided is whether he or she committed the *actus reus* ('did the act or made the omission charged against him'). If the jury is satisfied that the defendant did commit the *actus reus*, it must find accordingly. If it is not, it must acquit (Criminal Procedure (insanity) Act 1964, s. 4, as inserted in 1991).

Under s. 5 of the 1964 Act (as amended in 1991), if the accused is found unfit to plead, and the jury determines that he or she did the act or made the omission as charged, then the court may make:

(a) an admission order to a hospital approved by the Secretary of State;

(b) a guardianship order under the Mental Health Act 1983;

(c) a supervision and treatment order; or

(d) an order for the accused's absolute discharge.

(See **Chapter 23**.)

See also D. Carson, 'Prosecuting People with Mental Handicaps' [1989] Crim LR 87 and R. D. Mackay, 'The Decline of Disability in Relation to the Trial' [1991] Crim LR 87.

9.9 Plea of Guilty

If the defendant pleads guilty to all the charges, then the sentencing procedure begins. If he or she pleads guilty to some charges and not guilty to others, then sentencing on the guilty plea(s) is postponed until the trial on the not guilty pleas(s) has ended.

What if one defendant pleads guilty and another pleads not guilty? The usual course is for sentencing to take place at the end of the trial of the defendant who has pleaded not guilty. The judge is then in a better position to sentence the defendant who has pleaded guilty, in the light of evidence which has been heard. (See **11.2.5** for details.)

9.10 Plea of Not Guilty

If the defendant pleads not guilty to some or all of the charges, a trial will normally commence. But sometimes the prosecution will not proceed further. There are two main possibilities:

(a) The prosecution offers no evidence. The defendant is then entitled to a verdict of not guilty. This course would be taken where, for example, evidence has come to light since committal which suggests the defendant is not guilty.

(b) The prosecution asks that the count(s) to which the defendant has pleaded not guilty remain on file, marked 'not to be proceeded with without leave of this court or of the Court of Appeal'. The prosecution usually adopts this course when the defendant has pleaded guilty to some counts, but not all, and when proving the case would be a waste of court time in view of the guilty pleas entered. In practice, the counts left on the file are not reactivated unless, for example, the Court of Appeal sets aside the convictions on the other counts because the defendant's guilty pleas were involuntary (see **9.16** and **11.2.3**).

9.11 Ambiguous Pleas

The defendant may give an ambiguous answer when asked how he or she pleads, e.g. to a count of assault occasioning actual bodily harm: 'Guilty, but I didn't mean to hit him.' If so, the judge should explain the elements of the offence and try to ensure that the defendant pleads unambiguously. If the plea remains ambiguous, a plea of 'not guilty' should be entered (compare **5.1.4** and see **11.2.6**).

9.12 Guilty to an Alternative Offence

9.12.1 ALTERNATIVE OFFENCE INCLUDED IN OFFENCE CHARGED

Under the Criminal Law Act 1967, s. 6, if the defendant is charged with one offence, he or she may plead guilty to, or be found guilty of, any offence included in the offence charged. This can happen where the alternative offence is included (either expressly or by implication) in the offence charged.

For example, the offence of robbery is committed when a person commits theft together with actual or threatened violence. Therefore, if a person is charged with robbery, he or she may be found guilty of theft by the jury or plead 'guilty to theft, but not guilty to robbery'.

9.12.2 PROSECUTION PROCEDURE

If the defendant wishes, for example, to plead guilty to theft, but not guilty to robbery as charged, the prosecution can either:

(a) Accept the plea. The defendant is acquitted on the offence charged, and has pleaded guilty (and hence falls to be sentenced) on the alternative offence.

(b) Reject the plea. A plea of not guilty is entered, and a trial will be held. The guilty plea to the lesser offence must in these circumstances be treated as a nullity (*R* v *Hazeltine* [1967] 2 QB 857).

Note that if prosecuting counsel is minded to accept the plea, he or she will usually ask the judge whether it is proper to do so. The judge's decision on this point must then be accepted. A defendant often offers a plea to an offence he or she sees as less important than the one charged and which is thus likely to attract a lighter sentence.

9.12.3 WHERE DEFENDANT DISPUTES PART OF PARTICULARS

What if the defendant wishes to plead guilty to the offence charged, but disputes some part of the particulars? For example, Tommy Tucker is charged with the theft of £500 from Terence Thompson. He says he stole only £150. The position is that he should plead guilty, but counsel on his behalf should put forward Tommy's version in mitigation. The judge *may* then wish to hold a '*Newton*-style' hearing on the facts before sentencing. (See **14.4**.)

9.13 Pleas to Alternative Counts

Look again at the section above on 'Alternative Counts' (**9.2.3**). Where the defendant offers a guilty plea to the charge under s. 18, it would clearly be a waste of time to put the counts under s. 20 and s. 47. So this is not done, and the alternatives are not proceeded with. But if the defendant pleads guilty to, say, the s. 47 offence, the prosecution may well wish to proceed to trial on the s. 18 and s. 20 offences. A trial on those disputed counts will then follow. Such counts should therefore appear in the indictment in *decreasing* order of gravity, *viz*, s. 18, then s. 20, then s. 47.

9.14 Other Pleas

There are other pleas which occur very rarely in practice:

(a) *Autrefois acquit* and *autrefois convict* (see below).

(b) Pardon, i.e. the defendant has been pardoned for the offence.

(c) Demurrer (a written version of the motion to quash the indictment).

(d) Plea to the jurisdiction, i.e. the court has no power to try the case.

9.14.1 THE MEANING OF *AUTREFOIS ACQUIT* AND *AUTREFOIS CONVICT*

In essence, these pleas aver that the defendant has, on a previous occasion, been acquitted or convicted of the offence charged. The plea is made in writing by defence counsel on behalf of the defendant, normally before arraignment. If the prosecution does not accept the plea, it joins issue through a written replication, signed by an officer of the Crown Court.

The question of whether *autrefois* applied was formerly decided by a jury. Now, by CJA 1988, s. 122: 'Where an accused pleads *autrefois acquit* or *autrefois convict* it shall be for the judge, without the presence of a jury, to decide the issue.'

If the judge decides that *autrefois* does not apply, then the indictment is put in the usual manner, and the defendant pleads guilty or not guilty.

The principle behind a plea of *autrefois* is the rule against double jeopardy — nobody shall be tried to acquittal or conviction for the same offence twice. That principle applies also to summary proceedings in the magistrates' court. There, however, there is no special plea or procedure — the issues are canvassed on a not guilty plea.

9.14.2 WHEN DOES *AUTREFOIS* APPLY?

The leading case is *Connelly* v *DPP* [1946] AC 1254. The principles which it lays down may (at the risk of over-simplification) be summarised as follows:

(a) The defendant cannot be tried for an offence identical in law and on the facts to one of which he or she has been acquitted or convicted previously.

(b) The defendant cannot be tried for a crime of which he or she could, on a previous indictment, have been convicted by way of a verdict of guilty of a lesser offence. So if the defendant is acquitted of murdering V, he or she can raise *autrefois* if subsequently charged with the manslaughter of V. The reason is that the verdict of manslaughter was one which was open to the jury in the earlier trial. By deciding to acquit, it implicitly found the defendant not guilty of manslaughter as well as murder.

(c) The defendant cannot be tried for a crime, proof of which would necessarily, and as a matter of law, entail proof of another crime of which he or she has already been acquitted.

9.14.3 THE JUDGE'S DISCRETION

Even where a prosecution does not strictly fall within the three categories above, there are circumstances in which the judge may exercise a discretion to halt the prosecution as oppressive in view of previous proceedings against the defendant.

This might happen, for example, where the offence charged is *substantially or in effect* the same as one of which the defendant has previously been acquitted or convicted. In

Connelly, the court was divided as to whether such cases fell within the ambit of *autrefois*. In any event, as Lords Devlin and Pearce pointed out, there is a judicial discretion to stop a prosecution which offends the principles underlying *autrefois*. For example, in *R* v *Moxon-Tritsch* [1988] Crim LR 46, the defendant was the driver in an accident in which her passengers were killed. She was fined and disqualified for careless driving. A private prosecution was then brought for causing death by reckless driving. The trial judge held that the proceedings were oppressive, and ordered that the count lie on the file marked 'not to be proceeded with'.

9.14.4 ISSUE ESTOPPEL

Assume that a plea of *autrefois* is not available to the defendant on the above principles. Is the prosecution estopped from raising an issue of fact which has been decided in the defendant's favour at an earlier trial?

In *DPP* v *Humphreys* (1976) 73 Cr App R 95, the facts were that H had been charged with driving while disqualified. The only issue at trial was whether a police officer had correctly identified H as the driver on that particular day. H was acquitted and then charged with perjury for swearing that he had not driven during the year in question. The officer was allowed to give the same evidence. He was supported by other witnesses (not reasonably available at the first trial) who testified that H had driven on other occasions during that year. The House of Lords upheld H's conviction for perjury (reversing the Court of Appeal). It held:

(a) it was not a case of 'double jeopardy';

(b) nor was it an abuse of the court's process; and

(c) the doctrine of issue estoppel has no application to the criminal law.

9.15 Plea Bargaining

Frequently, defence and prosecution counsel will have discussions as to the charges, which may result in agreement being reached. The usual basis of such agreement is either:

(a) If the defendant pleads guilty to one or more counts in the indictment, the prosecution will not proceed with the remainder (see **9.9** above).

(b) If the defendant pleads guilty to a lesser offence, the prosecution will accept the plea, and not press for trial on the more serious offence (see **9.12** above).

This form of plea bargaining is widely accepted by the courts. It saves time and money, and avoids what can be the agonising experience of a trial for the defendant and witnesses. (Such discussions usually occur before a trial starts but can happen at any time before the jury retires to consider its verdict.)

For a case where the Court of Appeal said that the Crown was clearly wrong on the facts to accept a plea to a lesser offence, see *R* v *Stubbs* (1989) 88 Cr App R 53. See also the ***Professional Conduct Manual***, *R* v *Turner* [1970] 2 QB 321 and para. 1.6 of Annexe H in the Code of Conduct.

Sometimes there is discussion between prosecution and defence not only as to the counts in the indictment to which the defendant will plead guilty, but as to the facts which form the basis of the plea. On occasion this may result in an agreement as to the facts on which the plea of guilty is entered. In *R* v *Beswick*, *Times*, 10 October 1995, the Court of Appeal dealt with the situation where agreement had been reached between prosecution and defence counsel as to the facts upon which a plea of guilty was to be based, and the judge declined to give effect to that agreement. Their Lordships set out five principles for the guidance of the court in such cases:

(1) Whenever the court has to sentence an offender it should seek to do so on a basis which is true. The prosecution should not, therefore, lend itself to any agreement with the defence which was founded on an unreal and untrue set of facts.

(2) When that had happened, the judge was entitled to direct the trial of an issue (i.e. a *Newton* hearing (see **14.4.2**)) in order to determine the true factual basis for sentence.

(3) Such a decision did not create a ground upon which a defendant should be allowed to vacate his or her plea of guilty, provided he or she does admit his or her guilt of the offence to which he or she has pleaded guilty.

(4) The decision that there should be a trial of an issue meant that the judge was entitled to expect the assistance of prosecuting counsel in presenting evidence, and in testing any evidence called by the defence. The agreement which the prosecution had previously entered into with the defence must be viewed as conditional on the approval of the judge. If the judge's approval is not forthcoming, the defence cannot seek to hold the prosecution to the agreement.

(5) Before the trial of an issue was embarked on, the judge might consider whether there was any part of the agreement by which the prosecution should be bound. Counsel should also consider which issues are to be tried, and which of the prosecution statements were relevant to them.

9.16 Involuntary Pleas

If the defendant is subjected to pressure, so that he or she pleads guilty involuntarily, then the plea is a nullity. On appeal, the Court of Appeal will quash the conviction and order a retrial.

Such pressure may allegedly have come from defence counsel, e.g. defence counsel says to the defendant 'You have no chance of being acquitted. Whether you are guilty or not, you should plead guilty. That way you will get a more lenient sentence'. That would make any subsequent plea of guilty a nullity. Of course, counsel should advise on the strength of the prosecution case and the credit which the defendant will get for a plea of guilty. But the defendant should be left in no doubt that it is his or her decision. It is safest to say 'Only plead guilty if you are guilty'.

The pressure to plead guilty may be alleged to have come from the judge. The classic case is where counsel goes to see the judge in his or her private room, and the defendant then decides to plead guilty as a result of what counsel says took place (see **9.17** and **14.1**). See also para. 2.3 of Annexe H in the Code of Conduct.

9.17 Seeing the Judge about a Plea

Sometimes counsel will ask to see the judge in his or her private room in order to get an indication on sentence. Many judges will not agree to this, and the Court of Appeal has expressed reservations about the practice. If the judge agrees to see counsel for this purpose:

(a) Counsel for both the prosecution and the defence should be present.

(b) A shorthand writer should be present, so there can be no dispute about what was said.

(c) Any indication by the judge will usually be in the broadest terms, e.g. 'On what I have read and heard from you, I do not think an immediate custodial sentence will be imposed'.

(d) There should be no indication of a more severe sentence in the event of not guilty plea or a more lenient one for a guilty plea.

The most obvious situation in which such a course is adopted is where the defendant really knows that he or she is guilty, but is afraid to plead guilty because of the fear of a custodial sentence. Once the air has been cleared by the judge indicating to counsel that prison is not in prospect, the defendant can decide on a plea with clearer judgment. The process can lead to misunderstanding, however, and the Court of Appeal has emphasised point (d) above. It has also stressed that such discussions should take place only where necessary. (See *R* v *Smith* [1990] Crim LR 354 and, generally, *R* v *Turner* [1970] 2 QB 321. See also **14.1** and the ***Professional Conduct Manual***.)

9.18 Changing the Plea

At any stage of the trial, the defendant may change his or her plea from not guilty to guilty. Defence counsel asks for the indictment to be put again, it is put, and the defendant pleads guilty to the count in question. The jury then returns a formal verdict of guilty on the judge's direction. The defendant will get some credit for a guilty plea, but not as much as if the plea had been guilty from the start.

At any time before sentence is passed, the defendant can also change a guilty plea to not guilty with the judge's consent. One reason for consenting might be that the defendant was not represented at the time of the original plea.

9.19 Exercises

(**Note**: These are intended for self-assessment. Suggested solutions may be found in the **Appendix** of this Manual.)

(1) Michael Masters is seen on 14 February 1996 trying to take something from Mary Martin's handbag. When interviewed by the police, he tells them that he wanted to take hold of her wallet, but withdrew his hand when he saw he was being watched. Draft an indictment for trial at the Bluebridge Crown Court containing one count only.

(2) Would it make any difference to your answer if the Bluebridge magistrates had dismissed the charge in relation to the handbag, but committed Michael for trial on a charge of receiving stolen credit cards found on him at arrest?

(3) Noreen Naylor is lawfully searched by the police on 15 March 1996. They find in her jeans pocket 18.6 grams of cocaine. Draft an indictment containing a single count, for trial in the Newtown Crown Court.

(4) Peter Parsley is charged in an indictment containing a single count alleging that 'on the 18th day of May 1996 he raped or indecently assaulted Polly Pepper'. What should the defence do?

(5) Robert Rawlings is arrested as he runs from the scene of a burglary of a house. On him he has a set of skeleton keys which the police say were used to effect entry to the house in question. Robert has already been charged with robbery as a result of a street mugging which took place two months previously. Should the offences of burglary, going equipped and robbery be charged in the same indictment?

(6) Would it make any difference to your answer to (5) if Richard Rendell is also charged with robbery arising from the street mugging, the allegation being that he acted as look-out for Robert?

(7) Assume that you act for Richard, in the situation outlined in (5) and (6) above. Assume also that Robert has, in an interview with the police, stated that the

robbery was all Richard's idea. What application can you make on Richard's behalf at the trial of both on an indictment for the various offences?

(8) Simon Schofield is found, two hours after the burglary of a jeweller's shop on 19 June 1996, with some of the proceeds of the burglary. A man similar in appearance to Simon was seen running away from the jeweller's just after the alarm went off. Draw up an indictment for Simon's trial in the Blackbridge Crown Court. The goods taken from the jeweller's shop consist of six necklaces and four bracelets. When found, Simon had one necklace and all the bracelets. The jeweller's shop is at 108 High Road, Blackbridge, and is owned by Stanley Sutton.

Multiple-choice Questions (based on Chapters 6 and 9)

1. Astrid is charged alone with shoplifting. She elects jury trial and is committed for trial to the Crown Court. She wants to get maximum publicity for the case in order to encourage any defence witnesses to come forward. She asks for reporting restrictions to be lifted. The magistrates:

[A] must grant her application unless the prosecution opposes it;
[B] must refuse the application if they believe it will prejudice her right to a fair trial;
[C] must grant her application;
[D] must grant her application if it is in the interests of justice to do so.

2. Charles is charged in an indictment containing counts of causing grievous bodily harm with intent and forgery (the alleged offences relate to unrelated factual situations). At Charles' trial his counsel objects to the indictment on the ground that the counts are improperly joined. The trial judge (i) rules that the counts are improperly joined and (ii) orders that the indictment be severed.

The judge was:

[A] Right on point (i) and acting beyond his powers on point (ii).
[B] Right on point (i) and acting within his powers on point (ii).
[C] Wrong on point (i) and acting beyond his powers on point (ii).
[D] Wrong on point (i) and acting within his powers on point (ii).

Tutorial Questions

R v *LEWIS and others*

Aim: To consider on behalf of the prosecution which counts can properly be included in one (or more) indictments against Lewis and the others. After reading the papers carefully, you should consider what counts should be included in the indictment(s). Once you have done this, try to draft your own indictment, setting the counts out properly (in terms both of form and content).

IN THE CROWN COURT SITTING AT LEWES

R v *Lewis and others*

Instructions to Counsel for the Prosecution

Counsel has herewith:

1. Bundle of depositions and witness statements
2. Antecedent history of the accused

Counsel is instructed

(i) to prosecute in this matter and
(ii) to settle the appropriate indictment.

The four accused were committed to stand trial on a single charge of robbery, contrary to the Theft Act 1968, s. 8, by Brighton Magistrates' Court on 3.9.96.

Case Summary
On 12.4.96 a branch of the South Downs Building Society was held up at gunpoint by two masked men. One kept watch by the door, observing both the people inside the branch and passers-by. The other demanded money from a cashier. On obtaining a holdall containing £15,967, the two men fled on foot. They were pursued by a passer-by and one of the men stopped and shot the pursuer, a Mr Goodbody. They then made good their escape, using a car parked nearby.

The prosecution case at committal was that three of the accused, namely Lewis, Duke and Ella, were involved in the actual robbery with Ella as the driver of the escape vehicle, a stolen Ford Escort XR3i. The fourth accused, Peterson, stored the vehicle in his garage for several days prior to the robbery.

Committal charge
Against Finlay LEWIS, Arthur DUKE, Gerald ELLA and Leonard PETERSON

You are charged that, on the 12th day of April 1996, you did rob Mary Penny of £15,967, contrary to the Theft Act 1968, s. 8 (1).

<u>WITNESS DEPOSITION</u>

Statement of: Mary Penny
Age: Over 21
Occupation: Building society cashier
[Usual declaration omitted]

Dated 3rd May 1996

I am a cashier for the South Downs Building Society. I work in the Churchill Square Branch. I have been there for about 4 years.

I remember the 12th of April 1996. I was at work that morning. At about 10 am two men entered the branch. Both were wearing dark-coloured donkey jackets which had orange fluorescent material on the top half. They had on dark balaclava helmets with 'Porky Pig' masks. They were both carrying what looked like sawn-off shotguns.

One of the men shouted for everyone to get on the floor. There was some screaming and the same man shouted to shut up.

He came to my window and said 'fill this with money and nobody will get hurt.'

He produced a nylon holdall and passed it through the window. I looked to the manager who indicated that I should do as the man asked.

I emptied the contents of the tills into the bag. This was both cash and cheques. Then I gave it back to the man at the counter.

All this time the other man had just stood by the entrance door, pointing his gun at the staff and customers.

The man with the holdall joined the other one by the door. One of them shouted 'Nobody move and you won't get hurt' and they both ran out. I think it was the man with the holdall who shouted.

I had pressed the silent alarm as the man approached my window and about two minutes after the men left, several police officers arrived.

I would describe the man with the holdall as about 6 feet tall and medium build. His voice was unusual. He had an accent. Irish is how I would describe it.

I saw his hands when he gave me the bag — they were white.

On the 26th of April I attended an identification parade at Brighton Police Station where I saw a number of men. They all looked about the same height and build as the man with the holdall.

They each said the words 'fill this with money and nobody will get hurt'. I picked out the 5th man. I am sure he was the man with the holdall.

I did not get a good look at the second man. I think he was about 2 inches shorter than the other one, again medium build. I would not recognise him again.

The whole incident lasted for about 5 minutes.

I did not see the face of either man. I did not see their hair, they were both wearing balaclava helmets.

Their jackets were not tight on them. They could have been slimmer than medium build.

I saw no distinctive features on either man. The voice was distinctive.

I would call it Irish. I have no Irish relations or friends. I have not been to Ireland on holiday. I have never been to Scotland.

I can recall the voice of the man with the holdall. I am sure that the man I picked out at the identification parade had the same voice. I am not mistaken. I am not an expert on voices or regional accents.

Signed: Mary Penny
Signature witnessed by: D. Law, DS

WITNESS DEPOSITION

Statement of: Reginald Goodbody
Age: Over 21
Occupation: Retired grocer
[Usual declaration omitted]

Dated 3.5.96

(Witness sworn)

On the 12.4.96 I was in Brighton for some shopping. My wife was with me.

We started looking around the shops in Churchill Square. Just after 10 o'clock we were going past a small parade of shops when two men ran out of the South Downs Building Society premises there.

I was about 20 yards away from them. They ran towards me and my wife. They had a bag and guns. They were wearing balaclava helmets. They had workmen's jackets on — black I think, with orange patches.

I realised they had robbed the Building Society and I put up my arms to try and stop them. One got past me but I caught hold of the bag that the other one was carrying.

We got into a bit of a struggle over the bag. I think people were coming out of the Building Society by now.

The other man ran back and shouted at me to let go. When I said No, he shot me in the leg with his gun.

I fell over and let go of the bag. Both of them ran off.

The one I was struggling with was about my height and build. I am 6 feet tall and weigh about 13 stone. The other one was about the same. I can't recall him clearly.

I would not recognise either of them again. Their features were quite obscured by their helmets.

I went to hospital in an ambulance with my wife. The Royal Sussex Hospital in Brighton.

I was there for 8 days. My leg was badly damaged by the gun. It was a shotgun cartridge. I lost some blood and quite a bit of muscle and flesh in my calf.

I now have to walk with a stick. I find my mobility is very restricted. I attend the hospital physiotherapy department every week to build my leg up.

The one with the bag shot me. The gun did not go off in the struggle — I am quite sure.

I do not think it can have been an accident — he deliberately took aim and fired. There was nothing I could do.

The man who shot me shouted at me to let go of the bag. I cannot recall his exact words. He did not have an accent. I did not notice any accent.

The other one never spoke at all.

Signed: R. Goodbody

Signature witnessed by: D. Law, DS

STATEMENT OF WITNESS

(MCA 1980, s. 102; CJA 1967, s. 9; MCR 1981, r. 70)

Statement of:	Brenda BROWSE
Age:	Over 21
Occupation:	Housekeeper

[Usual declaration omitted]

Signed by: B. Browse
Signature witnessed by: D. Law, DS 494P

Dated 11.5.96

On the 12th of April 1996 I left my home to meet a friend in Brighton. We had arranged to meet by the Oxfam shop, just along the road from Churchill Square. I got there early, at about 9.30 am. There were several cars parked around the area but I did not take any notice of them. I went to a cafe over the road for a cup of tea.

While I was in the cafe, I could see the road ahead — Mountfort Road. There was a dark blue Ford Escort parked there with a man sitting behind the wheel. The car was there the whole time I was in the cafe. At about 10 o'clock, as I was about to leave, two men came running along the road, shouting something. The man in the car started the engine and the two men leaped into the car. It tore off down the road, towards the junction by the cafe and straight over without waiting to see if anyone was crossing the road.

I was astonished by this behaviour and made a note of the car registration number. It was E838 JPO.

I would not recognise the two men who jumped into the car again but both were wearing workmen's jackets with orange fluorescent patches like Council workmen wear. I think they both had dark hair.

The man in the car was quite slim with dark wavy hair, fair-skinned and in his early twenties. I would recognise him again.

I am willing to attend court to give evidence.

Signed: B. Browse
Signature witnessed by: D. Law, DS

STATEMENT OF WITNESS

Statement of:	Brenda BROWSE
Age:	(Details as above)
Occupation:	
Address:	

Dated 15.5.96

Further to my statement of 11th May 1996, on the 15th of May 1996 I was asked to attend Brighton Police Station. I was met by Inspector Charger who explained that there was going to be a parade where the man I saw in the Ford Escort might be. He explained that the man might not be there and I was to look at all of the men very carefully. He said only if I was sure I saw the same man, I should stop and touch him on the shoulder.

I was escorted into a waiting room by a WPC and eventually taken to a large room with several men lined up against one wall. I went to one end of the line and walked along it. The seventh man was the one I had seen driving the Ford Escort on the 12th of April. I was quite sure and I touched him on the shoulder. He did not do anything. The Inspector asked me to leave the room as the parade was now over.

I was then brought to a room where I wrote this statement.

Signed: Brenda Browse
Signature witnessed by: D. Law, DS

STATEMENT OF WITNESS

Statement of:	David LAW
Age:	Over 21
Occupation:	Detective Sergeant 494P, Brighton C.I.D.

[Usual declaration omitted]

Signed: D. Law
Signature witnessed by: A. Libby, DC 675P

Dated 18.5.96

On 12th April 1996 at 12.10 pm, as a result of information received, I went to 33 Dials Lane in Brighton where I found a navy blue Ford Escort XR3i which appeared to have been abandoned in a hurry. The doors were wide open. Under the driver's seat were some shotgun cartridges. The registration number of the vehicle was E838 JPO.

I had reason to believe that this vehicle had been used in an armed robbery which had occurred earlier that day in Brighton and I requested that a Scenes of Crime Officer attend the location in Dials Lane.

On 11th May 1996, I went to a private house at 72 Power Station Row, Southwick. The door was opened by a woman who identified herself as Sharon Ella. I asked her if I could speak to Gerald Ella — she replied that he was not in. Subsequently, I attended the rear of the house where colleagues had apprehended Gerald ELLA, while he was climbing over a fence in the garden of number 72.

I said to him, 'Are you Gerald Ella?' He replied, 'What if I am?' I said to him, 'I have reason to believe you were involved in an armed robbery on the South Downs Building Society in Brighton on the 12th of April, specifically as the driver of the getaway vehicle.' He replied, 'You've got a very good imagination for a copper'.

I then told him that his fingerprints had been identified on the getaway vehicle, the navy blue Ford Escort. He seemed to be about to fall down so I grabbed him and said, 'I am arresting you for your part in the South Downs robbery on the 12th of April 1996. You do not have to say anything unless you wish to do so, but what you say may be given in evidence.' He made no reply and was taken to Brighton Central Police Station under escort.

He was later seen by myself and DC Libby in an interview room at Brighton Central at 10.25 pm on the 11th. He was reminded of the caution and I then asked him if he was prepared to talk to us about the robbery. He indicated that he did not wish to talk to us and he was returned to his cell at 10.28 pm.

I was present at 7.35 am on the 12th of May 1996 when ELLA was charged with robbery, the charge was read over to him, he was cautioned and made no reply.

At 2.40 pm on the 12th of May I interviewed Arthur DUKE at Brighton Central Police Station where he was in custody. DC Libby took a contemporaneous note of what was said. At the end of the interview, DC Libby read the record to DUKE who signed each page as a correct record. The interview concluded at 3.02 pm.

At 6.00 am on the 13th of May 1996 I went to 22 Bramber Street, Brighton. There I saw a man I now know to be Finlay LEWIS. I said to him, 'Are you Finlay Lewis?' He said, 'Yes, why?' I told him that he had been implicated in the robbery of the South Downs Building Society in Brighton and he replied, 'Someone's a grass. I'm saying nothing till I see my solicitor.'

After a brief search of the premises, I told LEWIS that he was under arrest for robbery and cautioned him. He replied 'I'll be wanting a word with my solicitor.' He was then taken to Brighton Central Police Station and booked into a cell.

I saw LEWIS again at 2.10 pm that day in the interview room, together with DC Libby. The interview was recorded by DC Libby and ended at 2.25 pm. DC Libby read his contemporaneous notes over to LEWIS who then signed each page as correct.

At 4.45 pm on the 13th of May 1996 LEWIS was charged with robbery, the charge was read over to him, he was cautioned and made no reply.

Signed: D. Law
Signature witnessed by: A. Libby

STATEMENT OF WITNESS

Statement of:	Alan LIBBY
Age:	Over 21
Occupation:	Detective Constable 675P, Brighton C.I.D.

[Usual declaration omitted]

Signed by: A. Libby
Signature witnessed by: V. Worthy, PS 111P

Dated 18.5.96

At 6.00 am on the 12th of May 1996, I went to a private flat at 344 Lewes Road, Brighton, together with several other officers. The door was answered by a man I now know as Arthur DUKE. I said to DUKE, 'I have reason to believe that you were involved in an armed robbery last month on a Brighton building society. Have you got anything to say?' He replied, 'You've got the wrong man this time.' I asked if we could look round his flat and he said 'Yes'.

On the floor of a wardrobe in the bedroom I found a balaclava helmet. A shoebox in the same wardrobe contained six shotgun cartridges. Hanging in the wardrobe was a navy blue donkey jacket with an orange fluorescent upper half. I said to DUKE, 'Where did you get this jacket?' He said, 'I've had it for a while now. I wear it if I get any building site work.' I then showed him the balaclava and cartridges and said, 'How do you explain these then?' He did not reply.

I said, 'I am arresting you for robbing the South Downs Building Society in Brighton on the 12th of April this year.' I cautioned him and he made no reply. He was taken to Brighton Central Police Station.

At 2.40 pm on the same day, I was present when DS Law interviewed DUKE at Brighton Central Police Station. I recorded the interview contemporaneously. At its conclusion I read the record over to DUKE who then signed each page as a correct record. The interview was terminated at 3.02 pm. I produce the record of interview, AL/1.

At 5.25 pm on the 12th of May 1996 DUKE was charged with robbery, the charge was read over, he was cautioned and made no reply.

On the 12th of May at 10.50 pm, I went to 65 Brighthelmstone Street where I saw a man I now know to be Leonard PETERSON. I said to him, 'Are you Lennie Peterson?' He said, 'That's right. Who are you?' I showed him my warrant card and explained that I was investigating the robbery of the South Downs Building Society.

I said, 'I have reason to believe that you garaged the car for the gang before the robbery. What have you got to say?' He said, 'I know nothing about it.' I said, 'It's right that you've got a lock-up garage at the back of the house, isn't it. That's where the car was kept.' He replied, 'Who's been talking out of turn?'

I said, 'The car was stolen on the 5th of April — that's a week before the robbery. It had to be kept somewhere, out of sight. I think you warehoused it for the gang. For all I know, you stole it, too.' He said, 'Look, I'm no car thief. Gerry ELLA asked me to keep it safe for him until he needed it. He brought it round on the 5th and took it away on the 12th. That's all I know.'

I told him he was being arrested for the robbery and cautioned him. He made no reply and was then taken to Brighton Central Police Station.

At 7.30 pm on the 13th of May 1996 at Brighton Central Police Station PETERSON was charged with robbery, the charge was read over to him, he was cautioned and replied, 'I've been very silly and it's all for nothing. What can I say.'

On the 13th of May at 2.10 pm, I attended an interview of Finlay LEWIS by DS Law in an interrogation room at Brighton Central Police Station. I recorded the interview contemporaneously and produce the record, AL/2.

Signed: A. Libby
Signature witnessed by: V. Worthy

Extracts from interview of Arthur Duke by DS Law, recorded by DC Libby (AL/1):-

Q. Do you want us to wait for your lawyer?

A. No, let's get it over.

Q. As I mentioned on the way here, we've found some fingerprints on the Escort and it looks like they are yours.

A. Oh yeah.

Q. I'm serious. Those prints place you in the car. Take them together with what we found in your home . . .

A. All right. It was never meant to end up the way it did.

Q. What do you mean?

A. The old man. Finlay's always been stupid but that tops the lot.

Q. So it was Finlay that shot Mr Goodbody?

A. Yes.

Q. Is that Finlay LEWIS?

A. Yes. I should never have agreed to take part in it. Finlay had it all set up before I got invited. His original partner had to drop out — he's on remand in Brixton at the moment.

. . .

A. Finlay had Gerry ELLA and Len PETERSON lined up. He knew Gerry from Wandsworth and Len was a friend of Gerry's.

. . .

A. I kept watch while Finlay played the hard man with the cashier. Everything went smooth as silk until the old man grabbed Finlay's bag. I couldn't believe what they were doing. Just as I went back to help, Finlay's gun went off and the old boy went down. I don't know whether it was an accident or not.

Extracts from interview of LEWIS by DS Law, recorded by DC Libby (AL/2):—

Q. I am refusing to delay this interview so that you can have your solicitor present because I believe that delay may prevent recovery of the stolen money.

A. No reply

. . .

Q. . . . remind you that you are under caution . . .

Q. This was a very serious offence. I tell you now — I'm more worried about the guy that got shot than the money. Have you got anything you want to say?

A. No reply

Q. Look I'll be straight with you. We've got a confession from Arthur and he's dropped you right in it.

A. I don't believe it.

Q. Have a look at this. (Hands piece of paper to Lewis)

A. Well, it seems like you know it all. Why bother talking to me?

Q. We need to get your side of things, to see how everything fits together.

A. There's no point in holding back now — so much for honour amongst thieves. It was Arthur's idea — he'd planned it for weeks before he spoke to me. We decided that we needed a driver and I knew Gerry from our time in Wandsworth.

Q. You mean Gerry ELLA and HMP Wandsworth in South London?

A. That's right.

. . .

Q. Who got the car?

A. That's down to Gerry. I don't know where it came from — he just got it for the day. The first time I saw it was when I got in it after the job.

Q. Who did what in the shop?

A. I asked for the cash while Arthur kept everyone calm.

Q. With a sawn-off?

A. You don't want heroes in a situation like that.

Q. Like Reg Goodbody?

A. Is he the old boy? He never should have interfered. He got what was coming to him.

Q. From you?

A. No way. That was Arthur. I could have got the bag away from the old man but Arthur got impatient with him.

. . .

Q. So where's the money now?

A. Money? That's rich. Lots of it was cheques. The rest, well, I'll need a nest egg for when I get out, eh?

Q. So you won't tell me where it is?

A. No reply

. . .

Summaries of the antecedent histories of the accused men:—

Finlay LEWIS (Age 40) Born Stornaway, Outer Hebrides.
18 previous convictions including 2 for wounding (s. 18 OAPA) and 3 for armed robbery. Last conviction was at Portsmouth Crown Court for robbery in May 1988. Sentenced to 10 years' imprisonment. Released June 1995.

Arthur DUKE (Age 43) Born Catford, London.
8 previous convictions, mainly for offences of dishonesty. 1 recorded for robbery. Last conviction was at Brighton Magistrates' Court in February 1991 for a fraud on the Department of Health and Social Security. On committal to the Crown Court, sentenced to 6 years' imprisonment. Released April 1994.

Gerald ELLA (Age 26) Born Worthing, West Sussex.
6 previous convictions, all for theft of cars, except the last one. In 1989 a 3-year term of imprisonment was imposed by Inner London Crown Court. In September last year, Brighton Magistrates' Court fined him £250 and banned him from driving for 1 year for driving whilst unfit through drink or drugs.

Leonard PETERSON (Age 55) Born Brighton.
16 previous convictions, all for petty offences of dishonesty. Imprisonment has been ordered in the past, but the last conviction was in 1979 and resulted in a conditional discharge.

If you would like to try your hand at drafting an indictment in a simpler case, try the following short problem.

R v *ADAMS*

Arthur ADAMS was charged with stealing from Jane BROWN a handbag containing a purse, lipstick and £20 in money. He elected for trial on indictment and he has recently been transferred for trial at Casterbridge Crown Court on that charge. The papers have been sent to you by the CPS and you have been asked to draft an appropriate indictment.

There is evidence to the effect that John SMITH was amongst the crowds in the area of Trafalgar Square at around 11 pm on New Year's Eve 1996 when he was suddenly jostled. He felt inside his jacket pocket, where he had been carrying his wallet, and found that it was missing. He reported the matter to the first police officer he saw. Jane BROWN's evidence is that at around 1 am on New Year's Day 1996 she was in Trafalgar Square when a youth violently wrenched her handbag away from her. Shortly after, she believed she saw amongst the crowds the person who had taken her handbag. She pointed him out to a police officer who arrested him. That person was Arthur ADAMS.

He was searched, and found to have £300 in cash on his person (none of which could be positively identified as having been stolen from either John SMITH or Jane BROWN) together with a wallet containing a cheque card personalised in the name of John SMITH. Subsequently SMITH confirmed that the wallet found in ADAMS' possession was the one which he (SMITH) had lost earlier that night.

ADAMS made a statement to the police in which he said that (i) he had found the wallet on the ground about half an hour before he was arrested and had been waiting for a suitable opportunity to hand it to the police (ii) the wallet was empty when he found it and (iii) he was not the person who had taken Jane BROWN's handbag, she being mistaken in her identification of him.

Having drafted the indictment, consider any objections which the defence might raise against it either on arraignment or at a pre-trial hearing.

TEN

CROWN COURT: PRE-TRIAL ISSUES

This chapter covers a series of issues relating to preparation for trial in the Crown Court, which are dealt with in the Criminal Procedure and Investigation Act ('the Act').

10.1 The Criminal Procedure and Investigation Act

At the time of writing, the Act had just received the Royal Assent. Its effect upon criminal procedure is likely to be radical, particularly since for the first time the defence will be expected to disclose its case in advance of trial. In this chapter, the central provisions of the Act are summarised. These deal with the duties of the prosecution and the defence in relation to disclosure, and the powers of the court in relation to preparatory hearings and pre-trial hearings. Care should be taken, however, to establish which of the Act's provisions are currently in force.

In addition to the Act itself, the Home Office has produced a Code of Practice which is intended to govern the duties of police officers in the conduct of investigations, and which fills in a lot of the detail necessary to understand the way in which the new scheme of disclosure is to work. This Code is intended to be the equivalent to the Codes of Practice under the Police and Criminal Evidence Act 1984 (see **2.2**) and is subject to approval by affirmative resolution of both Houses of Parliament.

10.2 Disclosure

An important issue in criminal procedure is the extent to which the prosecution and the defence must before trial disclose to each other the information pertaining to the case. Concentrating for the moment upon the prosecution, there is a central distinction between:

(a) the disclosure by the prosecution of its case, i.e. the evidence upon which it will rely at trial; and

(b) the disclosure of other material pertaining to the case, which it does not intend to use — 'used material'.

As far as Crown Court trial is concerned, it is clear that the prosecution has an obligation to disclose its case to the defence, in the sense described in (a). In practice, the bulk of this evidence will be contained in the bundle of documents resulting from the accused's committal by the magistrates. Any gaps will then be filled in by notices of additional evidence.

At common law, the prosecution has also had a duty to disclose to the defence any unused material, i.e. the material described in (b) above. This duty was refined and extended in the wake of a series of high-profile miscarriage of justice cases, and reached its high-water mark in the case of *R* v *Ward* [1993] 1 WLR 619 (see **11.5.2.1**). There were protests from the police and the Crown Prosecution Service among others that the duty upon the prosecution had become too onerous, and that it resulted in the abandonment of cases where the court ordered the disclosure of sensitive or confidential material. On the other hand, there were those who were anxious to preserve the prosecution's obligation to disclose relevant material, so that the defence (which usually lacks investigative resources) could be aware of any potentially helpful information which the prosecution held, but had decided not to use.

The Royal Commission on Criminal Justice, chaired by Lord Runciman, recommended in 1994 that the prosecution duty of disclosure should be brought within a more restrictive framework, and that it should be tied to a measure of defence disclosure. The notion that the defence should be under an obligation to disclose its case was a novel one, and was argued by some to undermine the prosecution's burden of proof. Nonetheless, restrictions on prosecution disclosure more radical than those suggested by the Runciman Commission and accompanied by a proposal for defence disclosure, formed part of the Criminal Procedure and Investigation Bill when it was introduced in Parliament in November 1995.

The scheme of the legislation is that there is a statutory duty upon the police officer investigating an offence to record and retain information and material gathered or generated during the investigation. The prosecution should, in what the Act calls 'primary prosecution disclosure', inform the defence of certain categories of that material which it does not intend to use at trial (as stated, there is a separate obligation to inform the defence of material which it *does* intend to use). The defence then has a duty to inform the prosecution of the case which it intends to present at trial. The prosecution then has a duty to present further material to the defence — 'secondary prosecution disclosure'. The legislation makes provision for applications to be made to the court in certain circumstances where there is a dispute about whether the prosecution should disclose certain material; and there are sanctions laid down for defence failure to disclose or disclosure which is false or inconsistent.

10.2.1 THE INVESTIGATOR'S DUTY

Section 23 of the Act requires the Secretary of State to prepare a Code of Practice which will govern investigations carried out by police officers. By s. 26, those other than police officers charged with the duty of conducting criminal investigations (e.g. customs officers) must have regard to the Code's provisions.

The Code of Practice makes the investigator responsible for ensuring that any information relevant to the investigation is recorded and retained, whether it is gathered in the course of the investigation (e.g. documents seized in the course of searching premises) or generated by the investigation (e.g. interview records). Where there is any doubt about the relevance of material, the investigator should retain it. The duty to retain material includes, in particular, the following categories

(a) crime reports, including crime report forms, relevant parts of incident report books and police officers' notebooks;

(b) final versions of witness statements (and draft versions where they differ from the final versions) and any exhibits mentioned;

(c) interview records (written or taped);

(d) expert reports and schedules;

(e) any material casting doubt upon the reliability of a confession;

(f) any material casting doubt on the reliability of a witness.

But the duty to retain material does not extend to draft statements of opinion prepared by expert witnesses, routine exchanges of material or material purely ancillary to that in the above categories.

The material must be retained at least until criminal proceedings are concluded, and in accordance with a policy which the chief officer of police develops for each area.

Where the investigator believes that the person charged with an offence is likely to plead not guilty at a summary trial, or that the offence will be tried in the Crown Court, he or she must prepare a schedule listing material which has been retained and which does not form part of the case against the accused. If the investigator has obtained any sensitive material, this should be listed in a separate schedule. Sensitive material is material which the investigator believes it is not in the public interest to disclose. The Code gives a number of examples, which range from material relating to national security to material given in confidence, and includes material relating to informants, undercover police officers, premises used for police surveillance, techniques used in the detection of crime, and material relating to a child witness generated, for example, by a local authority social services department.

The investigator should draw the prosecutor's attention to any material which might undermine the prosecution case. The disclosure officer (defined as 'the person responsible for handling the administration of a criminal investigation') must certify that to the best of his or her knowledge and belief the duties imposed under the Code have been complied with.

After the defence has complied with *its* duty of disclosure (see **10.2.3**), the investigator must look again at the material retained, and draw the prosecutor's attention to any material which might reasonably be expected to assist the defence disclosed. Again, the disclosure officer must certify compliance with the duties imposed by the Code. If the investigator comes into possession of any new material after complying with the duties described above, then this must be treated in the same way.

If the prosecutor so requests, the investigator must disclose to the accused:

(a) material which might undermine the prosecution case;

(b) where the accused has given the prosecutor a defence statement (see **10.2.3**), material which might reasonably be expected to assist the defence which the accused has disclosed;

(c) any material which the court orders be disclosed.

10.2.2 PRIMARY PROSECUTION DISCLOSURE

Section 3 requires the prosecutor to disclose previously undisclosed material to the accused if, in the prosecutor's opinion, it might undermine the case for the prosecution. If there is no such material, then the accused must be given a written statement to that effect. Prosecution material includes material which the prosecutor possesses or has been allowed to inspect under the provisions of the Code (see **10.2.1**). It may be disclosed either by giving it to the defence, or allowing the defence to inspect it at a reasonable time and place. This step is called 'primary prosecution disclosure', and it must be carried out within a time limit which is to be laid down by statutory instrument. Material must not, however, be disclosed under this provision if a court has concluded that it is not in the public interest that it be disclosed, i.e. that it is sensitive (see **10.2.5**). By s. 4, if the prosecutor has been given a document indicating any non-sensitive material which has not been given to the accused, that document must be given to the accused at the same time as primary prosecution disclosure takes place.

10.2.3 DEFENCE DISCLOSURE

By s. 5, once primary prosecution disclosure has taken place and the case is committed to the Crown Court, the accused must give a defence statement to the prosecutor, within a time limit which will be laid down by statutory instrument. The defence statement is a written statement setting out in general terms the nature of the defence and the matters on which the accused takes issue with the prosecution, with reasons.

Note: There is no question of the defence having to disclose 'unused material'.

If the defence statement discloses an alibi, particulars of alibi must be given, including the name and address of any alibi witness, or information which might be of use in finding the witness, if his or her name or address is not known. This provision replaces s. 11 of the Criminal Justice Act 1967, although a similar definition of alibi evidence is adopted — 'evidence tending to show that by reason of the presence of the accused at a particular place or in a particular area at a particular time he was not, or was unlikely to have been, at the place where the offence is alleged to have been committed at the time of its alleged commission' (for interpretation of this definition see **6.3.2** and **11.7.1.1**).

10.2.4 SECONDARY PROSECUTION DISCLOSURE

Once the defence has served a statement, the prosecutor must disclose to the accused any previously undisclosed prosecution material 'which might be reasonably expected to assist the accused's defence as disclosed by the defence statement' (s. 7). If there is no such material, the prosecutor must give to the accused a statement to that effect. This process is termed 'secondary prosecution disclosure', and must be carried out within a time-limit to be laid down by statutory instrument. The methods of disclosure are identical to those set out in respect of primary prosecution disclosure, and the process is subject to the same exception in respect of material which the court orders should not be disclosed because it would not be in the public interest to do so.

10.2.5 REVIEW BY THE COURT

The prosecutor may make application to the court that material should not be disclosed, either at the primary or the secondary stage, on the basis that it is not in the public interest to disclose it. Although the legislation does not specifically so state, such application is likely to be on the basis that the material in question falls within one of the categories of 'sensitive' material outlined in the Code (see **10.2.1**). For its part, the defence can, under s. 8, apply to the court for an order that the prosecutor should disclose any material which might be reasonably expected to assist the accused's defence. Such application may only be made, however, after the defence has served a defence statement.

10.2.6 CONTINUOUS REVIEW

The prosecutor remains under a continuing duty to review questions of disclosure (s. 9). If he or she, at any time before the accused is acquitted or convicted, forms the opinion that there is material which might undermine the prosecution case, or be reasonably expected to assist the accused's defence, then it must be disclosed to the accused as soon as reasonably practicable (provided that the court has not ruled against disclosure in respect of that material).

For its part, the court must keep under review the question of whether it is still not in the public interest to disclose material affected by its order (s. 15).

10.2.7 SANCTIONS FOR DEFENCE DISCLOSURE

Integral to the scheme of the disclosure provisions is the notion that, if the defence fails to make disclosure, it will not trigger off the prosecution's obligation to make secondary disclosure (which is of material which may reasonably be expected to assist the defence advanced in the defence statement).

Section 11 lays down additional sanctions to which the defence will be liable if it is deficient in its duty of disclosure. They apply if the defence:

(a) fails to give a defence statement under s. 5;

(b) does so after the deadline laid down by statutory instrument;

(c) sets out inconsistent defences in its statement;

(d) puts forward a defence at trial which is different from the defence statement;

(e) at trial adduces evidence of alibi without having given particulars of alibi in the statement;

(f) at trial calls an alibi witness without having given details of that witness in the statement.

If any of these conditions apply then, under s. 11(3):

> *(a) the court or, with the leave of the court, any other party may make such comment as appears appropriate;*
> *(b) the court or jury may draw such inferences as appear proper in deciding whether the accused is guilty . . .*

In deciding what to do where the accused has put forward different defences, however, the court is to have regard to the extent of the difference and whether there is any justification for it.

10.2.8 SUMMARY TRIAL

The prosecution's duty of primary disclosure will apply wherever there is to be a summary trial in respect of which the accused pleads not guilty (s. 1(1)(a)). In addition, the defence may make voluntary disclosure (s. 6) which will trigger off the prosecution obligation to make secondary disclosure. In the event that the accused discloses inconsistent defences or a defence inconsistent with that later advanced at trial, however, similar consequences will follow to those which result in the Crown Court (see **10.2.7**).

10.3 Preparatory Hearings

By s. 29, a Crown Court judge may, on application or otherwise, order a preparatory hearing if a case is likely to be so long or complex that substantial benefits are likely to result. (This procedure does not, however, apply to serious or complex fraud, in which case s. 7(1) of the Criminal Justice Act 1987 would apply.)

The preparatory hearing takes place before the jury is sworn, but it marks the start of the trial. It may be held for any of the following purposes:

(a) identifying issues likely to be material to the jury's verdict;

(b) assisting its comprehension of any of the issues;

(c) expediting proceedings;

(d) assisting the judge's management of the trial.

10.3.1 POWERS OF THE JUDGE AT A PREPARATORY HEARING

The judge has the power at the preparatory hearing (s. 31) to order the prosecutor to give the court and the accused a written statement of its case, including the principal facts, the witnesses, any relevant exhibits, any proposition of law relied on, and any consequences which appear to flow from any of these matters. Where the judge has ordered the prosecution to give such a statement, he or she may also order the accused to give the court and the prosecutor a written statement in general terms of the nature of the defence, and the principal matters disputed, as well as any points of law and relevant authorities. Where the judge has decided to hold a preparatory hearing, he or she may require the prosecution or defence to supply such case statements in advance of the hearing (s. 32).

At the preparatory hearing itself, the judge may also make a ruling as to the admissibility of evidence and rule on any other question of law relating to the case (s. 31(3)). Any such ruling or order made by the judge shall have effect throughout the trial, unless there is an application to vary or discharge it, in which case the application must be decided in accordance with the interests of justice (s. 31(11)).

Although a party may depart from a case disclosed as a result of the judge's order at a preparatory ruling, comment may be made by the court (or by a party with the leave of the court) at trial, and 'the jury may draw such inference as appears proper'. A similar sanction attaches to a failure to comply with any requirement imposed under s. 31.

10.3.2 APPEALS FROM PREPARATORY HEARINGS

An appeal lies to the Court of Appeal from any ruling by the judge on the admissibility of evidence or other question of law, but only with the leave of the judge or of the Court of Appeal (s. 35). There is a similar possibility of appeal to the House of Lords, with the usual conditions (s. 36). The preparatory hearing may continue notwithstanding that an appeal is in progress, but no jury may be sworn until the appeal has been determined or abandoned. The policy is clearly to ensure that points of law are comprehensively dealt with before the court embarks upon a long and complex trial which may prove abortive due to a wrong decision on a point of law made at the preparatory hearing.

10.3.3 REPORTING RESTRICTIONS

By virtue of s. 37, any preparatory hearing (or appeal from it) may not be reported except in so far as the trial judge or the appellate court permits, until the trial is concluded. The court may order that these restrictions shall not apply if it decides that it is in the interests of justice to do so. Contravention of the reporting restrictions is an offence (s. 38).

10.4 Pre-Trial Hearings

Preparatory hearings apply to cases which are long and/or complex. A more limited set of provisions applies to run-of-the-mill cases, and these are contained in ss. 39 and 40. At any time after proceedings for trial have been committed to the Crown Court and before the start of the trial, the judge makes, at a pre-trial hearing, a ruling as to the admissibility of evidence or any other question of law, either on application by a party or of the judge's own motion. The ruling remains binding until the end of the trial, unless a judge decides to vary or discharge it (which may be on the application of a party). The judge who varies or discharges need not necessarily be the judge who made the original ruling. No application to vary or discharge may be made unless there has been a material change of circumstances since the ruling (or the last application) was made. It is apparent that these provisions envisage that the judge who conducts the pre-trial hearing may not be the trial judge, and that the extent to which the original rulings should be binding must be limited accordingly. There is, however, no right of appeal from the judge's ruling other than at the conclusion of the case in the usual way. There are reporting restrictions similar to those in respect of preparatory hearings (s. 41).

ELEVEN

JURY TRIAL

11.1 Plea and Directions Hearings

In an attempt to reduce the number of cases where the defendant was expected to plead not guilty but in fact pleaded guilty (so called 'cracked trials'), the Lord Chief Justice issued the *Practice Direction: Crown Court (Plea and Directions Hearings)* [1995] 1 WLR 1318. This Direction applies to all cases (except serious fraud cases which have their own provisions for a preliminary hearing under s. 7 of the Criminal Justice Act 1987).

The Direction stipulates that at the plea and directions hearing ('PDH'), pleas will be taken. If the defendant pleads guilty, the judge should proceed to sentencing whenever possible (although it may be necessary to adjourn in order for a pre-sentence report to be prepared).

In cases where the defendant pleads not guilty, the prosecution and defence will be expected to inform the court of:

(a) the issues in the case;

(b) whether the defendant or any witness is suffering from a mental or medical condition, and whether the prosecution will agree to defence witnesses who are ill giving written evidence;

(c) the number of witnesses who will be giving evidence orally or in writing;

(d) any additional witnesses likely to be called by the prosecution and the evidence they are expected to give;

(e) any formal admissions under s. 10 of the Criminal Justice Act 1967;

(f) any alibi which the defendant will rely on (which should already have been disclosed in accordance with s. 11 of the Criminal Justice Act 1967);

(g) any point of law or question of admissibility which is likely to arise in the trial;

(h) any applications for leave to give evidence via live television links or pre-recorded interviews or for the use of screens so that the identity of the witness remains secret;

(i) estimated length of trial;

(j) availability of witnesses and advocates.

The Direction envisages that the PDH will normally be conducted by the trial judge.

The PDH is normally held in open court and all defendants should be present unless the court otherwise directs.

The PDH should normally take place within six weeks of the committal of the case to the Crown Court if the defendant is on bail, and within four weeks if he is in custody. When the magistrates commit the case to the Crown Court, they should (after consultation with the Crown Court listing officer) specify the date on which the PDH should take place.

The defence should inform the prosecution, the court, and the probation service as soon as it is known that the defendant intends to plead guilty to all or part of the indictment.

Finally, the Practice Direction requires the defence solicitors to apply to the court for the case to be listed for mention if they are unable to obtain instructions from the defendant. If the defendant fails to attend this hearing, the judge is likely to issue a warrant for his arrest.

In *R* v *Wright* (1990) 90 Cr App R 325, it was held that a decision taken at a pre-trial review (the precursor to the PDH) may be reconsidered at the trial itself if there is good reason to do so (for example, if new arguments come to light). Presumably, the same principle applies to the PDH.

11.2 The Arraignment

At the arraignment (which should take place at the PDH), the indictment is 'put' to the defendant, in that he or she is asked to plead guilty or not guilty. The proceedings will go something like this:

Clerk of the Court: 'Are you Michael Smith?'
Smith: 'Yes.'
Clerk: 'Michael Smith, you are charged in an indictment containing one count of robbery contrary to s. 8 of the Theft Act 1968. The particulars of the offence are that on 8 May 1996 you robbed Alice Jones of £45 in cash. Michael Smith, to this indictment do you plead guilty or not guilty?'

If the indictment contains more than one count, each count will be put to the defendant separately, so that a plea is entered on each. The defendant must enter his or her plea personally (not through counsel or solicitor).

The defendant must he present to enter his or her plea. If the defendant fails to attend, the judge will issue a bench warrant for the defendant's arrest. If (having been present at the start of the trial) the defendant subsequently misbehaves or absconds, the judge has a discretion to continue with the trial in the absence of the defendant. However, if the defendant is absent through illness (again having been present to enter a plea of guilty or not guilty) the trial can only continue in the absence of the defendant if the defendant consents to this.

11.2.1 PROCEDURE ON A PLEA OF GUILTY

If the defendant pleads guilty to all the counts on the indictment, the prosecution will summarise the facts of the offence(s) and tell the court about the defendant's antecedents, that is basic details about his or her life (education, employment, income, etc.) based on what the defendant has told the police, together with details of any relevant previous convictions. The court will in fact have a complete list of this defendant's previous convictions, but will invite the prosecution to read out only those that are relevant, which will usually mean fairly recent ones.

11.2.2 THE *NEWTON* HEARING

In *R* v *Newton* (1982) 77 Cr App R 13, the defendant was charged with buggery of his wife. He claimed that she consented to this (not a defence, but relevant to sentence) but the prosecution alleged that she had not consented. The judge wrongly accepted the prosecution version without hearing evidence of the issue of consent. The Court of Appeal held that where there is a substantial divergence between the two stories (that is, a divergence which will have a material effect on the sentence imposed) the judge can reject the defence version only after hearing evidence of what happened.

Therefore, where the defendant has pleaded guilty, if there is a substantial conflict between the prosecution and the defence (i.e., there is sharp divergence between the prosecution version of the facts and the defence version of the facts), the judge must either accept the defence version and sentence accordingly or hear evidence of what happened and then make a finding of fact as to what happened, and sentence accordingly.

If the judge decides to hear evidence, then the evidence is heard without a jury. The parties are given the opportunity to call such evidence as they wish and to cross-examine witnesses called by the other side (for further details on *Newton* hearings, see **12.4.2**).

11.2.3 PROSECUTION OFFERING NO EVIDENCE; LEAVING COUNTS ON THE FILE

If the defendant pleads not guilty to some or all of the counts on the indictment, the next stage (which will take place some time after PDH) is to empanel a jury. However, it may be that new evidence has come to light showing that the wrong person has been charged or considerably weakening the case against this defendant, or it may be that a vital witness has refused to testify (and although a person can be compelled to give evidence, a reluctant witness nearly always does more harm than good). In that case the prosecution will offer no evidence against the defendant, in which case a finding of not guilty is entered under CJA 1967, s. 17. An alternative to offering no evidence is for the prosecution to ask the judge to direct that one or more counts be left on the file marked not to be proceeded with without the leave of the Crown Court or the Court of Appeal. The advantage of this is that if the prosecution obtain a conviction on another count but the defendant successfully appeals against that conviction, the prosecution could (with leave) proceed on the other counts. Leaving a count on the file is not an acquittal, whereas if the prosecution offers no evidence this does result in an acquittal.

11.2.4 'PLEA BARGAINING' WITH THE PROSECUTION

If there are several counts on the indictment, the defendant might be willing to plead guilty to some but not to others. If that is acceptable to the prosecution, the counts to which the defendant pleads not guilty are either 'left on the file' or else the prosecution offers no evidence in respect of those counts.

11.2.5 DIFFERENT PLEAS FROM DIFFERENT DEFENDANTS

If there is more than one defendant and one pleads guilty and the others not guilty, it is a matter for the judge whether to sentence the one who has pleaded guilty immediately or at the end of the trial of the others. The argument in favour of postponing sentence is that at the end of the trial, the judge will have a much better idea of who did what. However, it is a little more difficult if the defendant who pleads guilty also indicates that he or she is willing to 'turn Queen's evidence', giving evidence against his or her co-defendants. This will attract a very substantial discount in sentence, well beyond the one third normally credited to those who simply plead guilty. Such a person becomes a competent witness for the Crown after pleading guilty. However, if sentence is postponed, it may seem that the sentence imposed after the defendant has given evidence depends more on the quality of the evidence given than on the defendant's guilt; on the other hand if the defendant is sentenced before giving evidence, then he or she may have a change of mind and the lenient sentence given on the basis of the promised testimony cannot be altered (see *R* v *Stone* [1970] 1 WLR 1112). The Court of Appeal in *R* v *Weekes* (1980) 74 Cr App R 161 said that sentence should normally be postponed until after the trial of the other defendant. However, in

R v *Clement, The Times*, 12 December 1991 the court observed that it is a matter for the judge whether the defendant is sentenced sooner or later.

11.2.6 THE AMBIGUOUS PLEA

If the defendant pleads guilty but then advances mitigation which amounts to a defence, then the plea is ambiguous (e.g. guilty of theft but thought that the property was his or her own). In those circumstances, the law will be explained to the defendant, who will then be asked to plead again. If the plea remains ambiguous, a plea of not guilty will be entered on behalf of the defendant and a trial will take place in the usual way.

Sometimes a defendant will say to counsel, 'I didn't do it but I want to plead guilty to get things over and done with quickly'. In such a case, counsel should try to dissuade the client from pleading guilty to an offence which he or she denies. In particular, it should be pointed out that nothing can be said in mitigation which suggests innocence (since that would render the plea ambiguous) or even remorse (one cannot be remorseful for something one denies doing).

11.3 The Jury

11.3.1 WHO CAN SERVE?

The pool of potential jurors (the 'jury panel') is drawn by an officer of the Crown Court on a random basis from the register of electors aged between 18 and 70. The Juries Act 1974 (see s. 1 and sch. 1) sets out those people who may not serve on a jury. Anyone concerned with the administration of justice (lawyers, magistrates, police officers, probation officers, prison officers, etc.) is ineligible for jury service, as are the clergy and the mentally disordered. Others are disqualified from jury service. Anyone who has been sentenced to life imprisonment is disqualified for life; a custodial sentence (including a suspended sentence) disqualifies for ten years, as does a community service order; a probation order disqualifies for five years. Similarly, a person who is on bail at the time is disqualified. Of those who are eligible to serve, some have a right to be excused from jury service. This list includes members of parliament, medical personnel, full-time service personnel and those aged 65–70. The rest have the right (and duty) to serve when called to do so and will only be excused from jury service if they can show a good reason. The trial judge also has power to excuse from jury service a person who is not capable of acting as a juror because of physical disability. Furthermore, a person may be excused from jury service on the ground that he or she is practising member of a religious society or order, the tenets or beliefs of which are incompatible with jury service.

11.3.2 EMPANELLING THE JURY

A number of potential jurors come into the courtroom. The clerk reads out the names of 12 of them, selected randomly from the list of those present. The 12 go into the jury box. The clerk will also explain to the defendant that the list of names about to be called out will form the jury which will try the defendant but that he or she has the right to challenge jurors before they are sworn.

11.3.3 CHALLENGING POTENTIAL JURORS

There are two main types of challenge.

11.3.3.1 Stand by

The first type of challenge is the right of the prosecution to stand a juror by. Just as the juror starts to take the oath, the prosecuting counsel says 'Stand by'. The judge will then explain to that juror that he or she cannot sit on this jury but may be required to sit on another one. This challenge is confined to the prosecution, and prosecuting counsel does not have to give any reasons for the challenge. The fact that the prosecution would seem to have an advantage over the defence (who no longer has any right of peremptory challenge) led the Attorney-General to issue guidelines on the related issues of use of the stand by and jury vetting (see Appendix 4 to *Blackstone's Criminal Practice* for the full text). In many cases there will be no check at all on potential jurors. However, in ordinary cases the names of the potential jurors may be put through the Police National Computer to see if any have previous convictions which mean that they are disqualified from jury service or are unsuitable to serve on this particular jury. In cases involving national security and terrorism, however, a more thorough check is carried out, with use being made of Special Branch files. Unsuitable jurors can then simply be stood by. The other cases where use of the stand by is appropriate, according to the guidelines, is where the person is manifestly unsuitable to sit on this jury, and the defence agrees that he or she should not sit. An example might be the person who is clearly unable to read the words on the card which contains the jury oath and so is unsuitable for a case which involves perusal of documentary evidence.

It should be noted that the judge also has power to stand a juror by, but this power is exercised only very rarely. Some judges had used it (at the request of the defence) to try to secure a racially balanced jury so that some members shared the defendant's ethnic origin. However, in *R* v *Ford* [1989] QB 868 the Court of Appeal ruled that this practice was unlawful.

11.3.3.2 Challenge for cause

The other important form of challenge (and the only one open to the defence) is the challenge for cause. This challenge is used in cases where it is suspected that a potential juror might be biased. It should be remembered that although the names of potential jurors are available for inspection by the prosecution and defence, it is unlikely that any checks will have been carried out apart from the check for previous convictions carried out by the prosecution. The defence is unlikely to have information to show that a particular juror is biased (unless the defendant happens to recognise the person in question). Further (and this is different from the position in the United States) no questions may be asked of a potential juror unless the challenging party has already established a *prima facie* case that the person is likely to be biased (see *R* v *Chandler* [1964] 2 QB 322). An example of how this operates may be seen in the trial of the Kray brothers, presided over by Lawton J. A national newspaper had published a colourful account of the allegations against the Krays. The judge was persuaded that anyone who had read this material might well be biased against the defendants. He therefore allowed the defence to ask each juror whether he or she had read the material in question. If the juror said yes, that person was then successfully challenged.

To challenge for cause, counsel merely says 'challenge' before the juror takes the oath. If it is a straightforward case (e.g. the juror knows the defendant) counsel will simply state that this is the case and the judge will ask that person to leave the jury box. If it is more complicated, the jurors who have already been sworn and the rest of the potential jurors (the 'jury in waiting') will be asked to leave court and counsel will have to explain the basis of the challenge and (if the judge so directs) question the challenged juror.

In *R* v *Gough* [1993] AC 646 the House of Lords held that the test where bias is alleged is whether there is a 'real danger' that the juror is biased. See also *R* v *Wilson*, *The Times*, 24 February 1995, where convictions were quashed (and retrials ordered) because one of the jurors was the wife of a prison officer serving at the prison where the appellants had been held on remand. The Court of Appeal said that the test is one of *possibility* of bias rather than *probability* of bias and so it was not necessary to inquire into the juror's actual state of mind. There was a real danger that, consciously or not, she may have been biased against the appellants.

11.3.3.3 Replacement of juror

When a juror has been stood by or successfully challenged, he or she is replaced by another member of the jury in waiting.

11.3.4 DISCHARGE OF JURORS

11.3.4.1 Discharge of individual jurors during the trial

A jury always starts off with 12 jurors. However, under the Juries Act 1974, s. 16, up to three jurors may be discharged during the course of the trial in case of illness or other necessity (e.g. bereavement).

What constitutes necessity is a matter for the trial judge. In *R* v *Hanberry* [1977] QB 924 a juror was discharged because the trial went on longer than expected and she would otherwise have had to cancel a holiday.

If more than three jurors can no longer serve the trial has to be abandoned; a fresh trial will take place later.

11.3.4.2 Discharge of entire jury

The entire jury may be discharged if, for example:

(a) The jury hears evidence which is inadmissible and prejudicial to the defendant and the judge decides that a direction to ignore this evidence would not be sufficient (*R* v *Weaver* [1968] 1 QB 353).

(b) The jury cannot agree on a verdict (see **11.12.5** below).

(c) An individual juror has to be discharged and there is a risk that he or she may have contaminated the rest of the jury (e.g., because of knowing that the defendant has previous convictions or is facing further trials for other offences) (e.g., *R* v *Hutton* (1990) Crim LR 875).

If members of the jury misbehave during the course of the trial, the jury should be discharged if there is a 'real danger of prejudice' to the accused (*R* v *Spencer* [1987] AC 128). In *R* v *Sawyer* (1980) 71 Cr App R 283, for example, some jurors were seen in conversation with prosecution witnesses during an adjournment. The trial judge questioned them and it transpired that the conversation had been on subjects unconnected with the trial. The decision of the judge not to discharge the jury was upheld by the Court of Appeal.

Where the jury is discharged from giving a verdict, the defendant can be re-tried, as he is not regarded as having been acquitted.

11.3.5 START OF THE TRIAL

Once the jury has been empanelled, the trial begins with the clerk reading out the indictment and telling the jury that the defendant has pleaded not guilty. The jury is then told, 'It is your charge to say, having heard the evidence, whether he [or she] be guilty or not'.

11.4 Change of Plea

The defendant may change his or her plea from not guilty to guilty at any stage of the trial before the jury has returned a verdict. The defence simply asks for the indictment to be put again and the defendant pleads guilty. The jury must then return a formal verdict of guilty.

The defendant can change his or her plea from guilty to not guilty at any stage of the trial prior to the passing of sentence, but only at the discretion of the judge. The judge will want some explanation for the change of heart and may take into account matters such as the legal advice the accused has received, his or her age and level of intellect, and experience of criminal proceedings. See *R* v *Dodd* (1981) 74 Cr App R 50; *S* v *Recorder of Manchester* [1971] AC 481.

11.5 The Prosecution Case

After the indictment has been read to the jury, counsel for the prosecution opens the Crown's case:

> May it please your Honour [or your Lordship, if a High Court judge or sitting at the Old Bailey], members of the jury, I appear to prosecute and my learned friend Miss Green appears for the accused.

11.5.1 THE OPENING SPEECH

The purpose of the prosecution opening speech is to give the jury an overview of the prosecution case. The jury will be reminded of the charge(s) which the defendant faces, which should be explained to it in everyday language. Counsel will probably tell the jury what witnesses will be called by the prosecution and what it is hoped they will establish. Counsel will also mention the burden of proof and the standard of proof, and make it clear that anything said about the law is subject to what the judge will say in the summing up.

If counsel for the defence takes the view that an objection should be taken to the admissibility of some of the evidence which the prosecution will be calling (as disclosed to the defence in the bundle of committal statements, together with any notice of additional evidence), then he or she should inform counsel for the prosecution. The prosecutor will then omit any reference to the disputed material from the opening speech. The judge will then be asked to rule on the admissibility of the evidence at the appropriate moment (see **11.5.2.5**). It may be, however, that the disputed evidence is such an important part of the prosecution case that an opening speech would make no sense if no reference were to be made to that evidence; for example, the only evidence against the defendant is a confession, the admissibility of which is disputed. In that case, once the jury has been empanelled, the judge will be informed (either by the prosecution or the defence) that a ruling on a matter of law is needed at the outset. The jury will be sent out of the court and counsel will then seek the judge's ruling on the admissibility of the evidence. If the judge rules the evidence inadmissible, the prosecution will almost certainly have little option but to offer no evidence (see **11.2.3** above), in which case the jury will be called back into court and directed to acquit the defendant.

11.5.2 THE PROSECUTION EVIDENCE

At the conclusion of the opening speech, prosecuting counsel calls the evidence. It is the rule that the prosecution must call all the witnesses whose evidence was included in the bundle of statements sent to the magistrates' court in the transfer proceedings. If one witness is expected to duplicate the evidence of another (e.g. the second police officer present at an interview with the accused), the prosecution may 'tender' that second witness for cross-examination. This means that the witness is called into the witness box by counsel for the prosecution and having been identified and his or her relevance to the case established, he or she will be told to stay there in case the defence have any questions. The only exceptions to the rule that the prosecution must call (or tender for cross-examination) all the witnesses whose evidence was used in the transfer proceedings are those set out in *R* v *Armstrong* [1995] 3 All ER 831:

(a) the defence has consented to the written statement of that witness being read to the court — that witness will have been made subject to a conditional witness order at transfer; or

(b) counsel for the prosecution takes the view that the evidence of that witness is no longer credible; or

(c) counsel for the prosecution takes the view that the witness would so fundamentally contradict the prosecution case that it would make more sense for that person to be called as a witness by the defence.

The other side of the coin is that the prosecution can *only* call as witnesses people whose evidence was used at transfer proceedings or whose statements have been disclosed to the defence by way of notice of additional evidence. The notice of additional evidence procedure is used wherever the prosecution wants to use evidence which was not before the examining justices. A copy of the witness statement is served on the defence along with a notice saying that the prosecution will be adducing the evidence of this witness. The statement can be tendered in evidence (i.e. read to the court) unless the defence objects within seven days of the service of the notice, in which case the prosecution must either abandon that evidence or call the maker of the statement as a witness at the trial. There is no time limit within which a notice of additional evidence must be served, but if it is served just before the trial, so that the defence has had insufficient time to adjust its preparation in the light of the new evidence, then the judge should grant an adjournment. (For the position on disclosure of *unused* material, see **Chapter 10**.)

11.5.2.1 Taking evidence from the witnesses

Each witness called by the prosecution, having taken the oath (or affirmed) to 'tell the truth, the whole truth and nothing but the truth', is examined in chief by counsel for the prosecution (unless that witness is only being tendered for cross-examination) and may produce (i.e. identify) items of real evidence which then become exhibits in the case. Counsel must take great care not to lead the witness on matters which are contentious — if in doubt, ask your opponent if he or she will let you lead on specified matters.

Each witness is then subject to cross-examination by the defence. Cross-examination is not limited to matters arising from the examination-in-chief, but must be relevant to the issues arising in the case. The cross-examination is followed by re-examination by the prosecution; the rule against leading questions applies to re-examination and the questions must arise out of the cross-examination.

11.5.2.2 Formal admissions

If the defendant pleads not guilty then that puts the prosecution to proof of each and every element of the offence(s) on the indictment to which a plea of not guilty has been entered. The only exception to this is where the defence has made a formal admission under CJA 1967, s. 10. This provides that either party in a criminal case (though it is usually the defence) may admit any fact which would otherwise be in issue and this admission is conclusive evidence of the fact admitted. This admission may be made orally in court (by counsel) or in writing signed by the person making it, in which case the document will be read to the jury (but note that in the magistrates' court the formal admission must be in writing).

11.5.2.3 Reading witness statements

Formal admissions are not in fact very common. Usually, where evidence is not disputed by the defence, it will consent to the prosecution reading out the written statement of the witness who deals with the uncontroversial evidence (e.g. the loser of the stolen property where the defence case is not that the property was not stolen but rather that the defendant is not the thief). This is made possible by CJA 1925, s. 13. If a witness says some things which are not disputed by the defence but others which are, that witness will have to give oral evidence (since it would not be appropriate for the written statement to be read to the court) and it will no doubt become apparent from the cross-examination by the defence which part of that witness's evidence is disputed by the defence.

When the written statement of a witness is read to the court with the consent of the defence, the judge should explain to the jury that the contents of the witness statement are not in dispute and so the defence has consented to the statement being read to the jury without the maker having to attend court, thus saving time and money. The jury should be told that the evidence is just as good as evidence given 'live'. Counsel, in reading the statement, must read out the declaration signed by the maker of the statement, that it is true to the best of that person's knowledge and belief and is made knowing that a prosecution may be brought if the statement contains anything which the maker knows or believes to be false.

Note that where a statement is read to the jury because the maker is dead or too ill to attend court, the jury should be warned that the evidence needs to be viewed in light of the fact that the defence has not had the opportunity to cross-examine the maker of the statement.

11.5.2.4 Defence objections to prosecution evidence

If counsel for the prosecution agrees with the defence suggestion made before the start of the trial that certain evidence is inadmissible, the prosecutor should (via the Crown Prosecution Service representative or the police officer in charge of the case) warn the relevant witness not to give that particular evidence. If this involves evidence which will come into the possession of the jury (e.g. interview notes which count as real evidence and may be exhibited and so handed to the jury) this evidence may well have to be edited. In accordance with the *Practice Direction (Crime: Evidence by Written Statements)* [1986] 1 WLR 805, this should be done after consultation between both counsel and the judge.

If, on the other hand, the prosecution does not agree that the evidence in question is inadmissible, the judge will have to rule on the matter. As stated above, the prosecution opening speech will omit reference to the disputed material unless the evidence is so fundamental that a preliminary ruling has to be sought from the judge before an opening speech can sensibly be made. In other cases, the objection is taken either at the start of the evidence of the particular witness (immediately after he or she has taken the oath and been identified) or else at the point when the witness is about the deal with the disputed matter. When the objection is to be taken is a matter for counsel. At the appropriate time one of them (usually, but not always, the defence) will say that a point of law now arises and the jury will be told to leave court. In some cases, the objection takes the form of argument by counsel on a point of law (e.g. whether something is or is not hearsay). However, in some cases the judge cannot determine the admissibility of the evidence without hearing evidence. This hearing of evidence, by the judge in the absence of the jury, is known as a *voir dire* ('trial within a trial'). If the witness has not already taken the oath, he or she will take a special form of oath (or affirmation) to 'true answer make to all such questions as the court shall demand of me'.

The evidence on the *voir dire* is confined to the question of the admissibility of the evidence which the prosecution wishes to call in the main trial. This device is most commonly used where the defence wishes to exclude a confession made to the police and invoke PACE 1984, s. 76 requiring the prosecution to prove beyond reasonable doubt that the confession was not obtained by oppression and is reliable. The truth of what the accused said is irrelevant; all that matters is the circumstances in which the defendant made the confession. The procedure for taking evidence on the *voir dire*, however, is just like the trial itself, with examination-in-chief, cross-examination, and re-examination. Under s. 76 the prosecution evidence is called first, with the defence being able to call evidence (if it so wishes) afterwards.

At the conclusion of the *voir dire* or the submissions of counsel the jury returns to court and the trial continues, either with or without the disputed evidence (depending on the judge's ruling).

Note that if the accused denies uttering the words alleged, then this is not a matter for a *voir dire*; it is simply a question of whom the jury chooses to believe. However, if there is also an allegation of oppression or unreliable circumstances, the defence can ask the judge for a ruling on the admissibility of the confession, following a *voir dire*, on the assumption that the defendant did confess as alleged but without prejudice to his or her right to say to the jury that he or she did not confess at all if the judge rules the 'confession' admissible.

It should be noted that if inadmissible evidence is heard by the jury the judge has to consider whether the prejudicial effect can be cured by an appropriate direction in the summing up or whether the entire jury should be discharged and a new trial take place.

11.6 Submission of No Case to Answer

When the prosecution has called all its witnesses, counsel will say 'That is the case for the prosecution'. At the close of the prosecution case the defence may, if it wishes, make a submission that there is no case to answer (colloquially called 'a half-time submission').

This submission is made in the absence of the jury. Counsel for the defence makes the submission and counsel for the prosecution has the right to reply.

The submission is governed by the principles laid down in *R* v *Galbraith* [1981] 1 WLR 1039 (see p. 1042, per Lord Lane CJ):

(a) The submission should succeed if the judge comes to the conclusion that the prosecution evidence, taken at its highest, is such that a jury, properly directed, could not properly convict on it. In this case the judge should direct the jury to acquit on the count(s) in respect of which the submission has succeeded. If there are other counts on the indictment and either no submission was made in respect of them or a submission was made but failed, the trial proceeds on those counts.

(b) The submission should fail if the strength or weakness of the prosecution case depends on the view to be taken of the reliability of a witness and, on one possible view, there is evidence on which a reasonable jury, properly directed, could convict. In this case, the matter should be left to the jury and the trial should be allowed to take its course with the jury being left in ignorance about what has happened.

The basis for this distinction is that questions of the credibility of witnesses are matters of fact which are within the exclusive province of the jury. However, the words of Lord Lane must not be taken too literally. Regard should be had to the ruling of Turner J in *R* v *Shippey* [1988] Crim LR 767. His Lordship found no case to answer because of 'really significant inherent inconsistencies' in the complainant's evidence, which he found to be 'frankly incredible'. In other words, the judge can have regard to the sheer improbability of what the witness says and to internal inconsistencies in the evidence. If no reasonable jury could believe the witness, then the submission of no case to answer should succeed.

Note that where the only evidence against the accused is identification evidence, the special considerations highlighted in *R* v *Turnbull* [1977] QB 224 should be borne in mind and the case withdrawn from the jury if the evidence is weak.

If the judge wrongly refuses to uphold a submission of no case to answer this constitutes an error of law. Any evidence called afterwards (that is by the defence) is irrelevant on appeal as no evidence would have been called by the defence if the submission had been upheld. So if in the course of giving evidence the accused makes damaging admissions, those admissions will have to be ignored by the Court of Appeal. See *R* v *Abbott* [1955] 2 QB 497 and *R* v *Juett* [1981] Crim LR 113.

11.7 The Defence Case

The defence is under no obligation to call any evidence and so it would be possible for counsel for the defence to address the jury on the basis that the prosecution evidence has failed to show beyond reasonable doubt that the defendant is guilty. This may be appropriate where there is only just a case to answer. However, the Criminal Justice and Public Order Act 1994, s. 35, enables adverse inferences to be drawn by the jury if the accused either fails to give evidence or fails without good cause to answer which is put to him or her; it follows that the accused should, in the vast majority of cases, be advised to give evidence. If a defendant decides not to give evidence, despite the advice to the contrary of counsel, that defendant should be asked to endorse a note on counsel's brief confirming that he or she has chosen not to give evidence (see *R* v *Bevan* (1993) 98 Cr App R 354).

The defence case may start with an opening speech outlining the evidence the defence will be calling and showing how it will rebut the evidence called by the prosecution. In fact, opening speeches are rarely made by the defence (unless the case is a complex one). In any event, the defence is not allowed to make an opening speech unless it will be calling at least one witness as to the facts of the case, in addition to the evidence of the defendant. So if the only defence evidence is from the accused and/or character witnesses, there can be no opening speech.

11.7.1 THE DEFENCE EVIDENCE

If the defendant does give evidence, then he or she must be called as the first defence witness (unless the judge gives leave to the contrary) (PACE 1984, s. 79).

Each defence witness (including the defendant, if he or she gives evidence) takes the oath (or affirms) and is then examined in chief on behalf of the defendant, cross-examined by the prosecution and (if necessary) re-examined on behalf of the defence.

There is nothing to stop the defence from reading out written witness statements, with the consent of the prosecution, but this very rarely happens.

11.7.1.1 Alibi evidence

If the defendant wishes to adduce evidence of an alibi (i.e. that he or she was somewhere else at the time of the commission of the offence), then he or she can only do so as of right if the procedure laid down in CJA 1967, s. 11 has been complied with. This requires the defence to serve a notice of alibi on the prosecution either at or within seven days of committal. This notice must contains details of the defendant's whereabouts at the time of the offence and must give the names and addresses of any witnesses whom the defence proposes to call to support the alibi. A notice must be given even if the only evidence of the alibi will come from the defendant him- or herself (*R* v *Jackson* [1973] Crim LR 356. If the notice procedure is not complied with (e.g. the notice is served late), then the evidence of the alibi can only be adduced with the leave of the trial judge. If the prosecution has had sufficient time to check the alibi, then leave should be given. If it has not had sufficient time to investigate, then the trial should be adjourned to enable it to do so rather than refusing to admit what may be vital defence evidence, unless the defence has either deliberately misled the prosecution or refused to give any details (see *R* v *Sullivan* [1971] 1 QB 253 and *R* v *Jacks* [1991] Crim LR 611).

If the defendant does not adduce evidence of an alibi which has been the subject of an alibi notice (e.g. the defendant has a change of mind, or the alibi has been shown to be false), then the notice, which is given by the defendant's solicitors on the defendant's behalf, can be adduced as part of the prosecution case or be put to the defendant as a previous inconsistent statement (*R* v *Rossborough* (1985) 81 Cr App R 141).

11.7.1.2 Expert evidence

The defence may not call any expert witness without leave of the judge if it has not disclosed the expert's written report to the prosecution before the trial. See the Crown Court (Advance Notice of Expert Evidence) Rules 1997 (S.I. 1987 No. 716). When the Criminal Procedure and Investigation Bill becomes law, these two requirements of pre-trial disclosure by the defence will be subsumed within the general disclosure provisions applicable to the defence (see **Chapter 10**).

11.8 Closing Speeches

At the close of the defence case the prosecution may make a closing speech. The prosecution has no right to make a closing speech if the defendant is unrepresented and has called no witnesses as to the facts of the case apart from his or her own testimony. In a fairly straightforward case the prosecution will usually forgo a closing speech.

The defence always has the right to make a closing speech and this right should never be waived. It is a vital speech, giving counsel the chance to show how reasonable doubt has been cast on the prosecution case.

11.9 Two or More Defendants

Where two or more defendants are charged in the same indictment (and remember that joinder must satisfy the requirements of r. 9 of the Indictment Rules), and those defendants are separately represented, their cases will be presented in the order in which their names appear on the indictment. So if the indictment is against D1, D2 and D3, the order is:

D1 opening speech
D1's witnesses (including D1 if he or she wants to give evidence)
  Examination-in-chief by D1's counsel
  Cross-examination on behalf of D2
  Cross-examination on behalf of D3
  Cross-examination by prosecution
  Re-examination by D1's counsel (if necessary)
D2 opening speech
D2's witnesses (including D2 if he or she wants to give evidence)
  Examination-in-chief by D2's counsel
  Cross-examination on behalf of D1
  Cross-examination on behalf of D3
  Cross-examination by prosecution
  Re-examination by D2's counsel (if necessary)
and so on.
Closing speeches are in the order: prosecution, D1, D2, D3.

If the defendants are jointly represented, then they are regarded as putting forward a joint defence. Their counsel may make an opening speech. Then D1 may give evidence, followed by D2, then D3, then any other witnesses the defence wish to call.

11.10 The Summing Up

The judge's summing up follows the defence closing speech. It should contain the following matters:

(a) *The respective functions of judge and jury:* Questions of law are for the judge and questions of fact are for the jury. The judge is entitled to express a view on the facts but should always make it very clear that if he or she should seem to be expressing a view on the facts then the jury must regard itself as free to disregard what the judge has said about the facts. In *R* v *Jackson* [1992] Crim LR 214, the Court of Appeal approved a direction in these terms:

> It is my job to tell you what the law is and how to apply it to the issues of fact that you have to decide and to remind you of the important evidence on these issues. As to the law, you must accept what I tell you. As to the facts, you alone are the judges. It is for you to decide what evidence you accept and what evidence you reject or of which you are unsure. If I appear to have a view of the evidence or of the facts with which you do not agree, reject my view. If I mention or emphasise evidence that you regard as unimportant, disregard that evidence. If I do not mention what you regard as important, follow your own view and take that evidence into account.

(b) *Burden and standard of proof:* The prosecution has brought the case and it is for the prosecution to prove it, not for the accused to prove his or her innocence. Before convicting, the jury must be satisfied so that they are sure (a preferred formulation to the time-honoured 'beyond reasonable doubt'). The judge should not expand on what is meant by 'sure', as this is likely to generate confusion. However, if the jury later seeks further guidance, the judge can tell the jurors that they need to be as sure as they would be to make a decision which is very important in their own lives. If the case (exceptionally) involves a burden on the defendant (e.g. to show lawful authority or reasonable excuse for possession of an offensive weapon: Prevention of Crime Act 1957, s. 1) then the jury must be told that the standard is to the balance of probabilities, more likely than not. See *Ferguson* v *The Queen* [1979] 1 WLR 94 and *R* v *McVey* [1988] Crim LR 127.

(c) *The law and the evidence:* There should be an explanation of the law involved and how it relates to the facts of the case. The judge should remind the jury of the main features of the prosecution and defence evidence, even if the case is a straightforward one (see *R* v *McVey* [1988] Crim LR 127 and *R* v *Gregory* [1993] Crim LR 623). This involves fitting the evidence that has been heard into the legal framework of the charge(s) so that the jury knows what the prosecution must prove and what (if anything) the defence has said in response. In going through the evidence which has been heard, the judge must be careful to present both the prosecution and defence stories even-handedly (*R* v *Marr* (1989) 90 Cr App R 154). If there is an appeal, the Court of Appeal will look at the overall effect of the summing up (*R* v *Berrada* (1989) 91 Cr App R 131). In *R* v *Spencer*, *The Times*, 14 July 1994, the defendant's conviction was held to be unsafe as a result of excessive and largely one-sided comments made by the judge when directing the jury. It was said by Henry LJ that some comment is permissible, but not to the extent that the rehearsal of the evidence is interrupted and the jury's task made more difficult.

(d) *Identification evidence:* If the case against the accused depends on identification evidence, there should be a warning about the special need for care when examining identification evidence as a witness may appear convincing yet also be mistaken. The factors which should be taken into account in assessing the quality of the evidence should be set out. See *R* v *Turnbull* [1977] QB 224.

(e) *More than one count or defendant:* If there is more than one count or more than one defendant, a warning must be given that each count and each defendant must be considered separately. Where evidence is admissible against one defendant but not the other (e.g. a police interview in which a defendant implicates himself or herself and a co-accused), the judge must instruct the jury to disregard the evidence in so far as it relates to the other defendant.

(f) *Previous convictions:* If the defendant's previous convictions have been revealed, the judge must tell the jury that they are relevant only to the defendant's credibility as a witness and are not evidence that he or she has committed the present offence(s) (*R* v *McLeod* [1994] 3 All ER 254).

Where the defendant has no previous convictions, the jury should be directed that this is relevant both to the credibility of the defendant as a witness and to the likelihood that he or she committed the offence (*R* v *Vye* [1993] 1 WLR 471 and *R* v *Teasdale* [1993] 4 All ER 290).

(g) *Failure by accused to testify:* In *R* v *Cowan and others* [1995] 4 All ER 939 the Court of Appeal considered what should be said in the summing up if the defendant decides not to testify. The judge must remind the jury that the burden of proof remains on the prosecution. The jury must also be directed that:

(i) (as provided by s. 38(3) of the Criminal Justice and Public Order Act 1994) an inference from failure to give evidence could not on its own prove guilty;

(ii) it had to be satisfied (on the basis of the evidence called by the prosecution) that the prosecution had established a case to answer before inferences could be drawn from the accused's silence; and

(iii) it could only draw an adverse inference from the accused's silence if it concluded that the silence could only sensibly be attributed to the accused having no answer to the charge or none that would stand up to cross-examination.

(h) *Reaching a verdict:* Finally the judge will tell the jury that at this stage at least he or she can only accept a unanimous verdict (and that they should not at this stage concern themselves with the possibility of a majority verdict) and the judge will suggest that the jury elect a foreman to chair its discussions.

11.11 Bail

Once a defendant who was on bail before the trial has surrendered to the custody of the court at the start of the trial, he or she will only be released from custody if the judge grants bail. So a very brief bail application has to be made at the lunchtime adjournment and the end of each day. Such application should be made in the absence of the jury (as refusal might prejudice them against the accused). Some judges will withhold bail at lunchtime (e.g. where there is a risk that the defendant might come into contact with jurors); others grant bail but forbid the defendant to leave the court building or require the defendant to remain in the company of his or her solicitor. Once the judge has begun summing up the case to the jury, the defendant's chances of bail are, for some judges, slim; it is said that the prospect of imminent conviction is a good incentive to abscond.

11.12 The Verdict

11.12.1 THE JURY'S RETIREMENT

The jury is put in the charge of a jury bailiff, who takes an oath to take it to a private place and not to allow anyone to speak to it. The jurors then go off to the retiring room to consider their verdict.

Section 13 of the Juries Act 1974 (amended by s. 43 of the Criminal Justice and Public Order Act 1994) enables the court to allow the jury to separate after (as well as before) it has been sent out to consider its verdict. Formerly, separation was only permitted before the jury had been sent out to consider its verdict.

In *R* v *Oliver*, *The Times*, 6 December 1995, the Court of Appeal gave guidance on the directions which should be given to a jury which is allowed to separate before delivering its verdict. The jury must be warned that:

(a) it may only decide the case on the basis of the evidence it has heard in court; and

(b) jurors must not talk to anyone about the case except other jurors and even discussions with other jurors may only take place while they are deliberating in the retiring room.

Where a jury is sent to an hotel overnight, it must be told not to continue its deliberations in the hotel but only to discuss the case when it has returned to court the following day (otherwise, discussions might take place without all jurors being present): *R* v *Tharakan* [1995] 2 Cr App R 368.

When deliberating, the jury is allowed to have with them it exhibit in the case. In *R* v *Tonge* (1993) 157 JP 1137 the Court of Appeal considered what should be done if the jury (after it has retired) asks to hear the tape recording of the defendant's interview at the police station. It was said that if the tape recording has not been played in open court during the trial and the jury asks to hear the tape, it should usually be played in open court. However, if the tape has already been played in court, the jury may be allowed to hear it again in the jury room.

If the jury has any queries about the evidence, it passes a note to the judge via the jury bailiff. The judge will send for the jury and will deal with its query in open court, with both counsel and the accused present, having sought submissions from both counsel (*R* v *Gorman* [1987] 1 WLR 545).

Each time the jury comes into court, it is asked by the clerk 'Have you reached a verdict upon which you are all agreed?' If it has come back with a query, the answer will of course be no. If it has come back with a verdict the answer should be yes. A verdict must be taken on each count of the indictment separately. However, if two counts were in the alternative, if the jury convicts on the first count, it will be discharged from giving a verdict on the second.

11.12.2 ALTERNATIVE VERDICTS

It is possible for the jury to acquit the defendant of the count on the indicment but convict of another offence, a 'lesser included offence'. This is only possible if CLA 1967, s. 6 applies. This provides that where allegations in an indictment amount to or include, whether expressly or by implication, an allegation of another offence which may be tried on indictment, then the jury may acquit of the offence charged and convict of that other offence.

'Express inclusion' means that if certain words are deleted, you are left with the allegation of another offence: e.g. the indictment alleges that 'AB on 1st January 1996 entered 4 Gray's Inn Place as a trespasser and stole therein a television set, the property of the Inns of Court School of Law'. If the words 'entered 4 Gray's Inn Place as a trespasser and' are deleted, that leaves a valid count alleging theft. So if the jury feels that the prosecution has failed to prove trespass, an essential ingredient of burglary, but none the less find that the defendant stole the goods in question, it can convict of theft.

'Implied inclusion' means that the lesser offence is either a necessary step towards committing the offence charged on the indictment or else is an offence which, in the vast majority of cases, is a step on the road to committing the offence charged. See *Metropolitan Police Commission* v *Wilson* [1984] AC 242. So, for example, theft is a valid alternative verdict to a charge of robbery (where the jury decides there was no assault); indecent assault is a valid alternative to rape. Section 47 of the Offences Against the Person Act 1861 is a valid alternative to s. 20 of that Act (*R* v *Savage* [1992] 1 AC 714); s. 20 is a valid alternative to s. 18 of the Act (*R* v *Mandair* [1995] 1 AC 208).

In *R* v *Mearns* [1991] 1 QB 82 the Court of Appeal held that common assault, a summary offence under CJA 1988, s. 40, cannot be a valid lesser included offence as the jury can only convict of a s. 40 offence if it appears on the indictment. However, this decision needs to be seen in the light of certain statutory provisions which apply to other s. 40 offences. The Theft Act 1968, s. 12(4) provides that taking a conveyance without the owner's consent is a valid alternative verdict to a charge of theft and the Road Traffic Offenders Act 1988, s. 24 provides that careless driving is a valid alternative verdict to a charge of dangerous driving or causing death by dangerous driving.

Of course a jury will only be aware of its power to convict of a lesser included offence if it is told that it can do so; and even if the possibility is raised by counsel, the judge can decide to direct the jury not to consider that possibility. So what attitude should the judge take? In *R* v *Fairbanks* [1986] 1 WLR 1202 the Court of Appeal said that if there was an alternative and less serious offence to that charged, the judge should put the alternative offence to the jury if it was necessary in the interests of justice to do so. The court seemed to create a presumption in favour of leaving the lesser offence to the jury. The defence might argue that the jury might think that the defendant was innocent of the offence charged but guilty of something and so convict as charged to prevent the defendant getting off scot-free; the prosecution might argue that if the jury took the view that the defendant was guilty of something, albeit not the offence on the indictment, it would be wrong for him or her to be acquitted altogether.

In any event, in *R* v *Maxwell* [1990] 1 WLR 401 the House of Lords took a more restrictive view. In that case, the defendant was charged with robbery but would have been willing to plead guilty to burglary. The prosecution declined to add a plea of burglary to the indictment and to accept the defendant's plea to that rather than to robbery. Defence counsel asked the judge to leave theft to the jury as an alternative to robbery. The judge refused and his refusal was ultimately upheld by the House of Lords. It was said that, in view of the way the prosecution has presented the case, the essential issue was whether or not violence had been used; the theft was trivial in comparison. To have left theft to the jury would have been to distract it from the main issue in the case. As such it represented an unnecessary and undesirable complication. This decision appears to say that the judge should give great weight to the view of the prosecution before letting the jury consider a lesser offence.

It will only be in the interests of justice as far as the accused is concerned if he or she has had the opportunity of fully meeting the alternative charge in the course of presenting the defence case. Would the cross-examination of prosecution witnesses have been different? Would the defence have called different witnesses or presented its case differently? In other words, it is the same test as that applied if the court is asked to add a count to an indictment during the course of the trial. See *R* v *Wilson* (1979) (supra).

Where a judge refuses to leave an alternative offence to the jury, the Court of Appeal will only quash a conviction for the offence charged on the indictment if satisfied that the jury convicted the defendant only because it was reluctant to allow him to get away completely with his misconduct (see *R* v *O'hAdhmaill*, *The Times*, 13 February 1996).

It would of course be inappropriate to leave a lesser offence to the jury if it is inappropriate to the way in which the defence has been conducted; e.g. if the defence is one of alibi.

In *R* v *Salter* [1993] Crim LR 891 a jury sent out to consider an allegation of rape asked if it could convict of attempted rape. The judge allowed them to return a verdict of guilty to attempted rape. It was held by the Court of Appeal that where a jury is directed after it has retired that it may bring in a verdict on an alternative offence, this should only be done if the judge has first discussed with counsel the precise formulation of the direction to the jury and canvassed the possible need to remind it of any relevant evidence.

Note that a verdict on a lesser offence is only possible if the jury acquits of the offence actually on the indictment. In *R* v *Collison* (1980) 71 Cr App R 249, for example, the jury was unable to agree on an acquittal. To enable it to convict of a lesser offence, that offence had to be added to the indictment as a new count (and the decision to do this even though the jury had been considering its verdict for some time was upheld as the defence would not have been conducted any differently).

11.12.3 MAJORITY VERDICTS

The Juries Act 1974, s. 17 provides that a majority verdict may be accepted after the jury has been out for two hours or such longer time as the judge thinks appropriate given the nature and complexity of the case. A *Practice Direction (Crime: Majority Verdict)* [1970] 1 WLR 916 adds a further 10 minutes to the two hours to give the jury a chance to settle down and elect a foreman.

In the summing up (as we have seen) the judge tells the jury that he or she can only accept a unanimous verdict. And for the first two hours (and ten minutes) of the jury's deliberations the judge has no choice. However, after at least two hours ten minutes have elapsed, the judge may (if he or she thinks it appropriate) give the jury the majority verdict direction. That direction asks the jury to make a further attempt to reach a unanimous verdict, but says that if it is unable to do so, then a majority verdict can be accepted.

The only permissible majorities are:

12 jurors: 11–1 or 10–2
11 jurors: 10–1
10 jurors: 9–1

The latter two cases are where one or two individual jurors have been discharged due to illness or other necessity. If the jury is down to nine people, then the only permissible verdict is a unanimous one.

Before the majority verdict direction has been given, whenever the jury returns to court the clerk asks 'Have you reached a verdict upon which you are all agreed?' Once the majority verdict direction has been given the question becomes (assuming there are 12 jurors): 'Have you reached a verdict upon which at least ten of you are agreed?' If the answer is 'Yes', the foreman is asked (for each count on the indictment) whether they find the defendant guilty or not guilty. If the jury finds the defendant not guilty, nothing further is said (so it is never known whether the acquittal was 12-0, 11–1 or 10–2); if it finds the defendant guilty the foreman will ask how many jurors find the defendant guilty (to make sure that the verdict is a lawful one and not, say, 9–3 and to provide a piece of information which may be relevant in the event of an appeal, as the Court of Appeal may be slightly more willing to overturn a majority conviction).

If the response to the question is that it has not reached a verdict upon which at least ten are agreed, the judge will ask it if there is any possibility of it reaching a verdict, whether it be unanimous or by majority. If the answer is 'yes' (or 'maybe'), the judge will probably give the jury more time (though of course he or she should never say how long — that would be to exert undue pressure). If the answer is 'no', the judge will almost certainly discharge that jury from giving a verdict.

11.12.4 REACHING A VERDICT

No pressure should be put on the jury to reach a verdict. An example of the attitude of the Court of Appeal is to be found in *R* v *Duggan* [1992] Crim LR 513. The judge said to the jury that it was important that the jury should not feel under pressure, and that if necessary hotel accommodation would be provided for the jurors. The appeal against the conviction which followed soon after the judge's words was allowed because some of the jury had expressed anxiety about commitments at home and the thought of not being able to go home might have exerted undue pressure on them. Presumably, the judge should simply have sent the jurors to a hotel without giving them advance warning of this possibility.

Another form of pressure was considered in *R* v *Watson* [1988] QB 690. In that case the Court of Appeal provided a model direction to be given to a jury which is having trouble in reaching a verdict. Essentially, the judge may encourage the jurors to listen to each other's views, pooling their wisdom and experience, and engaging in give and take provided that each remained within the scope of his or her oath. However, if the judge gives such a direction, there must be no reference to the cost and inconvenience that would be caused by the need for a re-trial if it could not reach a verdict. See also *R* v *Boyes* [1991] Crim LR 717.

The *Watson* direction was considered in *R* v *Buono* (1992) 95 Cr App R 338. It was held that there should rarely be any need for a *Watson* direction, but if one had to be given it should be given either during the summing up [which the present writer thinks unlikely ever to be justified] or after the jury has been given a reasonable time to consider a majority verdict direction: the *Watson* direction should never be given at the same time as a majority verdict direction. Further, the judge should not add to the words of the model direction given by the Court of Appeal in *Watson*.

Where the defendant is charged with a number of offences and the jury indicates that it has agreed on verdicts on some, but not all, of the offences, it is good practice to take the verdicts on those counts upon which the jury is agreed before it carries on considering the other counts (*R* v *F* [1994] Crim LR 377).

11.12.5 DISCHARGE OF THE JURY

If the jury cannot reach a verdict within what the judge holds to be a reasonable time, the jury will be discharged. This does not count as an acquittal and there is every chance that there will be a re-trial. There is no need for fresh committal proceedings. In the event of the second jury being 'hung', the prosecution is likely to let the matter rest there.

11.13 Sentence

If the defendant is convicted of some or all of the counts on the indictment, the judge will proceed to hear the defendant's antecedents (including any relevant previous convictions) from prosecuting counsel, just as on a plea of guilty (see **11.2.1** above). Obviously, there is no need for the prosecution to summarise the facts as the judge has just presided over the trial.

It is possible that a pre-sentence report will have been prepared already, but this is very unlikely. Normally, the case will have to be adjourned (with the presumption in favour of bail created by BA 1976, s. 4 still applying to the defendant) for the preparation of a report, although the court may dispense with a report if it takes the view that a report is unnecessary. If the case is adjourned in this way, prosecuting counsel may ask to be excused from attendance at the subsequent hearing. Once a report is available, counsel for the defence makes a plea in mitigation in the usual way.

TWELVE

APPEALS TO THE COURT OF APPEAL

12.1 The Criminal Division of the Court of Appeal

The Criminal Division of the Court of Appeal entertains appeals from the Crown Court on all matters relating to a trial on indictment, and appeals against any sentence imposed by the Crown Court following a committal for sentence. Appeals on matters not relating to a trial on indictment, such as when the Crown Court hears an appeal from a decision of the magistrates, are heard in the High Court, either on appeal by way of case stated, or on an application for judicial review.

The following have all been held to be matters relating to a trial on indictment:

(a) A ruling given at a pre-trial hearing (*R* v *Southwark Crown Court, ex parte Johnson* [1992] COD 364, DC).

(b) An order staying the whole or part of an indictment (*R* v *Manchester Crown Court, ex parte DPP* [1993] 2 WLR 846, HL).

(c) A decision, after argument, as to the date of the trial (*R* v *Southwark Crown Court ex parte Ward*, *The Times*, 19 August 1994).

12.1.1 COMPOSITION OF THE COURT

If the Court of Appeal is hearing an appeal against conviction, the court must comprise at least three judges. Very occasionally, if the court is dealing with a case of exceptional difficulty, the court will consist of five judges. If the court is dealing with an appeal against sentence, it is usual for two judges only to sit. However, it is rare to have more than one judgment delivered, in order to make for certainty of the law.

The Court of Appeal itself consists of 28 Lords Justices of Appeal, and a number of ex-officio judges including the Lord Chief Justice. In addition, the Lord Chief Justice may ask either of the following to sit in the Criminal Division:

(a) any High Court judge, who may deal with any case that comes before the Court of Appeal, except a case in which he was either the trial judge or passed sentence; or

(b) in certain circumstances, circuit judges, who may sit in appeals specified as suitable by the Lord Chancellor, except that they may not sit on any appeal from the decision of a High Court judge (s. 9(1) of the Supreme Court Act 1981, as amended by s. 52 of the CJPOA 1994).

12.1.2 THE COURT'S REGISTRAR

The administrative work of the Criminal Division is carried out by the Registrar of Criminal Appeals, who receives all notices and applications, and in turn serves all relevant notices on the parties to the appeal. In addition, the Registrar will obtain necessary transcripts, exhibits or other material. Certain additional powers have been conferred on him by virtue of the Criminal Appeal Act 1995. See **12.6.1** below.

12.1.3 THE RIGHT OF APPEAL

The statute governing the right to appeal is the Criminal Appeal Act 1968, as amended by the Criminal Appeal Act 1995 referred to in this chapter as the CAA 1968 and the CAA 1995 respectively. The changes effected by the CAA 1995 came into effect on 1 January 1996, unless otherwise indicated.

12.2 The Appeal Against Conviction

By virtue of CAA 1968, s. 2, as substituted by CAA 1995, s. 2, a person convicted on indictment may appeal on the single ground that the conviction is 'unsafe' (see **12.2.2**). Leave to appeal is always required (see **12.2.3**).

12.2.1 GROUND OF APPEAL: THE 1968 ACT

Prior to 1996, the Court of Appeal would allow an appeal if one of the three grounds of appeal, discussed in paragraphs (a) to (c) below, were made out. The proviso to this was that the Court of Appeal could dismiss the appeal if no miscarriage of justice had actually occurred. This was known as 'exercising the proviso'. In this situation, the Court of Appeal in effect agreed that a ground of appeal had been made out, but that the ground was so trivial that the jury would inevitably have come to the same conclusion.

(a) *That the conviction was unsafe or unsatisfactory:* In deciding whether the conviction was unsafe or unsatisfactory, the court considered the case as a whole and asked itself the subjective question, 'whether we are content to let the matter stand as it is, or whether there is not some lurking doubt in our minds which makes us wonder whether an injustice has been done'. See *R* v *Cooper* (1969) 1 QB 267, per Widgery LJ, applied in *R* v *O'Leary* (1988) 87 Cr App R 387.

(b) *That the trial judge had made a wrong decision on a question of law:* If the appeal was on the basis of a wrong decision by the trial judge on a question of law, even if this could be demonstrated, the Court of Appeal still had to consider whether the judgment of the trial court should be set aside on that account. In effect it considered the proviso. See *R* v *Moghal* (1977) 65 Cr App R 56 and **12.3.4** below.

The following are typical examples of appeals on a question of law, which were decided before 1996:

(i) The wrongful admission or exclusion of evidence. If the jury would inevitably have come to the same conclusion, though the point of law was established, the proviso was applied.

(ii) Defects in the indictment. Where the indictment, for example, was bad for duplicity, or fell foul of the Indictment Rules 1971, r. 9, (SI 1971/1253), the court quashed the conviction only if the defect was serious.

(iii) Absence of corroboration. If there was no corroboration when it was required, the conviction was usually quashed, and the court only rarely applied the proviso.

(iv) A wrong direction as to the burden and standard of proof. If the trial judge failed to direct the jury on the burden or standard of proof, or directed it incorrectly, the conviction was usually quashed, and the court only rarely applied the proviso.

(v) A wrong rejection of a submission of no case to answer. If the trial judge wrongly rejected a submission of no case to answer, the appeal succeeded and the proviso was not applied. Had the judge not erred in law, the defendant would have been acquitted, and no matter what evidence was adduced in the trial subsequently, the acquittal would not have been affected. See *R* v *Cockley* (1984) 79 Cr App R 181.

(vi) A failure to deal with the essential thrust of the defence case in the summing-up. See, for example, *R* v *Jones* [1987] Crim LR 1701.

Note that the aim of a summing up is essentially practical. The fact that it contains something questionable from an academic point of view has been held not to give grounds for appeal (see *R* v *Ferrier; R* v *Barr, The Times*, 3 May 1995).

(c) *That there had been a material irregularity in the course of the trial*: An appeal on the basis that there has been a material irregularity succeeded if there had been a procedural error during the trial. But the irregularity must be major and material, i.e. serious enough to have affected the outcome of the trial.

The following are examples of irregularities discussed prior to 1996:

(i) Where the prosecution was wrongly allowed to make a speech. This was unlikely to be sufficiently material for the conviction to be quashed and the proviso was usually applied.

(ii) The constitution of the jury. Any suggestion that the jury was not properly constituted will be rebutted by the Juries Act 1974, s. 18, which says that no conviction will be quashed for this reason. But where, for example, a jury, having convicted one defendant, then sat on the trial of a former co-defendant who was being tried separately, the conviction was likely to be quashed. See *R* v *Gash* [1967] 1 WLR 454.

(iii) Interventions by the judge. If there was a large number of interventions by the judge, which effectively prevented the proper development of the defence case, then conviction was likely to be quashed. See *R* v *Matthews & Matthews* (1984) 78 Cr App R 23; *R* v *Gunning* (1994) 98 Cr App R 303; and *R* v *Ahmed, The Times*, 9 March 1995.

(iv) Improper basis for decision. In *R* v *Blackford* (1989) 89 Cr App R 239, the judge made a decision on a false basis of fact, and the resultant conviction was quashed.

(v) A failure by the prosecution to disclose to the defence material documents or information which should have been disclosed may be a material 'procedural' irregularity (see *R* v *Maguire* [1992] QB 936, CA).

(vi) A refusal by the judge to exercise a discretion in favour of the defence. The Court of Appeal was generally reluctant to interfere with the exercise of the judge's discretion, and would usually only do so if the discretion was exercised on the wrong basis (e.g. *R* v *Morris* [1991] Crim LR 385) or if the discretion was not exercised at all (e.g. *R* v *Dubarry* (1976) 64 Cr App R 7).

(vii) Errors on the part of defence counsel. The Court of Appeal will rarely allow an appeal on the basis that the defence counsel's actions had been mistaken or unwise (see e.g. *R* v *Satpal Ram, The Times*, 7 December 1995) but where it was shown that a decision not to call evidence was made without proper discussion and against all the promptings of reason and good sense, the court quashed the conviction (*R* v *Clinton* [1993] 1 WLR 1181, CA). See also *R* v *Swain* [1988] Crim LR 109; *R* v *Ensor* [1989] 1 WLR 497; and *Sankar* v *State of Trinidad and Tobago, The Times*, 28 December 1994, PC.

12.2.2 GROUND OF APPEAL: THE 1995 ACT

The CAA 1995 abolishes the three grounds of appeal and the proviso, replacing them with the single test of the safety of the conviction.

The CAA 1995, s. 2 provides as follows:

> *2.—(1) In section 2 of the 1968 Act (disposal of appeal against conviction), for subsection (1) (grounds on which Court of Appeal are to allow to or dismiss appeal), including the proviso, substitute—*
> *'(1) Subject to the provisions of this Act, the Court of Appeal—*
> *(a) shall allow an appeal against conviction if they think that the conviction is unsafe; and*
> *(b) shall dismiss such an appeal in any other case'.*

The Act does not contain any definition of the word 'unsafe'. However, it is generally assumed that the new test is designed to simplify the original tri-partite test outlined above. The old case law will therefore remain of assistance in determining what may or may not be 'unsafe' and it seems likely that many of the old cases would be decided in the same way today. In particular, the court may still apply the 'lurking doubt' test enunciated in *R* v *Cooper* (see **12.2.1(a)**).

12.2.3 LEAVE TO APPEAL

By virtue of the CAA 1968, as amended, leave to appeal against conviction is always required. This leave may be given by the trial judge or the Court of Appeal itself.

The CAA 1968, s. 1 provides as follows:

> *(2) An appeal under this section lies only—*
> *(a) with the leave of the Court of Appeal; or*
> *(b) if the judge of the court of trial grants a certificate that the case is fit for appeal.*

This provision removes a distinction drawn under the 1968 Act between questions of law and questions of fact or mixed law and fact. This was often difficult to determine, and this difficulty is now removed.

12.2.4 APPEALS AFTER A PLEA OF GUILTY

The defendant may appeal against conviction after a plea of guilty, but only in the following circumstances:

(a) where the defendant did not appreciate the nature of the charge; or

(b) where the defendant did not intend to admit that he or she was guilty of the charge. This would include cases where the defendant was pressured into pleading guilty by either counsel or the judge; or

(c) where on the admitted facts he or she could not in law have been convicted of the offence charged.

12.2.5 SINGLE RIGHT OF APPEAL

Under CAA 1968, the appellant has the right to bring an appeal before the Court of Appeal. If that appeal is dismissed, he or she has no right to bring a second appeal on the same matter (see *R* v *Pinfold* [1988] QB 462). Two apparent exceptions to this rule were recognised in *Pinfold:*

(a) where an appellant seeks to revive an abandoned appeal;

(b) where, owing to some defect in the procedure, the appellant has, on the first appeal being dismissed, suffered an injustice such as where he or she was not notified of a hearing date.

It appears that the appellant has a separate right of appeal on the basis that the proceedings were a nullity, as the powers of the Court of Appeal to issue a *venire de novo* exist independently of CAA 1968. See also *R* v *Larning* (1989) 90 Cr App R 450.

12.2.6 APPEALS IN THE CASE OF DEATH

Prior to CAA 1995, there was no procedure whereby the conviction of a deceased person could be challenged on appeal. CAA 1995, s. 7 inserts an entirely new provision into CAA 1968. Section 44A now gives a person approved by the Court of Appeal the right to begin or continue an appeal after the death of the deceased.

The persons approved by the Court of Appeal under s. 44(A)(3) must be one of the following:

(a) the widow or widower of the deceased;

(b) his personal representatives;

(c) any other person who, by family or other similar relationship with the deceased, has a substantial financial or other interest in the determining of the appeal.

The application for approval must be made within one year of death (s. 44(A)(4)).

12.3 Evidence

Under CAA 1968 as amended by CAA 1995, s. 4, the Court of Appeal may receive any evidence if it considers that it is necessary or expedient in the interest of justice.

CAA 1968, s. 23 as amended provides as follows:

(1) For purposes of an appeal under this part of this Act [appeals against conviction and/or sentence and references to the Court of Appeal By the Home Secretary] the Court of Appeal may, if they think it necessary or expedient in the interests of justice—
(a) order the production of any document, exhibit or other thing connected with the proceedings, the production of which appears to them necessary for the determination of the case;
(b) order any witness who would have been a compellable witness in the proceedings from which the appeal lies to attend for examination and be examined before the court, whether or not he was called in those proceedings; and
(c) receive any evidence which was not adduced in the proceedings from which the appeal lies.
(2) The Court of Appeal shall, in considering whether to receive any evidence, have regard in particular to—
(a) whether the evidence appears to the Court to be capable of belief;
(b) whether it appears to the Court that the evidence may afford any ground for allowing the appeal;
(c) whether the evidence would have been admissible in the proceedings from which the appeal lies on an issue which is the subject of the appeal; and
(d) whether there is a reasonable explanation for the failure to adduce the evidence in those proceedings.
(3) Subsection (1)(c) above applies to any evidence of a witness (including the appellant) who is competent but not compellable.
(4) For purposes of an appeal under this Part of this Act, the Court of Appeal may, if they think it necessary or expedient in the interests of justice, order the examination of any witness whose attendance might be required under subsection (1)(b) above to be conducted, in a manner provided by rules of court, before any judge or officer of

the Court or other person appointed by the Court for the purpose, and allow the admission of any depositions so taken as evidence before the Court.

The following points may be noted about this section:

(a) The test for receiving evidence is that of the interests of justice.

(b) The section permits any evidence to be called before the Court of Appeal, whether or not it was called at the trial.

(c) If evidence is to be received, the matters contained in s. 23(2) are important. These points, however, are merely matters to which the court should have regard and not conditions for the admissibility of the evidence.

(d) Section 23(2)(a) provides that the evidence must be 'capable of belief', replacing the old test of 'Likely to be credible'. In *R* v *Parks* [1961] 1 WLR 1484, it was held that the test there was whether the witness's proof of evidence is intrinsically credible, and whether it fits in with at least some of the other evidence in the case. The latter part of the test may still be applicable.

(e) As to whether there is a 'reasonable explanation' for the failure to adduce evidence at the trial, the case of *R* v *Beresford* (1971) 56 Cr App R 143, on precisely similar words decided that the test was whether the evidence could have been obtained with 'reasonable diligence'.

(f) *R* v *Guppy, The Times*, 8 March 1994, a decision on the old law, held that on a true construction of ss. 11(3) and 23(1)(c), the Court of Appeal is empowered to receive fresh evidence of any witness, including the appellant, on an appeal against sentence. It would seem that this decision would be followed under the new formulation of s. 23(1)(c).

(g) In *R* v *Ahluwalia* [1992] 4 All ER 889, the fresh evidence which the appellant wished to adduce raised a defence which was not raised at the trial (psychiatric reports as to the appellant's diminished responsibility). The Court of Appeal admitted the reports as fresh evidence, concluding that there may have been an arguable defence which, for some unexplained reason, was not raised at the trial.

12.4 Appeal against Sentence

The right of appeal against sentence after conviction on indictment is found in CAA 1968, s. 9. However, the Court of Appeal has always recognised that judges approach the question of sentencing in different ways, and must be allowed a measure of discretion in their approach. Thus, the court will not interfere merely because it would have passed a somewhat different sentence in a particular case.

The following are the most widely accepted grounds of appeal:

(a) The sentence is wrong in law. Where the judge passes a sentence which he has no jurisdiction to pass, such as a sentence of imprisonment on someone under the age of 21 years, the Court of Appeal will interfere. However, appeals on such grounds are rare.

(b) The sentence is wrong in principle. This contention covers two situations:

  (i) Where the appellant argues that entirely the wrong type of sentence was imposed, such as a sentence of custody when non-custodial measures were appropriate.

  (ii) Where the judge combines two sentences which are inconsistent with each other, such as a sentence of imprisonment and a probation order.

(c) The sentence is manifestly excessive. Here the appellant is arguing that the right type of sentence has been imposed, but that in the circumstances it is too severe.

(d) The judge took the wrong approach to sentencing. If the trial judge, in passing sentence, has taken into account an irrelevant consideration, such as the fact that the appellant has alleged that the police officers had fabricated their evidence, the sentence is likely to be reduced.

(e) The judge followed the wrong procedure prior to sentence. If, following a plea of guilty, there has been a dispute as to the facts of the case, and the judge accepts the prosecution version without any inquiry or investigation, then the Court of Appeal may feel obliged to reduce the sentence. See *R* v *Newton* (1982) 77 Cr App R 13 and, generally, **Chapter 14**.

(f) Disparity. Any disparity between the sentence imposed on co-defendants is probably best seen as merely a factor that the Court of Appeal will take into account when considering an appeal against sentence. It is unlikely, on its own, to support a successful appeal against sentence, but the view of the court has been inconsistent. On the one hand the court says that if the disparity is so marked that one of the former co-defendants is left with a burning sense of grievance, then it would be right to interfere (see *R* v *Dickinson* [1977] Crim LR 303). On the other hand, the court has also expressed the view that the mere fact that one sentence is wrong (the lighter sentence) is no reason for altering the right sentence and making two wrong sentences (see *R* v *Stroud* (1977) 65 Cr App R 150).

12.5 Procedure for Appeal Against Sentence

Preliminary note: The procedure is the same whether the appeal is against conviction or against sentence.

Within 28 days of the conviction (or sentence if the appeal is against sentence), notice of appeal, or notice of application for leave to appeal, should be served on the Crown Court at which the proceedings took place. The notice should be served together with a document containing the grounds of appeal. Both documents are in standard form, with a space at the bottom for the appellant to fill in the grounds. If grounds are settled by counsel, they will be typed on to a separate sheet and attached.

Detailed guidance on the preparation of grounds of appeal may be found in 'A guide to Proceedings in the Court of Appeal Criminal Division' (1983) 77 Cr App R 138. Students are also referred to the ***Drafting Manual***, **Chapter 24**.

The 28-day time limit may be extended under CAA 1968, s. 18(3), but there must be substantial grounds for so doing.

12.5.1 TRANSCRIPTS

The Crown Court sends the notice and grounds to the Registrar of the Court of Appeal. The Registrar may then order a transcript of any necessary part of the trial or summing-up, as specified by counsel in the grounds of appeal. It is rare to request a transcript of the entire case, and counsel should not do so unless it is essential.

12.5.2 GROUNDS OF APPEAL

Once counsel has received a copy of the transcript the grounds of appeal can then be set out in full, as counsel will now have, for example, the exact words with which the judge directed the jury.

No particular form of words is required when settling the grounds of appeal, but each point on which appeal is being made should be clearly identified. It is often convenient to make these points in chronological order. The grounds should refer to the transcript by page and paragraph number, and should cite any authorities upon which counsel proposes to rely. If counsel wishes to call a witness at the appeal, the reason why such a course is necessary should be explained fully.

In complicated cases, counsel may send the court a document expanding the grounds of appeal, and outlining the arguments he or she intends to place before the court. This may save time, and therefore expense, at the hearing of the appeal itself. Counsel has an obligation to ensure that skeleton arguments are placed before the Court of Appeal in good time, and not the evening before the hearing (*R* v *Muller, The Times,* 8 April 1992).

The Court of Appeal often reminds counsel not to make an appeal unless it is properly arguable. (See also section 6 of Annexe H to the Code of Conduct.)

12.5.3 THE SINGLE JUDGE

The application for leave to appeal, and any other applications (see **12.6** below), is placed before the single judge. No oral submission or arguments are heard by the single judge, who decides the matter on the basis of the papers before him or her.

If the single judge refuses to grant leave, the appellant has 14 days to renew the application before the full court, whose decision is final. When applying for leave to the single judge, or to the full court, the appellant should bear in mind the court's power to order 'loss of time' (see **12.7.1** below).

The court has power to extend the 14-day time limit, but very rarely does so.

If the single judge grants leave to appeal, the registrar ensures that all the matter is ready to be put before the Court of Appeal and prepares a summary of the case, to be read by the members of the Court of Appeal who will hear the case. Summaries of cases are now usually available to counsel in the case (*Practice Direction (Criminal Appeals: Summaries)* [1992] 1 WLR 938). Where the appeal is against conviction, the court will consist of at least three judges; in the case of an appeal against sentence, it will consist of two judges.

12.6 Powers of the Single Judge

Most of the powers of the Court of Appeal, short of deciding the appeal itself, are exercised by the single judge of the court under CAA 1968, s. 31. The single judge has power to:

(a) Grant leave to appeal.

(b) Allow the appellant to be present at the hearing of the appeal. Under CAA 1968, s. 22(1) the appellant is entitled to be present at the hearing of an appeal even if he or she is in custody. However, if he or she is in custody, he or she is not entitled to be present if the appeal is on the ground of law alone, nor on any preliminary application, without leave.

(c) Order a witness to attend for examination. The court may order a witness to appear before it, in pursuance of an appeal under CAA 1968, s. 23. This has the advantage of allowing both parties to the appeal to cross-examine.

(d) Allow bail pending the appeal hearing. Under CAA 1968, s. 19, the court has the power to grant bail to an appellant pending the hearing of the appeal. However, bail is granted only rarely, and only where it appears that the appeal is likely to be successful; or where the sentence is so short that it is likely to have been served before the appeal can be heard. In deciding whether to grant bail, the true test is, 'are there exceptional circumstances which would drive the court to the conclusion that justice can only be done by the granting of bail?' (*per* Geoffrey Lane LJ in *R* v *Watton* (1978) 68 Cr App R 293).

(e) Make, vary or discharge orders as regards, for example, whether the appellant is in custody or on bail pending re-trial.

(f) Make orders as to the costs of the appeal, including legal aid.

(g) Give directions for loss of time (see **12.7.1**).

12.6.1 POWERS OF THE REGISTRAR

By virtue of CAA 1968, s. 31(A), inserted by CAA 1995, s. 6, certain of these powers may be exercised by the Registrar. These are:

(a) to extend the time within which notice of application for leave to appeal may be given;

(b) to order a witness to attend for examination;

(c) vary the conditions of bail granted by either the Court of Appeal or the Crown Court. However, he or she may not do so unless satisfied that the prosecution does not object to the variation (s. 31(A)(3)).

If the Registrar refuses any of these applications, the appellant may apply to the single judge.

12.7 Powers of the Court of Appeal

12.7.1 FOLLOWING APPEAL AGAINST CONVICTION

Having heard the appeal against conviction the Court of Appeal may do any of the following:

(a) Dismiss the appeal.

(b) Allow the appeal and quash the conviction.

(c) Allow part of the appeal and dismiss the other part. If it does this the court may pass a new sentence on the remaining conviction, but this must not be greater than the sentence as a whole passed by the convicting court (CAA 1968, s. 4(3)). For example, the defendant is convicted of two offences and sentenced to one year's imprisonment on each to run consecutively. On appeal, one conviction is quashed. The Court of Appeal may increase the sentence on the remaining conviction to up to two years, this being the total imposed by the convicting court.

(d) Find the appellant guilty of an alternative offence. Under CAA 1968, s. 3, if the appellant has been convicted of one offence, but the jury, under CLA 1967, s. 6, could have found him or her guilty of another offence, then the court may substitute a conviction for that other offence. Thus, if the jury has convicted of murder, the court may substitute a verdict of guilty of manslaughter. Further, if the defendant is charged with two counts in the alternative, and is convicted on one but the jury is discharged from giving a verdict on the other, the court may reverse the verdicts. The court must consider that the jury was satisfied of facts which proved him or her guilty of the other offence. See *R* v *Spratt* [1980] 1 WLR 554. Section 4(3) (above) applies.

(e) Determine the appeal summarily under CAA 1968, s. 20. If the Registrar considers that an appeal has no real merit, he or she may put it before the court for 'summary determination'. The court may, if it is of the same opinion, simply dismiss it without a full hearing and without hearing argument from either side. This process is to discourage vexatious or frivolous appeals, and applies to all appeals, whether on points of pure law, fact, or mixed fact and law.

(f) Order a re-trial. Under CAA 1968, s. 7, the court may order a re-trial if it considers that a re-trial is required in the interests of justice. The power to order a re-trial is generally available, whether the appeal is on the basis of fresh evidence, or because of some irregularity or misdirection in the trial.

(g) Make an order for loss of time. Under CAA 1968, s. 29(1), any time spent in custody pending the determination of the appeal is to be reckoned as part of the term of any custodial sentence which has been imposed, subject to any directions to the contrary that the court may give. In *Practice Direction (Crime: Sentence: Loss of Time)* [1980] 1 WLR 270, it was indicated that such directions would be made in the following circumstances:

(i) If leave to appeal is refused by the single judge, unless the grounds of appeal have been settled by counsel. It would be unfair to penalise the appellant for following the advice of counsel.

(ii) If leave to appeal is refused by the full court, even if the grounds of appeal have been settled by counsel. The appellant has renewed his or her application in the face of the single judge's opinion that leave should not be granted, and thus is not protected from a direction for loss of time even if the grounds are settled by counsel.

In addition, the Court of Appeal has inherent powers, independent of CAA 1968, to issue a writ of *venire de novo.* If there has been such an irregularity at the trial that the trial can be said to have been a nullity, and the appellant was never in danger of a valid conviction, then the court may order the writ of *venire de novo* to be issued and the appellant may be re-tried. The irregularity has to be so fundamental that there could not be said to have been a trial (*R* v *Rose* [1982] AC 822).

See also 'The Court of Appeal Retrials and Tribulations', Patrick O'Connor [1990] Crim LR 615.

12.7.2 FOLLOWING APPEAL AGAINST SENTENCE

Having heard the appeal against sentence the court may:

(a) Quash any sentence or order which is the subject of the appeal.

(b) Impose any sentence that was available to the Crown Court, except that it may not deal with the appellant, taking the sentence as a whole, more severely than he or she was originally dealt with.

12.7.3 FOLLOWING AN APPEAL AGAINST SENTENCE AFTER SUMMARY CONVICTION

Under CAA 1968, s. 10, the Court of Appeal also has the power to deal with an appeal against a sentence imposed by the Crown Court after the defendant has been convicted summarily. Section 10 covers two separate situations:

(a) After committal for sentence. A defendant who has been summarily convicted and committed to the Crown Court for sentence may appeal against that sentence if:

(i) the sentence was to imprisonment or detention in a young offender institution for a term of six months or more; or

(ii) the sentence was one which the magistrates did not have power to pass; or

(iii) the sentence included disqualification from driving, a recommendation for deportation, or activation of a suspended sentence.

(b) Breach of a probation order or conditional discharge. A defendant who has been summarily convicted of an offence which puts him or her in breach of a probation order or conditional discharge, and who is sentenced by the Crown Court for the original offence, may appeal against that sentence in the same circumstances as set out in (a) above.

12.8 Other Methods of Appeal

12.8.1 THE ATTORNEY-GENERAL'S REFERENCE

Under CJA 1972, s. 36(1), where a defendant has been acquitted following a trial on indictment, the Attorney-General may refer any point of law that arose in the case to the Court of Appeal for its opinion. The purpose is to prevent potentially false decisions becoming too widely accepted. Whatever conclusion the Court of Appeal reaches on the point of law, the acquittal is not affected.

In order to bring proceedings under s. 36, the Attorney-General serves a notice on the defendant within 28 days, containing the point of law to be argued, a summary of the argument, and the authorities the Attorney-General relies on. The Court of Appeal must hear the argument from the Attorney-General or his representative, and may hear submissions from the defence.

Under s. 36(3) the Court of Appeal may refer the point to the House of Lords, either on its own initiative or following an application from either party. The House of Lords then considers the matter and gives its opinion

12.8.2 REFERENCE BY THE ATTORNEY-GENERAL ON A MATTER OF SENTENCE

Under CJA 1988, ss. 35 and 36, the Attorney-General may refer a sentence, which includes any order made by a court when dealing with an offender, to the Court of Appeal for review if:

(a) he considers that the sentence was 'unduly lenient'. This may, but need not, be because the Attorney-General considers that the judge had erred in law as to his powers of sentence; and

(b) leave of the Court of Appeal is granted; and

(c) the offence was triable only on indictment, or was triable either way but specified as reviewable in an order made by the Home Secretary.

By the Criminal Justice Act 1988 (Reviews of Sentencing) Order 1994 (SI 1994 No. 119), indecent assault, threats to kill, cruelty to a person under 16, and attempts or incitement to commit any of these offences were specified as reviewable.

If an offender is sentenced for two separate matters, only one of which is triable only on indictment or specified as reviewable, they are to be treated as having been passed in the same proceeding if they are passed on the same day, or passed on different days but ordered to be treated as one sentence by the sentencing court. Thus, sentences may be reviewed by the Court of Appeal even though they do not fall within (c) above.

The procedure for bringing a sentencing reference is the same as for bringing an appeal against sentence (see **12.5** above). The Court of Appeal may quash any sentence, and impose such a sentence as it thinks appropriate, provided it is a sentence which the Crown Court had power to pass.

The correct approach to sentencing references was set out by the Court of Appeal in *Attorney-General's Reference (No. 4 of 1989)* [1990] 1 WLR 41:

(a) The sentence must be *unduly* lenient, that is it must fall out of the range of sentences which the judge could reasonably consider appropriate.

(b) Assuming that it is unduly lenient, the court still has a discretion as to whether to exercise its powers.

(c) the court's powers are not confined to increasing the sentence.

12.8.3 REFERENCE TO THE COURT OF APPEAL BY THE HOME SECRETARY

Under CAA 1968, s. 17, where a person has been convicted on indictment, the Home Secretary may refer the case or any point arising in the case, to the Court of Appeal.

The reference is made by the Home Secretary in the exercise of his discretion, and the policy adopted by the Home Secretary is not one which fetters that discretion (*R* v *Secretary of State for the Home Department, ex parte McCallion* [1993] COD 148, DC).

If the whole case is referred, it is treated as if it were an appeal to the Court of Appeal by the defendant. This means that the defence then has the power to raise any questions of law, fact, or mixed law and fact. The defendant may, but need not, apply for a reference to be made, and in any event the defendant cannot be prejudiced by the reference as the court has no power to order loss of time in these circumstances.

If the reference relates to a point arising in the case, but not the case as a whole, the court will provide the Home Secretary with its opinion on that point.

Note: References by the Home Secretary will be abolished by CAA 1995, s. 3, which will come into effect when the Criminal Cases Review Commission is introduced (see **12.11**).

12.9 Appeal to the House of Lords

Under CAA 1968, s. 33, either the prosecution or defendant may appeal from any decision of the Court of Appeal to the House of Lords if:

(a) leave is granted by either the Court of Appeal or the House of Lords; and

(b) the Court of Appeal certifies that the case raises a point of law of general public importance which ought to be considered by the House of Lords. There is no appeal against the court's refusal to grant a certificate. See *R* v *Tang, The Times*, 23 May 1995.

One of the effects of s. 33 is that the prosecutor may appeal to the House of Lords against the order of the Court of Appeal quashing the appellant's conviction. If the prosecutor is successful in the House of Lords, the conviction will be restored.

12.10 Reference to the European Court of Justice

Under SI 1972 No. 1786, the Court of Appeal has power to refer a case to the European Court of Justice at any time before the determination of the appeal. (See *Archbold*, 1994 edn, paras. 7–302 to 7–304 or *Blackstone's Criminal Practice*, D25.3 for details.)

12.11 The Criminal Cases Review Commission

Part II of the CAA 1995 establishes the Criminal Cases Review Commission, to examine representations alleging a miscarriage of justice. The Commission will carry out any necessary investigation and refer cases to the courts, if appropriate. This takes over the present function of the Home Secretary.

12.12 Some Points to Note about the Commission

(a) The Commission is a body corporate, independent of government and the courts. It shall consist of at least 11 members, of whom at least one-third are legally qualified, appointed by Her Majesty on the recommendation of the Prime Minister. Further, at least two-thirds shall be persons who have knowledge or experience of any aspect of the criminal justice system, and at least one of them should have such knowledge in relation to Northern Ireland.

(b) The Commission may refer to the Court of Appeal any conviction or sentence following a trial on indictment, such a reference being treated for all purposes as an appeal by the person concerned under CAA 1968 s. 1 (CAA 1995, s. 9). Section 11 makes similar provisions in relation to a person convicted in a magistrates' court, referring the matter to the Crown Court.

(c) No reference should be made unless the conditions contained in s. 13 are satisfied. Section 13 provides as follows:

> *13.(1) A reference of a conviction, verdict, finding or sentence shall not be made under any of sections 9 to 12 unless—*
> *(a) the Commission consider that there is a real possibility that the conviction, verdict, finding or sentence would not be upheld were the reference to be made,*
> *(b) the Commission so consider—*
> *(i) in the case of conviction, verdict or finding, because of an argument, or evidence, not raised in the proceedings which led to it or on any appeal or application for leave to appeal against it, or*
> *(ii) in the case of a sentence, because of an argument on a point of law, or information, not so raised, and*
> *(c) an appeal against the conviction, verdict, finding or sentence has been determined or leave to appeal against it has been refused.*
> *(2) Nothing in subsection (1)(b)(i) or (c) shall prevent the making of a reference if it appears to the Commission that there are exceptional circumstances which justify making it.*

(d) The reference may be madc without any application to the Commission from the convicted person (s. 14(1)).

(e) In deciding whether to refer the matter, the Commission shall have regard, under s. 14(2) and (3) to the following matters:

   (i) any application or representations made to the Commission by or on behalf of the person to whom it relates;

   (ii) any other representations made to the Commission in relation to it;

   (iii) any point on which it desires the assistance of the Court of Appeal; and

   (iv) any other matters which appear to the Commission to be relevant.

(f) The Commission, when referring a matter, shall inform the court and any likely party to the proceedings, of its reasons for making the reference (s. 14(4)). However, the court is not restricted to dealing with the matter on the point referred to, and can examine the whole case (s. 14(5)).

(g) Where the Commission decides not to make a reference after an application has been made to it, the Commission shall give the applicant the reasons for its decisions.

(h) Section 5, part I of the Act inserts a new s. 23A into the CAA 1968, enabling the Court of Appeal to direct the Commission to investigate and report to the court on any relevant matters that should be resolved. The Commission shall then investigate the matter as it thinks fit and report to the Court of Appeal (s. 14). Sections 17 and 18 provide detailed rules as to obtaining documents which may assist in the exercise of the Commission's functions, and s. 19 empowers the Commission to comply investigating officers to carry out any necessary inquiries on the Commission's behalf.

(i) Matters may also be referred to the Commission by the Secretary of State, when considering whether to exercise the prerogative of mercy in relation to a conviction. This would arise when the criteria for reference are not made out, but there are matters which cause doubt about the safety of the conviction (see s. 16).

For a useful article on the Criminal Appeal Act 1995, see *Archbold News* 1995, 9, 3–6.

Multiple-choice Questions (based on Chapters 10 and 11)

1. Linzi appears before the Denton Crown Court to answer an indictment containing a single count of burglary, the particulars being that she entered the house of her next door neighbour and stole a hair-drier. Linzi says that the neighbour gave her permission to go into the house and borrow things whenever she wished, but admits that having borrowed the hair-drier she later decided not to return it. At her trial, her counsel asks the judge to direct the jury that it may acquit of burglary but convict of theft. Which one of the following statements correctly represents the law?

[A] The jury can only convict Linzi of theft if the indictment is amended so as to include a count alleging theft.
[B] The judge may direct the jury that it is entitled to acquit of burglary and convict of theft if he or she considers that it is in the interests of justice to do so.
[C] The judge must direct the jury that it may only consider the offence which appears on the indictment.
[D] The judge must direct the jury that it is entitled to acquit of burglary and convict of theft.

2. Edward is convicted in the Middlemarch Crown Court of burglary and sentenced to two years' imprisonment. He appeals against his conviction. Depending on the facts and evidence put before the Court of Appeal, which one of the following options is open to the Court of Appeal?

[A] Order a retrial.
[B] Make a direction for loss of time.
[C] Substitute a verdict of guilty of theft.
[D] Exercise any of the above powers.

Tutorial Questions

You have here the brief for an appeal to the Court of Appeal against conviction — *R* v *Lewis and Duke*. This is a continuation of the case used at the end of **Chapter 9**.

In the brief are the papers that would normally be available to counsel in order to advise on appeal and settle Grounds of Appeal.

For Lewis and Duke, prepare your appeal for the defence. Consider the arguments for and against the appeal.

Finally, consider ancillary points — e.g. whether Lewis or Duke should apply for bail pending the hearing; whether they can (or must) be produced in court for the hearing.

Lewis and Duke were convicted of the present offences on 5 January 1996. They received substantial terms of imprisonment.

R v *LEWIS AND DUKE*

Counsel has herewith extracts from notes supplied by N. B. Good, Esq. who was Defence counsel for the applicants at their trial.

Counsel is instructed

(i) to draft Grounds of Appeal against conviction for the applicants and

(ii) to advise on the merits.

Both applicants were convicted by a jury at Lewes Crown Court of robbery, contrary to s. 8(1) of the Theft Act 1968. Duke was also convicted of wounding with intent to cause grievous bodily harm; Lewis was convicted of this although not alleged to have actually committed the wounding.

Leave to appeal will undoubtedly be required from the single judge, no certificate having been granted by the trial judge.

As counsel was not instructed for the Defence at trial, instructing solicitors should make one or two points clear. First, the applicants were on trial for an armed robbery with two other men, Gerald Ella and Leonard Peterson, both of whom pleaded guilty to their parts in the incident. The applicants were separately accused of wounding Mr Goodbody with intent (OAPA, s. 18).

Ella turned Queen's evidence at trial and appeared as a witness for the Crown. His evidence was potentially very damaging for the applicants.

The judge allowed the Crown to adduce Duke's interview after a *voir dire.* The Defence made no objection to the Crown adducing Lewis's interview in evidence, subject to both interviews being edited to remove any references to the applicants having criminal records. The Crown agreed to this.

Duke did not testify in either his defence or on the *voir dire.* Lewis did testify in his own defence, alleging mistaken identity and fabrication.

Extracts from Defence counsel's notes of the trial follow.

Prosecution Case

1. *Cross-examination* of Gerald Ella (for Lewis and Duke)

I am not making the whole thing up.
Lewis and Duke planned the thing from start to finish.
I am not lying about this, they know it's true.
It is right that I have not been sentenced yet, but I am only doing this because I want to tell the truth.
I was a willing party to the plot but those two schemed it all, without them it would never have come off.

---

2. *Voir dire* (on Duke's interview)

Examination-in-chief of DS Law
I told Duke that we had his fingerprints from the Ford Escort.
At that time I thought there was a strong possibility that some of the prints we found might belong to Duke.
Some time after that interview occurred, I was informed by our forensic laboratory that none of the prints taken from the car matched Duke's fingerprints.

Cross-examination of DS Law (for Duke)
When I told Duke we had his prints, I genuinely thought that was the case.
It was not a deliberate lie.
I didn't need to lie, he knew what we'd found at his place.
I would describe it as unfortunate, that's all.

Judge's decision on voir dire:
. . . I am not satisfied that it has been demonstrated that DS Law lied to the defendant, Duke. It seems to me that there was a simple error of judgment. DS Law made an assumption which was very likely to be correct but later proved to be incorrect. I am not persuaded that the confession has been shown to be so unreliable that I should exclude it from the trial . . .
. . . I am bound to say, in any event, that there is no basis for the exercise of any discretion that I might have under s. 78 of the Police and Criminal Evidence Act to exclude the confession, as Mr Good argued.

---

3. *Cross-examination* of DS Law (for Lewis)

Lewis did take part in the interview, as recorded by DC Libby. DC Libby and I did not put our heads together and make up the interview.
Everything happened as recorded in the notes.
Lewis signed each page of the notes.

I don't agree that the signature looks 'nothing like' Lewis's.
Lewis actually spoke those words, they are not a figment of my imagination.

Defence Case

4. *Examination-in-chief* of Lewis

I know nothing about this robbery except what I've read in the newspapers.
I do know Gerald Ella but, until we were both arrested for this, I had not seen him for about 4 years.

5. *Judge's decision on an application by Crown to cross-examine Lewis under Criminal Evidence Act 1898, s. 1(f)*

I am satisfied that the cross-examination of both Gerald Ella and DS Law was such that no jury could be left with the thought that Lewis alleged them to be merely mistaken. Indeed, Mr Good has not sought to persuade me to the contrary. I have no hesitation in permitting the Crown to use Lewis's criminal record to show the jury his true character.

---

6. *Cross-examination* of Lewis

It is correct that I have several previous convictions.
About 18 altogether.
Some of them for robbery.
They were armed robberies.
Yes, they involved guns but no-one was ever hurt.
My last conviction was at Portsmouth Crown Court in 1988.
That was for an armed robbery.
I was sentenced to 10 years' imprisonment.

---

7. *Judge's Summing-up* (Extracts)

. . .

You may have heard something about the standard of proof, members of the jury. Well, the Court of Appeal has said there is no magic formula to help us judges to help you. But I can tell you that the defendants should only be convicted if you are persuaded in your own minds of their guilt. If in doubt, acquit.

. . .

As to Count 2, wounding with intent. You've heard Lewis testify that he was not there, and I shall be dealing with his testimony later. As to the law — the Crown do not say he was the man who pulled the trigger but they do say that Lewis must have agreed with Duke before the robbery that, in the event of trouble, they would use their guns. Or else, why carry them?

Even if there was no agreement, which you may think is so unlikely as to be fantastic, the Crown say that simply by standing by and watching Duke shoot Mr Goodbody, Lewis is as guilty as Duke. It's what we lawyers call aiding and abetting.

. . .

Miss Penny was quite clear that the masked man who spoke to her had an Irish accent. Whatever it was, she picked out Lewis as that masked man at a parade, having heard him utter that same phrase. You may think she is unlikely to forget the sound of that voice, members of the jury. Anyway, you had the benefit of hearing Lewis for yourselves. We know he comes from the Outer Hebrides originally and he hasn't lost his accent. Could you have thought he was Irish?

. . .

Ella's testimony was, you may think, quite persuasive. He is, on his own admission, an accomplice of the others. Until recently, I would have had to give you a complicated direction about his evidence. Now things are simpler. We can look more realistically at each witness's evidence on its own merits.

I caution you to take care when examining Ella's testimony — he is, after all, a self-confessed criminal but I need say no more about it.

. . .

DS Law told us about the frank admissions made by Lewis once he was incarcerated in Brighton Police Station and realised the game was up. You heard Mr Good suggest to DS Law that he'd made it all up with DC Libby — a suggestion hotly refuted by these two officers, who both have many years' experience in enforcing law and order. You may think, as I do, that Lewis's interview had the ring of truth about it. That's a matter for you.

A similar point was put to Gerald Ella — that he was lying to lighten his own sentence. I shall be dealing with Ella at the end of this trial, members of the jury, so don't worry about that.

As a result of this cross-examination of the Crown's witnesses, I allowed the Crown's application to cross-examine Lewis about his chequered past. What did that tell you about the sort of man Lewis really is? A man experienced in the ways of violence and armed robbery? There it is, I say no more about it.

. . .

Finally, you must consider the evidence against each man separately and on each count separately. You may recall that we heard the interviews of Lewis and Duke in which each clearly damned the other as well as himself. What they say about the other one outside the witness box is not evidence in the case and you must do your best to ignore it.

Note for Appeal. After the jury retired to deliberate (2.15 pm), the usher caught one of them slipping back into the jury room. The judge was informed and, in court, asked the juror where she had been. She said she had left to telephone her husband to say she might be late home (this was at 3.15 pm). No one saw her either leave the jury room or use the telephone. The judge rejected my suggestion to discharge her and allowed her back into the jury room.

The subsequent guilty verdicts (delivered at 3.45 pm) were unanimous.

APPENDIX

THE VICTIM IN COURT

The purpose of this appendix is to alert you to the very particular and special problems faced by the victims of crime, especially those who appear as witnesses in any criminal proceedings. It is a large and complex area, and this section can do little more than draw your attention to the issues involved. While it is intended as background reading only, you should not underestimate its importance in the conduct of your professional life.

The appendix deals only with The Victim's Charter, but students are also referred to The Code for Crown Prosecutors, and statements from the Crown Prosecution Service. Students should also be aware that a new Victim's Charter will be published in May 1996, but too late for inclusion in this edition of the Manual.

Note that the word 'victim' is technically correct only after a verdict of guilt has been recorded. Until then, the word 'complainant' would probably be more accurate. However, for the sake of simplicity, the word 'victim' is used throughout this chapter.

Note also that much of what is said relates to all witnesses, and not just those who are the victims of crime, and the word 'victim' should be understood to include other witnesses where appropriate.

History and Background

Until the middle of the nineteenth century, the person primarily responsible for the prosecution of offences was the victim himself. Consequently, he played a central role in the criminal justice system. With the introduction of efficient police forces, which took over the prosecuting role, the victim was reduced to the status of a mere witness, and any rights he may have had came to be ignored by the system. Indeed, many victims have found that the criminal justice system has served them so badly as to be a greater trauma than the offence itself. Some say that they would never again report an offence and face the criminal justice process a second time.

In recent years, a number of steps have been taken to try and redress the balance:

(a) 1964 saw the introduction of the Criminal Injuries Compensation Board (CICB) which has power to make *ex gratia* payments to victims of crime following an application to them by the victim. However, many victims knew neither that the scheme existed, nor how to make the application.

(b) In 1972, the court was given, for the first time, a power to make compensation orders to benefit victims in suitable cases. Similar problems of ignorance existed as with the CICB. This power has recently been extended by the CJA 1988, and students should refer to the sentencing section of this Manual for details.

(c) In 1974, the first victim support scheme was established in Bristol. Since then, such groups have proliferated, with now some 350 groups throughout the UK.

They are nationally organised, under the title of Victim Support, a registered charity, with a detailed Code of Practice to ensure consistency. Victim Support gives assistance to victims of offences immediately after they have been committed, throughout any court proceedings, and thereafter for as long as such support is needed. Special projects have been organised to improve skills in dealing with the most sensitive cases, such as cases involving racial harassment, the families of murder victims and child victims of offences. Recent research, by Mike Maguire and Claire Corbett, entitled 'The Effects of Crime and the Work of Victim Support Schemes', established that those who had been visited by Victim Support made a better recovery than those who did not. The writer is indebted to Victim Support for their assistance in writing this section of the Manual.

(d) In 1988, a working party, under the chairmanship of Lady Ralphs, CBE, JP, DL examined how a court appearance could be made less of an ordeal for the victim, and reported its findings under the title *The Victim in Court.* Following this, in 1990, the Government introduced *The Victim's Charter: A Statement of the Rights of Victims of Crime.*

The Victim's Charter

The Victim's Charter describes itself as a statement of the rights of people who have become victims of crime. However, it should be remembered that the Charter is not a statute, and does not have the force of law. Rather, these rights are an outline of what victims of crime may expect from the criminal justice system.

The Charter is in four parts, as set out below.

RECENT CHANGES

The first part of the Charter sets out briefly the changes that have taken place over recent years to improve the position of victims of crime. These changes include:

(a) Information for Victims.

One of the major complaints made by victims of crime is the lack of information available to them. Many will have had little or no previous contact with the police, the courts etc., and have very little idea of how the system works; nor has it been explained in a way which the victim can understand. Further, information has rarely been forthcoming about the progress of the case itself — whether any one has been arrested, whether bail has been granted, when a trial is to be expected and so on.

In order to give victims more information, the Home Office has produced two leaflets entitled *Victims of Crime* and *The Witness in Court.* The first should be made available to all persons who report crime to the police. It explains how to obtain compensation (from both the CICB and the court) and how to obtain information about crime prevention and about the progress of their case. The second leaflet explains what is involved in being called as a witness and giving evidence in court.

(b) Rape victims.

Home Office circular 69/1986 to chief police officers offers advice on the treatment of rape victims and victims of domestic violence. It includes suggestions for the provision of suitable facilities for the examination of witnesses, references to advice and counselling services and police training.

The Criminal Justice Act 1988 provides for the anonymity of rape victims from the moment the allegation is made throughout her life, regardless of whether or not any proceedings follow.

(c) Compensation.

The Criminal Justice Act 1988 contains provisions to increase greatly the use of compensation by the court. Students should consult the Sentencing section of this Manual for details.

THE TREATMENT OF THE VICTIMS OF CRIME

This is the most important part of the Charter, setting out in detail how victims should he treated, and what they are entitled to expect. These details are set out in a number of paragraphs, outlined below. As a guiding principle, the Charter affirms that all victims are entitled to sympathy and respect, while particular consideration will be given to those who are especially vulnerable, such as children and the victims of sexual or violent crimes. Further, while justice is dispensed openly, the media have a particular responsibility not to violate needlessly the victims privacy by turning the proceedings into a public spectacle.

(a) Reporting the crime.

The police should:

(i) respond to complaints of crime as promptly and as courteously as possible;

(ii) make readily available the Home Office leaflet *Victims of Crime*;

(iii) provide the victim with the name, station and telephone number of the officer in charge of the case;

(iv) ensure that they have all relevant details of the loss or injury suffered. This will then be passed on to the CPS which may then deal properly with the question of compensation if the offender is convicted;

(v) outline to the victim the investigatory process and especially tell the victim if a suspect is found, if he or she is charged or cautioned, if he or she is to be tried, and the results of that trial.

(b) Victim Support.

The police should inform the local Victim Support scheme about the victims of crime unless specifically asked not to. Victims can get in touch with the scheme themselves.

(c) Criminal Proceedings.

After a brief description of the way criminal proceedings are conducted, the following duties are outlined:

(i) the police will tell the victim, wherever practicable, of a decision to caution (as opposed to prosecuting) and remind the victim of how he or she may sue for compensation in a civil action;

(ii) if proceedings are undertaken, the CPS will check that the case includes a statement of the victim's injury or loss;

(iii) the police will take careful note of any fears that the victim may have that he or she will suffer further attacks, or retaliation. These will be communicated to the prosecution, and may be reported to the court when considering bail;

(iv) after any serious offence, particularly of violence, the victim should be told, normally by the police, if the accused is released on bail.

(d) Going to Court.

A common complaint of all witnesses (and not only witnesses!) is that they are called to attend court, perhaps at an inconvenient time, only to find that the case is adjourned, and they may have to go back another day. On some occasions this may be unavoidable, as where the accused changes his pleas. However, if this is the case, it is good practice for defence representatives to ensure that the court is informed of a change of plea without delay.

In any event, the following assertions are made in the Charter:

(i) the CPS will consider carefully whether witnesses will be required and will avoid calling them unnecessarily;

(ii) witnesses should always receive the 'Witness in Court' leaflet. In addition, many magistrates' courts produce their own leaflet, giving details of how to get to the court, where to park and so on — a practice to be encouraged.

(e) At Court.

Two major developments are highlighted by the Charter:

(i) In many courts, particularly magistrates' courts, witnesses are required to attend at the start of the day's business, but the case may not be called on for some considerable time leading to a sense of frustration and anger. In an attempt to counteract this, magistrates' courts are now urged to adopt a 'block listing' scheme, which gives the witness a definite time to attend. Note that while this has met with resistance in some courts, where it has been introduced, the system seems to work well, though the evidence is purely anecdotal. Thus the witness will be warned to attend at, for example, 10.00 a.m. or 11.30 a.m. In a handful of courts, the scheme is even more sophisticated, cases being timed for every half-hour or even every 15 minutes. Early fears that this would lead to much wasted court time do not, by and large, seem to have been justified. No research has been conducted on this issue.

(ii) Many courts sit in old buildings, where space is limited, and there will often be only one waiting area. It can be very intimidating for the victim of an offence — particularly an offence of violence — to have to sit in close proximity to the offender for a substantial period of time while waiting for the case to be called on. All courts are now being urged to provide separate waiting-rooms for prosecution and defence witnesses. The Home Office has revised the Design Guide it issues to Magistrates' Courts Committees when planning new buildings to incorporate separate waiting-rooms. Similar design standards apply to Crown Courts, some of which now have separate doors leading from the witnesses' waiting-room into the courtroom, so that witnesses can avoid contact with the public when going into the witness-box. Note that all Crown Courts now have a Victim Support witness service.

(f) Giving Evidence.

Arrangements to assist a witness giving evidence include:

(i) refreshing memory from the witness's statement, where appropriate;

(ii) live television links, to enable a child to give evidence outside the courtroom in cases involving sex, violence or cruelty. This avoids the child seeing his or her attacker in court.

You should consult the ***Evidence Manual*** on both these points.

(g) How the Case is Presented.

This paragraph of the Charter stresses that the burden is on the prosecution to prove their case beyond reasonable doubt, and the fact that it may fail to do so is a judgment on the strength of the prosecution case as a whole, and not a judgment on the victim. This is a point that victims often fail to appreciate.

It is the duty of the defence to put forward matters in mitigation as instructed by their client. However, matters may be put forward with which the victim strongly disagrees, but which he may have no opportunity to challenge. He may, for example, not be present in court and only learn of the matters raised in mitigation later. Even if he is present in court, the proceedings do not allow for him to reply, and the Charter states that it would not be right for the prosecution to reply (unless the matters raised are about the facts of the offence — see **Chapter 14**). Further, the court does not comment on the plea in mitigation, and so the victim does not know exactly what has been accepted, and what has not.

The Charter makes two points in answer to this:

(i) the victim can be reassured that the court will not simply accept at face value defence claims which push blame on the victim;

(ii) the prosecution must be ready to intervene when necessary to correct anything misleading, particularly where it attempts to denigrate the character of the victim.

These points are under continuing development and review.

(h) Compensation.

Where an offender is convicted, the court must always consider ordering him to pay compensation to the victim. Students should consult the Sentencing section of this Manual for details.

(i) Hearing the Result of the Case.

The victim may choose to remain in court until the end of the case, though many choose not to do so. The victim can expect to be told the result of the court case, and it 'may be practical' for the police to pass on the information. Such communication has proved problematic in the past, and work is being done to tackle the problem.

(j) Publicity.

Court proceedings are open, and all details may be reported, except for the offence of rape and other sexual offences, where certain restrictions apply; see **'Recent Changes'** above. However, newspapers occasionally publish material about the private life of the victim which amounts to an invasion of privacy. The question of what controls there should be over the publication of such material is under review.

(k) Offenders in Custody.

A difficulty experienced by some victims is on the release of the offender from custody. If the offender has been released on parole, particularly if a considerable amount of time was spent in custody prior to the trial (which would be treated as part of his sentence) then he may be released after what, to the victim, appears to an alarmingly short period. This can be particularly difficult if the victim and the offender live close to each other. This problem is not resolved by the Charter, which states that it is not generally practicable to tell the victim's family of the imminent release of a prisoner. However, if the victim is afraid that the prisoner, when released, will be a threat, the police should be told. They can then take specific precautions, if necessary.

If a prisoner subject to a life sentence is to be released, however, the Probation Service will be involved in making plans for his future, including arrangements for supervision. The Probation Service will get in touch with the victim and/or his family to see if they have any anxieties about the offender's release. Such anxieties may, if appropriate, be met by imposing restrictions on where the offender lives or works.

STANDARDS FOR THE CRIMINAL JUSTICE SERVICES

Part 3 of the Charter provides a checklist of questions for organisations involved in the criminal justice system, to test how well victims of crime are being treated by the system. Some examples are given below.

(a) The police

- (i) Is the victim given a contact at the police station to answer questions about the case?
- (ii) How is the victim kept in touch with the course of proceedings?
- (iii) Is it someone's job to tell the victim the outcome of court proceedings?

(b) Magistrates' courts

- (i) What arrangements are there to receive visitors (including witnesses) at court and give them directions? Are there good signs and notices?
- (ii) When compensation is ordered, does the court give victims adequate information about progress in securing it?

QUESTIONS FOR THE FUTURE

The final part of the Charter raises questions for discussion. These questions include:

(a) How can the family of a murder victim reply to things which may be said in court about their relative? Additional distress can be added to an already acutely distressed family if it is alleged by the defence that the victim was, for example, a drunkard or a drug addict. Such allegations may well affect neither guilt nor sentence, and so the prosecution will make no challenge and the trial judge will not comment. It thus appears to the victim's family that totally unfounded allegations have been accepted.

(b) If a compensation order is made, but the original estimate was incorrect, how can this be put right?

(c) Given that, with the volume of business going through the courts, priorities have to be set, how should those priorities be judged? Clearly a case involving child cruelty or sexual abuse will always be given a high priority. But how should the system weigh the need for swift action in crimes of disorder against other serious crimes, such as drug trafficking, where there is no identifiable victim?

(d) The courts frequently require a report from the Probation Service on the offender. Should the court also be required to consider a report on the effect of the crime on the victim? If so, should one be made in every case? Who would make it?

The Charter raises these issues for discussion only at this stage. You should be alert to such discussion from both sides of the profession, from organisations such as Victim Support and the Probation Service, and in the press generally.

There are two other problems that also need to be discussed:

(a) What right of redress does the victim of an offence have, if the rights outlined above are not complied with?

(b) Who pays? Additional duties are placed by the Charter on various bodies, but no additional resources are made available.

SENTENCING

THIRTEEN

INTRODUCTION

The Sentencing part of the Manual contains 13 chapters. This chapter includes an outline of the courts' sentencing powers, and **Chapter 14** describes the procedure between conviction and sentence. The remaining chapters do not purport to give complete coverage of the knowledge required for the sentencing part of the course. Rather, their purpose is to introduce the topics, to supply some basic information about the law and how it works in practice, and to provide a foundation for the lectures.

The material below goes beyond references to statutes and decided cases. It also directs attention to the statistics on how courts tend to use their sentencing powers, and how they approach sentencing for the different kinds of offences. (The latest statistics on the use of sentencing powers for offenders aged 21 and over convicted of indictable offences are to be found in **Figure 13.1** at the end of this introduction.) It also draws upon research into the factors which seem to weigh more or less heavily with courts when sentencing. During the 1980s it was an increasing feature of the Court of Appeal's guideline judgments on sentencing that the court would refer to the sentencing statistics and the aims of sentencing, as well as to the law itself. These chapters build upon that approach.

13.1 The Duties of Counsel

Most persons who are prosecuted plead guilty, which means that the criminal law and the laws of evidence hardly come into play in those cases. But in all cases of a plea of guilty or a conviction the court will pass sentence. In a small number of these it may be necessary to hold a *Newton* hearing in order to establish a factual basis for sentencing (*R* v *Newton* (1982) 77 Cr App R 13); the burgeoning case law may be found in D. A. Thomas (ed.), *Current Sentencing Practice;* in all cases, before sentence is passed, counsel may be called upon to make a plea in mitigation. This task places emphasis not only on advocacy skills but also on knowledge of the sentencing system and how it works. In addition to the detailed provisions of the Criminal Justice Act 1991 there has been further legislation on sentencing in 1993 and 1994. Courts may need the assistance of counsel in avoiding sentences which are unlawful or even unprincipled. Thus, there is a longstanding duty of counsel to prevent a court from passing an unlawful sentence:

> It was a matter for regret that in those three cases counsel had not considered, either in advance, or as soon as the sentence or order had been made, what power the court had to pass the sentence or make the order. It cannot be too clearly understood that there is a positive obligation on counsel, both for the prosecution and for the defence, to ensure that no order is made which the court has no power to make.

(*R* v *Komsta* (1990) 12 Cr App R (S) 63, in accord with such earlier decisions as *R* v *Clarke* (1974) 59 Cr App R 298.) Strong words on the same point were spoken by the Court of Appeal in *R* v *Hartrey* [1993] Crim LR 230.

A similar duty has recently been recognised in respect of guideline judgments and major decisions of principle:

> It seems to all members of the court that the time has come when counsel for the prosecution should draw the court's attention to guideline cases, not to ask for any particular penalty, but because a court is entitled to have its attention drawn to any guidelines which the Court of Appeal has laid down.

(*R* v *Panayioutou* (1989) 11 Cr App R (S) 535; the decision concerned compensation orders, and the term 'guideline' was used by the Court in a broad way to refer to any decisions on major issues of sentencing principle.) Occasionally, the Court of Appeal has encouraged counsel to cite appropriate appellate decisions when mitigating at trial (*Ozair Ahmed* (1994) 15 Cr App R (S) 286).

There is also increasing recognition of the duty of the sentencer to give counsel an opportunity to make submissions for or against a particular type of sentence:

> The Court has repeatedly held that if a judge is contemplating passing a sentence which is within his power but which a defendant or his counsel may not be anticipating, the judge is under a duty in fairness to the defendant to give notice of what is in his mind, so that counsel may have the opportunity of making submissions to him on that issue.

(*R* v *Scott* (1989) 11 Cr App R (S) 249, at p. 253.)

These decisions underline the importance of an understanding of sentencing practice and a knowledge of the sources for checking matters of detail.

13.2 Finding the Details of Sentencing Law

What are the principal sources? The statutory provisions and the cases are organised according to subject-matter in the regularly updated encyclopaedia *Current Sentencing Practice*, and there are also substantial sections on sentencing in *Blackstone's Criminal Practice* and in *Archbold*. Reports of Court of Appeal decisions are published each month in the *Criminal Law Review* (Crim LR), and there is a series of reports consisting entirely of sentencing appeals — *Criminal Appeal Reports (Sentencing)* (Cr App R (S)). However, these official reports convey only one part of the picture. In order to grasp the practical issues, the good advocate will also be familiar with the statistical trends in the use of sentences, will be aware of the latest research findings on factors which appear to influence courts in deciding to impose one sentence rather than another, and will also have an awareness of developments in penal policy (for example, the prisons, and statements of Government policy) insofar as they may affect sentencing. Some extracts from the Criminal Statistics are provided below. The best way to keep abreast of developments is to look through the relevant journals, notably *Criminal Law Review*, *British Journal of Criminology* and *Howard Journal of Criminal Justice*.

Legislative provisions on sentencing are scattered throughout the statute book, in such places as the Road Traffic Acts, the Magistrates' Courts Act 1980 and the Drug Trafficking Act 1994. For many years the most important statute has been the Powers of Criminal Courts Act 1973 (PCCA), which was intended as a consolidating statute. It includes most of the courts' general powers to impose non-custodial sentences. However, during the 1980s the pace of change quickened, and significant sentencing reforms were introduced by the Criminal Justice Acts of 1982 and 1988. By far the most important statute now is the Criminal Justice Act 1991, most of the provisions of which came into force on 1 October 1992. The CJA 1991 created a new sentencing framework, and also altered many of the details of particular forms of sentence (technically, by way of amendments of the PCCA 1973. The 1991 Act has itself been amended by the Criminal Justice Act 1993, and the Criminal Justice and Public Order Act 1994 contains further sentencing charges). The purpose of the paragraphs below is to give an outline of the courts' sentencing powers, leaving the details to the chapters that follow.

13.3 Outline of Principal Sentences

Before considering the choice of sentence, counsel and the court must consider two preliminary issues. One is the maximum sentence for the offence: this will usually be found in the statute creating the offence, but the legislature does alter maximum penalties from time to time. For example, CJA 1991 reduced the maximum for theft from ten to seven years' imprisonment, and the maximum for non-residential burglary from 14 to ten years. The other matter is the powers of the court: magistrates' courts are restricted by maximum fines and are limited to six months' custody (or 12 months on two or more convictions). The Crown Court is subject to limits when hearing appeals from magistrates' courts.

The framework of sentencing established by the CJA 1991 may he seen as a pyramid, in the following form:

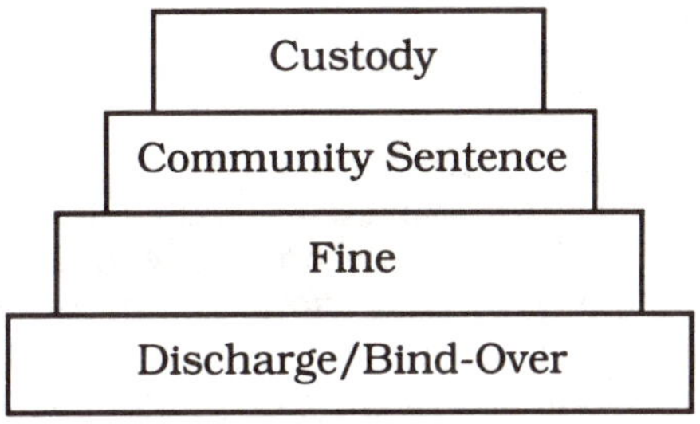

Starting at the base of the pyramid, the least that a court can do on conviction is to grant an absolute discharge (PCCA 1973, s. 1A substituted by CJA 1991, sch. 1). A stronger alternative is the conditional discharge, governed by the same statutory provisions, which discharges the offender on condition that he or she commits no further offence within a specified period of up to three years. If there is a further offence in that period, he or she is liable to be sentenced both for the new offence and for the original offence too. Some courts use, as an alternative, the power to bind over an offender to keep the peace, under one of several powers such as the Justices of the Peace Act 1361.

On the next level of the pyramid is the fine. The Crown Court may impose unlimited fines for indictable offences, unless the particular statute states otherwise. Whenever the Crown Court imposes a fine, it must also fix a term in default (PCCA 1973, s. 31A, as amended by CJA 1991). Magistrates' courts are limited to certain maxima, expressed in terms of five levels of fines. Most triable-either-way offences are on level 5, whereas offences triable summarily only are placed on different levels according to their relative seriousness (CJA 1982, s. 37(2), as amended by CJA 1991).

On the next higher level of the pyramid are community sentences, of which there are three main forms for adults — probation, community service and combination orders. A court may only make such an order if it is of the opinion that the offence is 'serious enough to warrant' a community sentence (CJA 1991, s. 6(1)). Some offences may be at a level where the court feels that the choice lies between a high fine or a community sentence, but most of the offences for which community sentences are considered will be too serious for a fine. A *probation order* places the offender under the supervision of a probation officer for a specified period between six months and three years (PCCA 1973, s. 2, as amended by CJA 1991, s. 8). Certain additional requirements may be included in a probation order (PCCA 1973, s. 3, as amended by CJA 1991, s. 9). A *community service order* requires the offender to perform unpaid work for between 40 and 240 hours, as specified by the court (PCCA 1973, s. 14, amended slightly by CJA 1991, s. 10). *A combination order* is a more restrictive order, part probation (from one to three years' supervision) and part community service (between 40 and 100 hours) (CJA 1991, s. 11). (In 1995 a fourth form of community sentence, the *curfew order with electronic monitoring*, was made available to courts in some areas: CJA 1991, ss. 12–13.) Before making a community order the court must always obtain the consent of the offender, and must usually obtain and consider a pre-sentence report (CJA 1991, s. 7(3)). When choosing among community orders, the court is required to select the order 'most suitable for the offender' and to ensure that the restrictions on liberty imposed by the order are commensurate with the seriousness of the offence (CJA 1991, s. 6(2)).

A custodial sentence may only be imposed if one of three justifications in CJA 1991, s. 1 applies. In most cases, the court will need to be satisifed that the offence was 'so serious that only [a custodial] sentence can be justified' (CJA 1991, s. 1(2)(a)). The Act goes on to provide that aggravating and mitigating factors that bear on the seriousness of the offence(s) must be taken into account (s. 3(3)). The court may then take account of any other mitigating factors (s. 28), and this may have the effect of reducing the sentence from custody to a community sentence. All these matters are discussed in **Chapters 21** and **22** below. They are equally relevant in determining length of sentence, because s. 2(2)(a) provides that the sentence shall be 'for such term . . . as is commensurate with the seriousness of the offence.' The power to suspend a sentence of imprisonment of up to two years remains (PCCA 1973, s. 22, as amended by CJA 1991, s. 5), but is now restricted to 'exceptional circumstances'.

The two other justifications for custody are invoked less frequently. The Criminal Justice Act 1991, s. 1(3) provides that a court may impose custody if the offender refuses consent to a community order. Section 1(2)(b) provides that custody may be imposed for a violent or sexual offence if 'only such a sentence would be adequate to protect the public from serious harm.' On this point, s. 2(2)(b) also provides that, for a violent or sexual offence, the sentence may be longer than commensurate if this is 'necessary to protect the public from serious harm from the offender.'

This pyramid of measures does not exhaust the court's powers and duties at the sentencing stage. In every case where there is death, injury, loss or damage, the court has a duty to consider ordering the offender to pay compensation to the victim (PCCA 1973, s. 35, as amended by CJA 1988). There are other forms of sentence not mentioned above, such as disqualification from driving, forfeiture of property connected with the commission of a crime (PCCA 1973, s. 43, as amended by CJA 1988), deprivation of profits of a drug trafficking offence (Drug Trafficking Act 1994, a mandatory procedure), and deprivation of profits of any other offence (Proceeds of Crime Act 1995).

Where the offender is aged under 21, the court's powers differ from those outlined above. The details are given in **Chapter 24**. Custody for young offenders is called 'detention in a young offender institution'. Where the offender is under 18 he or she will normally be dealt with in a youth court (CJA 1991, s. 70), and the powers are limited: detention in a young offender institution is only available from the fifteenth birthday, and its length must be between two months and two years (CJA 1991, s. 63, as amended). In exceptional circumstances custodial sentences are available for those under 15 and also for longer periods (Children and Young Persons Act 1933, s. 53). The statutory framework for fines, community sentences and custody established by the CJA 1991 applies to all young offenders. Two additional forms of community order are available. The *attendance centre order* requires a young offender under 21 to attend for a certain number of hours (the absolute maximum is 36) at an attendance centre (CJA 1982, s. 17). The *supervision order* requires a young offender under 18 to undergo supervision by the local authority, and certain conditions (such as intermediate treatment) may be included (Children and Young Persons Act 1969, s. 7). Both supervision orders and attendance centre orders are available from the age of 10, whereas probation, community service orders and combination orders are available only from the age of 16. When a court imposes a fine or a compensation order on an offender under 16, it must order the parents to pay in most circumstances.

There is also a different range of powers when the court is dealing with a mentally disordered offender. In addition to all the measures mentioned above, there are further possibilities such as a hospital order (Mental Health Act 1983, s. 37) and a hospital order with restrictions (Mental Health Act 1983, ss. 37 and 41). If a probation order is made, the court may add a requirement as to treatment for a mental condition. However, before imposing any custodial sentence on a mentally disordered offender, a court must obtain and consider a medical report and must take account of the likely effect of prison on the mental condition and on any treatment that may be available for it (CJA 1991, s. 4).

There is a separate set of penalties for road traffic offences, in addition to many of the general measures listed above, but they are outside the scope of the Manual.

Figure 13.1 Percentage of persons aged 21 and over sentenced for indictable offences by sex and type of sentence or order

England and Wales — Percentage of total persons sentenced

Sex and year	Total number of persons sentenced	Absolute or conditional discharge	Fine	Probation order	Community service order	Combination orders	Imprisonment: Fully suspended	Imprisonment: Partly suspended	Imprisonment: Un-suspended	Otherwise dealt with	Total immediate custody	Total community sentences
Males												
1983	100	9	47	6	7	*	11	2	18	1	19	13
1984	100	9	45	7	7	*	11	2	18	2	20	14
1985	100	9	43	7	7	*	12	2	19	1	21	14
1986	100	10	41	7	7	*	12	1	20	1	21	15
1987	100	10	41	8	7	*	12	1	20	1	21	15
1988	100	10	42	8	7	*	12	1	19	2	20	15
1989	100	12	43	8	6	*	11	1	18	2	19	14
1990	100	13	43	8	7	*	10	1	17	2	17	15
1991	100	15	39	8	8	*	10	1	18	2	18	16
1992(1)	100	17	37	9	9	0	8	0	17	3	18	18
1993(1)	100	18	38	10	11	2	1	*	18	3	18	23
Females												
1983	100	21	46	17	2	*	7	1	4	1	5	19
1984	100	22	43	17	3	*	8	1	5	1	6	20
1985	100	23	41	18	3	*	8	1	6	1	7	20
1986	100	24	38	19	3	*	8	1	6	1	7	22
1987	100	26	36	18	3	*	8	1	7	1	8	22
1988	100	27	35	18	3	*	8	1	6	1	7	22
1989	100	28	34	17	3	*	9	1	6	2	7	20
1990	100	32	32	18	4	*	8	0	5	2	6	21
1991	100	34	28	17	4	*	8	0	6	2	6	21
1992(1)	100	36	27	16	5	0	7	0	6	2	6	22
1993(1)	100	34	31	17	6	1	2	*	7	2	7	24

(1) Improvements in the data collection methods used by the Metropolitan Police District have led to an increase in the number recorded as sentenced of about 2% in 1993 and 1% in 1992 for indictable offences.

FOURTEEN

PROCEDURE BETWEEN CONVICTION AND SENTENCE

14.1 Advance Indications of the Sentence

If he or she wishes, a Crown Court judge may — prior to the indictment being put to the accused — indicate that the sentence either will or will not take a particular form, regardless of how the accused pleads (see *R* v *Turner* [1970] 2 QB 321, at 327). Usually such indications are given to counsel privately in the judge's room, and are then transmitted to the accused.

It is vital that, if an indication of sentence is given, it is not made conditional on how the accused pleads. If the judge were to promise a non-custodial sentence in the event of a guilty plea, and either expressly say that the promise would not apply were the accused to be convicted by a jury, or simply not state what would happen in that event, then the accused would be placed under intolerable pressure to plead guilty. In fact, his or her plea of guilty would, on appeal, be treated as a nullity. The Court of Appeal would quash the conviction and order a re-trial at which, presumably, the accused would plead not guilty (see **9.15, 9.16** and **12.3.6**).

Anything the judge says privately to counsel about sentence should be passed on to the accused. The court will then be bound by what the judge has indicated, even if there is an adjournment prior to sentence and a different judge actually deals with the accused (see *R* v *Moss* (1984) 5 Cr App R (S) 209).

Making pre-trial promises about sentence, made only in the minority of cases, restricts the court's freedom of action when the time to sentence arrives. It can do little to influence the plea because of the rule that the promises must not be conditional on how the accused pleads. Perhaps their greatest value is in a case where defence counsel suspects that the client really wants to plead guilty but is terrified that the result will be a custodial sentence. This saves a lot of court time, and is good for the accused as well, because the eventual sentence will reflect the credit he or she has earned by this plea.

No advance indications of sentence are given in the magistrates' courts because nothing is known of the accused or his or her offence prior to the hearing. A Crown Court judge, however, can familiarise himself or herself with the case by reading through the committal statements. He or she is also entitled to see the accused's written antecedents and list of previous convictions. Thus the papers in the case give the judge an adequate basis for such indications as to the sentence he or she considers proper to pass.

14.2 Advising on Sentence

Counsel has to rely upon knowledge of the tariff for the offence in question and on prior experience (if any) of the judge. There are suggestions (see *R* v *Cain* [1976] Crim LR

464) that, when completely unsure as to what the penalty is likely to be, counsel can ask the judge for a private *and confidential* indication of what the latter has in mind. In basing advice on such an indication, counsel would not reveal to the accused that he or she had seen the judge. In the light of *R* v *Turner*, however, it is highly unlikely that this procedure would now be approved by the Court of Appeal, and it is rarely, if at all, resorted to in practice. Either the judge gives a '*Turner*-type' indication which can be passed on openly to the accused, or he or she tells counsel nothing at all about the probable sentence.

An accused should always be told, assuming he or she does not know it already, that credit is given to an offender who pleads guilty. He or she receives a lighter sentence than he or she would have done had he or she pleaded not guilty and been found guilty by a jury. Strong advice, stressing the advantage of a guilty plea from the point of view of the eventual sentence, is permissible (*R* v *Peace* [1976] Crim LR 119), but it must not be so strong as effectively to deprive the accused of his free choice as to how he pleads (*R* v *Inns* (1975) 60 Cr App R 231). See also *R* v *Keily* [1990] Crim LR 204, *R* v *Smith* [1990] 1 WLR 1311, *R* v *Pitman* [1991] 1 All ER 468, CA and *R* v *Thompson* (1995) 159 JP 568.

14.3 Adjournments

The court does not necessarily sentence the offender on the day on which he or she pleads guilty or is found guilty. It has power to adjourn prior to passing sentence. The Crown Court's power to adjourn is one which it possesses at common law; a magistrates' court's power to do so is governed by MCA 1980. During the period of an adjournment before sentence, the offender is remanded in custody or on bail. He or she has a prima facie right to bail by reason of BA 1976, s. 4, but bail may be refused, not only on the grounds which apply before conviction as well, but also on the ground that the adjournment is for the purpose of preparing a report and it would be impracticable to do that if the offender were at liberty (see BA 1976, sch. 1, part I, para. 7). Where an offender remanded for reports is granted bail the court may, at its discretion, include a condition that he or she must be available for interview, etc. so that the report can be compiled (BA 1976, s. 3(6)(d)).

14.3.1 ADJOURNMENTS FOR REPORTS

Independent reports on offenders are often a vital factor in the sentencing decision, coming from sources such as probation officers and social workers producing pre-sentence reports, or from doctors and psychiatrists producing medical reports. Where an accused intimates an intention to plead guilty and it seems likely that the court will need reports before sentencing, they are prepared before the hearing if that is at all possible. If, however, the accused is pleading not guilty it is unlikely that reports will be prepared. Even if pleading guilty, reports are not prepared automatically. Sometimes the court can properly proceed without reports, but in many cases the sentencer's provisional view of the proper sentence will be such that to pass it without consulting a report would either be positively unlawful or at least bad sentencing practice. The court must then adjourn for reports. Two or three weeks will probably be sufficient, although the Crown Court could in theory adjourn for any period. Section 10(3) of MCA 1980 provides that when magistrates adjourn for reports it must be for not more than four weeks if the offender is remanded on bail, and not more than three weeks if he or she is in custody.

Section 10(3), which applies to adjournments for any type of report, is supplemented by s. 30 of the 1980 Act which applies only to medical reports. The main difference between the two sections is that under s. 30 the magistrates can adjourn for a medical report even before convicting the accused, provided they are satisfied that he or she committed the *actus reus* of the offence charged. This may enable them to make a *hospital* order without finding the accused guilty. Adjournments under s. 10(3), on the other hand, presuppose that the magistrates have convicted the accused. In addition, provisions under ss. 35 and 36 of the Mental Health Act (MHA) 1983, allow both the

Crown Court and magistrates' courts to remand offenders to a hospital for the preparation of reports.

14.3.2 ADJOURNMENTS WHERE THERE ARE SEVERAL ACCUSED

Sentencing joint offenders together should ensure consistent treatment for them all, with any disparity in sentence being justified by the differing degrees to which they were involved in the criminal conduct or by differences in their records.

If there are consistent pleas between the accused there should be no problem. But, if one accused (A1) pleads guilty and another accused (A2) pleads not guilty, then difficulties arise. A2 obviously cannot be sentenced unless and until he or she is convicted by a jury. The desirability of dealing with A1 and (if convicted) A2 together has led to a general rule that sentence on A1 should be postponed until after the trial of A2. This has the additional advantage of allowing the judge to hear the evidence called at A2's trial, and proportion his or her sentence according to which, if either, of the accused apparently played the leading role in the offence(s) (see *R* v *Payne* [1950] 1 All ER 102).

However, a special problem arises if A1 is going to be called by the prosecution at the trial of A2, since he or she might be tempted to give false evidence minimising his or her own part in the crime. For this reason, it used to be the practice in such cases to depart from the general rule and sentence A1 before A2's trial (*R* v *Payne, supra*). More recently, the Court of Appeal has indicated strongly that the general rule should always be followed, notwithstanding that Al will be a prosecution witness (see *R* v *Weekes* (1982) 74 Cr App R 161). Perhaps, though, the matter should be left to the discretion of the trial judge, who is in the best position to balance the interests of the co-accused (that the accomplice, when he or she testifies, should have no motive for giving false evidence) against the wider interests of justice (that confederates in crime should be sentenced together so as to avoid unjustified differences in sentence).

If the accomplice is sentenced before testifying for the prosecution, defence counsel in mitigation may outline the evidence his or her client proposes to give. This will no doubt secure a significant reduction in sentence. Should the accomplice fail to give the evidence thus foreshadowed, his or her sentence may *not* be increased (*R* v *Stone* [1970] 1 WLR 1112).

The desirability of sentencing confederates in crime together applies when they are to be dealt with in the magistrates' court just as much as when they are to be dealt with in the Crown Court.

14.3.3 ADJOURNMENTS WHERE THERE ARE OUTSTANDING CHARGES

It is desirable that an accused with several charges outstanding against him or her should be sentenced on one occasion for all matters in respect of which he or she is ultimately convicted. If he or she is sentenced piecemeal by different judges (or even by the same judge on different occasions) there is a danger that the aggregate sentence will be out of proportion to the overall gravity of his or her conduct. There is also a danger that the first judge, dealing perhaps with the less serious offences, will pass a non-custodial sentence and thus create a dilemma for the second judge. The latter may feel that a custodial sentence is necessary for the offences with which he or she is dealing, but to pass such a sentence might prevent the earlier non-custodial sentence running its natural course. To avoid such difficulties, it is better that one sentencer should deal with everything on one occasion, even if this means adjournments and some extra administrative work behind the scenes.

Much will depend on whether or not the offences have been joined in the indictment, under r. 9 of the Indictment Rules 1971. A court and jury can try only one indictment at a time, so sentence on one indictment where the accused is found guilty may have to be postponed until trial of a second indictment. Furthermore, where an accused has indictments outstanding against him or her at different locations of the Crown Court, it will be necessary for one location to transfer its indictment to the second location (see *R* v *Bennett* (1980) 2 Cr App R (S) 96).

14.4 The Facts of the Offences

If the accused pleads guilty, the first stage in the procedure (before sentence is passed) is for the prosecution to present the brief facts of the offence. In the Crown Court this is always the task of counsel, or solicitor with rights of audience in the Crown Court, for the prosecution must be legally represented for proceedings on indictment (*R* v *George Maxwell Developments Ltd* [1980] 2 All ER 99).

In the magistrates' court, the prosecution case will be presented by a Crown Prosecutor (or by an agent instructed by the CPS). The procedure before sentence is passed is essentially the same in both the Crown Court and magistrates' courts, but it is less formal in the latter.

14.4.1 PRESENTING THE FACTS

The prosecuting advocate in the Crown Court has the benefit of the statements from the committal proceedings. Counsel summarises the prosecution case based on these statements. He or she will probably describe in sequence: (i) the circumstances, method and gravity of the offence; (ii) the manner in which the offender was arrested; and (iii) his or her questioning at the police station.

Concerning the advocate's account of the offence itself, details which should be included will obviously vary according to the nature of the offence. The degree of planning which apparently preceded the commission of the offence is always a relevant factor, as is any other aggravating factor, e.g. breach of trust in an offence involving dishonesty committed by an employee against his or her employer.

As to the arrest and questioning of the offender, the judge will want to know whether the offender was frank and cooperative with the police. If he or she was, that is useful mitigation. Also, what the offender said to the police may foreshadow what defence counsel will say in his or her speech in mitigation about the way the offence was committed, the motive for it, and the offender's degree of involvement in it if it was a joint offence. Where the offender followed up verbal admissions by making a written statement under caution, the advocate can either read it out in full or give the gist of it, whichever seems more convenient.

When presenting the facts, the prosecuting advocate should not try to make the offence seem as serious as possible so as to obtain a heavy sentence. Traditionally, the prosecution has taken a neutral attitude to the sentence which ought to be passed, not asking for any particular sentence. So, the advocate must present the facts fairly in the light of the prosecution evidence contained in the committal statements, conceding to the defence those points in mitigation which are apparent from the statements, but equally giving full weight to any aggravating factors which make the offence a serious one of its type. In particular, if the offender (in his or her statements to the police) or defence advocate (in mitigation) puts forward a version of the facts of the offence which does not accord with the evidence the prosecution has available, the advocate should indicate that he or she cannot accept what the defence is saying about the offence.

Two further points should be made:

(a) Prosecuting advocate should apply for compensation, confiscation or forfeiture if appropriate.

(b) Both prosecuting and defence advocate should draw the court's attention to any limits on its sentencing powers (*R* v *Komsta* [1990] 12 Cr App R (S) 63). In addition, prosecuting advocate should also mention guidelines cases (*R* v *Panayioutou* [1989] 11 Cr App R (S) 535. See also *R* v *Hartrey* (1993) 14 Cr App R (S) 507.

14.4.2 DISPUTES ABOUT THE FACTS AFTER A GUILTY PLEA

By pleading guilty an offender does not necessarily concede that the prosecution case against him or her is correct in its entirety. He or she admits, of course, that he or she committed the offence described in each of the counts of the indictment to which he or she enters a guilty plea, and if the defence advocate says anything in mitigation which is inconsistent with the pleas the judge will ignore that part of the mitigation or invite the defence to consider a change of plea. But the particulars about an offence given in a count of an indictment are so basic that they only partially reveal whether the offence is a serious or trivial one of its type. Thus, it occasionally happens that an offender quite properly pleads guilty and then, after the facts have been presented by the prosecuting advocate, denies that his or her crime was as grave as has been alleged. However, the sentence can be significantly affected by whether the judge accepts the prosecution statement of facts or the defence mitigation.

Guidance in these circumstances is given by *R* v *Newton* (1982) 77 Cr App R 13, followed in *R* v *Costley* (1989) 11 Cr App R (S) 357. After the guilty plea, the judge may either:

(a) hear whatever evidence the parties wish to call on the disputed issue, and come down on one side or the other (this is usually referred to as a '*Newton* hearing'); or

(b) act merely on the basis of counsels' respective submissions, in which case he or she must accept the defence version as far as possible; or

(c) empanel a jury to decide the issue. In such a case a count will be added to the indictment by way of amendment and a trial on that count will ensue.

Defence solicitor and counsel have a duty to notify the Crown that a guilty plea will be put forward, but that the prosecution version of the facts would be contested, so that the prosecution could ensure the presence of any necessary witnesses, to enable a *Newton* hearing to proceed (*R* v *Mokun* [1992] Crim LR 98, CA; *R* v *Gardener* [1994] Crim LR 301).

When the judge conducts a *Newton* hearing, the rules of evidence should be strictly followed, and the judge should give himself or herself the same directions which he or she would give to a jury, for example, in accordance with the guidelines in *Turnbull* (*R* v *Gandy* (1989) 11 Cr App R (S) 564). Further he or she should openly direct himself or herself that the facts have to be proved to the criminal standard, though failure to do so will not necessarily be fatal (*R* v *Kerrigan* (1992) 156 JP 889, CA).

It is not right, on a *Newton* hearing, to sentence the defendant on the basis of a more serious offence than charged. In *R* v *Druce* (1993) 14 Cr App R (S) 691, CA, the prosecution alleged rape although the charges were unlawful sexual intercourse and indecent assault. The Court of Appeal held that if that was the prosecution case, he should have been so charged. The judge had no alternative but to deal with the case by giving the defendant the benefit of the doubt, and proceed on the basis that the complainant had consented.

It should be noted that the defence cannot frustrate the *Newton* inquiry procedure by declining to give evidence. In these circumstances, where the basic facts are not in dispute, the judge is entitled to draw inferences from these undisputed facts (*R* v *Mirza* (1992) 14 Cr App R (S) 64, CA).

Where the alleged facts relied upon by the offender to reduce the gravity of the offence are exclusively within his or her knowledge, so that the prosecution cannot reasonably be expected to call evidence in rebuttal, the judge is entitled to reject the offender's evidence of what happened as unbelievable, notwithstanding that it is the only evidence there is (*R* v *Kerr* (1980) 2 Cr App R (S) 54); and see *R* v *Hawkins* (1983) 7 Cr App R (S) 351 where it was said that the judge is entitled to reject the defence version without hearing evidence if the story is 'incredible').

Occasionally, a defendant will decide to change his plea halfway through the trial, after at least some evidence has been given for the prosecution. In these circumstances, the judge should hear evidence from the defendant and then decide upon the version of facts upon which he is going to sentence, forming his view on the whole of the evidence which was given. See *R* v *Mottram* [1981] 3 Cr App R (S) 123 and *R* v *Archer* [1994] Crim LR 80.

Section 2(2)(b) of the Criminal Justice Act 1991 provides for the imposition of longer than normal sentences where the offence is of a violent or sexual nature and the court is of the opinion that it is necessary in order to protect the public from harm from the offender. In such a situation, the court must hold a *Newton* hearing to resolve any important issue relevant to sentence. See *R* v *Oudkerk* [1994] Crim LR 700.

Credit should be given for a plea of guilty, since court time has been saved, even if the judge rejects the version of the facts put forward by the defendant, taking the view that the plea was put forward on a false basis: *R* v *Williams* (1990) 12 Cr App R (S) 415.

If the judge wrongly is to hold a *Newton* hearing, the Court of Appeal, may vary the sentence to one which is appropriate on the basis that the defendant's version of events is correct (*R* v *Mohun* (1993) 14 Cr App R (S) 5).

See *R* v *Cranston* (1993) 14 Cr App R (S) 103, CA, for a recent example and note that further guidance has been provided by the Court of Appeal in *R* v *Beswick* (1996) 160 JP 33. See **9.15**.

14.4.3 DISPUTES ABOUT THE FACTS AFTER A VERDICT OF GUILTY

Post-conviction disputes about the circumstances of the offence are not limited to cases where the offender pleaded guilty, for a jury's verdict of guilty after a not guilty plea is not necessarily a total vindication of the prosecution's case. In such cases it is for the judge to form a personal view of the evidence adduced before the jury, and decide what the facts of the offence were. He or she should not ask the jury the reasons for its verdict or what facts it found proved (*per* Humphreys J in *R* v *Larkin* [1943] KB 174, although that case recognised an exception to the rule where the jury finds the accused not guilty of murder but guilty of manslaughter, and may be asked whether the verdict was on the basis of provocation, diminished responsibility or something else). The judge is not obliged to adopt as a basis for sentencing the least serious version of events consistent with the jury's verdict (*R* v *Solomon* (1984) 6 Cr App R (S) 120), but should be 'extremely astute' to give the benefit of any doubt to the offender (*per* Watkins LJ in *R* v *Stosiek* (1982) 4 Cr App R (S) 205). In *R* v *Wood* (1991) 13 Cr App R (S) 207, the Court of Appeal said that it would only interfere with the finding of fact by a judge after hearing evidence in exceptional circumstances.

The view the judge takes of the facts must naturally be consistent with the jury's verdict. Thus, if the jury refuses to find the accused guilty as charged but only convicts him or her of a lesser offence, the sentence must be appropriate to the lesser offence, notwithstanding that the judge is convinced there should have been a conviction for the more serious offence (*R* v *Hazelwood* (1984) 6 Cr App R (S) 52 and *R* v *Dowdall* (1992) 13 Cr App R (S) 441, CA).

14.5 Character and Antecedents Evidence

After the prosecution summary of the facts or (in the case of a not guilty plea) immediately after the guilty verdict, the Crown Prosecutor in the magistrates' court or prosecuting counsel in the Crown Court provides the court with information about the character and antecedents of the offender. Information about the character of the offender will be wholly or principally concerned with the matter of his or her previous convictions, if any. Information about antecedents deals with his or her general background and circumstances.

14.5.1 THE ANTECEDENTS

By virtue of the *Practice Direction (Crime: Antecedents)* [1993] 1 WLR 1459, standard forms should be used for both the personal details of the defendant and previous convictions. The forms are to be completed by the police and each document typed. Most of the personal information is to be provided by the defendant while in custody following arrest. The information will not be verified. Where information is refused, or is not available, this should be stated on the form. The personal information will include such matters as the defendant's age, education, employment and domestic circumstances.

The standard forms and additional information should be provided to the court as set out below.

> *2. Provision to court and parties*
>
> *(a) The Crown Court antecedents will be prepared by the police immediately following committal proceedings or upon receipt of a notice of appeal.*
>
> *(b) Ten copies of the set of antecedent documents will be prepared in each case. Two copies to be provided to the Crown Prosecution Service direct, the remainder to the court. The court will send two copies to the defence and one to the probation service. The remaining copies are for the court's use, including one for the notetaker.*
>
> *(c) The antecedent documents must be served as above, within 21 days of committal in each case. Any points arising from the antecedent information are to be raised with the police, by the defence solicitor, at least seven days before the listing so that the matter can be resolved prior to the hearing.*
>
> *(d) Seven days before the listing hearing date, the police will check the conviction details and any additional convictions shown will be listed on an additional Form MG16A and served as above to the attached to the documents already supplied. Details of any additional outstanding cases will also be provided at this stage.*
>
> *3. Additional information*
>
> *(a) Paragraph 12 of Form NIB74C should be used to identify any current orders breached, outstanding offences known and liability for driving disqualification (if known). Details of outstanding fines will not be shown.*
>
> *(b) Where more than four previous convictions are recorded, paragraph 13 must contain a summary of the total convictions recorded in the following format:*
>
> *Offences against the person*
> *Offences against property*
> *Fraud and kindred offences*
> *Theft and kindred offences*
> *Public disorder offences*
> *Others*
>
> *(c) Paragraph 13 should also show details of the time spent in custody on the impending case.*

Should the defence challenge anything in the antecedents, the antecedents officer and any other witnesses may have to be called, as the prosecution is expected to provide proper proof of what it has alleged, i.e. evidence of a type which would be admissible in a trial of a not guilty plea. If it fails to provide such proof, the judge should ignore the challenged allegation, and state that he or she is ignoring it (*R* v *Campbell* (1911) 6 Cr App R 131). It follows that where the prosecution does not have proper proof of an allegation prejudicial to the offender, it should not make the allegation in the first place (see *R* v *Van Pelz* [1943] KB 157 and *R* v *Wilkins* (1977) 66 Cr App R 49). Where the prosecution does propose to adduce first-hand antecedents evidence of a factual nature, but it realises that the facts may well be challenged by the defence, it should give notice of the proposed evidence (*R* v *Robinson* (1969) 53 Cr App R 314). It is not entirely clear whether the prosecution is ever entitled to refer to the offender as having criminal associates. In *R* v *Bibby* [1972] Crim LR 513 it was held that it was unfair of the antecedents officer to say that B mixed with criminals, but in *R* v *Crabtree* [1952] 2 All ER 974 Lord Goddard CJ held such evidence to be acceptable provided the officer could speak from his personal knowledge. In the light of these cases the safest rule for a police officer giving antecedents evidence must be to restrict himself or herself to what is on the antecedents form, and not start making additional allegations likely to be disputed by the defence.

14.5.2 PREVIOUS CONVICTIONS

Prior to CJA 1991, the CPS would make available to the courts a list of previous convictions, which would be read out at court. Spent convictions were not mentioned, but even if convictions were not spent, the court was unlikely to require all the convictions to be read out.

Section 29(1) of CJA 1991, as originally drafted, provided that the court was not entitled to regard an offence as more serious by reason of any previous convictions of the offender. This provision led to an inconsistent approach to sentencing by the courts and was very unpopular. It was replaced by s. 66(b) of CJA 1993 in the following terms:

> *In considering the seriousness of any offence, the court may take into account any previous convictions of the offender . . ..*

The full implications of this provision have not yet been fully investigated. It seems clear, however, that the court 'should clearly identify which convictions . . . are relevant for this purpose and then consider what the effect . . . is in relation to seriousness': The Magistrates' Association, Sentencing Guidelines [1993].

14.5.3 SPENT CONVICTIONS

The Rehabilitation of Offenders Act 1974 (ROA) was passed with the aim of helping criminals who had decided to 'go straight' to live down their past. Its main effect is that, once a certain time (the 'rehabilitation period') has elapsed from the date of an offender's conviction, the conviction becomes spent and the offender, in respect of that conviction, is a rehabilitated person. As a rehabilitated person he or she is, for most purposes, treated as if he or she had never committed or been convicted of the offence.

Whether a conviction is capable of becoming spent depends upon the length of the sentence imposed for the offence. The length of the sentence, assuming that it is within the limit, also governs the length of the rehabilitation period.

Section 7 of ROA 1974 provides that the ban on revealing or asking questions about spent convictions does *not* apply in criminal proceedings. But Lord Widgery CJ, in *Practice Direction (Crime: Spent Convictions)* [1975] 1 WLR 1065, stated that neither judge nor counsel should refer to a spent conviction where 'such reference can be reasonably avoided'. Mention of a spent conviction always requires the judge's authority, that authority being given only where the interests of justice so require. At the sentencing stage, the list of previous convictions given to the court should mark those which are spent. When passing sentence the judge should say nothing about spent convictions unless it is vital to do so to explain the penalty he or she has decided upon.

Presumably, the above still applies after CJA 1991.

14.5.4 DEFENCE QUESTIONS

If a police officer has testified about the offender's antecedents and previous convictions, defence counsel can ask him or her questions. The questioning is unlikely to be hostile in nature, but counsel might wish to confirm that his or her client was cooperative when questioned about the offence or that he or she showed signs of genuine remorse. If there has been a change in the offender's circumstances since the antecedents were prepared the officer can be asked if he or she knows anything about that. Upon the officer leaving the witness box the prosecution case is closed.

14.6 Reports

After information as to the character and antecedents has been presented to the court the judge — if he or she has not already done so before court — reads any reports which have been prepared about the offender. Sometimes sentence may properly be passed without the benefit of reports, but there are many occasions when the court must have them either because there is a statutory provision to that effect or because good sentencing practice demands it.

14.6.1 THE NECESSITY FOR PRE-SENTENCE REPORTS

A pre-sentence report is defined by s. 3(5) of CJA 1991 as a report in writing which is made or submitted by a probation officer or social worker with a view to assisting the court to reach the most suitable method of dealing with the offender, and contains such information as may be specified by the Secretary of State.

Under s. 3(1) of CJA 1991, when a court is forming any necessary opinion under s. 1 or s. 2 of that Act (whether a custodial sentence should be imposed and the length of that order) the court is under a duty to obtain and consider a pre-sentence report. Section 3(1) does not apply, however, if the offender is aged over 18, and in the circumstances of the case, the court is of the opinion that it is unnecessary to obtain a pre-sentence report (s. 3(2) as amended by the Criminal Justice and Public Order Act 1994, sch. 9, para. 40). This would apply where the sentence was clear, and the report would, in practice, make no difference.

Failure to obtain a report does not invalidate a sentence, but any court sitting on appeal against sentence must obtain one and consider it, unless it is of the opinion that it is unnecessary (s. 3(4) and s. 3(4A), as amended by Criminal Justice and Public Order Act 1994, sch. 9, para. 40).

Where the offender is aged 17 or under, by virtue of s. 3(2A) as amended as above, the court must obtain a report unless either:

(a) the offence is triable only on indictment, and the court is of the opinion that it is unnecessary to obtain one; or

(b) there already exists a report, and the court has considered the information. If more than one report exists, the court should consider the most recent.

When making any of the following orders, the court, under s. 7(3), is under a duty to obtain and consider a pre-sentence report, unless it considers it unnecessary (s. 7(3A), inserted by CJPOA 1994, sch. 9, para 14):

(a) a probation order which includes additional requirements authorised by the Powers of Criminal Courts Act 1973 (PCCA), sch. 1A;

(b) a community service order;

(c) a combination order; and

(d) certain supervision orders.

Section 7 contains provisions relating to failure to obtain a report, and offenders under 18 which are parallel to those in s. 3 above.

A probation officer writing a report will draw upon many sources. Of prime importance is the interview with the accused. He or she may also visit the accused's home and speak with members of the family. With permission, he or she might talk to the accused's employer, although great care would obviously have to be taken not to jeopardise continued employment. He or she will also have access to background sources of information such as police antecedents and any records the probation service has of previous contact with the accused. If the accused has recently been released from a custodial sentence, the probation officer could consult the authorities at the relevant establishment to see what effect the sentence apparently had on him or her. Where medical or psychiatric reasons seem to have contributed to the offence, assistance might be sought from the accused's doctor, and the report might suggest the preparation of full medical reports.

14.6.2 CONTENTS OF A PRE-SENTENCE REPORT

The pre-sentence report replaces the social inquiry report, and indicates a shift in emphasis in the presentation of reports. By s. 3(5) a pre-sentence report is defined as a report in writing which:

(a) with a view to assisting the court in determining the most suitable method of dealing with an offender, is made or submitted by a probation officer or by a social worker of a local authority social services department; and

(b) contains information as to such matters, presented in such manner, as may be prescribed by rules made by the Secretary of State.

In the White Paper (para. 3.10 and 11) the Government outlined the purpose of the pre-sentence report:

> The purpose of requiring the courts to consider a report by the probation service when a custodial sentence is contemplated will be to provide the court with detailed information about how the offender could be punished in the community, so that option can be fully considered. Its purpose will not be to make recommendations about sentencing or to be a plea in mitigation.

In addition, the Green Paper entitled 'Punishment and Supervision in the Community' described (at para. 9.6) what such a report should contain:

> The reports should include: information about the offence and the offender's attitude towards it, background information about the offender, an assessment of the offender's ability and willingness to stop committing crimes, and a detailed programme of supervision to achieve this. Preparing a report of this sort needs skill in assessing the likely outcome of various sentencing options; these assessments can be made only against a background of detailed knowledge about court practice, about the resources available for supervising offenders together with knowledge and understanding of offending; judgements involving issues of public safety have to be made; and those preparing the reports exercise their discretion in ways which can have serious and lasting consequences for offenders under sentence.

The most significant change bought about by the new Act is that the report will no longer contain a recommendation, made by the probation officer or social worker involved, as to the appropriate sentence. On the other hand, it appears likely that the contents of reports will need to reflect a clear understanding of sentencing principles and practice. It may also be the case that reports will have to deal with the various factors in the commission of the crime that may or may not make it 'serious' for purposes of s. 1(2)(a).

Pre-sentence reports are discussed in detail in **Chapter 17**.

14.6.3 THE PRESENTATION OF PRE-SENTENCE REPORTS

A representative of the probation service should always be available at court to hand in reports and assist the court in any other way he or she can (e.g. by interviewing an offender so as to bring an old report up to date). Unless required to do so by the defence, the probation officer who prepared a report need not attend when its subject appears to be sentenced, although may choose to do so if, for instance, the offence was committed while on probation. Such a practice is confirmed by s. 3(5) which indicates that the report is 'made or submitted' by a probation officer or social worker. The report would then be presented by a liaison officer. It is clear from s. 3(5) that the pre-sentence reports must be in writing. This ends the occasional practice of probation officers or social workers giving their report orally in court.

A copy of the report must be given to the offender or his or her legal representative, except that in cases of unrepresented juveniles it should be given to their parents (PCCA 1973, s. 46). It is considered bad practice to read out the whole of a pre-sentence report in open court since it may well contain matters which, in the offender's best interests, should not be publicly emphasised. The defence, in mitigation, may, however, refer the sentencer to passages in the report or perhaps read isolated sentences which are especially favourable. The defence can challenge allegations made in the report by requiring the probation officer concerned to attend for questioning in open court.

14.6.4 OTHER REPORTS

In addition to pre-sentence reports, the court may be assisted by the following types of report:

(a) *Medical reports* These may be on the offender's physical condition or on his or her mental condition or on both. If an offender is remanded on bail, it may be made a condition of bail that he or she attend a hospital, etc. for the preparation of medical reports (see BA 1976, s. 3(6)(d) and MCA 1980, s. 30 (2)). If remanded in custody, he or she may be examined by the prison medical officers. Also, there is now the possibility under the Mental Health Act (MHA) 1983 of a remand to a mental hospital for reports in cases where the court is considering a hospital order under s. 37 of the MHA 1983. A hospital order can only be made on the basis of reports from two doctors, one of whom must be a psychiatrist.

A copy of a report on an offender's mental condition must be given to his or her counsel or solicitor, but the offender personally is not entitled to a copy. If unrepresented, he or she should be told the gist of what is in the report (MHA 1983, s. 54(3)). The psychiatrist who prepared the report may be required to attend court to give oral evidence.

(b) *Reports on juveniles* Having found a juvenile guilty, the youth court sometimes remands him or her in care for two or three weeks so that a detailed report can be prepared. Such a report will deal with intelligence, aptitudes, attitudes to those in authority, relationships with peers and many other matters. The school he or she attends (or fails to attend) may also submit a report, together with a record of attendance.

(c) *Remand centre reports* There is nothing to stop the court adjourning for a remand centre report on a young offender (under the age of 21), if it considers that that would be helpful. Generally, reports on the behaviour of offenders held at custodial institutions are more likely to be prepared for the assistance of the Court of Appeal than for sentencers at first instance. In determining an appeal against a custodial sentence, the Court of Appeal is quite often given information about the appellant's progress in prison, young offender institution, or whatever, during the period between the passing of the sentence and the hearing of the appeal.

14.7 Defence Mitigation

After the judge has read the reports the defence has the opportunity to present mitigation on behalf of the offender. If he or she wishes, defence counsel may call character witnesses. The offender personally will not be called unless either there is a dispute about the facts of the offence, or it is a road traffic case and he or she would be liable to mandatory disqualification unless he or she can show special reasons for not disqualifying. In most cases there will not be any character witnesses, and defence counsel will proceed immediately to make a plea in mitigation. (See ***Advocacy Manual***.)

There is no set pattern for mitigation, and what ought to be said will obviously vary from case to case. However, a plea in mitigation will usually include a discussion of the facts of the offence, the circumstances which led up to it, and the offender's personal circumstances. As regards the potential sentence, one possible approach is to discuss all the available sentences, explaining why they would not be appropriate in this case, concluding with the sentence that is thought appropriate. However, counsel should bear in mind the seriousness of the offence in deciding what is appropriate. If the offence is so serious that only a custodial sentence would be justified, the judge's patience should not be tried by discussing non-custodial sentences at length. Conversely, counsel will look foolish if he or she virtually concedes that the offender must go to prison, and then the judge imposes a community sentence.

The fact that the defendant has pleaded guilty has always been seen as an important point in mitigation, and has been said to reduce the sentence by as much as a third. Section 48 of the Criminal Justice and Public Order Act 1994 is an attempt to place this on a statutory footing. Section 48 reads as follows:

> *(1) In determining what sentence to pass on an offender who has pleaded guilty to an offence in proceedings before that or another court a court shall take into account—*
>
> *(a) the stage in the proceedings for the offence at which the offender indicated his intention to plead guilty, and*
>
> *(b) the circumstances, in which this indication was given.*
>
> *(2) If, as a result of taking into account any matter referred to in subsection (a) above, the court imposes a punishment on the offender which is less severe than the punishment it would otherwise have imposed, it shall state in open court that it has done so.*

The provision contained in s. 48(2) is a new one, but it should be noted that the section does not go on to provide that failure to comply invalidates the sentence.

Other matters which are generally accepted as being good mitigation include the youth of the offender or his or her age; previous good character; that the offender had assisted the police; that the offender has expressed genuine remorse or made attempts to compensate the victim; that the offender was under some sort of particular stress at the time of the offence; and the potential effect on the offender's family in the event, for example, of a custodial sentence. For a more detailed discussion on mitigation, see the later chapters of this Manual, and the ***Advocacy Manual***.

One important point to bear in mind is that counsel almost always has the most up-to-date information on the offender. The antecedents are taken at the time of the arrest, which may have been some considerable time before the trial, and in any event are only an outline of the offender's circumstances. There is not always a pre-sentence report, and even if there is, it may also be out of date, or not contain the information that is required. Consequently, courts are increasingly looking to counsel to provide accurate, detailed, up-to-date information concerning the offender.

Sometimes, when counsel has concluded his or her mitigation, the judge asks the offender whether he or she personally has anything to say. After that it is for the judge to pronounce sentence.

14.8 Pronouncing Sentence

A Crown Court judge sitting alone will normally pronounce sentence immediately after defence mitigation (or after giving the offender the opportunity to make a personal statement). If he or she is sitting with lay magistrates and the decision is a difficult one, they sometimes retire to consider it. Similarly, a lay bench of magistrates may wish to retire to consider sentence, and they may also ask their clerk to retire with them to advise on their sentencing powers. In the magistrates' court, the decision on sentence may be taken by a majority but it is pronounced by the chairman of the bench.

Crown Court judges are encouraged to give their reasons for deciding upon a particular sentence. They should certainly give reasons when the sentence prima facie seems a severe one in the circumstances of the case (see *R* v *Newman* (1979) 1 Cr App R (S) 252 and ss. 1(4) and 2(3) of the CJA 1991). The reasons will be brief and couched in language which the offender may be expected to understand. The judge might say why he or she could not follow a recommendation in the pre-sentence report that the offender be given a non-custodial sentence; or, if he or she does pass a non-custodial sentence, the offender might be warned that this really is a last chance and if he or she offends again the penalty will be severe; or, where the offender is going to prison for the first time after a series of convictions which were dealt with by other means, he or she could be told that he or she still has time to reform but if he or she does not learn his or her lesson now he or she is in danger of becoming an habitual criminal who will spend half his or her life in prison. Occasionally the judge's comments on passing sentence get him or her into trouble. It may be evident that he or she has taken irrelevant matters into account, and for that reason passed a sentence which is more severe than would otherwise have been passed. The Court of Appeal is then likely to reduce the sentence, even if it was a proper sentence in itself.

In a few cases, statute obliges the court to give reasons for its decisions. For instance, both the magistrates and the Crown Court must explain a decision not to activate a suspended sentence if they are dealing with an offender who is in breach of such a sentence. In other cases (notably the making of a probation order, community service order, combination order) the offender's consent to a proposed sentence is required. In yet other cases (e.g. suspended sentences) the effect of the sentence must be explained to him or her by the court. See the later chapters of this Manual for details.

The Crown Court may vary or rescind a sentence within 28 days of its being passed (if the offender was jointly indicted with other accused the period is 56 days from the passing of the sentence or 28 days from the conclusion of the joint trial, whichever expires sooner). The variation must be made by the Crown Court judge who originally passed the sentence, but if he or she was then sitting with lay justices they need not be present for the variation. It is clear that the power to vary may be used to correct technical errors in the original sentence or to alter it in the offender's favour. The extent to which a sentence may be fundamentally varied to the offender's detriment is unclear. The Crown Court's power to vary sentence is now contained in s. 47 of SCA 1981.

Once the statutory period for variation has expired a court may *not* vary its sentence even if, through inadvertence, it failed to consider including in the sentence an order which really ought to have been included.

Magistrates' courts may also vary or rescind a sentence at any time if it is considered to be in the interest of Justice to do so (MCA 1980, s. 142) (see **5.1.1**).

14.9 Taking Other Offences into Consideration

An offender is sentenced for the offences to which he or she pleads guilty or of which he or she is found guilty. In deciding on sentence, the judge or magistrates must not be influenced by any circumstances which lead them to think that the offender may also have committed other offences with which he or she has not been charged (e.g. *R* v *Courtie* [1984] AC 463). There is one major exception to this rule, namely the practice of taking other offences into consideration.

Other offences taken into consideration when sentence is passed (or 't.i.c.'s as they are colloquially known) are offences of which the offender is never convicted, but which are admitted by him or her in court and, at his or her request, are borne in mind by the judge when passing sentence for the offences in respect of which there is a conviction ('conviction offences'). The sequence of events leading up to offences being 't.i.c.'ed will vary from case to case. Typically it will involve a suspect who has been arrested on suspicion of one or more crimes, admitting at the police station that he or she committed those crimes, and making it obvious that he or she is going to plead guilty. The police may then ask him or her about other similar offences which they believe he or she may have committed, but which, in the absence of an admission from him or her, they will find it difficult to prove. Since he or she is resigned to having to plead guilty to the offences for which he or she was arrested, the suspect often decides to make a clean breast of everything on the understanding that some or all the offences he or she is now being asked about will not be the subject of separate charges but will merely be taken into consideration. A list is then drawn up of the offences to be 't.i.c.'ed and the suspect signs the list. The offences for which he or she was arrested and with which he or she was charged are then prosecuted in the normal way, and, if the matter is to be dealt with in the Crown Court, appear as counts on the indictment. He or she duly pleads guilty. Then at some convenient stage during the procedure before sentence is passed, prosecuting counsel mentions to the judge that the offender wants other matters considered. The judge is handed the list of offences signed by the offender at the police station, and he or she (or the court clerk) asks whether he or she admits committing them and whether he or she wants them taken into consideration. Assuming the offender answers 'yes' to both questions, the judge may, at his or her discretion, comply with the request. Prosecuting counsel should be in a position to give the judge brief details of the nature of the offences. The sentence the judge eventually passes for the conviction offences will no doubt be somewhat more severe than it would have been in the absence of 't.i.c.'s, but the addition to the sentence will almost certainly not be as great as the penalty for the offences would have been had they been prosecuted separately. Thus, the system of taking offences into consideration has advantages for offenders. It also has advantages for the police, because they clear up offences which might otherwise have remained unsolved. This is why the system flourishes even though it has no solid basis in law.

The following points about taking offences into consideration should be noted:

(a) The sentence the court may pass is restricted to the maximum permissible for the offence(s) of which the offender has been convicted. This does not in practice deter the courts from 't.i.c.'ing offences because maximum penalties are usually far higher than a sentencer would wish to impose even for a grave instance of the offence in question. It is thus possible to add something to the sentence to reflect the 't.i.c.'s without exceeding the maximum penalty.

(b) Which offences to charge and which to refrain from charging in anticipation of their eventually being taken into consideration is essentially a matter for the police and the prosecution. Sometimes the most serious offences are charged and later appear on the indictment, while other less grave but broadly similar crimes are taken into consideration. Or perhaps the most recent offences will be charged and the remainder 't.i.c.'ed. On occasions, the 't.i.c.'s vastly outnumber the conviction offences (see e.g., *R* v *Sequeira* (1982) 4 Cr App R (S) 65).

(c) Offences should not be taken into consideration unless the offender clearly requests the sentencer to do so. The offender should also admit in open court that he or she committed the offences (R v *Griffiths* (1932) 23 Cr App R 153). It is not, however, necessary to put the particulars of each offence to him or her one by one. Usually the offender is asked whether he or she signed at the police station the list of other offences, whether he or she admits committing those offences, and whether he or she wants them considered.

(d) Since the taking of an offence into consideration does not, as a matter of strict law, amount to a conviction, the offender is unable to bar a subsequent prosecution for the offence by reliance on a plea of *autrefois convict* (*R* v *Nicholson* [1947] 2 All ER 535). However, the police do not in practice prosecute for matters which have already been 't.i.c.'ed because to do so would undermine a system which they themselves find very convenient. If a prosecution were to be brought, the court would almost certainly pass a nominal sentence such as an absolute discharge.

(e) Although the 't.i.c.' system is geared to offenders pleading guilty, there is nothing to stop the prosecution using a short adjournment after the accused has been found guilty on a not guilty plea to ask him or her whether, given the outcome of the trial, he or she would now like other offences considered.

(f) The court is not obliged to comply with a request to take offences into consideration. It is generally bad practice to 't.i.c.' offences of a different type from the conviction offences, and the court should never consider offences which carry endorsement of the driving licence and disqualification if the conviction offences are not so punishable (*R* v *Collins* [1947] KB 560). The reason for this is that taking endorsable offences into consideration will not entitle the court to endorse the licence/disqualify if the conviction offences are non-endorsable, whereas if the offences are prosecuted in the normal way endorsement would be virtually certain and disqualification a possibility.

(g) The practice of taking offences into consideration is as common in the magistrates' courts as it is in the Crown Court. However, magistrates should not 't.i.c.' offences which are triable only on indictment (see *R* v *Simons* [1953] 1 WLR 1014).

(h) The court should state when passing sentence how many other offences it has taken into consideration.

14.10 Legal Representation

The offender can, of course, represent himself or herself if he or she so wishes, and present his or her own mitigation. If the offence is a trivial one, for which he or she is obviously only going to be fined, he or she would be well advised not to employ a lawyer because his or her solicitor's bill will exceed any slight reduction in the fine which might be achieved by eloquent mitigation. In more serious cases, especially where the offender's liberty is at stake, legal representation is desirable.

Legal representation not only assists the offender but it should assist the court, in that the lawyer can clarify the issues, highlight those matters which are in the offender's favour and remind the judge that although the offender might qualify for a custodial sentence, the court is still under a duty to consider whether such sentence is appropriate having regard to the mitigating factors available and relevant to the offender (see *R* v *Cox* [1993] 1 WLR 188). The court will not want to resort to the drastic expedient of prison unless there is really no alternative. The same applies whenever a custodial sentence of any description is contemplated for a young offender. So, in these types of cases the offender is not merely allowed to have legal representation, but is positively encouraged to have it by the offer of legal aid.

The general effect of the relevant legislation is that, when dealing with an offender who is not legally represented in court, the court *must* give him or her an opportunity to apply for legal aid before doing any of the following:

(a) Passing a sentence of imprisonment if the offender has never previously been sentenced to imprisonment (PCCA 1973, s. 21).

(b) Passing a sentence of detention in a young offender institution or custody for life (CJA 1982, s. 3).

(c) Making an order for detention under CYPA 1933, s. 53 (CJA 1982, s. 3).

Situation (a) above applies both to the passing of an immediate sentence of imprisonment and to the passing of a suspended sentence, but in deciding whether an offender has previously been sentenced to imprisonment a suspended sentence which has not been brought into effect must be ignored. Points (b) and (c) apply irrespective of whether the offender has previously received the sentence in question.

The court must not pass the relevant sentence on an unrepresented offender unless either:

(a) he or she applied for legal aid and the application was refused on the ground that it did not appear his or her means were such that he or she required assistance; or

(b) having been informed of his or her right to apply for legal aid and having had the opportunity to do so, he or she refused or failed to apply.

Since legal aid in criminal proceedings is hardly ever refused on grounds of the applicant's means, the effect of the legislation is that, if the court is considering a first sentence of imprisonment, etc. for an unrepresented offender, it must (if it has not been done already) tell him or her that he or she can apply for legal aid and grant him or her an adjournment of sufficient length to make the application and instruct solicitors. If the offender fails to use the adjournment for the purpose for which it was granted, that is his or her fault, and the court at the resumed hearing can pass whatever sentence it considers appropriate even if the offender is still unrepresented.

If s. 21 of PCCA 1973 is not complied with, but a sentence of imprisonment is nonetheless passed on an offender who has not previously been so sentenced, it would seem that the consequences of the error depend on which court makes it. If it was a magistrates' court which failed to comply with s. 21, the Crown Court (which hears appeals against sentences passed in the magistrates' courts) must replace the sentence of imprisonment with a sentence the magistrates could lawfully have passed on the occasion on which they dealt with the offender. So the replacement sentence cannot be a sentence of imprisonment (*R* v *Birmingham Justices, ex parte Wyatt* [1976] 1 WLR 260). If it was the Crown Court which forgot about s. 21, the Court of Appeal can uphold the lower court's sentence if, notwithstanding the procedural irregularity, it considers that the sentence was the appropriate one for the offender (*R* v *McGinlay* (1976) 52 Cr App R 156). Presumably the same consequences will flow from breach of any of the other sections requiring the court to allow time for an application for legal aid to be made.

14.11 Differences Between Sentencing Procedure in the Crown Court and in the Magistrates' Courts

The procedure before sentence is passed is essentially the same whatever the court. The practice of taking other offences into consideration and the power to defer sentence are equally applicable to both the Crown Court and the magistrates' courts. For minor driving matters, the court relies merely on the endorsements, if any, on the offender's licence.

FIFTEEN

PENAL POLICY AND SENTENCING POLICY

15.1 Introduction

Current sentencing practice and current sentencing policy reflects nearly a hundred years of enquiry, precedent and the deliberations of successive governments. Perhaps more than any other branch of the law, sentencing practice has been built up gradually, so that it is very difficult to understand current dilemmas without realising how sentences have evolved.

The Criminal Justice Act 1991, most of which came into force on 1 October 1992, is currently the major legislation governing the aims and practice of sentencing. The Act was intended to be revolutionary — to change the basis on which all sentencers consider sentences. It set out, for the first time, a detailed set of prescriptions for the way in which sentencers should think about sentences for different kinds of offences and different offenders. Before the Act, sentencers could for the same offender, decide to give precedence in their consideration of sentencing to deterring others, or to reforming that offender, or to providing compensation for the victim, or to marking the seriousness of the offence (see **Chapter 16** for a discussion of these philosophies of sentencing). As a result, prior to the Act, different sentencers could, quite properly, give different sentences. The Criminal Justice Act 1991 attempted to produce greater uniformity in the sentencing process, through elevating one particular philosophy of sentencing (making the sentence proportionate to the seriousness of the offence) over others.

However, certain provisions in the Act attracted considerable criticism from magistrates and others and, as a result, two of the major provisions were abolished in 1993. These were the calculation of financial penalties by using a unit fine system, and the prohibition of sentencers being able to take into account previous convictions unrelated to that offence. Some would now say that the major principle of the Act — to make all sentences proportionate to the seriousness of the offence — has been put into jeopardy (for example, because previous convictions may now be taken into account, and so sentences will not relate solely to the present offence). It is certainly true that sentencers remain confused by the changes. On financial penalties, for example, there is now no nationally prescribed way of calculating how the penalty should be related to the means of the offender to pay.

Research findings on the operation of the new Act are still being analysed, but preliminary findings suggest that practice is varying considerably between different courts. Courts are interpreting the provisions of the Act and subsequent legislative changes in slightly different ways. It is always true that any major change in sentencing, such as the Criminal Justice Act 1991, takes some considerable time to settle down. Counsel starting practice in 1997/8 will need to bear in mind that there are likely to be differences between the courts in which they practise. It makes it doubly important for counsel to go into court and listen to previous cases before they make a plea in mitigation in a court in which they have not previously appeared.

15.2 The Manual, Lectures and Tutorials in Sentencing

There is no accepted textbook or 'cookbook' on sentencing — either for counsel or for sentencers! Clearly, sentences must be within the range specified in the statute defining the offence for which the defendant has been convicted. In England and Wales, however, the permitted maxima for offences reflect the worst possible case and hence give little guidance to sentencers for common instances of that offence. It is very rare for any other statutory guidance to be given in statutes setting out the offence. Guidance for sentencers comes from a wide range of sources, including the statutes setting up each sentence, the guideline decisions of the Court of Appeal, publications of the Magistrates' Association (such as their guidelines), research reports on the effectiveness and use of different sentences, the experience of probation officers, doctors and others set out in their reports to the courts, Home Office publications on the effect of gender and of race (required to be produced for sentencers by CJA 1991, s. 95), and, not least, the mitigation speeches of counsel or solicitors.

The practice of sentencing is hence constantly changing. There is no textbook because any textbook would almost immediately become out of date. The role of this Manual and of the lectures in sentencing cannot, therefore, be to give students a potted guide to sentencing. Instead, they aim to give an appreciation of the factors which are currently moulding sentencing, such that, as changes occur, they can be slotted in to counsel's framework of understanding. In particular, they aim to:

(a) Provide an appreciation of the more common statutory sources, decisions of the Court of Appeal and other factors affecting sentencers.

(b) Relate these to the actual pattern of sentencing in the courts.

(c) Relate the statutory possibilities to the facilities which are most commonly available in different parts of the country. Particularly in relation to community sentences and the mentally disordered, the actual sentences which are given are strongly affected by the availability of particular types of programmes or residential accommodation (hostels, attendance centres, treatment programmes, types of community service, etc.).

(d) Attune the student to the way sentencers are thinking and what they are trying to achieve by their sentences.

(e) Relate all these to what happens in court and the role of the different participants between conviction and sentence.

The aim of this chapter is to set out the way in which the sentencing structure has developed, current patterns of sentencing, and the major provisions of CJA 1991. Subsequent chapters deal in more detail with specific sentences (imprisonment, community sentences, etc.) and with kinds of offenders for whom special sentences have been developed (the young, the mentally disordered, the dangerous).

Tutorials in sentencing provide an opportunity to ask about any of these aspects, but also, more importantly, the opportunity to practise preparing and making speeches in mitigation on real-life examples.

Since sentencing provisions, sentencing policy and sentencing practice are constantly changing, these materials can only form a first building block in the materials that will be needed as you pursue your career at the Bar. Written materials of value include not only case reports but statistical studies. It is very much worth amassing such a collection, using these materials as a beginning for that. In particular, the booklet *The Sentence of the Court* (published by HMSO) is revised periodically to provide magistrates and others with official guidance on how sentences might be used. Case reports on sentencing can be found particularly in the *Criminal Appeal Reports (Sentencing)* and the *Criminal Law Review*. Articles on the effectiveness of different sentences and on sentencing practice may be found in journals such as the *British Journal of Criminology, the Criminal Law Review*, and the *Howard Journal*.

15.3 Changes Affecting Mitigation

Over this century, there has been a continuous *increase* in the number of different types of sentences made available to the courts. This has affected the role of counsel in three ways:

(a) sentencers require more *information* from professionals in the courtroom (including counsel) before passing sentence, and expect those professionals to be able to discuss, where appropriate, the merits of different kinds of sentence;

(b) more *professionals* are involved in the sentencing process, with whom counsel must interact, and must know their roles;

(c) mitigation has become, as a result, a more complicated and more important task, which requires considerable *preparation*.

The Criminal Justice Act 1991 has continued these trends. It has introduced more sentences. More pre-sentence reports are being prepared by probation officers, and these reports will contain, in certain instances, not only the opinion of the probation officer as to the appropriate sentence, but also a sentence plan for supervision. Defence counsel will need to be familiar with the local facilities for community sentences and with the appropriate forms of supervision (and so must make a practice of talking to the local probation liaison officer for the court before finalising mitigation). Counsel must be able to anticipate what kinds of sentences may be suggested by the probation service and what will be found realistic by the sentencer, and be prepared to put forward what is best for his or her client and to discuss this, as necessary, with the judge.

One of the major difficulties in this process is that the current existing sentences have been introduced at different times and that there has been no overall review of how they will fit into the schema proposed in the CJA. To understand sentencing today, it is necessary to appreciate this history. This Chapter hence first considers current sentencing practice in the courts and then gives a brief résumé of the major developments in sentencing which affect current practice, before turning to the CJA 1991 and subsequent legislation. Finally, we shall consider how this affects mitigation.

15.4 Parameters of Current Sentencing Practice

Since the decisions of the Court of Appeal largely focus on serious cases involving substantial terms of imprisonment, it might be thought that most defendants are sentenced to imprisonment. However, both at the magistrates' court and at the Crown Court, this is far from the case.

Considering only male defendants aged 21 and over, custodial sentences were given to only 7% of defendants in the magistrates' court and 54% of defendants at the Crown Court in 1994. Hence, even at the Crown Court, immediate custody is not inevitable. Overall, taking both courts together and looking at indictable offences, the most common sentence in 1994, as it has been for many years, was a financial penalty (36%), with 20% getting immediate custody, 16% an absolute or conditional discharge, 11% a community service order, 11% a probation order, 2% a combination order and only 1% a suspended sentence. Women are more commonly given sentences at the lower end of the tariff, but the pattern of offences for women is different from that for men. The number of suspended sentences being given has fallen dramatically since the new provision in the Criminal Justice Act 1991 that it can only be justified by 'exceptional circumstances' of the case, and the restricted interpretation of such circumstances in *R* v *Okinikan* (1993) 14 Cr App R (S) 453.

1993 was the first complete year during which the Criminal Justice Act 1991 was in force. The first few months of the Act showed a significant decrease in imprisonment, but in 1993 and to an even greater extent in 1994 there have been substantial rises in both the proportion of people sent to prison and the lengths of imprisonment given, in parallel with ministers' advocacy of the need for more severe punishment of serious and violent offending. The last few years have shown that there can be substantial shifts in sentencing practice, according to public and judicial mood, in the space of a few months, and counsel should be aware that this may occur in the future.

15.5 Major Developments in Sentencing Policy

The sentences available to the courts have been expanded greatly in number and type since the turn of the century. The ways in which the courts are supposed to use them reflect the philosophies of punishment dominant at the time of their introduction (see **Chapter 16** for a discussion of the different philosophies of punishment). The imposition by the CJA 1991 of one particular philosophy as pre-eminent (retribution) has not been accompanied by any review of sentences and so it is necessary to describe briefly how the current existing sentences have been introduced in order to see how courts are intended to use them today.

15.5.1 THE BEGINNING OF THE CENTURY: TARIFF RETRIBUTIVE SENTENCING

Current sentencing policy has its roots in practice at the turn of the century. In 1905 the only penalties for offenders aged 17 and over were death, imprisonment, penal servitude, fines and common law binding-over powers, the latter with or without supervision by the Police Court Mission volunteers (the forerunners of the probation service) in the magistrates' court in some towns. The major attitude to sentencing at this time was an attempt to produce a complete tariff of sentences by offence. At the higher courts, the judges prescribed particular lengths of imprisonment or penal servitude for a 'typical' case of, say, burglary. Sentencing was hence basically a *tariff* based on the *offence*, the seriousness of the offence, and mitigating circumstances concerned with the offence. It espoused a *retributive philosophy*.

15.5.2 THE FIRST CHANGE: REHABILITATION AND REFORM

The first major change came in 1907–8, ushering in a long period of rehabilitation and reform as the primary penal philosophy, which lasted until the late 1960s and early 1970s. Probation was the prime rehabilitative sentence, which was designed to *reform* the offender through training and supervision, i.e. to attempt to change his or her attitude towards committing crime through a constructive regime of work, education and training supervised by a probation officer. Probation is, in fact, one of many examples in the penal system of voluntary or informal practices (such as the Police Court Mission) developing in response to immediate problems and later being legalised and taken over by the state (the probation service).

The task of sentencing when several different sentences are available, embodying different philosophies, was quickly recognised by the judiciary as having become more difficult. It is exemplified in this comment by McCardie J, one that would probably be echoed by many judges today: 'Anyone can try a case. That is as easy as falling off a log. The difficulty comes in knowing what to do with a man once he has been found guilty' (from Page, L., *The Sentence of the Court*, London, Faber and Faber, 1948, p. 31). By 1948, it was recognised that sentencers were going to need more information on the offender, as well as on the offence, and the probation service was given the task of producing reports on offenders before sentence was passed (now termed pre-sentence reports). In appropriate cases, medical reports should also be prepared. Defence legal representatives had to be shown these reports before mitigation, thereby permanently changing the nature of mitigation from a rhetorical plea for mercy to its current form of a reasoned exercise in persuasion, grounded and argued from a basis of information about the offence and the offender.

In 1948, as well, new sentences were introduced. Detention centre and attendance centre for offenders under 21 were introduced to provide different types of training and life style for those offenders not meriting the then standard custodial sentence for younger offenders, borstal. Probation provisions were consolidated, and the court *required* to consider 'the circumstances, including the nature of the offence and the offender' before sentencing an offender to probation. The condition of a maximum 12 months of mental treatment could now be added if the offender agreed to a probation order, provided reports were received from two doctors recommending this. Absolute and conditional discharges were introduced.

One category of offender had been severely neglected for many years. Sentences for mentally disordered offenders in higher courts were lacking until the CJA 1948 with its provisions for mental treatment with a probation order. Magistrates' courts had had powers to certify imbeciles or lunatics. Probation orders with condition of mental treatment, however, could only be given with the defendant's consent, and it was not until 1959 in the Mental Health Act (now under the Mental Health Act 1983) that courts were given powers to give compulsory sentences involving treatment for mentally ill offenders who were not feeble-minded or 'moral imbeciles' from an early age. These were the Hospital Order and the Restriction Order (Hospital Order with secure confinement). For both of these, two doctors' reports had to be produced to the court.

What was driving this expansion of sentencing powers? As explained above, in 1901 the major penal philosophy was straight retribution — a tariff based on the offence. By 1910 the words used were changing subtly towards bringing in a reformative ideal — that punishment could change the offender and make him or her into a new person, not just through the old idea of the prisoner contemplating his or her sins sitting in a cell, but through active intervention by prison officers and the example set by them. This reformative movement grew in strength in the 1920s and 1930s, when active intervention started incorporating the idea of rehabilitative programmes for training offenders to provide them with skills on their release — or discussion sessions with probation officers using the social work skills of individual casework to solve individual problems within the family. The growth of non-custodial sentences originally had these idealistic and rehabilitational aims, but by the 1960s the growing crime rate — and growing prison population, which made it difficult to run rehabilitative programmes in prison — started putting the emphasis on a new aim: to keep people out of prison. Prison was seen as positively harmful and as encouraging rather than diminishing criminal habits. Those who did not need it should not get it.

15.5.3 KEEPING PEOPLE OUT OF PRISON — NON-CUSTODIAL ALTERNATIVES

As the prison population kept on growing a more administrative and practical aim appeared in penal policy. The Home Office did not just want offenders kept out of prison because they could better be rehabilitated in the community, but because prisons were becoming increasingly overcrowded. None the less, the late 1960s and early 1970s saw the peak of the rehabilitative philosophy. And then came the shocks.

First, a number of research studies doing evaluations of both prison and non-custodial sentences showed that supposedly rehabilitative measures did not seem to have much effect on reconviction rates. The review by Brody in 1978 summed up the sudden unpleasant shock that it seemed as though 'nothing works' — a view that has held sway until the early 1990s, when a more limited treatment ethos is beginning to appear (that it is possible to focus on *offending behaviour* and produce effective programmes for sex offending, tackling drink or drug problems, or diffusing anger in violent offenders).

Secondly, the continuing increase in crime rates in the 1970s and 1980s put more pressure on prisons and the criminal justice system in general in purely numerical terms. Staff just tried to cram them in and had no energy or time for anything else like penal philosophy.

Thirdly, the lack of investment in prisons during the 1950s and 1960s started showing through. The buildings were in a poor state — and, despite the prison building programmes of recent years, are still often in a poor state. The overcrowding in the local prisons often cannot be resolved because there is nowhere to move prisoners to while the wing is being rebuilt.

Responding to the need to keep people out of prison unless they really needed to be there, the Home Office devised yet more alternatives to custody from which sentencers could choose. The 1967 Criminal Justice Act introduced suspended sentences. The 1971 Act introduced a condition of attendance at a Day Training Centre with a probation order, the community service order, the possibility of deferring sentence for up to six months, provisions for criminal bankruptcy and increased provisions for compensation orders. The 1982 Act made compensation orders a sentence in their own right — that if an offender did not have sufficient funds both to pay a fine and to pay compensation to the victim, then the sentence could be compensation alone.

Though sentencers were being offered ever more sentences to suit the individual circumstances of offenders and the type of offence committed, the amount of guidance offered as to how to use this range was fairly limited. The Court of Appeal had, by the late 1970s and early 1980s, started to produce 'guideline cases' for sentencers, but the number of offences and sentences covered was relatively small, particularly for offences heard at the magistrates' court. The role of probation officers in preparing reports for courts had become very significant, particularly for the range of offences whose seriousness might denote either a custodial sentence or one of the range of non-custodial sentences.

15.5.4 THE 1980s: 'JUST DESERTS' AND REPARATION

The penological pragmatism of the 1970s, stressing the need to keep minor offenders out of prison, drew from a range of penal philosophies — retribution, deterrence, rehabilitation. The 1980s saw the growing importance of reparation as an additional element, and the increasing dominance of one particular philosophy, 'just deserts'.

The idea of reparation is for the offender to recompense the individual victim, or society, for the harm he or she has done through the offence. It may be direct reparation to the victim, as in compensation orders (the payment of money to the victim through the court, for the loss, damage or injury suffered), or indirect reparation as in community service orders. Here the offender is ordered to do a certain number of hours work for the community. Both forms of reparation have become more popular since they were introduced in the early 1970s. Sentencers are now instructed that they should give reasons if they do not make a compensation order in a case where there is an identifiable victim and injury, loss or damage (CJA 1988). Community service has been emphasised in the CJA 1991.

At this point, given the decline in the rehabilitative ideal, it could not be said that any particular penal philosophy was dominant. However, in the CJA 1991, the American 'justice movement' or 'just deserts' principle has been made dominant. The new model puts back a focus on the offence rather than the offender — a return to the retributive mood of the beginning of the century. In America, it has incorporated much-reduced discretion for sentencers — mandatory or advisory guidelines for judges and a reduced role for parole.

In England and Wales, so far, there has been no imposition of rules by Parliament on the judiciary equivalent to those in America, though the proposals in the 1996 White Paper (*Protecting the Public*, HMSO, Cm 3190) envisage mandatory minimum sentences and 'automatic' life sentences for serious, violent and drug offenders. There has in fact been considerable resistance to the idea that there should be such guidance from Parliament. We have no system of mandatory or advisory legislative guidance for sentencers. Our maxima reflect the worst possible case and so give little guidance on the ordinary case. In a few cases, Parliament has required reasons to be given when passing certain sentences — but has not put in place any real sanctions if the process does not happen. Court of Appeal cases have not provided a complete framework for sentencers. There is no manual which is publicly available containing the collection of these cases. There is no obvious and agreed sentencing system which sets out clearly the acceptable approach to take to cases. There is no way of having a discussion about what is happening in sentencing publicly — so that judges, the Bar, solicitors, probation officers and all those who have to provide information to sentencers can discuss what they are doing and what they should be doing in a regular forum.

Worse, England and Wales is amongst the highest in Europe in terms of the proportion of offenders given custodial sentences and the prison population. The Council of Europe publishes regular league tables. We appear at the wrong end. Perhaps another relevant statistic is that, in England and Wales, one-third of men will have a criminal conviction by the age of 28.

The growth in non-custodial sentences has not in fact led to a decreasing number of people sent to prison. In the last ten years, new sentences have really taken their clients from other non-custodial sentences, as opposed to making any dent on custody. This is clearly seen from **Figure 15.1.** Looking at the immediate imprisonment graph, it has hardly changed. Probation, discharges, community service have replaced fines as unemployment has bitten — but not custody. Sentence lengths have increased. The hardened mood against new threats — drugs in particular — has increased sentences for more serious crimes.

The pattern of sentencing immediately prior to the CJA 1991 was a pattern of wide discretion, and considerable disparity between courts in the pattern of sentences they were giving the offenders coming before them.

15.6 The Criminal Justice Act 1991

15.6.1 PRINCIPLES OF THE CJA 1991

The advent of CJA 1991 was intended to produce substantial changes in sentencing. For the first time, the Government decided to state relatively clearly and unambiguosly its sentencing philosophy. The White Paper introducing the Bill states:

> The Government's aim is to ensure that convicted criminals in England and Wales are punished justly and suitably according to the seriousness of their offences; in other words that they get their just desserts [sic]. No Government should try to influence the decisions of the courts in individual cases. The independence of the judiciary is rightly regarded as a cornerstone of our liberties. But sentencing principles and sentencing practice are matters of legitimate concern to Government, and Parliament provides the funds necessary to give effect to the courts' decisions.
>
> The sentence of the court prescribes the punishment for criminal behaviour. Punishment in proportion to the seriousness of the crime has long been accepted as one of many objectives in sentencing. It should be the principal focus for sentencing decisions. This is consistent with the Government's view that those who commit very serious crimes, particularly crimes of violence, should receive long custodial sentences; but that many other crimes can be punished in the community, with greater emphasis on bringing home to the criminal the consequences of his actions, compensation to the victim and reparation to the community. . . .
>
> The Government's proposals therefore emphasise the objectives which sentencing is most likely to meet successfully in whole or in part. The first objective for all sentences is denunciation of and retribution for the crime. Depending on the offence and the offender, the sentence may also aim to achieve public protection, reparation and reform of the offender, preferably in the community. This approach points to sentencing policies which are more firmly based on the seriousness of the offence, and just desserts [sic] for the offender. (From *Crime, Justice and Protecting the Public*, 1990, HMSO.)

Figure 15.1 Percentage of Male Offenders Aged 21 and Over Sentenced for Indictable Offences Who Received Various Sentences or Orders

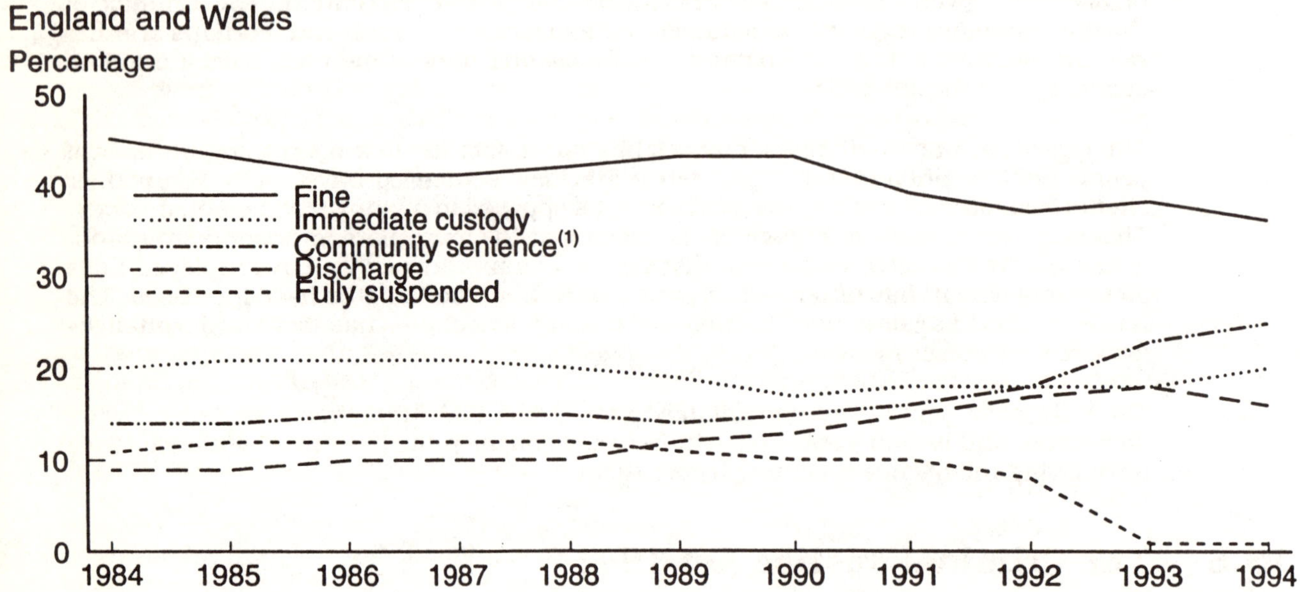

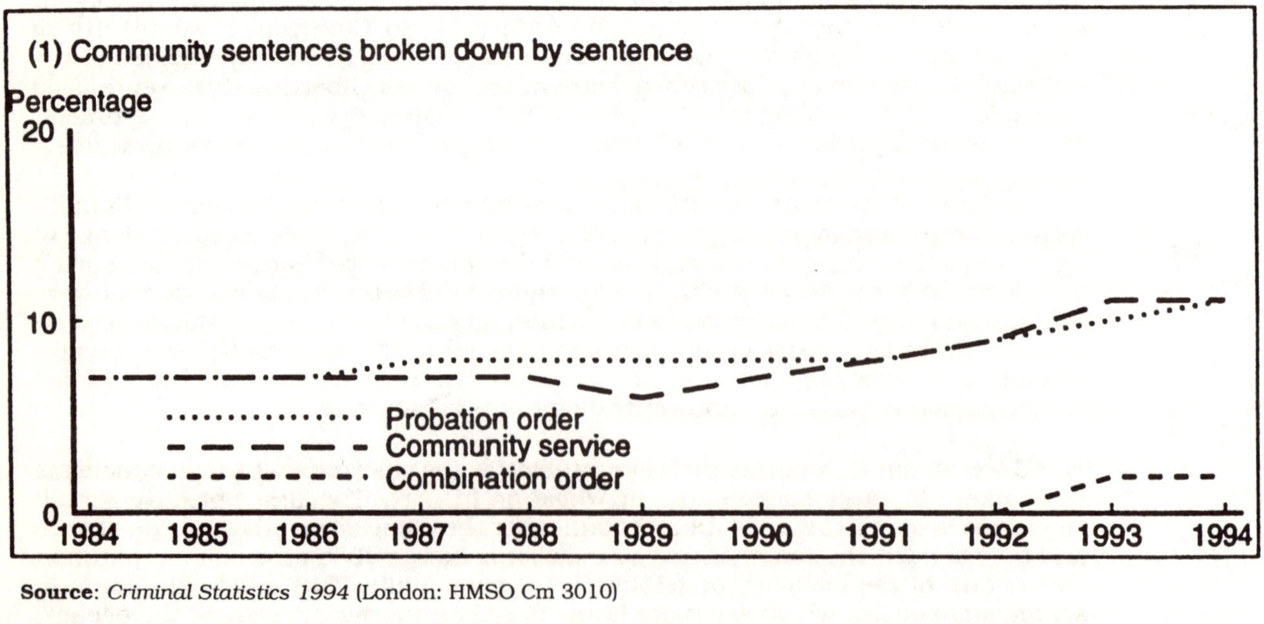

Source: *Criminal Statistics 1994* (London: HMSO Cm 3010)

The Government thus finally set out the relative priorities it would like the courts to give to the different philosophies of sentencing in dealing with offenders. Retribution or just desserts — concentrating on the seriousness of the offence — is to be the primary aim in sentencing. It will therefore be unlawful to pass a more severe sentence in the hope of achieving reform, or because of the prevalence of the offence. The sentence must be proportionate to the seriousness of the crime.

15.6.2 THE PYRAMID OF THRESHOLDS OF SERIOUSNESS

The Act makes a distinction between four different kinds of sentences graded according to the severity of their consequences to the offender. At the bottom of the pyramid are discharges, seen as the least severe sentences. Next come fines and other financial penalties. Then there are community orders or community sentences and finally, at the top of the pyramid of severity, custody. It is clear that the sentencer's choice between these four types should be governed by the seriousness of the offence. The Act and the associated documentation set out the 'custody threshold' of seriousness of offence which will need to be passed before an offender is given a custodial sentence. Similarly there is a 'community sentence threshold'.

Is there then no place for rehabilitation? What about all the community sentences which were originally introduced for rehabilitative or reparative reasons, such as probation or community service? Within the custody band, and within the financial penalties band, the choice of sentence (number of months of custody, or 'units' of fine) is indeed only to be made according to the seriousness of the offence. But *within* the community sentence band, the choice of sentence is to depend not only on proportionality to the offence, but also the individual problems of the offender and to his or her rehabilitation. Hence the choice between probation, community service, the new combination order, or a probation order with restrictions (such as attendance at a probation centre) should reflect both the seriousness of the offence (and the severity of the consequences of the community sentence to the offender) and the best sentence to suit the individual offender.

These principles are set out in the following sections of the Act:

The 'custody threshold'

> *. . . the court shall not pass a custodial sentence on the offender unless it is of the opinion—*
>
> *(a) that the offence, or the combination of the offence and one other offence associated with it, was so serious that only such a sentence can be justified for the offence.* (s. 1(2))

Proportionality within the custody band

> *The custodial sentence shall be—*
>
> *(a) for such term (not exceeding the permitted maximum) as in the opinion of the court is commensurate with the seriousness of the offence, or the combination of the offence and other offences associated with it.* (s. 2(2))

The 'community sentence threshold'

> *A court shall not pass on an offender a community sentence, that is to say, a sentence which consists of or includes one or more community orders, unless it is of the opinion that the offence, or the combination of the offence and one other offence associated with it, was serious enough to warrant such a sentence.* (s. 6(1))

Proportionality and suitability within the community sentence band

> *where a court passes a community sentence—*

> *(a) the particular order or orders comprising or forming part of the sentence shall be such as in the opinion of the court is, or taken together are, the most suitable for the offender; and*
>
> *(b) the restrictions on liberty imposed by the order or orders shall be such as in the opinion of the court are commensurate with the seriousness of the offence, or the combination of the offence and other offences associated with it.* (s. 6(2))

Proportionality within the band of fines and the principle of unit fines

> *the amount of the fine shall be the product of—*
>
> *(a) the number of units which is determined by the court to be commensurate with the seriousness of the offence, or the combination of the offence and other offences associated with it; and*
>
> *(b) the value to be given to each of those units, that is to say, the amount which, at the same or any later time, is determined by the court in accordance with rules made by the Lord Chancellor to be the offender's disposable weekly income.* (s. 18(2))

However, the word 'seriousness' is not defined within the Act and few clues are given in the Act as to how sentencers should interpret it, or which factors should be seen as mitigating or aggravating (see subsequent chapters for cases on mitigating and aggravating factors). In addition, *R* v *Baverstock* [1993] 1 WLR 202 sets out that even if the custodial threshold has been passed in relation to the seriousness of the *offence*, it is possible for a lesser sentence to be given if there are mitigating factors relevant to the *offender*.

15.6.3 THE MAGISTRATES' ASSOCIATION GUIDELINES

Sentencing guidelines for use by magistrates in the magistrates' court were introduced in June 1992 by the Magistrates' Association, the professional association for magistrates, and a revised version was produced in September 1993. They apply only to offenders aged 18 and over. They are only a voluntary code and have no legal force, but previous versions have been shown in a survey to be used by 89% of magistrates in road traffic cases and 75% in other cases (see M. Wasik and A. Turner, 'Sentencing guidelines in the magistrates' courts' [1993] Crim LR 345–56). For each non-motoring offence, the guidelines set out a guide to sentencing, in relation to some 'seriousness indicators' which may be present.

The guidelines indicate entry points for each type of offence — types of sentence which should be considered first for that kind of offence. They relate to what would be seen as cases of average seriousness. So, for example, for 'theft from vehicle' (Theft Act 1968, s. 1), the entry point is a community penalty, whereas for criminal damage it is a fine. At the most serious end, the offences for which not only should a custodial sentence be considered, but magistrates should be *committing the offender for sentence* at the Crown Court, are production, supply possession with intent to supply of Class A drugs, and possession with intent to supply of Class B drugs (unless small scale). The offences for which entry points are given as *custody* are: aggravated vehicle taking, assault on police, burglary of dwelling, driving whilst disqualified, violent disorder and wounding/GBH (Public Order Act 1986, s. 2). The offences for which entry points are given as a *community penalty* are affray, actual bodily harm, burglary of non-dwelling, common assault, dangerous driving, possession of Class A drugs, causing fear (or provocation) of violence (Public Order Act 1986, s. 4), handling, obtaining by deception, false representation in relation to social security, taking a vehicle without consent, theft from vehicle and theft in which a breach of trust is involved. All other offences listed have a *financial penalty* as the entry point. It should be noted that the entry points are based on a first-time offender pleading not guilty and that a guilty plea may 'be regarded as a mitigating factor for which a sentencing discount of approximately one third might be given'. Other mitigating and aggravating factors will also need to be taken into account for particular offences.

The sentencing guidelines also contain some suggested fines, which relate to offences of average seriousness committed by first offenders. The guideline fine for shoplifting is £280, for television licence evasion £180 and for driving with no insurance £570.

The sentencing guidelines of September 1993 clearly appear harsher than the previous 1992 ones and it was acknowledged that sentencing had moved 'up tariff', especially for offences of violence, house burglary, criminal deception or those involving hard drugs. Again, the lesson for counsel is that sentencing levels can change substantially over a 12-month period and that it is important to remain up to date with the penal mood and with any guidance being given to sentencers, whether by the courts or by bodies such as the Magistrates' Association.

It must be stressed that these sentencing guidelines are only suggestions for magistrates. The Home Office *Information on the Criminal Justice System in England and Wales* indicates clearly that there was still substantial regional and local disparity in sentencing levels around the country in 1991 and it is important that counsel attune themselves to local patterns of sentencing, particularly in courts at which they appear only rarely.

15.6.4 WHAT IS SERIOUSNESS?

In relation to probation, the national standards first issued in the spring of 1992 have set out some ideas of how probation officers should deal with ideas of seriousness in their reports (see **Chapter 19**). **Chapters 20—22** consider the current cases relating to seriousness for custody. In *R* v *Baverstock* [1993] 1 WLR 202, the Court of Appeal, addressing the question of seriousness in one of the first cases under the CJA 1991, affirmed the view taken in *R* v *Bradbourn* (1985) 7 Cr App R (S) 180 that there should be no additional definition of seriousness and courts should apply the ordinary, everyday meaning of the term. However, counsel will need to pay great attention to the guidance produced by the Court of Appeal in cases taken under the CJA 1991 to gain an idea of what factors they should bring out in mitigation. So, for example, *R* v *Cunningham* [1993] 1 WLR 183 shows that the prevalence of an offence is a legitimate factor in determining seriousness, because the seriousness of an offence is affected by the number of people it harms and the extent to which it harms them, taking into account the fact that prevalent offences can cause general fear among potential victims in the neighbourhood.

A difficulty in working out the relationship between seriousness and length of sentence is that the changes in the CJA 1991 on parole and remission have meant that it is not possible to compare sentence lengths before and after the Act, since the effective amount of time served in prison will be different. Indeed, *Practice Statement (Crime: Sentencing)* [1992] 1 WLR 948 states that a sentence passed under the new Act may well be different in length from one passed before the Act. The proper comparison is between the period likely to be served under the sentence imposed and the period likely to have been served under the sentence the judge would have imposed before the Act, but *R* v *Cunningham* [1993] 1 WLR 183 firmly stresses that no precise mathematical calculation can be made (and thus, by implication, appeals based on such calculations will fail, with the Court of Appeal being concerned essentially with whether the sentence complies with the new legislation, rather than its relationship with the old). If the proposals in the 1996 White Paper become law and are brought into force, the relation between sentence passed and sentence served will change again.

15.6.5 A DISTINCTION BETWEEN SERIOUS OFFENDERS AND THE REST

In addition to the focus on seriousness, the overall sentencing policy of the Government is now set more firmly than before on a course of bifurcation. This term, originally coined by Professor Bottoms, means that a distinction is drawn between sentencing for the serious, violent and dangerous — who should be given long periods of incarceration, and for whom a protective sentencing policy is envisaged — and sentencing for the majority of ordinary offenders. For ordinary offenders, prison will not be seen as a necessary, or even desirable, response, and a community alternative may be far better. Quoting the White Paper again:

> Most offenders can be punished by financial penalties — by paying compensation to their victims and by fines. When offences are too serious to be properly punished by financial penalties alone, the courts have a choice of community penalties, such as probation or community service, or of custody . . .
>
> For most offenders, imprisonment has to be justified in terms of public protection, denunciation and retribution. Otherwise it can be an expensive way of making bad people worse. The prospects of reforming offenders are usually much better if they stay in the community, provided the public is properly protected.

This has been embodied in the Act in s. 1(2)(b) and s. 2(2)(b), which state:

> [*the court shall not pass a custodial sentence on the offender unless it is of the opinion—*]
>
> *where the offence is a violent or sexual offence, that only such a sentence would be adequate to protect the public from serious harm from him.* (s. 1(2)(b))
>
> [*the custodial sentence shall be—*]
>
> *where the offence is a violent or sexual offence, for such longer term (not exceeding the maximum) as in the opinion of the court is necessary to protect the public from serious harm from the offender.* (s. 2(2)(b))

In *R* v *Baverstock* [1993] 1 WLR 202 it was held that the judge should clearly state under which section the sentence he or she is passing falls and why that is so. The judge is also required to explain his or her reasoning to the offender in ordinary language (s. 1(4) — though the Court of Appeal will not be sympathetic to appeals based on 'fine linguistic analysis' of sentencing remarks). The judge must give an express indication to counsel if he or she is considering imposing a longer sentence than is commensurate with the seriousness of the offence under s. 2(2)(b). Sentences for the violence and dangerousness are discussed further in **Chapter 23**.

15.6.6 HELP FOR SENTENCERS

In order to help sentencers with the new Act, a major training and information programme took place in 1992. Previous experience with substantial new legislation on sentencing, however, has proved that it is very difficult to change sentencing practice quickly over the whole range of sentencers and courts in England and Wales. Within the Act, the Government is relying on procedural criteria and information to help sentencers.

The Act provides that courts should consider a pre-sentence report before passing a custodial sentence (s. 3 — though it will not invalidate such a sentence if they do not). They should give their reasons for giving a custodial sentence (s. 1(4)). Sentencers should consider the circumstances of the case and also consider information about it (including any aggravating or mitigating factors — s. 3(3)). This of course implies that counsel will have a major role in helping to provide this information. Sentencers should take into account any information before the court which is relevant to the offender's attitude to the offence and his or her physical and mental condition.

15.7 The Proposals in the 1996 White Paper

The 1996 White Paper, *Protecting the Public*, HMSO, Cm 3190, departs significantly from previous forms of legislative guidance to sentencers, in proposing mandatory minimum sentences for certain types of serious crime (as in the US). Currently, we have sentencing maxima for all offences (set out in the statutes creating the offences), but no minima, and there is judicial discretion to pass any sentence beneath the maximum. Murder is the only offence for which there is only one sentence available to the judge — that of life imprisonment. There has been considerable debate recently as to whether this restriction should be retained, given the wide breadth of types of conduct classified as murder in English law, but the White Paper in fact proposes an extension of 'automatic' sentencing.

The White Paper proposals include the following:

(a) an automatic life sentence for offenders convicted of a second serious violent or sex offence, unless there are 'genuinely exceptional circumstances' (p. 46). The violent/sex offences are those currently able to attract a life sentence (attempted murder, manslaughter, robbery, wounding with intent, rape, etc.). As currently with discretionary life sentences under the Criminal Justice and Public Order Act 1994, the judge would have to set a minimum period to be served in relation to the need for retribution and deterrence (release then depending on the Parole Board's view of the continuing dangerousness of the offender);

(b) mandatory minimum prison sentences of seven years, unless there are genuinely exceptional circumstances, for those convicted of drug-trafficking offences involving class A drugs, who have two or more previous convictions for similar offences;

(c) mandatory minimum prison sentences of three years, unless there are genuinely exceptional circumstances, for those convicted of burglary of a dwelling, who have two or more previous convictions for similar offences;

(d) abolition of automatic early release and parole (although retention of a small discount on the sentence to be served for good behaviour, and retention of licence conditions on release for life sentence prisoners), with those sentenced to 12 months or more merely being supervised for a further period in the community. This means people will serve longer in prison for the same sentence length than they do currently.

It is envisaged that the proposals relating to 'automatic' life sentences and to sentences for burglary will substantially increase sentence lengths served for these offences. Unless there are significant changes in judicial sentencing patterns, with sentences passed decreasing to mitigate the effects of the abolition of early release, so will the proposals relating to release.

It is extremely difficult to predict if and when these proposals will be implemented (the White Paper envisages a rolling programme of implementation from 1997 to 1999, but a substantial number of new prisons would be needed). Even during the discussion and implementation period, however, previous practice would suggest that sentence lengths will start increasing substantially both generally (continuing the 1993/4 trends) and, more markedly, for these kinds of offenders. Counsel will need to keep up to date with Court of Appeal decisions in such cases and also sentencing trends in the particular Crown Courts in which he or she is practising.

15.8 The Role of Defence Counsel

The number of sentences available to the court has more than trebled since those being used in 1905. A range of both custodial sentences and community sentences is provided in all courts. We have seen that as the numbers and aims of sentences have changed, so the need for information in the process between conviction and sentencing has grown and grown. The CJA 1991 continues this trend. Even more work will need to be done by probation officers and by counsel and solicitors before the sentencing hearing.

This makes it essential that counsel should have full instructions from the defendant as to any mitigating or aggravating factors, and as to his or her financial and personal circumstances. Counsel should also liaise with the probation officer at court in relation to whether a pre-sentence report should be prepared, whether one exists and the availability of different community sentences in that particular local area. Possible sentences should be discussed with the client and all should be completed in sufficient time so that counsel can prepare the final mitigation, go into court and listen to previous cases, to see how that court views particular factors.

Mitigation plays a vital information-providing role for the judge. Currently, defence counsel is one of the major providers of information to the judiciary — in the study of mitigation in both magistrates and Crown Courts carried out by the author in the late 1970s, 18% of the reasons cited by sentencers in passing sentence as to why they had passed the sentence they did stemmed solely from the mitigation speech. Another 38% came from either the facts of the case (in a guilty plea) or from the antecedents and previous convictions, presented by the prosecution (Shapland, J., *Between Conviction and Sentence*, 1981, London, Routledge & Kegan Paul). The information-gathering and information-providing role of counsel is very important. Mitigation in particular is not just an exercise in rhetoric, but an exercise in persuasion. The best persuasion is based soundly on facts and moulded by an appreciation of how the sentencing and penal systems are put together.

SIXTEEN

THE AIMS OF SENTENCING

16.1 Introduction

What aims do the courts pursue when passing sentence? What aims should they pursue? These have often been regarded as academic questions, of no importance to the criminal practitioner. That view has always been an exaggeration: magistrates, trial judges and the Court of Appeal have from time to time proclaimed that the purpose behind a particular sentence is to rehabilitate the offender, or to deter others, or to protect the public, etc. But, as **Chapter 15** makes clear, the new legislation requires sentencers to consider the aims of sentencing more regularly and more rigorously. The Criminal Justice Act 1991 promote one aim of sentencing — 'just deserts' (proportionality) — to become the leading criterion for the imposition and the length of custodial sentences. You will therefore need to have a grasp of what the proportionality principle includes and what it excludes. To begin with, there are two short sections on the varieties of crime and on the prevention of crime.

16.2 Varieties of Crime

Whilst it is true to say that the vast bulk of summary offences are road traffic crimes, and that the vast bulk of indictable offences are crimes contrary to the Theft Acts, the wide variety of crimes which comes before the courts for sentence should not be overlooked.

In the magistrates' courts there are the many road traffic offences and property offences, but also a range of offences from non-payment of television licences to unlawful wounding, from selling alcohol without a licence to the discharge of oil from an oil tanker, from offences against the Health and Safety at Work Act to minor public order offences, from the sale of impure food to assault on a police officer.

The Crown Court is preoccupied chiefly with offences of theft, handling and deception, but it also has to deal with serious violence and sexual offences, public order offences, neglect and cruelty to children, possession of firearms, offences under the Official Secrets Acts, drug offences, pollution offences, and so forth.

Any sentencing system has to be able to adapt to and cope with this great variation in types of offence, as well as the differences among offenders and their previous records (considered further in **Chapters 20** and **21**).

16.3 Crime Prevention

'The ultimate objective of the Government is to reduce crime, particularly crimes committed by young people, before they embark on a career of criminality' (White Paper, *Crime, Justice and Protecting the Public*, para. 1.7). Most people would accept that it is preferable to prevent crimes from happening at all, rather than waiting until they do happen and then passing sentences for them. To this end a variety of crime prevention strategies has been adopted over the years — some of them well known, such as 'Neighbourhood Watch' schemes, others less well known. However, it is common for people to speak as if sentencing is the primary tool for the prevention of crime, and as if the sentences passed by the courts constitute the main hope for reducing the amount of crime in society. In its 1990 White Paper the Government has sounded a cautionary note on this argument: 'Punishment has a major part to play in reducing crime, but its role must not be over-stated'.

In fact, the role of sentencing is limited by the small proportion of all crimes which result in conviction in the courts. The 1988 British Crime Survey made enquiries of over 10,000 citizens, to try to discover how many crimes are committed but never reported by their victims. This survey, which focused on offences of theft, burglary, robbery, wounding and sexual offences, found that only about 41% of crimes are reported. By no means all the incidents reported as crimes were recorded by the police as such, so that the proportion of these crimes actually reported and recorded was only 26%. Of these, the police 'cleared up' fewer than one-third, with the result that only 7% of all crimes are reported, recorded and cleared up. Some of these were not prosecuted, some resulted in a caution, and some resulted in an acquittal; eventually only 3% ended in a conviction. (P. Mayhew et al., *The 1988 British Crime Survey*, Home Office Research Study no. 111, as presented in A *Digest of Information on the Criminal Justice System*, Home Office, 1991, p. 31).

Thus, the fact that a relatively small proportion of offences may come before the courts for sentence places a severe limitation on the ability of the courts to influence patterns of behaviour in society as a whole. This is not to suggest that sentencing is unnecessary: far from it, since the existence of the police, prosecutors, courts, the probation service and the prison service has an underlying general deterrent effect on behaviour. But we must be wary of believing that increases and decreases in the levels of court sentences will necessarily, or even probably, have an effect on the crime rate. Crime prevention strategies may prove to be more effective for these purposes than changes in sentencing practice.

16.4 Deterrent Sentencing

It could be argued that, although only a small proportion of crimes result in the offender being sentenced in court, those few sentences have a considerable deterrent effect. At the outset a distinction must be drawn between *general deterrence*, i.e. sentences aimed at deterring potential lawbreakers from committing crimes, and *individual deterrence*, i.e. sentences aimed at deterring the particular offender from committing further crimes.

16.4.1 INDIVIDUAL DETERRENCE

A sentencing strategy based on individual deterrence would presumably require courts to pass increasingly severe sentences on offenders if they repeat their offending, in the hope that eventually the sentences persuade the offender to 'go straight'. In practice this seems rarely to happen, as Lawton LJ recognised in *R* v *Sargeant* (1974) 60 Cr App R 74, at p. 77:

> Experience has shown over the years that deterrence of the offender is not a very useful approach, because those who have their wits about them usually find the closing of the prison gates an experience which they do not want again. If they do not learn that lesson, there is likely to be a high degree of recidivism any way.

The statistics certainly tend to show that most first offenders (71%) are *not* reconvicted within six years, whereas the vast majority of those with five or more previous convictions (87%) are reconvicted within six years. (See Philpotts, G. and Lancucki, L., *Previous Convictions, Sentence and Reconviction*, Home Office Research Study No. 53 (HMSO, 1979), p. 16.)

16.4.2 GENERAL DETERRENCE

From time to time courts have expressly justified sentences on grounds of general deterrence, often termed 'exemplary sentences'.

Two questions are raised by this practice. First, is it right to punish one person more severely in the hope that this sentence will deter others? Some would argue that this is justifiable for the protection of innocent victims, whereas others would vigorously assert that an offender does not lose all rights and should not be used as a mere pawn in social policy by increasing the sentence beyond what is proportionate.

Even for the protectionists, however, much may depend on the answer to the second question: Is it likely that the sentence will succeed in deterring some others? Here, the picture is much less clear than is sometimes supposed. One favourite anecdote is the 'exemplary' sentences handed down in the trials following the Notting Hill race riots of 1958: these were indeed followed by a lull, but increased policing and the removal of leading rioters from circulation may be stronger explanations. Moreover, one key factor is the risk of detection, or, to be more precise, offenders' beliefs about the risk of detection. If offenders think that the risk of detection is low, this may go a long way towards nullifying the effect of higher sentences imposed by the courts.

16.4.3 THE EFFECTIVENESS OF GENERAL DETERRENCE STRATEGIES

Does research cast any light on the effectiveness of general deterrence strategies? There are many difficulties in the way of conducting reliable research on general deterrence, and criminologists have not yet moved far beyond the proposition that extremely harsh punishments are likely to deter. There are likely to be variations according to type of offence, as recognised by Lawton LJ, in *R* v *Sargeant* (1974) 60 Cr App R 74, at p. 77:

> So far as deterrence of others is concerned, it is the experience of the courts that deterrent sentences are of little value in respect of offences which are committed on the spur of the moment, either in hot blood or in drink or both. Deterrent sentences may very well be of considerable value where crime is premeditated. Burglars, robbers and users of firearms or weapons may very well be put off by deterrent sentences.

The 1990 White Paper counselled caution on deterrent sentencing (para. 2.8):

> Much crime is committed on impulse, given the opportunity presented by an open window or unlocked door, and it is committed by offenders who live from moment to moment; their crimes as impulsive as the rest of their feckless, sad or pathetic lives. It is unrealistic to construct sentencing arrangements on the assumption that most offenders will weigh up the possibilities in advance and base their conduct on rational calculation. Often they do not.

The intention was that the CJA 1991, based as it is on proportionality to the seriousness of the offence, would reflect this caution. However, in *R* v *Cunningham* (1993) 14 Cr App R (S) 444 the Court of Appeal held that a trial judge had not been wrong to refer to the need for deterrent sentences for robbery. Lord Taylor, CJ, held that the phrase in s. 2(2)(a) of the Act — '*commensurate with the seriousness of the offence*' — does allow the sentencer to take account of deterrence: it means 'commensurate with the punishment and deterrence which the offence required'. This is an unexpected reading of the Act, made without support from the White Paper that preceded it. However, Lord Taylor went on to say that s. 2(2)(a) does prohibit the addition of any extra length to the sentence which by the above criteria is commensurate with the seriousness of the offence, 'simply to make a special example of the defendant'. It seems that general sentencing levels may be set by reference to deterrence, but that a court in a particular case may not pass an exemplary sentence that goes above the general level. The Government has now signalled its intention to move back towards deterrence in sentencing. The above quotation from the 1990 White

Paper is now out of favour, and the 1996 White Paper (discussed in **18.3**) proposes mandatory minimum sentences for repeat burglars and drug dealers which rely heavily on individual and general deterrence.

16.5 Rehabilitative Sentencing

In the 1960s there was considerable enthusiasm for sentences which were reformative or rehabilitative. The 1970s, however, saw the publication of two surveys of the available research on rehabilitative sentencing, both of which reached somewhat negative conclusions (in the United States, Martinson, R., 'What Works? Questions and Answers about Prison Reform', (1974) *Public Interest*, Spring, p. 22; in England, Brody, S. R., *The Effectiveness of Sentencing*, Home Office Research Study No. 35 (HMSO, 1975)). These conclusions have often been summarised in the pithy comment, 'Nothing works'. The reality is somewhat more complicated and more hopeful, as Brody argues ('Research into the Aims and Effectiveness of Sentencing' (1978) 17 *Howard Journal* 133 at p. 134):

> . . . both these publications presented similar evidence which has encouraged a widespread conviction that no one type of sentence works any better — that is, is no more effective in preventing reconviction — than any other. It has to be emphasised that even if it is true, research results have actually provided little evidence for such a belief. This is because, with one or two exceptions, only a very limited range of sentencing alternatives have ever been studied (and consequently only a relatively small proportion of the offender population has ever been considered).

It would therefore be more accurate to say that no sentence has been *proved* to be more effective than others, than to say that no sentence is more effective than others, in view of the limitations of the research. Brody continues in a more optimistic vein (at p. 135):

> One good reason for not completely abandoning a faith in rehabilitation is that a number of studies have shown that improvements *can* be effected in failure rates. What is strikingly consistent about these studies is that in all of them the treatment (whatever form it took) was effective only when it was applied to certain types of offenders, or simply when it was adapted to the particular requirements of individuals, or when it was aimed at modifying such specific aspects of behaviour as addiction or aggressiveness . . . There is nothing very astonishing in these discoveries. What is more surprising is that researchers have so rarely allowed for individual variations or 'interaction effects' in their research designs, but have expected one particular programme to work equally for all offenders.

To expect imprisonment to reform an offender is now rather far-fetched in most cases, for reasons which will be elaborated in **Chapter 21**. But there are forms of probation order which aim to rehabilitate, as well as the special measures for mentally disordered offenders. Success might be possible if forms of treatment programme can be matched to suitable offenders, and in this respect much depends on the helpfulness of the pre-sentence report (see **Chapter 17**).

16.6 Incapacitative Sentencing

The present sentencing system provides a degree of public protection by exerting a general deterrent effect on potential offenders and by keeping some offenders out of circulation, i.e. for any period when they are incarcerated. But it is sometimes argued that an incapacitative sentencing policy ought to be pursued in respect of certain groups of high-risk offenders. Such a policy has long been in existence in the shape of the sentence of life imprisonment, a sentence which may only be imposed on certain offenders who meet the criteria of dangerousness laid down by the Court of Appeal in *R* v *Hodgson* (1967) 52 Cr App R 113. It is difficult to test whether all the discretionary life sentences which are imposed are necessary for public protection; no one knows. But questions have been raised about whether it is possible to identify other offenders who are so dangerous to the public that they ought to be given incapacitative sentences, longer than is proportionate to their current offences. The findings of research on this are not encouraging:

> In practice, assessments of dangerousness are no more than subjective expectations about the likelihood of any offender causing serious personal injury in the future. As these expectations naturally rely very heavily on knowledge of past behaviour, it is obviously an advantage to have the fullest possible accounts of offenders' histories and circumstances before coming to any decisions about them, but even so, no-one has been able to predict accurately more than half the time, and seldom as often as that. Most 'expert' predictions seem to be right for only one out of three individuals . . . The infrequency of really serious crimes of violence, their apparently generally random quality and the rarity of anything like a genuinely 'dangerous type' offers little encouragement for a policy which aims to reduce serious assaults by selective incapacitation of those with violent records. (Brody, S. and Tarling, R., *Taking Offenders out of Circulation*, Home Office Research Study No. 64 (HMSO, 1980), p. 37.)

Notwithstanding these doubts, the Criminal Justice Act 1991 includes two provisions for incapacitative sentencing. Section 1(2)(b) allows a court to impose a custodial sentence on a violent or sexual offender where only such a sentence would be adequate to protect the public from serious harm from the offender (even though the present offence is not serious enough); and s. 2(2)(b) allows a court to lengthen a term of imprisonment in such a case, if it appears necessary to protect the public from serious harm from the offender. These points are taken further in **Chapter 23.** For the present, it may be suggested that any policy of incapacitative sentencing for dangerous offenders must be based on hope rather than experience, and is likely to involve longer periods of incarceration unnecessarily for perhaps two-thirds of the offenders subjected to the policy.

16.7 Deserved Sentences and Proportionality

Recent years have seen a resurgence of the retributive justification for sentences, which proposes that an offender should be sentenced proportionately to the seriousness of the offence, because that is what he or she deserves. This approach does not dispute the underlying deterrent rationale for having a system of courts, law and sentencing. But it argues that sentencing offenders according to what they deserve for the offence committed conforms to fundamental principles of justice and fairness. Desert is seen as 'an integral part of everyday judgments of praise and blame' (Andrew von Hirsch, *Past or Future Crimes*, p. 52) which, transferred to the administration of criminal justice, means that sentences should 'express disapprobation of the conduct and its perpetrators'. This disapprobation should be proportionate to the seriousness of the offence.

There are those who say that English sentencing has always accepted the principle of proportionality. In fact, as is evident from the foregoing sections of this chapter, English sentencers have used various aims of sentencing on different occasions, often departing from proportionality in the hope of achieving deterrence or incapacitation. What was new about the Criminal Justice Act 1991 was the installation of proportionality as the leading aim in most cases. In the 1990 White Paper, the Government announced its policy thus (para. 2.2):

> Punishment in proportion to the seriousness of the crime has long been accepted as one of many objectives in sentencing. It should be the principal focus for sentencing decisions. This is consistent with the Government's view that those who commit very serious crimes, particularly crimes of violence, should receive long custodial sentences; but that many other crimes can be punished in the community, with greater emphasis on bringing home to the criminal the consequences of his actions, compensation to the victim and reparation to the community.

16.8 Sentencing and Victims' Rights

The last quotation makes it clear that the compensation of victims is to be regarded, in general, as a concurrent aim with proportionate sentencing. Consciousness of victims' needs and victims' rights has grown considerably in recent years. Victim support schemes have developed; greater efforts are being made to inform victims of the progress of 'their' case; facilities for victims at courts have seen some improvements; experimental schemes of mediation between victims and offender have been started; the State compensation scheme for the victims of violent crime, administered by the Criminal Injuries Compensation Board, has been brought to the attention of more victims; and courts are imposing more compensation orders on offenders in favour of victims. These developments, and further targets, were set out by the Government in its *Victim's Charter* (Home Office, 1990).

At the sentencing stage, s. 35 of PCCA 1973 empowers courts to order an offender to pay compensation to a victim for any injury, loss or damage caused (this section was amended by s. 104 of CJA 1988 so as to include compensation to the relatives of a deceased victim). Section 35 of PCCA 1973 empowers a court to make a compensation order as the sole order upon a convicted defendant, and also provides that courts should give priority to compensation when an offender has insufficient means to pay both a fine and compensation. Section 35 also imposes on courts the duty to give reasons for not making a compensation order in cases where there is a power to do so. These developments are discussed further in **Chapter 18**. In a few cases the courts have permitted the reception of a 'victim impact statement' in which the victim sets out details of the offence from his or her point of view, but the Court of Appeal has warned of the procedural difficulties of this practice (*R* v *Hobstaff* (1993) 14 Cr App R (S) 605).

16.9 Sentencing and the Avoidance of Discrimination

The Criminal Justice Act 1991 includes a provision which gives legislative recognition to the duty not to discriminate. Section 95(1) requires the Home Secretary to publish information annually which will facilitate the performance, by persons engaged in the administration of criminal justice 'of their duty to avoid discriminating against any persons on the ground of race or sex or any other improper ground'.

This is an important symbolic declaration. Its relevance to sentencing practice is established by the research of Dr Roger Hood, *Race and Sentencing* (1992). This large-scale study of sentencing in the West Midlands showed that there were significantly different patterns of sentencing blacks and whites at one of the court centres, where blacks were some 23% more likely to receive a custodial sentence than similarly situated white offenders. Taking account of the seriousness of offences and other variable factors, there were also significant differences in the lengths of the custodial sentences, with both Asians and blacks receiving longer sentences than their white counterparts. Similar differences were found in respect of non-custodial sentences, with blacks being given measures that were more severe than similarly situated white offenders.

It has sometimes been suggested that sentencers discriminate in favour of females, the so-called 'chivalry hypothesis'. It is true that the rate of imprisonment for women is far lower than for men, but a study of the crimes committed by men and by women suggests that the difference is more apparent than real:

> All of this seems to indicate that women are more minor offenders than men, and commit offences less frequently. It may be these factors which explain the different sentencing patterns for men and women, therefore, and not the fact that the defendants are female. (Morris, A., 'Sex and Sentencing' [1988] Crim LR 163, at p. 164.)

Research on sentencing by Farrington and Morris concluded that, taking into account the seriousness of the offence and previous record, men and women were dealt with in much the same way. But they also found that, whereas courts regarded the gravity of the offence as the most important factor when sentencing men, they regarded 'current problems' as the most important factor when sentencing women ('Sex, Sentencing and Reconviction' (1983) 23 BJ Crim 229). This may be supported by reference to the Home Office survey, in which probation was used for 6% of male offenders but 21% of female offenders (Moxon, D., *Sentencing Practice in the Crown Court*, Home Office Research Study No. 103 (HMSO, 1988), p. 54). Thus, some female offenders may be subjected to more 'interventionist' measures than their male counterparts. One effect of the Criminal Justice Act's emphasis on proportionality to the seriousness of the offence may be to reduce the scope for discrimination in sentencing.

SEVENTEEN

PRE-SENTENCE REPORTS AND DEFERMENT OF SENTENCE

17.1 Pre-sentence Reports

Probation officers have always assisted the court by preparing reports on offenders prior to sentencing. Prior to the Criminal Justice Act 1991 (CJA 1991), probation officers prepared social inquiry reports (renamed in the 1991 Act, pre-sentence reports). However, the only legal requirement for adult offenders was that such a report should be prepared before a community service order was passed. There was no statutory requirement to consider reports for other community sentences, such as probation, although it was good practice.

The CJA 1991 states that a court should obtain a pre-sentence report before making a probation order with additional requirements (see **Chapter 19**), a community service order, a combination order, or a supervision order with requirements (s. 7(3)). However, no community sentence will be invalidated if the court does not do so, but if there is an appeal, then the court hearing the appeal should obtain such a report and consider it. There are therefore very strong presumptions that a pre-sentence report should be obtained if such community sentences are being considered and obviously it would be good practice so to do.

The CJA 1991 also states that courts should obtain and consider a pre-sentence report before passing a custodial sentence (s. 3(1)), although if the offence is triable only on indictment, this will not apply if 'the court is of the opinion that it is unnecessary to obtain a pre-sentence report' (s. 3(2)). However, the majority of offences are triable summarily or on indictment and so a growth in the provision of pre-sentence reports is likely here too.

The probation service will have guidelines as to whether such a report should be prepared, but it is of course only counsel who will know whether he or she should suggest one of these community sentences in mitigation. Hence, defence counsel may need to suggest that such a report should be prepared — and should one of the requirements such as a hostel be seen as a likely and useful opportunity, then it may be necessary for counsel to raise this in discussion with the probation liaison officer present in court. Essentially, the probation officer is an extremely useful resource, both to the court in sentencing, and to counsel.

Probation officers stand as the gateway to many community sentences and provisions for mentally disordered offenders — in particular, the facilities that may be available locally as part of a probation order, and as providing information on the local provisions suitable for a client. They will also of course have information on bail hostels and whether places are available there, so that offenders without ties in the community who are remanded for reports can live at the bail hostel rather than being remanded in custody.

It is highly recommended that defence counsel should always go and talk to the probation officer for the court as to whether he or she has had any dealings with counsel's client and whether he or she has prepared a report or can help, and that this discussion should take place before the final talk to the client at court before a guilty plea. If the client is pleading not guilty, then the probation service, if the client agrees, may still be able to prepare a more limited pre-sentence report which does not in any way discuss the offence, and this may be useful where there is a clear possibility of their services being needed, or there is a suggestion of mental disorder.

17.1.1 NATIONAL STANDARDS FOR PRE-SENTENCE REPORTS

There are National Standards for pre-sentence reports (*National Standards for the Supervision of Offenders in the Community*, London: Home Office, 1995), which envisage that pre-sentence reports will be very close in practice to social inquiry reports. The Standards define a pre-sentence report as a report in writing with a 'view to assisting the court in determining the most suitable method of dealing with an offender which imposes a restriction on liberty commensurate with the seriousness of the offence'. The probation officer should summarise the offence factually and objectively and then draw on his or her professional experience to analyse the offender's behaviour and attitude to the offence. If applicable he or she should also describe the community sentence under which the offender could most appropriately be supervised and the risk of future offending reduced.

The pre-sentence report will start with a front sheet, which will give basic information about the offender, the offence and the court hearing. Following that will be the introduction, an analysis of the offence, focusing upon seriousness, relevant information about the offender, an analysis of the risk to the public of re-offending, and a conclusion.

The introduction should contain a summary of the sources drawn upon to prepare the report (documents seen, people interviewed, agencies consulted). It will say whether the offender is known to the probation or social services.

The analysis of the offence is designed primarily to assist the court's understanding of the nature and seriousness of the offence, and why the offender committed the offence at this time. It will bring out any factors which, in the opinion of the report writer, the court might see as aggravating or mitigating, but it will not necessarily highlight them as such. Hence, counsel will need to read the report carefully and may be able to build upon some of the factors mentioned briefly in the report. Again, although the report writer is required to form a judgment about the seriousness of the offence (and many probation areas use numerical seriousness scales for this purpose), the report will not express a firm judgment about seriousness, since this is seen as the task of the court. The analysis of the offence is very likely to contain not only an assessment of the context in which the offence occurred, but also an assessment of its consequences, including the impact upon the victim, and an assessment of the offender's attitude to the victim and the consequences of the offence.

Information about the offender will look at his or her personal and social circumstances to help the court decide on relevant sentences. The section on the risk of re-offending is designed to distil the previous information into a concise statement of the risk of re-offending and the risk of harm to the public. It should be followed by a conclusion which is normally intended to contain only one sentencing suggestion, unless the court has specifically asked for a range or number of options. Hence, counsel should be aware of this and, in the hearing which asks for a pre-sentence report, rehearse the need for the report to consider a variety of options where this is appropriate (for example, where local resources for mentally disordered offenders are scarce). Where the suggestion is for a community sentence, it is likely that a specific programme will be proposed. Any requirements which might be attached to a probation order should be set out in the report in the precise terms proposed. A supervision plan for a probation order may be attached.

It is anticipated that at the Crown Court, pre-sentence reports may be prepared on the day to avoid adjournments, in particular to avoid a remand in custody.

17.1.2 TO WHAT EXTENT DO SENTENCERS FOLLOW PRE-SENTENCE REPORTS?

Some research in the 1970s showed that magistrates followed probation officers' recommendations in social inquiry reports in around 80% of cases. This does not of course mean that magistrates were necessarily persuaded away from some course of action towards that recommended by the probation officer in those cases. It is possible that both agreed on the best sentence from considering identical information, or that the probation officers, knowing their local magistrates, were able to second guess them. Whichever reasons held, it is clear that, in the magistrates' court, the probation officers are an extremely useful and potentially powerful resource for sentencers.

In the Crown Court, Moxon's research has shown that social inquiry report recommendations are less often followed:

> Taking the disposals that featured most often in social inquiry report recommendations — the suspended sentence, probation and conditional discharge — only one third of recommendations were in line with actual sentences.

This is unsurprising, since the role of the probation service is to attempt to find the sentence which is best to prevent reoffending, which will often be a non-custodial sentence, and the tariff sentence may well be a substantial period of imprisonment. Moxon continues:

> However, there was good evidence that, where the court decided on a non-custodial sentence, the social inquiry report came into its own, exercising real influence over the choice between alternatives. Social inquiry reports are of particular importance if the court is considering either a probation order or a community service order. In all, those who were recommended for probation and those who were recommended for a community service order were three times as likely to receive these disposals as those for whom no such recommendation was made.

So in the Crown Court, and with more serious offences in the magistrates' court, it is necessary for counsel to be realistic in their sentencing suggestions, and it may not always be possible to follow the recommendation in any pre-sentence report. However, even with a long record of previous convictions, and a moderately serious offence, such as burglary, custody is not an automatic sentence, and reports can still be very useful. Guidance to the probation service in relation to the implementation of the CJA 1991 indicates that pre-sentence reports in the Crown Court may start to reflect current Crown Court sentencing practice more closely, in which case such reports are likely to become more important.

17.2 Deferment of Sentence

A court may defer sentence for up to six months, i.e. may require the offender to come back to the court (not necessarily before the same bench or judge, though efforts are made to ensure this) before he or she has been sentenced. The power is set out in s. 1 of PCCA 1973:

> *(1) Subject to the provisions of this section, the Crown Court or a magistrates' court may defer passing sentence on an offender for the purpose of enabling the court or any court to which it falls to deal with him to have regard in dealing with him to his conduct after conviction (including, where appropriate, the making by him of reparation for his offence) or to any change in his circumstances.*

The reasons can be various, but common ones include whether the offender will do what he or she and his or her counsel say in mitigation that they will do. This might be to get a job, or take voluntary treatment (though a straight probation order without conditions is more usual here), or to pay reparation to the victim or just to 'go straight' — another form of the 'last chance'. It is not possible to put a definite condition of paying compensation into deferment of sentence (the only definite way for the court to order compensation is via a compensation order made in conjunction with or instead of a sentence — and of course deferment happens *before* sentencing). However, defendants would be well advised to get ready to pay reparation if they say they are going to and that is taken up by the judge in deferment. Note that the offender has to consent to the deferment. If the offender successfully completes the period of deferment, he or she can certainly expect not to be sent to prison (a conditional discharge or a probation order is a more usual result).

But there are problems with the very vagueness of the order, and these are well set out in the case of *R* v *George* (1983) 6 Cr App R (S) 211 (judgment of Lord Lane CJ). A defendant definitely 'fails' if he or she commits another offence during the period of deferment. But the other expectations have often been less than clear. Following *George*, it can be stated that:

> The purpose of deferment is therefore to enable the court to take into account the defendant's conduct after conviction or any change in circumstances and then only if it is in the interest of justice to exercise the power. It will, one imagines, seldom be in the interests of justice to stipulate that the conduct required is reparation by the defendant.
>
> The court should make it clear to the defendant what the particular purposes are which the court has in mind under s. 1(1) of PCCA 1973 and what conduct is expected of him or her during deferment.
>
> The failure to do so, or more often the failure on the part of the defendant or his or her representatives to appreciate what those purposes are or that conduct is, has been a fruitful source of appeals . . . It is essential that the deferring court should make a careful note of the purposes for which the sentence is being deferred and what steps, if any, it expects the defendant to take during the period of deferment. Ideally the defendant himself or herself should be given notice in writing of what he or she is expected to do or refrain from doing, so that there can be no doubt in his or her mind what is expected of him or her.
>
> Thus the task of the court which comes to deal with the offender at the expiration of the period of deferment is as follows:
>
> First the purpose of the deferment and any requirement imposed by the deferring court must be ascertained. Secondly the court must determine if the defendant has substantially conformed or attempted to conform with the proper expectations of the deferring court, whether with regard to finding a job or as the case may be. If he or she has, then the defendant may legitimately expect that an immediate custodial sentence will not be imposed. If he has not, then the court should be careful to state with precision in what respect he or she has failed.
>
> . . . In many cases a short probation order may be preferable to a deferment of sentence. Such an order enables the defendant's behaviour to be monitored by the probation officer, and it ensures that formal notice of the requirements of the court are given to the defendant.
>
> On the other hand a deferment of sentence will be more appropriate where the conduct required of the defendant is not sufficiently specific to be made the subject of a condition imposed as part of a probation order without creating uncertainty in the mind of the probation officer and the defendant as to whether there has been a breach of the order; for example, where the defendant is to make a real effort to find work, or where the sentencer wishes to see whether a change in the defendant's attitude and circumstances, which appears to be a possibility at the time of deferment, does in fact come about. Again, deferment may be the appropriate course where the steps to be taken by the defendant could not of their nature be the subject of a condition, for example where he or she is to make reparation, or at least demonstrate a real intention and capacity to do so.

EIGHTEEN

DISCHARGES, COMPENSATION ORDERS AND FINES

18.1 Introduction

Most indictable offences (either-way offences and those triable only on indictment) result in either a fine or a discharge, often combined with a compensation order. This is because most either-way offences are tried in the magistrates' courts, which tend to use the fine most frequently. The Magistrates' Association guidelines (see **20.2.4**) tend to focus on fines, but they indicate that where aggravating features predominate in certain crimes, the court's 'entry point' should be a community sentence or, as the case may be, a custodial sentence. On the other hand, where mitigating features predominate in certain crimes, the 'entry point' should be a discharge.

In this chapter we first consider discharges and bind-overs, and then move on to compensation orders and fines. It is important to bear in mind throughout that in any case involving death, injury, loss or damage, the court is obliged to consider making a compensation order. The order may be added to any other form of sentence, or may be the sole order in the case.

18.2 Absolute Discharge

The absolute discharge is exactly that: the offender is discharged absolutely from punishment for the offence. The law is now contained in a new sch. 1A to the Powers of Criminal Courts Act 1973, substituted by sch. 1 to the Criminal Justice Act 1991. A Home Office booklet for sentencers, *The Sentence of the Court*, suggests that an absolute discharge might be appropriate in response to 'the triviality of the offence, the circumstances in which it came to be prosecuted, or factors relating to the offender'. In practice, absolute discharges are granted rarely (1% of cases in magistrates' courts, even less in the Crown Court). They seem to be reserved for cases where the court takes the view that the offender had little or no moral guilt, or is in dire circumstances (e.g. suffering from a terminal disease).

Cases in which an absolute discharge is appropriate should come before the courts only rarely, because they should usually be eliminated at the stage of deciding whether to prosecute. The initial decision is usually that of the police, and the Home Office circulars to police forces on the use of police cautions (No. 59/1990 and No. 18/1994) recommend the use of a caution instead of prosecution in cases where the likely penalty in court will be nominal, and in cases where there are factors personal to the defendant (old age, infirmity, mental illness or stress) which would make a prosecution particularly traumatic. In these cases the police are urged to caution the defendant formally, usually involving the attendance of the defendant at a police station to be cautioned by a uniformed senior officer. The police have been encouraged to use cautions more widely for adult offenders, and in consequence the 'cautioning rate' rose from a mere 3% during the 1980s to 26% of defendants aged 21 or over in 1993

(*Criminal Statistics 1993*, Table 5.5), but the latest Home Office Circular (No. 18/1994) aims to reduce the cautioning rate by restricting second and subsequent cautions.

There is a further filter in cases where the police decide upon prosecution and pass the papers to the CPS. According to the *Code for Crown Prosecutors*, issued under s. 10 of the Prosecution of Offences Act 1985, the CPS should consider 'whether the public interest requires a prosecution' in each case. The factors to be considered are similar to those enumerated in the police cautioning circular: a prosecution might properly be discontinued if the court 'would be likely to impose a purely nominal penalty' (such as an absolute discharge), and if the defendant is old, infirm, mentally ill or under great stress. If these filters work effectively, it will be rare that the courts will find a case in which an absolute discharge is the appropriate disposal.

18.3 Conditional Discharge

A conditional discharge, like an absolute discharge, now counts as a conviction for some purposes (CJA 1991 s. 29(4), as amended). The difference is that the court may discharge the offender 'subject to the condition that he commits no offence during such period, not exceeding three years', as the court may specify; and, if the offender does commit another offence during the specified period, the court which convicts him or her of that offence has the power to impose a sentence for the original offence as well (sch. 1A to the PCCA 1973, substituted by sch. 1 to the CJA 1991). In that sense the conditional discharge carries the threat of a more severe sentence if the offender fails to conform to the law during the specified period.

Discharges were given to some 16% of male indictable offenders aged 21 and over in 1994, and to some 32% of female indictable offenders aged 21 and over. It is an appropriate measure for a non-serious offence by someone with no previous convictions, or with a substantial gap since the last conviction. It sounds a warning, and reserves to the courts the power to re-sentence if a further offence is committed within the specified period. Conditional discharges have also been used in cases where the offender is thought to lack the means to pay an adequate fine. The point is illustrated by *R* v *McGowan* [1975] Crim LR 113. The defendant was convicted of handling seven stolen crabs. The judge was informed that the defendant was impecunious and that a fine would be difficult to pay. He therefore imposed a suspended sentence of 12 months' imprisonment. The Court of Appeal held that this was wrong in principle: the offence was not serious enough for imprisonment of any kind and, if a fine was not thought to be practical, the proper course was to move down to a conditional discharge.

18.4 Binding Over

This option may be seen as an alternative to a conditional discharge. Some courts seem to have a tradition of using the power to bind over instead of the power to grant a conditional discharge. This is a technical area of sentencing law, with several common law powers and ancient statutory powers still in force. The Law Commission has proposed its abolition (Law Com. No. 222, *Binding Over* (1994)).

One of the principal modern restatements of the power is in s. 1(7) of the Justices of the Peace Act 1968, which declares 'the power to bind over to keep the peace, and the power to bind over to be of good behaviour, a person who or whose case is before the court, by requiring him to enter into his own recognisances or to find sureties or both, and committing him to prison if he does not comply'.

The chief practical differences between the bind-over and the conditional discharge are twofold. First, the bind-over specifies a sum of money to be forfeited, and thus takes the form of a suspended fine. And second, a bind-over can be breached without the commission of a subsequent offence, if it is proved that the person has failed to keep the peace or to be of good behaviour.

18.5 Deferment of Sentence

Section 1 of the PCCA 1973 empowers a court to defer sentence on an offender for up to six months in order 'to have regard . . . to his conduct after conviction (including where appropriate the making by him of any reparation for his offence) or to any change in his circumstances'. The power is to be used where the court has in mind a severe sentence, often custody, but where it is thought that some promised change in the offender's circumstances in the coming months might dissuade the court from that course. There is a guideline case on the power to defer, *R* v *George* (1984) 6 Cr App R (S) 211.

18.6 Compensation Orders

18.6.1 INTRODUCTION

In 1990 the Government issued a document entitled *Victim's Charter: a Statement of the Rights of Victims of Crime* (Home Office, 1990). It includes a detailed description of rights and facilities for victims, and sets out standards which should be attained in dealing with victims by the police, the CPS, Victim Support, the probation service, and the courts.

In respect of compensation, there are two important features of the English system. First, there is the Criminal Injuries Compensation Scheme: the Criminal Injuries Compensation Board (CICB) is open to claims from anyone who suffers personal injury as a result of an offence of violence or as a result of an act of law enforcement. The Board does not deal with any claim in respect of an injury valued at less than £1,000. A new statutory scheme, under the Compensation for Criminal Injuries Act 1995, was introduced on 1 April 1996.

This leads on to a discussion of the second aspect of the English system, the compensation order. From the victim's point of view there are major differences between the two. A claim may be made to the CICB even though the offender is never traced, whereas a court can only make a compensation order if the perpetrator is convicted (and has the means to pay). On the other hand, claims to the CICB for State compensation are limited to crimes of violence, whereas courts are empowered to make compensation orders in respect of injury, loss or damage.

The CJA 1988 made important changes to the law on compensation orders, so that its key features are now as follows:

(a) In every case involving injury, death, loss or damage, a court must consider making a compensation order and must give reasons for not doing so if it decides not to exercise its power.

(b) In deciding whether to make a compensation order, and the amount of the order, a court must take account of the offender's means.

(c) If the court wishes to impose a fine as well as a compensation order, preference should be given to the compensation order if it appears that the offender has insufficient means to pay both.

(d) A compensation order may be made both for the offence of which the offender is convicted and for any offence or offences taken into consideration.

(e) A court may make a compensation order as the sole order on conviction.

18.6.2 THE IMPORTANCE OF COMPENSATION ORDERS

The importance of making compensation orders has been urged on the courts more and more, largely in response to the legitimate expectations of victims of crime.

Research into the opinions of victims of crime in the early 1980s showed that victims in general are far more concerned to receive some compensation (not necessarily full compensation) from the offender, than to see severe sentences meted out. As Shapland reported, on the basis of research which involved the interviewing of victims (Shapland, J., 'Victims, the Criminal Justice System and Compensation' (1984) 24 BJ Crim 131, at pp. 144–5):

> Victims were, again, not particularly punitive either in the sentence that they would wish their offender to get or in their reactions to the sentence that those offenders who were convicted finally received. Their suggested sentences seemed to be very much within those of current English sentencing practice. They did, however, feel that compensation for the offender should have played a much larger part than in fact it did (only 20% of victims whose offenders were sentenced received compensation orders and many of these were for small amounts). These reactions on sentencing are not just confined to the victims of violent crime, as in our study. The recent British Crime Survey . . . has also suggested that: 'victims' recommendations are broadly in line with present practice', and that compensation is important.

It was quite clear from the research that victims tend to attribute great significance to compensation:

> How, then, did victims view state compensation and compensation by offenders? They regarded compensation not as mainly a matter of money or of financial assistance (charitable or otherwise), but rather as making a statement about the offence, the victim and the position that the criminal justice system was prepared to give to the victim. Even the element of payment in proportion to suffering and loss was subordinated to this symbolic function. This was most obvious in victims' enthusiasm for compensation from offenders as part of the sentence of the court.

18.6.3 AWARDING COMPENSATION

It is not for the victim to apply to the court for compensation: the duty is upon the court to make an order unless it gives reasons for not doing so. Section 35(1A) of the PCCA 1973 states that the compensation order 'shall be of such amount as the court considers appropriate, having regard to any evidence and to any representations that are made by or on behalf of the accused or the prosecutor'. The Victim's Charter declares that it is the prosecutor's responsibility to inform the court about the victim's loss: among the questions it poses to prosecutors are, '(1) Do case papers routinely include information on the victim's injury or loss? . . . (6) Is the prosecutor invariably put in a position to assist the court in considering a compensation order?' (p. 24).

It is wrong in principle for a court to allow an offender to 'buy his way out of prison' by paying a substantial sum by way of compensation (*R* v *Copley* (1979) 1 Cr App R (S) 55). The voluntary payment of compensation may be regarded as evidence of remorse and therefore treated as mitigation, but it would be wrong to allow an offender's inability to pay compensation to the victim to increase the severity of the sentence (*R* v *Barney* (1989) 11 Cr App R (S) 448). The court has a duty to enquire into the offender's means, and should not impose a compensation order which is beyond those means (*R* v *Stanley* (1989) 11 Cr App R (S) 446). Where two or more persons are convicted of an offence, the compensation orders made against them should reflect the means of each individual, so that if one co-defendant is less wealthy than the others a lower compensation order should be imposed (*R* v *Bagga* (1989) 11 Cr App R (S) 497). Indeed, liability is joint and several, and if only one of the co-defendants has financial resources, it is quite proper to make a compensation order for the whole sum against that one (*R* v *Beddow* (1987) 9 Cr App R (S) 235).

Two further points about the use of the compensation order may be illustrated by reference to the decision in *R* v *Martin* (1989) 11 Cr App R (S) 424. The offender had attacked another woman, and was convicted of assault occasioning actual bodily harm and assault with intent to rob. The court sentenced her to 12 months' detention in a young offender institution (she was aged 20) and ordered her to pay £200 compensation to the victim. The propriety of the compensation order was attacked on two grounds. First, it was argued that it is wrong to make a compensation order which made it necessary for the offender to sell an asset (here, her car) which had no connection with the crime. The Court of Appeal held that the order was quite proper, although there are other decisions which emphasise the need for a court to be satisfied that the asset is sufficient to cover the amount of the compensation order (*R* v *Chambers* (1981) 3 Cr App R (S) 318, *R* v *Stewart* (1983) 5 Cr App R (S) 320). Secondly, it was argued that it is wrong to combine a compensation order with a substantial custodial sentence. The Court of Appeal held that this is not wrong, so long as the sentencer is satisfied that the offender has the means to pay the order.

18.6.4 THE LAWFULNESS OF COMPENSATION ORDERS

Section 35 of the PCCA 1973, as amended, empowers a court to make a compensation order '*for any personal injury, loss or damage resulting from that offence or any other offence which is taken into consideration by the court in determining sentence*'. Two restrictions are embodied in this provision. First, a compensation order should be made only if the loss or damage results from the offence: thus in a case of handling where the stolen goods are returned to the owner, there is unlikely to be any loss (*R* v *Tyce* [1994] Crim LR 71). Secondly, where a person is convicted on one or more specimen counts, it is unlawful to make a compensation order in respect of losses alleged to result from other offences that were neither charged nor taken into consideration (*R* v *Crutchley* [1994] Crim LR 309 (applying the same principle also to confiscation orders, see **18.8** below)).

18.7 Fines

The fine is the penalty imposed for the vast majority of summary offences, and also remains the most frequently imposed penalty for indictable offences. Its use has, however, declined, from some 60% of persons sentenced for indictable offences in the mid–1970s to 36% in 1994. This decline is often attributed to the rising unemployment of the 1980s, an explanation which immediately raises the question of the relation between the fine and the offender's means.

The maximum fine for most offences tried in the Crown Court is unlimited, but magistrates' courts are limited to a maximum fine of £5,000 (with a few exceptions), and the maxima for summary offences are ranged on five standard levels (levels 1 to 5) according to the relative seriousness of the offence.

18.7.1 TO FINE OR NOT TO FINE?

How should a court decide whether to fine an offender or not? If the case is not thought suitable for a conditional or absolute discharge (see **18.3** and **18.2**), then the court might presume that a fine is the appropriate measure unless the case is serious enough to warrant a community sentence (s. 6(1), discussed in **19.2** below).

There are two dangers to be avoided at this stage. One is that it is wrong to impose a fine on an offender simply because he or she has the means to pay, when a less wealthy offender would receive a custodial or community sentence. This is the principle of equality before the law, that an offender should not be able to buy his or her way out of prison (*R* v *Markwick* (1953) 37 Cr App R 125). The second danger is perhaps less noticeable: it is wrong to impose a more severe penalty on an offender simply because he or she appears to lack the means to pay a substantial fine. Research has shown that courts tend to fine unemployed offenders less frequently than employed offenders: in magistrates' courts the difference is between 43% for unemployed offenders and 54% for employed offenders (Home Office Statistical Bulletin 20/94, para. 12). Such a decision may be acceptable if the court then selects a less severe sentence than a fine, such as a conditional discharge. But it is wrong in principle for a court to move up to a more severe sentence simply because the offender lacks the means to pay a sizeable fine (see *R* v *McGowan* at **18.3**).

This issue is revisited below: for the present, the point is that the decision whether or not to impose a fine should be taken by reference to the seriousness of the offence, not by reference to wealth or poverty.

18.7.2 THE EFFECT OF THE CRIMINAL JUSTICE ACT 1991

Sections 17 to 24 of the 1991 Act made several changes in the system of fines. Section 17 raises the financial values of the scale of fines, so that a level 5 offence (the most serious) now carries a maximum fine of £5,000 in a magistrates' court. Section 18 introduced 'unit fines' whenever a magistrates' court imposed a fine on an individual; but the CJA 1993 has now abolished the 'unit fine' system, and so the principles of fining are the same for the Crown Court and magistrates' courts. Sections 22 and 23 introduce new levels of fines, and s. 24 provides for the recovery of fines by deductions from income support.

18.7.3 CALCULATING THE AMOUNT OF THE FINE

Section 65 of the CJA 1993 repeals ss. 18 and 19 of CJA 1991, and substitutes a new s. 18. The three basic principles are these:

> *18.—(1) Before fixing the amount of any fine, a court shall inquire into the financial circumstances of the offender.*
> *(2) The amount of any fine fixed by the court shall be such as, in the opinion of the court, reflects the seriousness of the offence.*
> *(3) In fixing the amount of any fine, a court shall take into account the circumstances of the case including, among other things, the financial circumstances of the offender so far as they are known, or appear, to the court.*

The new law seems rather less clear than the previous s. 18, and it is possible to read subsections (1), (2) and (3) as being inconsistent with one another. They should be interpreted, however, as successive steps to be taken by the court. First, the court should decide what fine would reflect the seriousness of the offence. Second, the court should adjust that to reflect the means of the offender — s. 18(5) adds that this may have the effect of increasing or decreasing the amount of the fine. In order to determine an offender's means, s. 18(1) requires the court to inquire into the offender's financial circumstances, and a new s. 20(1) (substituted by sch. 3 to the 1993 Act) empowers a magistrates' court to make a financial circumstances order requiring the defendant or the defendant's parent to disclose such details as are requested.

In taking the first step, magistrates' courts may consult the 'guideline fines' recommended in the Magistrates' Association Sentencing Guidelines (1993 revision). Some of these, for an average offence committed by a person of average means, are:

£360 — failing to stop/report an accident
£270 — theft (general); theft from shop; criminal damage; abstracting electricity
£180 — careless driving; possessing class B drug; cultivating cannabis; harassment, alarm or distress; making off without payment; obstructing a constable
£90 — drunk and disorderly.

In considering these guidelines, magistrates are encouraged to take account of factors that make the offence more or less serious, and then to take account of personal mitigating factors.

18.7.4 MAXIMUM REPAYMENT PERIOD

A number of decisions in the 1980s seemed to have settled the proposition that fines should normally be calculated so that they could be paid within 12 months (e.g. *R* v *Knight* (1980) 2 Cr App R (S) 82; *R* v *Nunn* (1983) 5 Cr App R (S) 203). However, in *R* v *Olliver and Olliver* (1989) 11 Cr App R (S) 10, the Court of Appeal held that there was nothing wrong in principle with the payment period being longer than 12 months, provided that it was not an undue burden and too severe a punishment, having regard to the nature of the offence and the offender. A period of two years would seldom be too long, and three years might be acceptable in an appropriate case. The court added (*per* Lord Lane CJ, at p. 15) that this was 'particularly important in the present climate, where every effort is required in the face of growing crime figures, to find alternatives to custodial sentences... it may well be that fines, where fines are possible, are the most effective and the most desirable alternatives to custody'.

The longer possible payment periods apply also to compensation orders.

18.7.5 IMPRISONMENT IN DEFAULT

One of the greatest practical problems with financial penalties is that if they are not properly calculated according to the offender's means, the offender may be unable to pay. The outcome is that an offence for which a fine was thought appropriate by the court results in a short prison term. Research suggests that, among those who do not pay fines, there are some who genuinely cannot pay because their means are inadequate (see Softley, P., *Fines in Magistrates' Courts*, 1978) and some who can pay but refuse to do so. It is often said that it is necessary to retain the sanction of imprisonment in order to put pressure on those who can pay but wish to avoid their obligations, but it has proved difficult to separate these people from cases of genuine hardship.

> The magistrates' courts, who are responsible for enforcing the collection of fines, have been asked to review their arrangements. Attachment of earnings is a valuable method and the principle could be extended to the attachment of [State] benefits. The Government is considering whether this is worthwhile. The Government believes that improved assessment and enforcement should reduce the number of people imprisoned for fine default. In 1988, 16,800 people went into custody for fine default. This compares with 18,700 in 1987 and over 24,000 in 1982 (1990 White Paper, para. 5.4).

Numbers have risen since then, with some 22,469 fine defaulters received into custody in 1994, despite a shortening of the periods to be served in default, and the Government is considering the use of community service for fine defaulters. The maximum periods of custody for the Crown Court are as follows:

Not exceeding £200	7 days
Over £200, up to £500	14 days
Over £500, up to £1,000	28 days
Over £1,000, up to £2,500	45 days
Over £2,500, up to £5,000	3 months

18.8 Forfeiture and Confiscation

It is important to note that there are now some mandatory provisions for forfeiture. These provisions apply in offences concerned with drugs, and they are aimed at depriving offenders of their profits. (In fact the provisions strike at gross receipts rather than profits: see *R* v *Smith* [1989] Crim LR 752.)

The principal statute is the Drug Trafficking Act 1994, and this imposes on the court a duty, in the case of every person convicted of one of the listed offences, to proceed through a series of decisions designed to result in the making of a confiscation order under the Act where the offender has assets. Although details of the legislation are not pursued here, it must be complied with in all drug trafficking and some other drugs cases. For a summary of the law, see D. A. Thomas, 'Confiscation Orders and Drug Trafficking' [1994] Crim LR 93.

The Proceeds of Crime Act 1995 consolidated and reformed the procedures for confiscating the profits of non-drug offenders.

NINETEEN

COMMUNITY SENTENCES

19.1 The Basis of the New Law

Since the mid-1960s several new forms of sentence have been introduced in order to provide courts with a wider range of options and thereby to reduce their use of custody. The suspended sentence, introduced in 1967, is discussed at **21.8**. In 1972 the community service order and day training centres were introduced. In 1982 the compensation order became a sentence in its own right, and 'Schedule 11' probation orders were introduced. Courts were frequently urged to use community service orders and probation orders as 'alternatives to custody', but overall the use of custody did not decline. Sentences such as the community service order became widely used, but often in the place of other non-custodial measures, and the imprisonment rate remained fairly constant.

In 1988 the Government proposed new initiatives to deal with more offenders in the community. The aim was to make certain non-custodial sentences more 'credible' in the eyes of courts, offenders and the public. The 1990 White Paper signalled a move away from the rhetoric of 'alternatives to custody' and towards a concept of 'punishment in the community' (paras. 4.1–4.3):

> The Government believes that more offenders should be punished in the community. There seems to be an assumption that custody is the only 'real' punishment. This is reinforced by confusing references to other penalties as 'alternatives to custody'. No other penalty can place the same restrictions on liberty as a custodial sentence; if it did, it would be another form of custody: so there can in reality be no 'alternative' to it, only other ways of punishing . . .
>
> The Government believes a new approach is needed if the use of custody is to be reduced. Punishment in the community should be an effective way of dealing with many offenders, particularly those convicted of property crimes and less serious offences of violence, when financial penalties are insufficient. The punishment should be in the restrictions on liberty and in the enforcement of the orders. All community service orders place some restrictions on the offender's liberty and so may probation orders when, for example, they require an offender to attend a day centre for a lengthy period. The discipline exerted by these orders on offenders may extend over many months. These orders intrude on normal freedom, and the court should be satisfied that this is justified.

The essence of the new approach, therefore, is that community sentences should be seen as tough and demanding, and that they should be used in some cases where custody was imposed prior to 1992. The 1991 Act provides a threshold test before a community sentence may be passed, and then provides further criteria for determining the type and quantum of the sentence — requirements which are analogous to those which ss. 1 and 2 of the 1991 Act apply to custody.

19.2 The Threshold Test for a Community Sentence

If a court is considering a community sentence, its attention must be drawn to s. 6(1) of the CJA 1991:

> *A court shall not pass on an offender a community sentence, that is to say, a sentence which consists of or includes one or more community orders, unless it is of the opinion that the offence, or the combination of the offence and one other offence associated with it, was serious enough to warrant such a sentence.*

The definition of a community sentence is discussed at **19.3**. The reference to 'the combination of the offence and one other . . .' incorporates the principles discussed at **20.5** below.

The main thrust of s. 6(1) is that a court should satisfy itself that the offence was 'serious enough to warrant' a community sentence. This wording differs from that of the threshold test for custody in s. 1(2)(a), i.e. 'so serious that only a custodial sentence can be justified'. The difference suggests that there might be cases in which a court may have to choose between a heavy fine and a community sentence, and that the two are not mutually exclusive. In other words, whereas it is the position under the 1991 Act that custody should only be imposed if a community sentence would be inadequate, it is not the position that a community sentence should only be imposed where a fine would be inadequate. Usually this will be the case: a community sentence will normally be considered more severe than a financial penalty. As para. 4.3 of the 1990 White Paper stated, 'punishment in the community should be an effective way of dealing with many offenders . . . when financial penalties are insufficient'. But the wording of s. 6(1) leaves open the possibility of imposing a community sentence where a heavy fine is a possible option.

19.3 The Definition of 'Community Sentence'

From the wording of s. 6(1) it will have been observed that a community sentence 'consists of one or includes one or more community orders'. Section 6(4) lists the six forms of community order:

(a) a probation order;

(b) a community service order;

(c) a combination order;

(d) a curfew order;

(e) a supervision order;

(f) an attendance centre order.

Supervision orders and attendance centre orders are available only for offenders under 21, and they are therefore discussed only in **Chapter 24**.

As for the community orders available for adults, it is clear that any of them may be combined with a fine or compensation order or both, thus sweeping away some of the restrictions which previously existed. However, orders (a), (b) and (c) may not be combined in any way (s. 6(3)), since the whole purpose of the new combination order (discussed at **19.7**) is to make provision for a combined probation and community service order. It should be noted that the curfew order is not yet available to all courts.

Although the 'cocktail sentences' that add fines to community orders may be lawful themselves, a court may only impose them if the conditions in s. 6(2) of the 1991 Act are also satisfied.

19.4 Proportionality and Suitability

The type and quantum of community order or orders are governed by the two requirements in s. 6(2):

> *... where a court passes a community sentence—*
> *(a) the particular order or orders comprising or forming part of the sentence shall be such as in the opinion of the court is, or taken together are, the most suitable for the offender; and*
> *(b) the restrictions on liberty imposed by the order or orders shall be such as in the opinion of the court are commensurate with the seriousness of the offence, or the combination of the offence and other offences associated with it.*

These requirements are consistent with the general policy of the 1991 Act. Section 6(2)(b) ensures that the proportionality principle applies to decisions on community sentences. Section 6(2)(a) aims to ensure that, within the framework of the proportionality principle, the selection of community orders(s) maximises the preventative and rehabilitative potential of the sentence. The 1990 White Paper commended the prevention of re-offending as an aim of the probation service (para. 1.9), and added that 'reforming offenders is always best if it can be achieved' (para. 2.6). Before pursuing this question of selecting the appropriate community order(s), each of the three orders available to adults must be described.

19.5 Probation Orders

The probation order has been used in courts for over a century, but the 1991 Act alters the statutory framework. In the past, a probation order was made 'instead of sentencing the offender'. Now probation is to be a sentence of the court, and is to be found in s. 8 of the CJA 1991. The principal provision is:

> *Where a court by or before which a person of or over the age of 16 years is convicted of an offence (not being an offence for which the sentence is fixed by law) is of the opinion that the supervision of the offender by a probation officer is desirable in the interests of—*
> *(a) securing the rehabilitation of the offender; or*
> *(b) protecting the public from harm from him or preventing the commission by him of further offences,*
> *the court may make a probation order ...*

A probation order may be for a period of six months to three years, as specified by the court. The offender must consent to the making of the order. The CJA 1991 makes it available for 16-year-olds in the new youth courts, whereas before the CJA 1991 it had started at 17 years.

Any award of compensation or restitution to the victim must be made using a separate compensation order and may not be a requirement attached to the probation order.

The sentencer may sentence the offender for one offence to both a probation order and a fine, or a suspended sentence, but may not make a probation order together with a community service order. Instead, the sentencer should then make a combination order (which combines community service with supervision).

19.5.1 WHAT HAPPENS IN A PROBATION ORDER?

The main idea of probation has not been changed by the Criminal Justice Act 1991. The key words are 'the supervision of the offender by a probation officer'. Probation officers are under a duty to 'advise, assist and befriend' offenders under their supervision, i.e. it is a helping role, but, because it is supervision, it is also a controlling role, since the offender must report to them as they order, and receive visits from them as required in his or her home. The two elements of care and control have always been present in probation and in the work of probation officers, and they have always produced a dichotomy in which there is tension between the need to respond to the offender's problems and the need to control and supervise the offender. The provisions of the CJA 1991 have not been universally popular with probation officers, as some see it as reflecting a move towards the controlling, rather than caring, end of probation.

There are National Standards (*National Standards for the Supervision of Offenders in the Community*, London, Home Office, 1995) for the supervision of probation orders. These include the requirements that:

(a) supervision should commence promptly;

(b) there should be a supervision plan, regularly reviewed;

(c) there should be frequent appointments with the offender in the first three months;

(d) records should be kept of all appointments;

(e) there should be prompt and effective action to enforce orders, including the taking of breach proceedings.

The objectives of a probation order are:

(a) confronting offending behaviour, challenging the offender to accept responsibility for his or her crime and its consequences;

(b) making offenders aware of the impact of the crimes they have committed on their victims, the community and themselves;

(c) motivating and assisting the offender towards a greater sense of personal responsibility and discipline, and to aid his or her reintegration as a law abiding member of the community;

(d) intervening to remedy practical obstacles preventing rehabilitation (e.g., education, training, skills needed for employment and action to counter drug or alcohol misuse, illiteracy or homelessness) and to help the offender acquire relevant new skills; and

(e) ensuring that the supervision programme for the offender is demanding and effective. (National Standards 1995.)

Probation officers, like counsel, also have two duties — in their case to the offender and also to the court as they are officers of the court.

19.5.2 NUMBERS OF PROBATION ORDERS

During the height of the rehabilitation philosophy period, probation orders were very popular, with over 15% of offenders over 21 being given probation before the Second World War. This fell to 7% by 1983, but is now rising gently (10% for males for indictable offences in 1993). The proposals in the CJA 1991 envisage probation becoming more important and being used for more serious offences. The Act forecast there being around 2,200 to 3,300 additional orders involving supervision, 11,250 additional pre-sentence reports, and the likelihood of more supervision after release, leading to a need for 550 additional probation officers/staff nationally.

19.5.3 PROBATION'S PLACE IN THE TARIFF

19.5.3.1 Use of probation in the Crown Court

Moxon's research is the first to explore what is actually happening in the Crown Court — as opposed to the tables in the *Criminal Statistics*, which merely delineate the kinds of offenders who get fines, probation, etc. He looked at a very large sample of Crown Court cases and at the factors which seemed to be related to getting different sentences. In relation to probation he states:

> Probation is very much an individualised disposal, intended for those who do not pose a sufficient threat to society to require custody but who are seen as in need of an element of supervision while at liberty to help in guiding them towards a more law-abiding way of life. It is accordingly seen as particularly appropriate for offenders with personal problems who might benefit from professional help. For the most part probation was not strongly associated with particular offences except that it was used disproportionately for sex offenders.

Figure 19.1 on p. 273 shows the factors associated with the use of probation by the Crown Court.

> A clear pattern discernible from the table is that those most likely to be given probation were offenders who had been involved in a fair amount of criminal activity — as indicated by the number of charges involved, offences taken into consideration, previous convictions and previous supervision.
>
> This is consistent with efforts to promote the use of probation as a fairly high tariff disposal — efforts which have contributed to an increase in the proportion of defendants who have previously served custodial sentences from 24% in 1981 to 32% in 1985. Defendants who had secured treatment for an addiction had often done so with probation help, and were clearly likely to need continuing

Figure 19.1 Use of probation as a proportion of all non-custodial disposals by factors related to the offence and the offender

Factors associated with higher use of probation	*Probation* % %	*Factors associated with with lower use of probation*	*Probation* % %
Treatment for addiction	59	Not mentioned	23
Good response to supervision	34	Poor response	0
Convicted on 4 counts or more	46	3 offences or less	22
Severe stress	44	Not mentioned	21
Female	42	Male	21
Unemployed	33	Employed	17
1 or more t.i.c.'s	38	No t.i.c.'s	23
Pleaded guilty	27	Pleaded not guilty	13
Property not recovered	27	Property recovered	13
3 or more previous convictions	31	2 or less previous convictions	20
Premeditated	25	Spontaneous	16

> support and supervision. The low use of probation for those who pleaded not guilty was almost certainly influenced by the fact that social inquiry reports (now termed pre-sentence reports) were much less likely to have been available in those cases: a social inquiry report was available in 82% of cases involving a guilty plea but in only 51% of contested cases.
>
> As with the suspended sentence, a probation order was sometimes used as a 'last chance' for those who might at last be breaking with a criminal past. (Moxon, *Sentencing Practice in the Crown Court.*)

Similarly, in a study of mitigation and sentencing in the late 1970s, probation appeared as an individualised measure. Invited to place sentences and orders on a notional tariff, counsel were able to place community service, even hospital orders, on such a scale. But probation, they said, was used for offences of very widely differing seriousness and for offenders with different problems (see Shapland, J., *Between Conviction and Sentence*, London: Routledge & Kegan Paul, 1981).

Such a pattern will of course cause problems if the 'just deserts' principle of the Criminal Justice Act 1991 is adopted as strictly the only philosophy of sentencing to be used. However, when discussing non-custodial sentences, the White Paper refers to the need that: 'Each order should be tailored both to the seriousness of the offence and the characteristics of the offender. A comparatively short order may make more severe demands on some offenders than more severe orders would on others'. It remains to be seen how this may work out in practice — it will certainly require a more sophisticated approach by sentencers, counsel and probation officers to reflect both factors in the discussion between conviction and sentence — and considerable preparation for the sentencing hearing by counsel.

19.5.3.2 Probation where there is mental disorder, drug or alcohol misuse

The position with regard to mental disorder or drug or alcohol misuse is rather more complicated and varies locally. Courts are ready to give probation orders in such cases, but local clinics may not be willing to take offenders under such a court order, because they feel that treatment has to be truly voluntary to be of benefit. Sometimes they will take the person if the treatment is not a condition of the order — i.e. a straight probation order is specified. Sometimes, the sentencer and the clinic and the offender will agree on voluntary treatment, with the actual disposal being a fine or conditional discharge or suspended sentence, etc. Local knowledge is essential.

19.5.3.3 Using probation as a 'last chance'

The last chance for the offender with a long string of convictions to break free of a pattern of crime has always been a favourite target of judges for probation. It has been given the blessing of the Court of Appeal in *R* v *Bradley* (1983) 5 Cr App R (S) 363 (judgment of Stocker J). This was a burglary case involving a long criminal record of burglary and theft. The court said the trial judge's sentence of four years could not be criticised, but 'this court takes the view, having read the probation report, that at least an attempt should be made to break the applicant's pattern of crime. It is quite clear from reading his record of convictions that he is set into a pattern of offending and that if he is not already institutionalised he shortly will be . . . it is worth taking a risk to see if the applicant's lifelong pattern of offending can be broken', and the court substituted probation.

19.5.3.4 The likely effect of the Criminal Justice Act 1991

There has been a definite attempt to move probation up the tariff in recent years and this is now very much encouraged by the Government. The National Statement of the Home Office on the priorities for the probation service in 1983–84 said that pre-sentence reports should concentrate on those at imminent risk of going into custody — and probation practice is following. It is, therefore, possible to suggest probation even for an offender with quite a high number of previous convictions. However, it should be stressed to clients that not cooperating with the probation officer preparing the pre-sentence report is likely to be disastrous for the client's chances of obtaining a community sentence.

The CJA 1991 also envisages requirements being attached to probation orders in relation to treatment for drug or alcohol abuse as well as for treatment for mental disorders (see **Chapter 23**). It must be said, however, that clinics offering such treatment can be very reluctant to admit offenders subject to an order of the court. They feel that such an order represents compulsion and that offenders need to prove to the clinic that they themselves wish to have such treatment. In such instances, counsel should consider suggesting to the court that a probation order without requirements, or another penalty, might be more appropriate, with the offender attending the clinic voluntarily. The advice of the probation service should be sought.

19.5.4 REVOCATION AND AMENDMENT

A probation order can be revoked either by the probation officer supervising the order or by the offender on application to the court which made the order (CJA 1991, sch. 2, part III). The order should be revoked if the probation officer feels that all the purpose of the order has been fulfilled, or if he or she finds the offender cannot comply with the terms of the order. If revoked, then any other order which could originally have been made by that court may be made. Overall more than 80% of orders are completed satisfactorily.

An order may also be amended (sch. 2, part IV). Again there needs to be an application to the court by the probation officer or the offender. Amendment may be used to cancel some requirements or to add new ones if the offender consents (except that a condition of mental treatment or treatment for drug abuse may not be added if the application occurs more than three months from the commencement of the order). The length of the order cannot be changed in this way; orders can only be lengthened if breached, shortened if discharged.

19.5.5 BREACH

The National Standards' provisions on enforcement (breach) of orders state that breach proceedings should be taken at any stage and without prior warning if the failure to comply is serious, such as an attempt to prevent its completion or serious misconduct. Where breach action is not being taken, on the first occasion of failure to comply with an order the offender should be given a formal warning in writing of the likely consequences of further failure. At most, two warnings within any 12-month period of the order may be given before breach proceedings are instituted.

The provisions for breach of a probation order have, under the CJA 1991, been brought into line with those for other community sentences and are dealt with in **19.10**. In *R* v *Oliver* (1992) 14 Cr App R (S) 457, the Court of Appeal found that sch. 2 to the CJA 1991 applies to probation orders made before 1 October 1992 (i.e. before the Act came into force). Hence the provisions set out in **19.10** are the only ones now in force.

Further guidance from *Oliver* shows that if an offender breaches a probation order and the breach is dealt with at the Crown Court, then the penalty which is given then may well be a custodial sentence. Obviously, when the original probation order was given, the court must either have decided that the offence was not sufficiently serious to merit a custodial sentence or the mitigating factors related to the defendant were sufficient to bring the sentence back below the custodial threshold. However, in breaching the probation order, the defendant is likely to have deprived himself or herself of much of that mitigation (contrition, etc.) and so may on breach be in danger of a custodial sentence.

19.5.6 REQUIREMENTS ATTACHED TO A PROBATION ORDER

A probation order can have various requirements (formerly termed conditions) attached to it: a requirement to receive mental treatment; a requirement of attendance at a probation centre (formerly termed a day centre or day training centre) for up to 60 days; a requirement of residence at a hostel; and indeed any other requirement which is written in the order. Conditions vary according to the facilities available locally, which will be run by the probation service or by local voluntary groups. In some areas there is group therapy available, in others drop-in centres for the long-term unemployed and socially inadequate, or for those with drink problems. In some areas there is specific alcohol abuse or drug counselling, and related programmes, and in others social skills training. It varies enormously around the country and it is essential that you should begin to build up a knowledge of the facilities available in the various areas in which you normally practise. Nonetheless you are likely to have to rely on the advice of the probation service as to what is currently available and whether your particular client fits the rules for acceptance onto the programme. All these requirements are those for which a pre-sentence report should be obtained and considered by the court (see **Chapter 17**).

19.5.6.1 Hostels

Probation hostels are run by the probation service or by voluntary agencies but approved by the probation committee. Their aim is to provide a 'stable and supportive atmosphere in which groups of up to 30 offenders may learn how to get on with their contemporaries and others, including those in authority' (*The Sentence of the Court* HMSO (5th edn) 1990). So they have three purposes: to provide residence for those of no fixed abode, to apply group therapy in modern group home techniques, and to have a fairly strict rule basis which the offender is supposed to learn to accept and thus learn to regulate his or her life, and not commit offences.

There is a shortage of hostels, though the Home Office is now trying to open more. It is important to suggest a hostel as a possible solution open to the solicitor for him or her to talk to the probation officer — or if there is a remand for a report, for you to talk to the liaison officer in appropriate cases. Before making a requirement that an offender must reside in a particular place on an order, the court *must* consider his or her home surroundings — and the name of the hostel must be specified in the order — so a place must be available. Someone can be remanded on bail to a hostel for three or four weeks to assess his or her likely response — then there should be a report from the hostel. The period of residence can be for any period not exceeding the term of the order but it may be helpful to have the supervision to extend for a time such as one year after the offender has left the hostel for the person to be helped to move into the outside world.

19.5.6.2 Probation centres

Until now, there have been two forms of day training centre (now renamed probation centre in the CJA 1991). One is the informal drop-in centre or other non-residential place often catering for particular groups and this may be mentioned in a pre-sentence report but may not be a legal requirement of an order. The other is a legal requirement to attend for up to 60 days at a centre approved by the local probation committee (sch. 1A to the PCCA 1973, para. 3, inserted by sch. 1 to CJA 1991). This requirement is supposed to be for offences relatively high up the tariff, i.e. for those in imminent danger of a custodial sentence (like all other requirements attached to a probation order it requires the consent of the offender). It has been criticised by Vanstone and others as being an extension of custody into the community without the cost and the overt position of making a custodial sentence. It is definitely an infringement on someone's liberty, so it should not be suggested for 'down tariff' offences or people who are inadequate, even if they have a long record of nuisance offences.

Few of these approved centres currently exist, though the numbers are growing. Again, the gateway to such a requirement is via the probation service and the pre-sentence report. For a requirement to attend a probation centre to be made, the court must consult a probation officer, it must be shown that arrangements can be made and the person in charge of the centre must consent to having that particular offender.

19.5.6.3 Requirements as to activities, etc.

The new sch. 1A to the PCCA 1973, inserted by CJA 1991, contains the provision that a probation order may require the offender to 'present himself to a person or persons specified in the order at a place or places so specified' (sch. 1A, para. 2(1)(a)) or 'participate or refrain from participating in activities specified in the order on (i) a day or days so specified or (ii) during the probation period or such portion of it as may be so specified' (sch. 1A, para. 2(1)(b)). It is this provision which allows the court to specify that certain offenders should attend group work sessions on controlling anger, treating sexual offences etc.

19.5.6.4 Requirements as to treatment for mental disorder

This is dealt with in **Chapter 23.** It is now governed by the CJA 1991.

19.5.6.5 Requirements as to treatment for drug or alcohol dependence

Paragraph 6 of the new sch. 1A to the PCCA 1973, inserted by the CJA 1991, provides a new power for the court to impose a requirement on an offender 'dependent on drugs or alcohol' to attend a treatment facility if the 'dependency is such as requires and may be susceptible to treatment'. One doctor's report recommending such a course of action is required. The treatment must be by a doctor (not a psychologist or other professional) and must be with a view to the reduction or elimination of the dependency. Like all other requirements of a probation order, this also requires the consent of the offender. During the passage of the Act, some doubt was expressed as to whether this power would often be used, given that offenders need to consent and that clinics are reluctant to take clients on court orders. It is likely that the response will vary between different areas of the country.

19.6 Community Service Orders

The community service order (CSO) is an order, which requires the offender's consent, by which he or she is ordered to perform between 40 and 240 hours' work (as specified) in the community. Community service is organised by the probation service, although much of the work is usually carried out under the supervision of voluntary workers and others involved in community projects. Section 14 of the PCCA 1973 states that a court must only make a CSO if it is satisfied:

(i) *after considering a report by a probation officer about the offender and his circumstances and, if the court thinks it necessary, hearing a probation officer, that the offender is a suitable person to perform work under such an order; and*
(ii) *that provision can be made under the arrangements for him to do so.*

The CSO was introduced in 1973 on an experimental basis, and made available to all courts in 1975. Since then, it has been widely used, accounting for 11% of all sentences on adult males for indictable offences in 1993. In the 17–20 age group, it accounted for 14% of male offenders and 7% of female offenders.

The CJA 1991 makes no changes to this statutory framework, although s. 10 makes a few consequential amendments of detail. The community service order has therefore been accepted into the new approach of 'punishment in the community' without demur, although National Standards have been introduced in an attempt to 'tighten' the organisation of community service and to ensure that there is a consistent policy on bringing breaches to the attention of the courts.

19.6.1 THE ORGANISATION OF COMMUNITY SERVICE

This is now governed by the National Standards. Offenders placed on a CSO will begin with a period of some 21 hours of 'assessment', when they carry out work under the close supervision of the probation service. After that, they will be placed on one of the schemes currently being run — which may involve such activities as working in a Salvation Army hostel, working in a hospital or with mentally handicapped children, making wooden toys for playgroups, painting community centres, etc. Work under a community service order is done in the offender's spare time, usually at weekends and in the evenings, and should be completed within 12 months of the court order. Where the offender is unemployed it may be possible for him or her to do community service during weekdays, but some areas do not permit unemployed offenders to complete their orders in this way.

It is the job of the probation service to ensure that each offender's attendance for work is monitored, although reliance may be placed on volunteer supervisors to report this. Over the years sentencers have complained, from time to time, about lax attitudes towards work attendance on CSO, some probation officers being more willing to accept excuses from offenders than others, and some officers rarely bringing offenders back to court for breach of the order. The 1995 National Standards for the Supervision of Offenders in the Community, Chapter 5, require the CSO work to be 'physically, emotionally or intellectually taxing'; they also require an offender to be brought back to court after three unexplained failures to attend work appointments.

19.6.2 THE PHILOSOPHY

What is the CSO designed to achieve, and what aims of sentencing does it fulfil? In proposing the CSO as a new measure, the Advisory Council on the Penal System put it this way (*Non-Custodial and Semi-Custodial Penalties* (1970)):

> . . . the proposition that some offenders should be required to undertake community service should appeal to adherents of different varieties of penal philosophy. To some, it would be simply a more constructive and cheaper alternative to short sentences of imprisonment; by others it would be seen as introducing into the penal system a new dimension with an emphasis on reparation to the community; others again would regard it as a means of giving effect to the old adage that the punishment should fit the crime; while still others would stress the value of bringing offenders into close touch with those members of the community who are most in need of help and support.

This passage may help to explain why the CSO has been welcomed and used relatively widely by the courts.

19.6.3 USING COMMUNITY SERVICE AS A SENTENCE

Formerly, the Court of Appeal held that a court should consider making a CSO in all cases where it is minded to impose a short custodial sentence. In *R* v *Clarke* (1982) 4 Cr App R (S) 197, Lord Lane CJ held that even when a court has formed the opinion that the case is so serious that a custodial sentence is necessary, the court should ask itself this: 'can we make a community service order as an equivalent to imprisonment, or can we suspend the whole of the sentence? That problem requires very careful consideration'. Since the 1991 Act the CSO is no longer an 'alternative to custody', but courts should still consider a CSO when the offence is serious enough for custody and there is substantial personal mitigation. The cases in which it might be appropriate to make a CSO may involve relatively serious offences which are either committed by a person of good character or committed in circumstances of strong mitigation. One example of this might be a house burglary committed by a young first offender (see *R* v *Brown* (1981) 3 Cr App R (S) 294 and *R* v *Mole* (1990) 12 Cr App R (S) 371); another example might be a burglary committed by an offender with a criminal record but who appears to have 'gone straight' for a number of years prior to the latest conviction (*R* v *Lawrence* (1982) 4 Cr App 2 (S) 69). Research shows that those offences which result in CSOs imposed in the Crown Court tend to have more aggravating features than cases resulting in any other non-custodial penalty: the three leading factors for CSOs in the 1988 study, *Sentencing Practice in the Crown Court*, were 'large sum involved', 'use of weapon' and 'serious injuries mentioned' (p. 45). What this suggests is that these were offences of moderate seriousness, for which the court selected a CSO on account of some extenuating or mitigating factors in the cases.

A court is required to consider a pre-sentence report before making a CSO, and this should assist in ensuring that a CSO satisfies the requirement of being 'the most suitable' order for the offender. As to the length of the order, the court should calculate the number of hours on the scale from 40 to 240 hours according to the seriousness of the offence(s).

19.6.4 BREACH OF COMMUNITY SERVICE

Most CSOs are completed satisfactorily. Some 75% run their course without the offender being returned to court either for breach or for a further offence. Since many of the offenders placed on CSOs are relatively young and do have previous convictions, and are therefore at high risk of re-offending, this suggests that the order is sufficiently demanding to keep most of them out of trouble for around 12 months. The powers of the courts on breach have been altered by the 1991 Act, and are dealt with at **19.10**.

19.7 Combination Orders

The courts have never had the power to make both a probation order and a CSO on an offender as the sentence for an offence. The CJA 1991 does not give them that power (s. 6(3)), but it does introduce an entirely new order which consists partly of probation and partly of community service. In other words, the law now permits probation and community service to be combined, but only under the restricted conditions of a combination order. The White Paper explained (1990, para. 4.16):

> Under this new order, an offender could be required to carry out a period of community service work while under the supervision of a probation officer and subject to any of the requirements which could be attached to a probation order. It would enable the courts to introduce an element of reparation but, at the same time, to provide the probation service with an opportunity to work with offenders, to reduce the likelihood of future offending . . .

Section 11 of the CJA 1991 provides that the probation component of the new order may be one to three years, whereas the community service component may only be 40 to 100 hours. The probation element is therefore uppermost, and indeed s. 11 provides that the court must consider that a combination order is desirable in order to secure the rehabilitation of the offender or to protect the public from harm from him or her or to prevent the commission by him or her of further offences — the same justifications as for a probation order. The probation component of a combination order may also include any of the additional requirements set out in sch. 1A to the PCCA 1973, inserted by sch. 1 to the CJA 1991.

By s. 7(3)(c) of the 1991 Act, a court is obliged to obtain and consider a pre-sentence report before forming an opinion on the suitability of a combination order for a particular offender.

The White Paper envisaged that combination orders 'should be particularly suitable for some persistent property offenders. About 10,000 of those in custody sentenced for burglary, theft, handling, fraud and forgery have three or more previous convictions' (para. 4.16). This suggests that combination orders are intended to be a fairly 'high tariff' measure, perhaps the most demanding of all the community orders. However, around three-quarters of combination orders are made by magistrates' courts, which may suggest that they are not always high on the tariff. The 1995 National Standards (a form of Home Office guidance) attempt to ensure that they are reserved for serious cases.

19.8 Curfew Orders

Section 12(1) of the 1991 Act empowers a court to make a curfew order, 'that is to say, an order requiring him to remain, for periods specified in the order, at a place so specified'. Section 13 of the CJA 1991 makes provision for the possibility of electronic monitoring of curfew orders. These provisions have been in force in three areas on an experimental basis since 1 April 1995.

19.8.1 REQUIREMENTS OF A CURFEW ORDER

What times and places may be specified in a curfew order? Section 12(2) outlines the limits on the power:

> *A curfew order may specify different places or different periods for different days, but may not specify—*
>
> *(a) periods which fall outside the period of six months beginning with the day on which it is made; or*
>
> *(b) periods which amount to less than 2 hours or more than 12 hours in any one day.*

Curfew of periods of less than two hours would hardly be sensible, and for more than 12 hours might impede too many ordinary obligations. Section 12(3) further provides that the requirements should avoid conflict with religious beliefs, work and attendance for education. Section 12(5) requires a court to explain the effect of the order, and the consequences of failure to comply with it, to the offender in court in ordinary language. There is no statutory requirement for a pre-sentence report before making a curfew order, although it may be added to another community order for which a pre-sentence report is obligatory.

19.8.2 PROBABLE USE OF A CURFEW ORDER

A kind of curfew order has been available to courts dealing with juvenile offenders since 1982, but it has been little used. The White Paper put forward the view that, for adults and young adults, 'curfews could be helpful in reducing some forms of crime, thefts of or from cars, pub brawls and other types of disorder. A curfew order could be used to keep offenders away from particular places, such as shopping centres or pubs, or to keep them at home in the evenings or at weekends' (1990, para. 4.20). A curfew order might well be added to another community sentence (e.g., probation), so long as s. 6(2)(b) on proportionality is complied with.

19.8.3 ELECTRONIC MONITORING

Section 12(4) requires that any curfew order should include provision for making a person responsible for monitoring the offender's whereabouts during the curfew periods. Section 13 further provides that a curfew order may include requirements for securing the electronic monitoring of the offender's whereabouts during curfew periods, but only if the court has been notified by the Home Secretary that arrangements are available. There were earlier trials with electronic monitoring, the results of which were distinctly unpromising: G. Mair and C. Nee, *Electronic Monitoring: the Trials and their Results* (Home Office Research Study no. 120, 1990). The Government is now trying again.

19.9 Selecting Community Orders

Having considered the types of community order available to courts when dealing with adult offenders, we must now return to the statutory criteria in s. 6(2), i.e. proportionality and suitability (see **19.4**).

There is little guidance on the question of proportionality. The CJA 1991 says that the restrictions on liberty must be 'commensurate with the seriousness of the offence' and that seems to require both an estimate of the relative seriousness of the offence and an assessment of the relative severity of the community order(s). On seriousness of the offence, the court is required by s. 7(1) to take account of 'all such information about the circumstances of the offence (including any aggravating or mitigating factors) as is available to it'. The discussion in **Chapter 20** is therefore relevant to this point. Equally, s. 20 allows the court to take account of any other mitigating factors. But what about the relative severity of community orders? Is a 120-hour CSO more severe or restrictive of liberty than a one year probation order with a requirement of attendance at a probation centre? Is a 240-hour CSO with an added fine more severe than a combination order? Guidance on these points is scanty, but the Act seems to envisage that courts might find that two or more community orders may be 'commensurate' in a given case, and that they should then decide between them on grounds of suitability for the offender. For example, both a certain length of probation order and a number of hours CSO might be considered proportionate, but the court might regard the former as more suitable for this offender.

The Act is somewhat clearer on the question of suitability. Section 7(2) permits a court to take account of any information about the offender which is before it. In many cases that will include a pre-sentence report. In all cases there should be details of any previous convictions, and they are relevant on suitability (although less so when assessing the seriousness of the offence).

19.10 Breach or Re-offending

Any one of the three community orders may be breached by an offender, e.g. by failing to attend when and where required, or by failing to notify the probation officer of a change of circumstances etc. The first stage in enforcement is a warning or administrative sanction by the supervising officer. The second stage, if the offender breaches again, is to return the offender to court. The National Standards relating to probation, community service and combination orders specify the circumstances in which a probation officer should take this action. The third stage is the court's decision, now regulated by sch. 2 to the 1991 Act.

If a breach is established, the court may fine the offender up to £1,000, or make a community service order of up to 60 hours, or (where the offender is under 21) make an attendance centre order. If one of these courses is taken, the original order remains in force. Paragraph 3(1)(d) of sch. 2 also provides that the court may decide to revoke the original order and deal with the offender again for the offence. It also adds that the court may assume, 'in the case of an offender who has wilfully and persistently failed to comply with those requirements, that he has refused' consent to a community sentence. This means that, according to s. 1(3) of the Act (see **21.5.4**), a custodial sentence becomes a possibility in these cases of persistent breach, even though the original offence was evidently not so serious that only a custodial sentence could be justified.

The above powers apply when the offender is brought back to the magistrates' court responsible for enforcing the order. If the original community order was made by the Crown Court, a magistrates' court can deal with the breach in any way other than revocation of the original order. If it regards this as the proper course, it must commit the offender to the Crown Court, which then may choose between the various powers set out in the previous paragraph.

The commission of a further offence during the currency of a community sentence does not constitute a breach of that sentence. However, the court may, in certain circumstances, revoke the order(s) and deal with the original offence as well as the new offence when passing sentence on the second occasion. The Crown Court has wide powers in this respect, varying according to whether the further offence results in conviction at the Crown Court, or in committal for sentence to the Crown Court. The powers of magistrates' courts outlined in para. 7 of sch. 2 are limited to cases in which the original community order was made by a magistrates' court: essentially, the magistrates may impose any sentence which they could have imposed for the original offence. If the community sentence was imposed by the Crown Court, the magistrates must commit the offender to appear before the Crown Court for revocation of the order but the Crown Court may revoke the community order and deal with the offender only if the order is still in force at the time of the proceedings (*R* v *Bennett* (1993) 15 Cr App R (S) 213).

When a court is dealing with an offender for the original offence, following revocation, it may have regard to the circumstances leading to the revocation. In *R* v *Oliver* (1992) 14 Cr App R (S) 457 it was argued that the imposition of a community sentence originally for the offence showed that it could not be considered to be sufficiently serious to justify a custodial sentence. This argument was rejected by the Court of Appeal which said (per Lord Taylor of Gosforth CJ):

> . . . there may well be cases where, notwithstanding that the offence itself passes the custody threshold, there is sufficient mitigation to lead the court to impose a community sentence. Nevertheless if a further offence was or offences were committed while the community sentence was in force . . . the defendant . . . would have deprived himself of much of the mitigation, such as good character, genuine remorse, isolated lapse and similar considerations, which had led the original court to pass a community rather than a custodial sentence.

In all cases in which the court re-sentences the offender, either for breach or for a further offence, it is required to take account of the extent to which the offender complied with the original order, i.e. giving credit for substantial part performance where that has happened (a principle established since *R* v *Paisley* (1979) 1 Cr App R (S) 196).

TWENTY

GENERAL PRINCIPLES AND THE CRIMINAL JUSTICE ACT 1991

20.1 Introduction

The general principles of sentencing are those which apply to most types of offence and most types of sentence. In this chapter we shall deal with the principles relating to aggravation and mitigation, previous record and multiple offences. These principles apply not only to the custodial sentences already considered, but also to non-custodial sentences. The Criminal Justice Act 1991 has made some alterations, with the result that the relevant principles now consist of a mixture of statute and common law. Within the provisions of the 1991 Act there is an important distinction between cases in which 'the seriousness of the offence' is the key issue, and others such as 'public protection' cases. However, this distinction will be explained more fully at the end of the Chapter, after the various principles have been outlined.

20.2 Aggravation, Mitigation and the Criminal Justice Act 1991

20.2.1 THE RESTRICTED SENSE OF AGGRAVATION AND MITIGATION

It has already been noted, in **Chapters 18 and 19**, that 'the seriousness of the offence' is a key issue in deciding questions relating to fines and community sentences. **Chapter 21** will show that 'the seriousness of the offence' is also central to decisions on custodial sentences. The common law approach was that, in assessing the seriousness of a case, a court would naturally consider factors which aggravate and factors which mitigate. However, this is a matter which must be approached carefully now that the 1991 Act is in force. In relation to custodial sentences, s. 3(3)(a) states that, in forming an opinion about the seriousness of an offence, a court:

> *. . . shall take into account all such information about the circumstances of the offence (including any aggravating or mitigating factors) as is available to it.*

Section 7(1) states the same principle with respect to community sentences. Do these provisions do anything other than confirm the common law approach?

The answer is that they achieve something different. What they say is that in determining the seriousness of *the offence* a court should take account of aggravating and mitigating factors which bear on the circumstances of *the offence*. This means that factors which bear on the offender are irrelevant for this purpose (e.g. the offender's bad criminal record), as are matters which have arisen since the offence (e.g. assistance to the police, a plea of guilty, reparation to the victim). Sections 3(3)(a) and 7(1) require the court to focus on the circumstances of the offence when assessing its seriousness.

Later in this Chapter the relevance of such factors as previous convictions and a plea of guilty will be considered. For the present, we must look in greater detail at those aggravating factors and those mitigating factors which bear on the seriousness of an offence.

20.2.2 AGGRAVATING CIRCUMSTANCES OF THE OFFENCE

To a large extent these vary with the type of offence under consideration. In offences of violence, the more violence that is used, the more serious the offence. In property offences, the more property that is taken the more serious the offence. The Court of Appeal precedents give plenty of examples of aggravating factors when discussing the various types of offence, and they can be consulted, by offence, in *Current Sentencing Practice.* One of the advantages of guideline judgments is that they usually contain a list of the major aggravating factors. For example, in the case of *Mussell* (1990), see **22.1.9**, the Court of Appeal identified certain aggravating features of burglary. When dealing with social security frauds in *R* v *Stewart* (1987) 9 Cr App R (S) 135, the Court of Appeal stated that the offence would be more serious where (i) the fraud was committed over a lengthy period, (ii) the fraud began by deliberate deception rather than by omission, (iii) the money was taken to finance lavish spending rather than the purchase of necessities, and (iv) the fraud was carefully organised. Further aggravating factors recognised in the various guideline decisions will be discussed in **Chapter 22** below.

The last factor mentioned in *Stewart*, i.e. careful organisation, is a more general aggravating factor, and one well supported by authority. A central element in seriousness is the culpability of the offender, and carefully planned offences are generally much more serious than sudden, momentary actions. Unprovoked offences are generally treated as more serious than provoked crimes. Moxon's survey of 2,000 Crown Court cases showed that four factors were strongly associated, in practice, with a high use of immediate custodial sentences (*Sentencing Practice in the Crown Court*, 1988, p. 9):

Where the victim was elderly	97% immediate custody
Where offender was ringleader	77%
Where offence planned/premeditated	71%
Where weapon used	71%

The effect of the first factor is confirmed by *R* v *Allen* (1988) 10 Cr App R (S) 466, where two young men had entered a house at night and, on finding a woman aged 82 in the house, had held her down on the floor until she told them where she kept her money. The Court of Appeal upheld sentences of six years for robbery, stressing the significance of the fact that the victim was elderly:

> Cowardice and brutality seem to know no bounds in this connection. It was said in this case that these two appellants did not know that this house was occupied or that they would encounter an old lady when they went inside. But having found her, they did not desist . . .

Turning to cases in which the offender was the ringleader, it must first be stated that offences committed by groups are often treated as more serious than offences committed by individuals, because of the fear which groups of people can cause. This factor often comes to the fore in public order cases, and an example is *R* v *Rogers-Hinks* (1989) 11 Cr App R (S) 234. The appellant was one of seven men convicted of affray following a large-scale disturbance involving football supporters on a North Sea ferry, resulting in extensive damage to the ship and fear among other passengers. The general level of the sentences passed at the trial was approved by the Court of Appeal, on account of the fear caused by the disturbance and the difficulty of controlling the disorder. The Court further made it clear that the trial judge was right to differentiate among the offenders according to the degree of their involvement. A sentence of eight years' imprisonment was upheld on the offender who was identified as the ringleader, who had not only joined in the fighting but had also seized a microphone and incited further disorder. Lesser sentences were imposed on the others.

It is also well-established that an offence will be aggravated if it is committed against a police officer (or other public servant), or by a police officer (or other public servant). The decision in *R* v *Nawrot* (1988) 10 Cr App R (S) 239 is one example of the former point, the Court of Appeal upholding a sentence of two years' imprisonment for punching a police officer on the jaw, knocking him unconscious. By the same token, police officers who commit offences of violence against suspects can expect to receive longer sentences. This may be seen as an aspect of the general proposition that people who offend whilst holding a position of trust deserve a more severe sentence for the breach of that trust. The guideline case of *R* v *Barrick* (1985) 7 Cr App R (S) 143 supports this, as does *R* v *Lowery* (1992) 14 Cr App R (S) 485 (see **21.8.2**).

Offences which are racially motivated should also be treated as aggravated. Thus in *Attorney-General's References Nos. 29, 30 & 31 of 1994* (1995) 16 Cr App R (S) 698, Lord Taylor CJ stated that 'it cannot be too strongly emphasised by this Court that where there is a racial element in an offence of violence, that is a gravely aggravating feature'. The Court of Appeal increased sentences for grievous bodily harm with intent from five to seven years' imprisonment on the ground that the trial judge had given insufficient weight to this element.

The Criminal Justice Act 1993 gives statutory authority to the existing principle that an offence committed whilst on bail for another offence should be treated as aggravated (see *Attorney-General's References (Nos. 3, 4 & 5 of 1992)* (1992) 14 Cr App R (S) 191). The new s. 29(2) of the CJA 1991 (substituted by s. 66(6) of the CJA 1993) declares that the court 'shall' treat this as an aggravating factor.

20.2.3 MITIGATING CIRCUMSTANCES OF THE OFFENCE

Once again, many mitigating factors are dependent on the type of offence committed. In this sense, 'mitigating' merely means 'reducing the seriousness of the offence' and includes such factors as the slightness of the injury caused, the smallness of the amount of money taken, etc. Most of the guideline judgments list such factors in relation to the offence concerned. For example, the judgment in *R* v *Stewart* (1987) 9 Cr App R (S) 135 states that a social security fraud will generally be less serious where the offence arose from an omission rather than a deliberate deception, or where the money was taken in order to buy necessaries.

Among the general mitigating factors which relate to the seriousness of the offence, the most important are those connected with culpability. An offence is usually less serious if it was committed impulsively rather than deliberately, recklessly rather than intentionally, and so on. Similarly, if the offender was close to having a defence to criminal liability, this will tend to reduce the seriousness of the offence. For example, in *R* v *Beaumont* (1987) 9 Cr App R (S) 342 the appellant's sentence was reduced by the Court of Appeal to reflect the fact that he had been entrapped into committing the offence: entrapment is no defence in English law, but it constitutes mitigation. Elements of duress, mistake of law and mental disturbance might have a similar effect. For present purposes, however, it is important to bear in mind that only mitigating factors which affect the circumstances of the offence (including the offender's culpability) are relevant to 'seriousness'.

20.2.4 THE MAGISTRATES' ASSOCIATION GUIDELINES

In 1989 and 1992 the Magistrates' Association, a voluntary body to which most of the 30,000 magistrates belong, issued to its members a set of sentencing guidelines covering many of the offences with which magistrates' courts frequently deal. Most road traffic offences and many non-motoring offences are listed. The most recent version was issued in 1993, taking acount of the 1991 Act and the amendments made by the 1993 Act. The main part of the guidelines consists of an offence-by-offence consideration of sentencing. Each page deals with an offence, states the maximum penalty, lists some 'seriousness factors', and then sets out some starting points for sentencing. Our interest here lies with the 'seriousness indicators'. These do not deal with personal mitigation (see **20.3** below): they list 'plus' and 'minus' factors related to the seriousness of each offence. For example, the 'plus' factors which may make theft offences more serious include 'large amount', 'planned', 'sophisticated', 'vulnerable victim', and 'adult involving children'. The 'minus' factors for theft offences include 'low value', 'impulsive action', and 'voluntary restitution'. Turning to offences of violence, the table of factors for assault occasioning actual bodily harm is as follows:

Plus	*Minus*
Deliberate kicking	Impulsive action
Extensive injuries	Minor injury
Group action	Provocation
Offender in position of authority	
Premeditated	
Victim particularly vulnerable	
Victim serving public	
Weapon	

These sentencing guidelines have no legal force. They appear to be widely used, but some courts are using altered versions and others find little use for them at all. The document itself urges magistrates to treat them as starting points, not finishing points. The lists of plus and minus factors are not intended to be exhaustive, and it remains for the court to take account of personal mitigating factors in each case. See **15.6.3**.

20.3 General Mitigating Factors

When the Criminal Justice Bill (which became the CJA 1991) was first presented to Parliament, there was no other provision on aggravation and mitigation apart from those already set out. It was protested that this would prevent the courts from taking account of long-established mitigating factors such as the plea of guilty, assistance to the authorities and other matters which had no bearing on the seriousness of the offence as such. Eventually various provisions were inserted into s. 28, the most important of which is the first:

> *(1) Nothing in this part shall prevent a court from mitigating an offender's sentence by taking into account such matters as, in the opinion of the court, are relevant in mitigation of sentence.*

This has two effects. First, it ensures that the common law principles of mitigating sentence survive the 1991 Act, so that all the pre-1992 precedents on this point remain authoritative. Secondly, it is confined to mitigating factors. So far as aggravating factors are concerned, the court may only take account of those which arise from the circumstances of the offence, not any conduct or events before or after the crime.

In many cases the mitigation is personal to the offender, relying on such matters as stress, financial difficulties, and family or other personal problems. Brief mention can now be made of three further types of mitigating factor which may be taken into account by virtue of s. 28(1): those associated with contributions to the smooth running of the system; those associated with good social deeds; and those stemming from the expected impact of the sentence on the offender.

20.3.1 CONTRIBUTING TO THE SMOOTH RUNNING OF THE SYSTEM

It is well established that a person who reports the offences to the police before he or she has been discovered deserves a significant sentence discount (*R* v *Whybrew* (1979) 1 Cr App R (S) 121). It is also well established that an offender who co-operates with the police should receive a discount which reflects the degree of help given. This may range from helping the police to trace stolen goods to 'turning Queen's evidence' and testifying against other offenders. Decisions such as *R* v *Lowe* (1977) 66 Cr App R 122 and *R* v *Sivan* (1988) 10 Cr App R (S) 282 show that it may not be easy for courts to calculate the proper size of the discount, bearing in mind that such offenders will probably have to be kept apart from other prisoners for their own protection, and may be in danger even after their release from custody.

The most frequent mitigating factor in this group is the plea of guilty. In general, a person who pleads guilty should receive a reduction in sentence which a person who is convicted after a trial should not receive. This established principle was confirmed by Lord Lane CJ, in *R* v *Costen* (1989) 11 Cr App R (S) 182, where he also set out four types of case in which the discount might properly be withheld:

(a) where a long sentence is necessary for public protection: *R* v *Stabler* (1984) 6 Cr App R (S) 129;

(b) where there had been a 'tactical plea': *R* v *Hollington and Emmens* (1985) 7 Cr App R (S) 364;

(c) where the offender had been caught 'red-handed' and there was no real defence: for recent examples, see *R* v *Landy* [1995] Crim LR 660 and *Hastings*, [1995] Crim LR 661

(d) where a single count had been brought as a specimen charge, as in *Costen* itself.

This guideline judgment has now been overtaken, to some extent, by s. 48 of the Criminal Justice and Public Order Act 1994, which states:

> *(1) In determining what sentence to pass on an offender who has pleaded guilty to an offence in proceedings before that or another court a court shall take into account:*
>
> *(a) the stage in the proceedings for the offence at which the offender indicated his intention to plead guilty, and*
> *(b) the circumstances in which this indication was given.*
>
> *(2) If as a result of taking into account any matter referred to in subsection (1) above the court imposes a punishment on the offender which is less severe than it would otherwise have done, it shall state in open court that it has done so.*

In broad terms this merely confirms the position at which the courts have arrived: Parliament's purpose in enacting the provision was apparently to give statutory authority to the notion that larger discounts should be given for earlier pleas. This had been recognised judicially in many cases, notably *R* v *Buffrey* (1993) 14 Cr App R (S) 411, where Lord Taylor CJ spelt out the 'general guidance' that 'something of the order of one-third would very often be an appropriate discount from the sentence which would otherwise be imposed on a contested trial'. Where the offender is given the maximum possible sentence despite having pleaded guilty, an appeal will usually succeed unless the case comes within one of the *Costen* exceptions above. (See, for example, *R* v *Sharkey and Daniels* (1995) 16 Cr App R (S) 257, where the Court of Appeal held that 'it is an erroneous approach to sentencing to refuse to give a discount for a plea of guilty, unless the case falls within a limited, albeit not closed range of cases where this court had held the maximum sentence to be appropriate even on a guilty plea'.)

Moxon's survey of Crown Court cases found an average reduction of some 22% in sentence lengths for those who pleaded guilty (*Sentencing Practice in the Crown Court*, p. 32), and Hood's more recent survey found an average reduction of some 30% in the length of sentences of those who had pleaded guilty (*Race and Sentencing*, 1992). The Magistrates' Association Sentencing Guidelines (1993) state, in respect of all offences: 'for a timely guilty plea allow a discount of about a third'.

20.3.2 MITIGATION FOR GOOD SOCIAL DEEDS

Both the newspapers and the law reports yield several examples of sentences being reduced for 'good deeds' which have no connection at all with the offence committed. Thus in *R* v *Reid* (1982) 4 Cr App R (S) 280 the Court of Appeal reduced a sentence for burglary to reflect the fact that, whilst awaiting trial, the offender had rescued three children from a blazing house. The Court commented that this suggested that 'the appellant was a much better and more valuable member of society' than his criminal activities would lead one to believe. Likewise in *R* v *Ingham* (1980) 2 Cr App R (S) 184, the Court reduced a sentence for burglary on the ground that 'this man shows some indications of social responsibility because he has done quite a lot of good voluntary work'. These practices suggest that to some extent sentencing involves the drawing up of a social 'balance sheet', and that counsel should take advantage of that in advancing mitigating factors.

20.3.3 EXCEPTIONAL IMPACT OF SENTENCE ON OFFENDER

Where the sentence for the crime would have an unusually harsh impact on the particular offender, this is a ground for imposing a less severe sentence. Examples would be where the offender is elderly and imprisonment would be more gruelling for him (*R* v *Varden* [1981] Crim LR 272), where the offender is pregnant (*R* v *Beaumont* (1987) 9 Cr App R (S) 342, the entrapment case mentioned in **20.2.3**), or where the offender has young children to care for (*R* v *Whitehead* [1995] Crim LR 755).

More controversial are those cases where the offender held a position of trust which has been lost, together with job prospects and pension rights, as a result of the conviction. The collateral effects of conviction for such a 'white collar' offender can be considerable: should they mitigate? In the guideline case of *R* v *Barrick* (1985) 7 Cr App R (S) 142 (see **22.1.8**) the Court of Appeal took the view that these collateral effects are insufficient to deflect courts from substantial sentences:

> Despite the great punishment that offenders of this sort bring upon themselves, the court should nevertheless pass a sufficiently substantial term of imprisonment to mark publicly the gravity of the offence.

The Court went on to say that 'it will not normally be appropriate in cases of serious breach of trust to suspend any part of the sentence'. Moxon's survey of Crown Court practice tends to suggest that some judges do mitigate on these grounds: not only did 20% of thefts in breach of trust result in a non-custodial sentence, but a further 29% resulted in a suspended sentence (*Sentencing Practice in the Crown Court*, pp. 34–35). However, the new restrictive provisions on suspended sentences (see **21.8.2**) may now make this less likely.

Moxon's research (*Sentencing Practice in the Crown Court*, p. 18) found that the following mitigating factors were most strongly associated with a low use of custody:

Use of unsuspended custody as a proportion of all sentences for offenders aged 17 or over, by factors relating to the offender

Factors associated with lower use of custody	*Unsuspended custody %*	*Factors associated with higher use of custody*	*Unsuspended custody %*
Good response to supervision	46	Poor response	93
Long time since offence	15	Not specified	50
Signs of reform	18	Not specified	50
Fixed address	47	No fixed abode	77
Female	28	Male	52
Employed	35	Unemployed	58
Secure job	32	Not specified	52
No previous convictions	35	One or more previous	54
Secure permanent home	32	Not specified	50
Compensation made/offered	32	Not specified	50
No breach of court order	45	In breach of order	62
No trouble since offence	34	Not specified	51
Treated for addiction	35	Not specified	50
Pleaded guilty	48	Pleaded not guilty	55

20.4 Previous Convictions

The 1991 Act included an apparently restrictive provision on previous convictions, which has since been repealed. We look first at the common law, then the 1991 Act, and then the 1993 amendments.

20.4.1 THE PRINCIPLE OF PROGRESSIVE LOSS OF MITIGATION

The 1990 White Paper made it clear that the intention behind this part of the 1991 Act was to give legislative force to the principle endorsed by the Court of Appeal in *R* v *Queen* (1981) 3 Cr App R (S) 245. A man with a 25-year history of convictions had been sentenced to 18 months' imprisonment for, essentially, stealing a cheque for £50. On appeal, counsel submitted that the sentence should be quashed because Queen had been sentenced on his record, and the Court replied that counsel was:

> . . . right in the enunciation of that principle. Of course no prisoner is to be sentenced for the offences which he has committed in the past and for which he has already been punished. The proper way to look at the matter is to decide a sentence which is appropriate for the offence for which the prisoner is before the court. Then in deciding whether that sentence should be imposed or whether the court can extend properly some leniency to the prisoner, the court must have regard to those matters which tell in his favour, and equally to those matters which tell against him; in particular his record of previous convictions. The matters have to be balanced up to decide whether the appropriate sentence to pass is one at the upper end of the bracket or somewhere lower down.

This has been called the 'principle of progressive loss of mitigation' (see Ashworth, *Sentencing and Criminal Justice*, Ch. 6): the idea is that a first offender can usually expect a substantially reduced sentence, but that with each subsequent conviction an offender progressively loses the mitigation which he or she had as a first offender. The idea also incorporates an important limitation: no matter how bad the record of previous convictions, this 'will not justify the imposition of a term of imprisonment in excess of the permissible ceiling for the facts of the immediate offence' (Thomas, *Principles of Sentencing*, p. 41).

It is this last point which the wording of s. 29(1) of the 1991 Act was designed to reinforce. A bad criminal record may not be an aggravating factor. Nor is the fact that the defendant has re-offended after receiving lesser sentences a good reason for imposing a more severe sentence than is appropriate to the seriousness of the offence. But, by virtue of s. 28(1), a court may regard a good previous record as a mitigating factor.

The hoped-for result of s. 29(1) was that minor persistent offenders would not receive substantial sentences. In particular, they should be dealt with by community sentences and not by custodial sentences if their offences are not serious enough for custody. The Court of Appeal took some steps in this direction in the first group of appeals decided under the CJA 1991. In *R* v *Bexley* [1993] 1 WLR 192 Lord Taylor of Gosforth CJ accepted that s. 29(1) 'embodies the principle established' before the Act in case law in cases such as *Queen* (above) and *R* v *Bailey* (1988) 10 Cr App R (S) 231.

A good example of progressive loss of mitigation is provided by *R* v *Cox* [1993] 1 WLR 188 (discussed at **21.5.2**): the reckless driving of the motorcycle was considered so serious that only a custodial sentence could be justified, but the Court of Appeal held that two mitigating factors took the case beneath the custody threshold. One was the appellant's youth (he was 18), and the other was his antecedent history (he had only one previous conviction). This decision shows the operation of the principle of progressive loss of mitigation, in that even an offender with one previous conviction can expect significant mitigation of sentence. It is not clear when all mitigation is lost and the offender reaches the 'ceiling', but presumably this is after three or four convictions.

20.4.2 THE NEW LAW ON PREVIOUS CONVICTIONS

Section 66(6) of the CJA 1993 repeals the original s. 29 and substitutes a new s. 29 into the CJA 1991. The main provision is the new s. 29(1):

> *In considering the seriousness of any offence, the court may take into account any previous convictions of the offender or any failure of his to respond to previous sentences.*

The effect of this provision remains unclear. Certainly it removes the (erroneous) belief that the post-1991 law prohibits all reference to previous convictions when considering the proportionate sentence. Whether it allows courts to treat a bad previous record as an aggravating factor is doubtful: Lord Taylor CJ has stated extra-judicially that the common law principle of progressive loss of mitigation, beneath a 'ceiling' set by reference to the seriousness of the current offence, is preserved by the new s. 29.

The new section includes a further element, however. It allows courts to take account of any failure of the offender 'to respond to previous sentences'. What this means is also unclear. An offender who has re-offended during the currency of an existing sentence (e.g., community service, probation, suspended sentence) may be said to have failed to respond. But can the same be said of an offender who re-offends soon after *completing* a community service order, or paying a fine, or being released from prison? At least the provision refers to the plural, response to previous sentences (one failure to respond is insufficient), but in other respects an authoritative Court of Appeal decision is awaited. (For further discussion, see Wasik and von Hirsch, 'Section 29 Revised: Previous Convictions in Sentencing' [1994] Crim LR 409.)

20.4.3 THE IMPORTANCE OF THE 'QUALITY' OF A CRIMINAL RECORD

In general, the relevance of a criminal record relates not only to the quantity of previous convictions but also to what might be termed the 'quality' of the record. Thus courts might view a criminal record differently according to the type of previous offences (similar to the present?), the seriousness of previous offences, the nature of previous sentences received, the frequency of previous convictions, the existence of a conviction-free 'gap' prior to this offence (see, e.g. *R* v *Fox* (1980) 2 Cr App R (S) 188 and note the mitigating effect of a gap in the Table in **20.3.3** above), and the age of the defendant when previously convicted. How can counsel make use of these factors when putting together a mitigation speech of behalf of an offender with previous convictions? (See Shapland, J., *Between Conviction* and *Sentence*, Routledge and Kegan Paul 1981, pp. 70–1.)

20.5 Multiple Offences

The problem here arises where a person is convicted of two or more offences at one court hearing, or where a person has been committed for sentence for two or more offences. How should a court approach the passing of sentence on one occasion for two or more offences? The problem might arise in a case where a defendant is convicted on an indictment charging, say, eight separate offences. Another possible example would be where a defendant is convicted of two offences and agrees that ten other offences should be 'taken into consideration', an informal procedure approved by the courts (*Anderson* v *Director of Public Prosecutions* [1978] AC 964). The numbers of convictions and of offences taken into consideration may vary, but the principles are the same.

20.5.1 THE CHANGE IN THE LAW

Originally, the 1991 Act stated that a court could only treat offences as sufficiently serious for a community sentence or for custody, as the case may be, if any two of the offences were (taken together) so serious that only a community sentence or custody would be adequate. This 'two offence' rule was designed to prevent the courts from aggregating a whole series of minor offences and sending the offender to prison.

However, this policy came under great strain when courts were confronted with offenders who had committed large numbers of relatively small offences, sometimes over 100. This led to the abolition of the 'two offence' rule by s. 66 of the CJA 1993, which substitutes new wording in s. 1(2)(a) of the 1991 Act and in other relevant sections. Courts may now aggregate all the 'associated' offences, whether convictions or offences taken into consideration, in deciding whether they are sufficiently serious for custody or for a community sentence. The approach in cases such as *R* v *Clugston* (1991) 13 Cr App R (S) 165 (three years' imprisonment upheld for 103 offences of obtaining £50 by deception with stolen cheques) therefore prevails over that in *R* v *Choudhary* (1991) 13 Cr App R (S) 290 (two months' detention quashed for 140 offences of theft of amounts between £20 and £30, because no individual offences were sufficiently serious).

It should be noted that a court can only take into account other offences 'associated with' that for which the offender now stands convicted. Section 31(2) of the 1991 Act states that an offence is 'associated with' another if:

(a) the offender is convicted of it in the proceedings in which he is convicted of the other offence, or (although convicted of it in earlier proceedings) is sentenced for it at the same time as he is sentenced for that offence; or

(b) the offender admits the commission of it in proceedings in which he is sentenced for the other offence and requests the court to take it into consideration in sentencing him for that offence.

Paragraph (b) refers to offences taken into consideration. Paragraph (a) seems to exclude cases in which a suspended sentence is activated. Thus in *R* v *Crawford* (1993) 14 Cr App R (S) 782 it was held that the offence in respect of which the suspended sentence was originally passed does not become an 'associated offence' when the sentence is activated in subsequent proceedings. However, if the original sentence was a conditional discharge, and a court subsequently revokes it (because of a breach) and deals with the offender for the original offence, that does become an 'associated offence' because it is an offence for which sentence is passed in the same proceedings (*R* v *Godfrey* (1993) 14 Cr App R (S) 804).

20.5.2 MULTIPLE OFFENCES AND LENGTH OF SENTENCE

If a court decides that the offences for which it is passing sentence are, taken together, so serious that only custody can be justified, then the length of the custodial sentence must be determined. Section 2(2)(a) states that the sentence must be for such term as is 'commensurate with the seriousness of the offence, or the combination of the offence and other offences associated with it'. This means that a court can take account of all the offences, including t.i.c's, for which it is passing sentence. A similar provision in s. 6(2)(b) governs the extent of the restrictions on liberty imposed by means of a community sentence.

So far as custody is concerned, this seems to mean that the common law principles relating to whether the prison terms should be *concurrent* or *consecutive* remain in vigour. The extensive caselaw on this point can be reduced to three basic principles:

(a) Where it can be said that the offences formed part of the same transaction, the sentences should generally be concurrent; the main exceptions to this are firearms offences (*R* v *Faulkner* (1972) 56 Cr App R 594) and offences committed whilst resisting arrest (*R* v *Kastercum* (1972) 56 Cr App R 298), which should receive consecutive sentences even where they arise out of the 'same transaction'.

(b) In all cases where the offences did not form part of a single transaction, the sentences should generally be consecutive (the principle applies to other forms of sentence — e.g. fines and community service order — as well as to custody). This applies particularly to offences committed whilst on bail (see *R* v *Baverstock* [1993] 1 WLR 202, and the new s. 29(2) of the CJA 1991).

(c) Where the court imposes consecutive sentences, it must not content itself by doing the arithmetic and passing the sentence which the arithmetic produces. It must look at the totality of the criminal behaviour and ask itself what is the appropriate sentence for all the offences taken together, by comparison with sentencing levels for other crimes. This principle is preserved by s. 28(2) of the 1991 Act.

20.6 General Principles and the Criminal Justice Act 1991

It will have been observed that many of the general principles discussed in this chapter relate to the seriousness of offences. It is important now to make the point that there are sentencing questions under the 1991 Act which are not governed by the seriousness of the offence; and therefore where the more restrictive provisions above are not applicable. Two main classes of case stand out:

(a) *'Public protection' cases.* If a court is seeking to justify the use of a custodial sentence under s. 1(2)(b), or to impose a longer-than-proportionate sentence under s. 2(2)(b), by reference to the need to protect the public from serious harm from a particular sexual or violent offender, there are no apparent restrictions on what it may take into account when forming its opinion. It can take account of previous convictions — indeed, it may well use them as the basis for predicting future conduct; and it can consider any other offences for which it is now passing sentence. It will usually have a pre-sentence report in such cases, and that report may well discuss the previous convictions.

(b) *'Suitability' in relation to community sentences.* As we saw in **19.4**, a court which makes a community order must satisfy itself that the order is 'the most suitable for the offender' (s. 6(2)(a)). To reach such a conclusion the court may have to consider previous convictions and other wider matters, and it is likely that a pre-sentence report would discuss previous record and previous sentences.

However, apart from these decisions, the court will be focusing on the seriousness of the offence, and will therefore be bound by the narrow conception of aggravating factors (relating only to the circumstances of the offence) and the new rules on taking account of other offences.

TWENTY-ONE

IMPRISONMENT

21.1 Introduction

Imprisonment is the most severe sanction which an English court can impose. Life imprisonment is the mandatory sentence for murder, and is the maximum sentence for several serious crimes, including manslaughter, attempted murder, causing grievous bodily harm or wounding with intent (Offences against the Person Act 1861, s. 18), robbery, rape, buggery, intercourse with a girl under 13, arson, and criminal damage endangering life. In practice life imprisonment is not used as the sentence for the most serious varieties of these offences, but is reserved for serious cases in which the offender is mentally unstable (see **Chapter 23**).

Apart from those crimes which carry the maximum of life imprisonment, each indictable offence has a maximum prison sentence assigned to it by statute. In theory these maxima should form a hierarchy, with the most serious offences carrying the longest sentences and the least serious carrying lower maxima. In practice there are several anomalies, although Parliament acts from time to time to raise or lower certain maxima. For example, the CJA 1988 raised the maxima for neglect of or cruelty to children to ten years; and for various corruption offences, to seven years. The 1988 Act also reduced to six months' imprisonment the maxima for common assault, driving whilst disqualified, and taking a motor vehicle without the owner's consent. The CJA 1991 reduced the maximum for theft from ten to seven years, and the maximum for non-residential burglary from 14 to ten years. The CJA 1993 doubled, from five to ten years, the maxima for causing death by dangerous driving and causing death by careless driving whilst intoxicated.

21.2 The English Prison System

What does imprisonment involve? In all cases it involves deprivation of liberty, but beyond that the 'pains of imprisonment' may vary considerably from institution to institution. The prison establishment in the English system may be divided broadly into three groups — local prisons, training prisons, and open prisons. The local prisons contain prisoners who are on remand awaiting trial, and also contain most sentenced prisoners who are serving terms of up to 18 months. Prisoners serving longer sentences will usually be sent to a training prison. Open prisons provide for those serving prison sentences who are thought not to be in need of security, and consequently the regimes in open prisons are considerably more flexible than in the closed prisons.

21.3 Some Problems of the Prison System

The prison system in England and Wales has been the subject of several major inquiries in recent years. Foremost among these is the Woolf Inquiry, set up after the acute problems of English prisons came to the notice of a wider audience in this country, and indeed in the world, as a result of the riots and disturbances at

Strangeways prison, Manchester, and at several other prisons during 1990. The Woolf Inquiry recommended sweeping changes in the organisation of the prison service and in its approach to its tasks. Prisons should be divided into smaller units, and there should be a stronger movement towards 'community prisons', closer to prisoners' homes and with improved visiting facilities. Integral sanitation should be installed in all cells, and a timetable should be set so as to end 'slopping out' at the earliest opportunity. Each prisoner should be entitled to a single cell, unless he or she wishes to share. Overcrowding, one of the greatest problems, should be tackled by means of a new Prison Rule to provide that no establishment should hold prisoners in excess of its certified normal accommodation (with only a limited power to derogate). There was a wealth of further recommendations aimed at improving security, control and justice within the prisons. (*Prison Disturbances April 1990: Report of an Inquiry by Lord Justice Woolf (parts I and II) and Judge Stephen Tumim (part II)*, Cm. 1456, February 1991.)

The Government now has little enthusiasm for the Woolf reforms, and the subsequent Learmont Inquiry into escapes from top security prisons has ushered in a greater emphasis on security. The Home Office wishes to see greater austerity in prisons, despite the experience of the 1990 riots, and despite the increased pressure on the prison system produced by the sharp rise in the prison population from 41,000 in early 1993 to 55,000 in mid 1996. However, at least two major recommendations from the Woolf Inquiry have been implemented. Integration sanitation has been put into cells, and 'slopping out' in English prisons ended in April 1996. A national Criminal Justice Consultative Committee has been established, with a view to promoting 'better understanding, cooperation and coordination in the criminal justice system'. This kind of development serves to underline the importance, for counsel as for others, of acquiring a basic knowledge of the prison system and the meaning of imprisonment.

21.4 Prison Policy and Sentencing Policy

It is sometimes said that, whatever the conditions in prison, 'prison works' because it keeps offenders out of circulation for a period of time and therefore protects society. This is true only to an extent. It is certainly true that escapes from prison are rare; indeed, escapes from local or training prisons are so rare that it may be concluded that the prisons provide almost 100% protection for society for the duration of the sentence. But in another sense the statistics are far less encouraging: over one half of male prisoners are reconvicted within two years of their release (at least 54%, according to Home Office Research Study No. 136, *Explaining Reconviction Rates* (1994)).

If the conditions inside the prisons have been so poor, why is it that so many offenders are reconvicted (many of whom return to prison)? One explanation is that one of the main subjects of discussion among inmates in prison is crime, and this leads to the view that prisons may protect the public in the short term but that in the longer term they have the opposite effect, since they breed crime. The Government propounded this view in its 1990 White Paper (para. 2.7):

> . . . however much prison staff try to inject a positive purpose into the regime, as they do, prison is a society which requires virtually no sense of personal responsibility from the prisoners. Normal social or working habits do not fit. The opportunity to learn from other criminals is pervasive. For most offenders, imprisonment has to be justified in terms of public protection, denunciation and retribution. Otherwise it can be an expensive way of making bad people worse. The prospects of reforming offenders are usually much better if they stay in the community, provided the public is properly protected.

The last point, about public protection through non-custodial measures, was discussed in **Chapter 19**. But the general drift of this view is that the public protection provided by prison sentences may be short term and therefore somewhat overstated.

21.5 The Criminal Justice Act 1991 and the Custody Threshold

21.5.1 THE STATUTORY FRAMEWORK

The policy behind the 1991 Act was the twin-track approach:

> . . . that those who commit very serious crimes, particularly crimes of violence, should receive long custodial sentences; but that many other crimes can be punished in the community, with greater emphasis on bringing home to the criminal the consequences of his actions, compensation to the victim and reparation to the community (1990 White Paper, para. 2.2).

Thus, when the White Paper stated that 'punishment in proportion to the seriousness of the crime . . . should be the principal focus for sentencing decisions', it indicated a more elongated scale of proportionality than that in use at the moment. At the lower end of the scale, prison should be replaced by community penalties (discussed in **Chapters 18** and **19**). At the higher end of the scale, the Government envisaged little change in the policy of long prison sentences for serious crimes.

The 1991 Act seeks to establish a framework for custodial sentencing which reflects both the proportionality principle and the policy of reducing the use of prison for non-serious offences. To this end, s. 1 introduces a 'custody threshold' which has to be surmounted before any court can impose a custodial sentence, and s. 2 imposes limits on the length of any custodial sentence. These provisions apply to custodial sentences for all offences except murder, to all courts and to all ages of offender, including those under 21.

The remainder of this chapter will examine the 'custody threshold' in s. 1. Three lawful grounds for a custodial sentence are provided: the seriousness of the offence; the protection of the public; and refusal of consent to a community order. Each of them will be discussed in turn, but the first is likely to be much the most important in practice. The Act also imposes requirements on courts to give reasoned explanations for custodial sentences, and these are set out in **21.5.5**.

21.5.2 CUSTODY BECAUSE THE OFFENCE IS 'SO SERIOUS'

The first 'custody threshold' is that established by s. 1(2)(a) as follows:

> . . . *the court shall not pass a custodial sentence on the offender unless it is of the opinion—*
> *(a) that the offence, or the combination of the offence and one or more offences associated with it, was so serious that only such a sentence can be justified for the offence.*

The phrase, 'or the combination of the offence and one or more offences associated with it', refers to offenders who are being sentenced for more than one offence: such cases were discussed separately at **20.5**. The focus here is on an offender being sentenced for one offence.

21.5.2.1 How should the courts interpret s. 1(2)(a)?

The pre-1991 precedents provided a few clear markers. The possession of a small amount of cannabis for personal consumption is unlikely to be sufficiently serious for custody (*R* v *Robertson-Coupar and Baxendale* (1982) 4 Cr App R (S) 150), as are consensual homosexual acts in public lavatories (*R* v *Dighton* (1983) 5 Cr App R (S) 233) and social security frauds without aggravating features (*R* v *Stewart* (1987) 9 Cr App R (S) 135).

Probably the leading case under the 1991 Act is *R* v *Cox* [1993] 1 WLR 188, where the court held that a course of reckless driving involving flagrant breach of traffic regulations was so serious that only custody could be justified, although it subsequently found personal mitigating circumstances which took the case below the custody threshold. Lord Taylor of Gosforth CJ held that an offence was 'so serious' if it was 'the kind of offence which . . . would make right-thinking members of the public, knowing all the facts, feel that justice had not been done by the passing of any sentence other than a custodial one', following the words of Lawton LJ in *R* v *Bradbourn* (1985) 7 Cr App R (S) 180. The same test was used in the companion case of *R* v *Baverstock* [1993] 1 WLR 202, where the Court of Appeal concluded that a relatively minor common assault was not sufficiently serious, but held that the combination of handling stolen goods (the offender acted as a lookout whilst others dismantled a stolen car) with an offence of theft from a motor vehicle committed whilst he was on bail for the handling offence amounted to conduct so serious that only custody could be justified.

The Court of Appeal has repeated the test of 'right-thinking members of the public' in several cases, but it is difficult to see in what way it affects the Court's decision. In *R* v *Keogh* (1993) 15 Cr App R (S) 279 the defendant had pleaded guilty to obtaining £35 by deception, having persuaded a cashier to allow him to 'exchange' goods which he had in fact taken from the shelves without authority. The Court of Appeal, referring to the test of 'right-thinking members of the public', held that the offence was so serious that only a custodial sentence could be justified. Similarly in *R* v *McCormick* (1995) 16 Cr App R (S) 134 the Court of Appeal upheld a custodial sentence for a woman of 47, with no previous convictions, who had been found guilty of stealing £17 from her employers by re-issuing used ferry tickets. The court reduced the sentence of 28 days' imprisonment so as to enable her immediate release, but insisted that her offence was so serious that only custody could be justified.

In two other theft cases, both involving vandalism, the court went further and based its reasoning on deterrence. Thus, in *R* v *Arslan* (1994) 15 Cr App R (S) 90 and in *R* v *Costello* (1994) 15 Cr App R (S) 240, the Court of Appeal upheld custodial sentences of four months and six months' imprisonment respectively on offenders who had drilled into the cash boxes of public telephones, stealing £82 in the first case and nothing in the second. The wording of the 1991 Act does not provide for deterrent sentences, however; it provides that the offence must, in itself, be so serious that only custody can be justified.

Turning to offences of violence, there is evidence of a fairly low custody threshold here too. In *R* v *Fenton* (1994) 15 Cr App R (S) 682 a driver who became involved in an altercation with another driver, in the course of which he pushed the other driver in the chest, pleaded guilty to common assault and was sentenced to 14 days' imprisonment. The Court of Appeal held that this offence was so serious that only custody could be justified, chiefly on the ground that 'such conduct can very easily develop into serious offences of violence'.

However, there are some cases where the Court of Appeal has quashed custodial sentences under s. 1(2)(a). Although almost all sentences of custody for burglary have been upheld, there are two decisions, one case of residential burglary (*R* v *Bennett* (1993) 15 Cr App R (S) 213) and at least two cases of minor commercial burglary (*R* v *Tetteh* (1994) 15 Cr App R (S) 46 and *R* v *Carlton* (1994) 15 Cr App R(S) 335) in which the court has regarded custody as out of proportion to the crime. In fairly minor cases of indecent assault there is a conflict in the case law (*cf. R* v *Orriss* (1994) 15 Cr App R (S) 185, and *R* v *Chagan* (1995) 16 Cr App R (S) 15, with *Townsend* [1995] Crim LR 180).

Overall, there is no clear pattern to these cases. Perhaps the most important point is that it is wrong to assume that the legal category of the offence is conclusive. This was the main implication of the pre-Act case of *R* v *Hearne and Petty* (1989) 11 Cr App R (S) 316; even if the case is one of burglary of a dwelling, counsel should urge the court to look at the particular facts and should not assume that custody is 'automatic', especially for a young offender. There may often be room for counsel to mitigate on the particular facts.

The relevance of previous convictions, aggravating and mitigating factors to findings of 'seriousness' was discussed in **Chapter 20**.

21.5.3 CUSTODY FOR 'PUBLIC PROTECTION'

The second custody threshold established by the 1991 Act is found in s. 1(2)(b):

> . . . *the court shall not pass a custodial sentence on the offender unless it is of the opinion—*
> *(b) where the offence is a violent or sexual offence, that only such a sentence would be adequate to protect the public from serious harm from him.*

This provision is unlikely to be invoked in many cases. On the face of the statute it is restricted to 'violent or sexual' offences, both of which are defined in s. 31(1):

> *'Violent offence' means an offence which leads, or is intended or likely to lead, to a person's death or to physical injury to a person, and includes an offence which is required to be charged as arson (whether or not it would otherwise fall within this definition).*

It will be seen that the definition is artificially extended so as to include arson, and also that the opening phrases are wide enough to encompass all attempted offences against the person, aggravated criminal damage contrary to s. 1(2), Criminal Damage Act 1971, many cases of dangerous driving, and other offences which would not normally be classified as 'violent'. An issue which has come before the Court of Appeal on more than one occasion is whether robbery falls within the definition of a 'violent offence' — the Court of Appeal appears to have strained to ensure that robbery is included (see, e.g., *R* v *Bibby* [1994] Crim LR 610 and *R* v *Cochrane* (1994) 15 Cr App R (S) 708).

The definition of 'sexual offence' in the 1991 Act was soon revealed to be inadequate (see *R* v *Robinson* (1993) 14 Cr App R (S) 448), and the Criminal Justice and Public Order Act 1994 substitutes a new definition into s. 31(1) of the 1991 Act:

> *'sexual offence' means any of the following—*
> *(a) an offence under the Sexual Offences Act 1956, other than an offence under section 30, 31 or 33 to 36 of that Act;*
> *(b) an offence under section 128 of the Mental Health Act 1959;*
> *(c) an offence under the Indecency with Children Act 1960;*
> *(d) an offence under section 9 of the Theft Act 1969 of burglary with intent to commit rape;*
> *(e) an offence under section 54 of the Criminal Law Act 1977;*
> *(f) an offence under the Protection of Children Act 1978;*
> *(g) an offence under section 1 of the Criminal Law Act 1977 of conspiracy to commit any of the offences in paragraphs (a) to (f) above;*
> *(h) an offence under section 1 of the Criminal Attempts Act 1981 of attempting to commit any of those offences;*
> *(i) an offence of inciting another to commit any of those offences.*

However, once it has been established that the offence with which the court is dealing falls within one of the above definitions, the court must be satisfied that only a custodial sentence would be adequate to protect the public from serious harm from the offender. There is no legal requirement to obtain a medical report unless the offender appears to be mentally disordered, but we have seen in **Chapter 16** above that a pre-sentence report will often be necessary. In deciding whether serious harm is likely to be caused by the offender, the court should be directed to the definition in s. 31(3):

> . . . *any reference, in relation to an offender convicted of a violent or sexual offence, to protecting the public from serious harm from him shall be construed as a reference to protecting members of the public from death or serious personal injury, whether physical or psychological, occasioned by further such offences committed by him.*

The nub of the definition therefore lies in 'serious physical or psychological injury', and it is clear that such offences must be likely to be committed by this offender, not by others — general deterrence is not a relevant consideration here.

Further discussion of factors which may or must be taken into account when applying s. 1(2)(b) will be found in **Chapter 23**. Few cases in which custody has been justified by reference to s. 1(2)(b) alone, i.e., where the offence was not also so serious as to qualify under s. 1(2)(a), have reached the Court of Appeal.

21.5.4 CUSTODY FOR REFUSING CONSENT TO A COMMUNITY SENTENCE

In **Chapter 19** we saw that one of the aims of the 1991 Act was to promote various community sentences, such as probation orders, community service orders, combination orders and so on. A court cannot make one of these orders unless the offender consents, and the question of the consequences of refusing consent therefore arises. Section 1(3) provides:

> *Nothing in subsection (2) . . . shall prevent the court from passing a custodial sentence on the offender if he refuses to give his consent to a community sentence which is proposed by the court and requires that consent.*

What this means is that a court may, if it thinks fit, impose a custodial sentence on someone who refuses to consent to a community sentence, even though the offence itself was not so serious that only a custodial sentence could be justified for it. In practice these circumstances are not likely to arise frequently, since the prospect of a custodial sentence will lead most offenders to give their consent even to an onerous non-custodial sentence. But s. 1(3) will be of practical importance in some cases where a court has to deal with breach of a community order: see **19.10**.

21.5.5 DUTY TO GIVE REASONS AND EXPLANATIONS

Section 1(4) imposes two duties on a court when it passes a custodial sentence. The first duty applies unless the custodial sentence is under s. 1(3) (refusal of consent): it must '*state in open court that it is of the opinion that either or both of paragraphs (a) and (b) of subsection (2) above apply and why it is of that opinion*'. The second duty is '*to explain to the offender in open court and in ordinary language why it is passing a custodial sentence on him.*' These were considered by the Court of Appeal in *R* v *Baverstock* [1993] 1 WLR 202, where Lord Taylor of Gosforth CJ held that:

> this should not normally be a two-stage process; in most cases the judge should be able at one and the same time to explain in ordinary language the reasons for his conclusions and tell the offender why he is passing a custodial sentence.

His Lordship added that the statutory provisions are not to be treated 'as a verbal tightrope', and the precise words used by the court are 'not critical'. These requirements apply equally to magistrates' courts, which are additionally required by s. 1(5) to record their reasons.

21.6 The Criminal Justice Act 1991 and the Length of Custodial Sentences

21.6.1 THE STATED LENGTH AND THE ACTUAL LENGTH

When the court states that a custodial sentence of so many months or years is imposed, it is important to know exactly what this means in terms of time to be served. That is discussed in **21.6.2**. After that, the two provisions on length of sentence of the 1991 Act are examined (s. 2(2)(a) and (b)), and finally there is reference to the suspended sentence of imprisonment.

21.6.2 EARLY RELEASE UNDER THE CRIMINAL JUSTICE ACT 1991

The general rule during the second half of this century was that prisoners were entitled to one-third remission on the sentence announced in court, which they would only forfeit if they committed disciplinary offences in prison. The effect of the 1991 Act was to abolish remission.

Since 1968 it has been possible for prisoners serving medium and long-term sentences to be released on parole after one-third of their sentence. Parolees receive supervision from the probation service, and fewer than 10% are recalled for breach of the conditions or the commission of a further offence. During the 1980s the use of parole became so widespread for those serving sentences of one to two years that concern was expressed that custodial sentences were being emptied of their meaning. The Carlisle Committee was appointed to review the position, and it recommended sweeping reforms (Report of the Review Committee, *The Parole System in England and Wales*, Cm 532 of 1988). Most of the Carlisle Committee's proposals found their way into the CJA 1991, part II. The parole system in its previous form is abolished.

The essence of the new arrangements for early release is that all parts of the sentence announced in court should have some meaning and some effect. All offenders serving custodial sentences of less than four years are granted conditional release after serving one half (s. 33(1)). The condition is that they do not commit another offence before the expiry of the full term of their sentence. If they do so, then they are liable to be ordered to serve the unexpired balance of their sentence, in addition to any sentence for the new offence (s. 40(2)). The 'unexpired balance' is that portion between the date on which the new offence was committed and the date on which their sentence would expire. In addition, those serving at least one year and under four years are released subject to licence until the three-quarters point of their sentence: during that period they are under the supervision of the probation service, and breach of licence may lead to proceedings (s. 38(1)). These arrangements cover all prisoners, and the discretionary elements in the previous parole system do not apply. Any disciplinary offences committed in prison may result in time being added on to the sentence.

The following provides an example of the operation of these provisions:

1. D is sentenced to 2 years' imprisonment.
2. 12 months later he is released on licence.
3. 15 months after sentence he breaches the conditions of his licence. He is then liable to serve up to 3 months' imprisonment until the expiry of his licence.
4. 18 months after sentence, his period of licence expires.
5. 21 months after sentence, D commits an imprisonable offence. He is liable to be recalled to serve the unexpired 3 months of his sentence.

For offenders serving four years or longer, a discretionary system remains. Such prisoners must be released on licence after serving two-thirds, but they may be released on licence after serving one half if the Parole Board and the Home Secretary agree (ss. 33 and 39). In all cases the licence continues until the three-quarters point in the sentence, and the last quarter consists of conditional release, with a liability to serve the unexpired portion if convicted of a new offence. The Act also introduces new provisions on the release of prisoners serving discretionary life sentences (s. 34). (For further discussion see M. Wasik, 'Early Release Arrangements' [1992] Crim LR 252.)

If one result of these reforms is to ensure that all parts of a custodial sentence have some meaning, another result is that many offenders, particularly medium-term prisoners, spend longer inside than they did under the previous parole system. The Carlisle Committee noted this, and insisted that it saw no reason to lengthen custodial sentences in this way. It therefore called for a reduction of at least 5% in sentencing levels in the courts, in order to ensure that the new Act did not inadvertently increase levels of punitiveness. In formal terms, it has long been a principle of sentencing that the court in a particular case should take no account of remission (*R* v *Maguire and Enos* (1957) 40 Cr App R 92) or parole (*R* v *Kenway and Cunningham* (1985) 7 Cr App R (S) 457) when calculating the length of a sentence. However, this principle has been abandoned for the purpose of calculating the appropriate length of custodial sentences following the changes introduced by part II of the CJA 1991. As the Lord Chief Justice said in his *Practice Statement (Crime: Sentencing)*, it is now necessary:

> to have regard to the actual period likely to be served and, as far as practicable, to the risk of offenders serving substantially longer under the new system than would have been normal under the old. Existing guideline judgments should be applied with these considerations in mind.

No formula was provided for the judges in the *Practice Statement*, and there is no evidence that it had a significant effect.

21.6.3 PROPORTIONALITY AND CUSTODIAL SENTENCING

Once a court is satisfied that an offence has overcome the 'custody threshold' established by s.1 of the 1991 Act, the length of the sentence is governed by s. 2. The main provision is the proportionality principle (s. 2(2)(a)), but it is as well to bear in mind that courts are permitted to exceed the proportionate sentence in limited circumstances when sentencing violent or sexual offenders for public protection (see s. 2(2)(b) and **21.7**).

Most cases will be governed by the first part of s. 2, which states:

> *(1) This section applies where a court passes a custodial sentence other than one fixed by law.*
> *(2) The custodial sentence shall be—*
> *(a) for such term (not exceeding the permitted maximum) as in the opinion of the court is commensurate with the seriousness of the offence, or the combination of the offence and other offences associated with it . . .*

The key phrase here is 'commensurate with the seriousness of the offence.' As noted in **16.4** above, this has been interpreted by the Court of Appeal in *R* v *Cunningham* [1993] 1 WLR 183 to mean 'commensurate with the the punishment and deterrence which the offence requires.' This makes it unlikely that, following the 1991 Act, there will be any significant reappraisal of sentence levels. Parliament has never undertaken such a task, preferring simply to alter a few maximum penalties from time to time. The courts, too, appear to have assumed that existing sentence levels, particularly for the more serious offences, do reflect proportionality. It will therefore continue to be important to understand the way in which the 'tariff' has been shaped in recent years and that is the subject of **Chapter 22** below.

21.6.4 PROPOSED CHANGES IN EARLY RELEASE

The 1996 White Paper, *Protecting the Public* (see **22.3**), makes far-reaching proposals for change of the early release arrangements introduced in 1992. The proposal is to move towards greater 'honesty in sentencing', which means reducing the gap between the sentence announced in court and the period served in custody. The proposed system will be complex, and there is no need to set out its details at this stage. But its essence lies in two changes. First, offenders sentenced to custody should generally serve the whole period, with a reduction of up to 20% as a reward for good behaviour in prison. Most prisoners could therefore expect to serve four-fifths of the time announced in court. Second, judges would be expected to adjust their sentences downwards so as to ensure that the change to 'honesty in sentencing' did not result in generally longer periods of incarceration.

21.7 Public Protection: The Exception to Proportionality

As mentioned earlier, there is only one group of cases in which courts are permitted to sentence above the level which is commensurate with the seriousness of the offence(s) committed. Section 2(2)(b) CJA 1991 provides that the custodial sentence shall be:

> *where the offence is a violent or sexual offence, for such longer term (not exceeding [the] maximum) as in the opinion of the court is necessary to protect the public from serious harm from the offender.*

The definitions of 'violent' and 'sexual' offences, and of serious harm, were discussed in **21.5.3**. Section 2(4) provides that discretionary sentences of life imprisonment and detention for life must also be justified according to s. 2(2)(b).

This 'public protection' provision is the equivalent to the threshold provision in s. 1(2)(b), but it is not limited to cases which qualified for custody under s. 1(2)(b). So long as the criteria in s. 2(2)(b) are fulfilled, it would not matter if the case qualified for custody under s. 1(2)(a). These 'public protection' sentences are aimed at so-called 'dangerous' offenders: the difficulties of predicting dangerousness were mentioned in **16.6** and are examined in **Chapter 23**.

If a court imposes a disproportionate custodial sentence for public protection reasons, there are various procedural requirements. By s. 2(3), the court must state in open court that s. 2(2)(b) applies and why it is of that opinion, and it must explain to the offender in open court and in ordinary language why the sentence is for such a term. The leading cases on s. 2(2)(b) include *R* v *Bowler* (1993) 15 Cr App R (S) 78; *R* v *Mansell* (1994) 15 Cr App R (S) 771 and *R* v *Fawcett* (1995) 16 Cr App R (S) 55, and these are discussed below at **23.2.3**.

21.8 Suspended Sentences of Imprisonment

The suspended sentence was introduced into English law in 1967 as the first of several measures designed to reduce the use of imprisonment by the courts. The legislative framework is to be found in the PCCA 1973, ss. 22 and 23, as amended by the Criminal Justice Act 1991, s. 5.

Essentially, a court is empowered to suspend, for a period of not less than one year nor more than two years, any sentence of imprisonment of two years or less. If the offender is convicted of an imprisonable offence committed within the operational period of the suspended sentence, the court which deals with the new offence must activate the suspended sentence and commit the offender to prison unless it would be 'unjust to do so'. The suspended sentence therefore operates as a definite threat to the particular offender. It should be noted that only a sentence of imprisonment can be suspended: this means that suspension is unavailable for custodial sentences for offenders under 21, which are termed 'detention in a young offender institution'.

21.8.1 THE DECISION SEQUENCE

Before imposing a suspended sentence of imprisonment, the court must go through the decision sequence indicated by PCCA 1973, s. 22(2), as substituted by CJA 1991, s. 5:

> *A court shall not deal with an offender by means of a suspended sentence unless it is of the opinion—*
>
> *(a) that the case is one in which a sentence of imprisonment would have been appropriate even without the power to suspend the sentence; and*
>
> *(b) that the exercise of that power can be justified by the exceptional circumstances of that case.*

This means that the court must first ensure that the case passes over the custody threshold established by s. 1 of the CJA 1991, usually, that the offence was so serious that only a custodial sentence can be justified. The second step is to decide on the appropriate length of the custodial sentence, applying s. 2(2)(a). The third step, if the appropriate length is two years or less, should be to decide whether or not the sentence should be suspended. This depends on the requirement of 'exceptional circumstances'.

21.8.2 'THE EXCEPTIONAL CIRCUMSTANCES OF THE CASE'

Following the implementation of the 1991 Act, a court may only suspend a prison sentence if this can be justified by the exceptional circumstances of the case. The intention was that this would result in far fewer suspended sentences than in previous years, and the hope was that most of those who had formerly benefited from suspension would instead qualify for a community sentence. Whether that hope will be realised remains to be seen, but the Government's intention to restrict the use of the suspended sentence has been successful. The Court of Appeal has already established the extremely narrow ambit of 'exceptional circumstances'.

In *R* v *Okinikan* (1993) 14 Cr App R (S) 453 the Court of Appeal held that:

> . . . taken on their own, or in combination, good character, youth and an early plea are not exceptional circumstances justifying a suspended sentence. . . . They may amount to mitigation sufficient to persuade the court that a custodial sentence should not be passed or to reduce its length.

This makes it clear that frequently-invoked mitigating circumstances cannot be regarded as 'exceptional'. A similar conclusion was reached in *R* v *Sanderson* (1993) 14 Cr App R (S) 361, where the appellant's good record, the fact that his wife and mother-in-law were dependent on him and his remorse were not regarded as 'exceptional'. In *R* v *Lowery* (1993) 14 Cr App R (S) 485 the offender was a police officer who had stolen money collected as fines, in order to help finance alterations to his house when his wife became disabled. He subsequently attempted suicide and was placed under psychiatric care. However, the court held that these were not 'exceptional circumstances' sufficient to justify suspension of the prison sentence for theft. It appears that in both this case and *Sanderson* (a case of unlawful wounding), the seriousness of the offence led the court to conclude that only an immediate custodial sentence would be adequate. This strict approach was restated in *Attorney-General's Reference (No. 5 of 1993)* (1993) 15 Cr App R (S) 201 and in *R* v *Bradley* [1994] Crim LR 381, but decisions of the Court of Appeal such as *R* v *Khan* (1993) 15 Cr App R (S) 320 (suspending a sentence of imprisonment on an elderly solicitor suffering from serious health problems), *R* v *French* (1993) 15 Cr App R (S) 194, and *R* v *Weston* [1995] Crim LR 900, are more flexible.

The use of the suspended sentence declined from 10% in 1991 to 1% in 1994. There is evidence that, at the level of Crown Court practice, 'exceptional circumstances' are being found rather more readily than the Court of Appeal's criteria would suggest: see N. Stone, 'The Suspended Sentence since the Criminal Justice Act 1991' [1994] Crim LR 399. However, some sentencers resent the restrictions imposed by Parliament and believe that suspended sentences should be more widely available: see Campbell, J. Q., 'A Sentencer's Lament on the Imminent Death of the Suspended Sentence' [1995] Crim LR 293.

21.8.3 ADDING A FINANCIAL PENALTY

To insert an immediate punitive impact into cases where a suspended sentence is imposed, there is a new s. 22(2A) of the PCCA 1973, introduced by CJA 1991, s. 5:

> *A court which passes a suspended sentence on any person for an offence shall consider whether the circumstances of the case are such as to warrant the imposition of a fine or the making of a compensation order.*

This is merely a duty to consider, but its manifest intent is to ensure that a higher proportion of suspended sentences are combined with a financial penalty. In the past, about one-fifth of Crown Court suspended sentences have been combined with a compensation order. (The principles relevant to fines and compensation orders were discussed in **Chapter 18**.)

21.8.4 BREACH OF SUSPENDED SENTENCE

If a person who is subject to a suspended sentence is convicted of an imprisonable offence committed during the operational period of the suspended sentence, the court which sentences him or her for the new offence must activate the suspended sentence unless it appears 'unjust to do so' (PCCA 1973, s. 23(1)). Moreover, the suspended sentence should run consecutively to any custodial sentence imposed for the new offence (*R* v *Ithell* [1969] 2 All ER 449). This severely restricts the sentencing powers of the second court, especially since the Court of Appeal has laid down that the fact that the new offence is of a different kind from the original offence is not a ground for failing to activate the suspended sentence (*R* v *Moylan* [1970] 1 QB 143). If the new offence is minor in nature and would not itself warrant a custodial sentence, this is a 'strong circumstance' for not activating the suspended sentence (*R* v *McElhorne* (1983) 5 Cr App R (S) 53; *R* v *Dobson* (1989) 11 Cr App R (S) 332), although recent decisions emphasise that a court may properly decide to activate the sentence in these circumstances, e.g., because of the rapidity with which the offender returned to crime (*R* v *Calladine* (1993) 15 Cr App R (S) 345; *R* v *Stacey* [1994] Crim LR 303).

21.9 Suspended Sentence Supervision Orders

Where a court imposes a suspended sentence of more than six months' imprisonment, it is empowered to add to that a suspended sentence supervision order. Section 26 of the PCCA 1973 states that the supervision should be for a period not exceeding the operational period of the suspended sentence; and, unlike probation, the offender does not have to consent to the supervision. The restriction to sentences of more than six months means that this order is only available in the Crown Court.

TWENTY-TWO

ASPECTS OF THE TARIFF

The aim of this chapter is to give an outline of certain aspects of the 'tariff', or 'going rate', for offences. Within the present context it is not possible to attempt a complete survey of all offences or of all Court of Appeal decisions. What can be conveyed is the basis of the tariff, the structure of the upper echelons of the tariff for serious offences, the relevance of guideline judgments and judgments on Attorney-General's references, and some aspects of the lower reaches of the tariff.

22.1 Structuring the Tariff

The 'going rate' of prison sentences for serious offences has developed since the late nineteenth century, and can be inferred from some of the judgments of the Court of Criminal Appeal in the first half of the twentieth century. However, it was not until 1975 that the Court of Appeal delivered a judgment that surveyed the upper echelons of the tariff and attempted to impose some logic on the different levels of sentence there. The leading case is *R* v *Turner* (1975) 61 Cr App R 67, where the court had to decide on the appropriate length of sentences for grave armed robberies. The court stated that 'it is not in the public interest that even for grave crimes, sentences should be passed which do not correlate sensibly and fairly with the time in prison which is likely to be served by somebody who has committed murder in circumstances in which there were no mitigating circumstances' (at pp. 90–1). The court took 15 years' imprisonment as the period likely to be served by such a murderer. That was equivalent to a determinate sentence of some 22 years, which, less the one-third remission which applied before 1992, would work out at 15 years in prison. So the court started from the position that determinate sentences should not usually exceed 22 years for non-murder offences.

Beneath this notional ceiling of 22 years should come, first, what Lawton LJ referred to as 'wholly abnormal' crimes — 'bomb outrages, acts of political terrorism and possibly in the future acts of political kidnapping'. Then, beneath that group of crimes, should come offences which are very grave but not 'wholly abnormal'. The court therefore concluded (at p. 91):

> . . . that the normal sentence for anyone taking part in a bank robbery or in the hold-up of a security or Post Office van, should be 15 years if firearms were carried and no serious injury done.
>
> . . . something must be added to the basic sentence passed on those who committed more than one robbery, but the maximum total sentence should not normally be more than 18 years. That is about the maximum sentence which should be passed for crimes which do not come into the category of offences on which we have put the description 'wholly abnormal'.

This framework is still used by the Court of Appeal as a means of ordering sentences at the top end of the scale, particularly in cases of armed robbery (see, e.g., *R* v *Copeland and Hegarty* (1994) 15 Cr App R (S) 601). It does not mean, however, that courts may never justifiably impose a determinate prison sentence longer than 22 years. In *R* v *Hindawi* (1988) 10 Cr App (S) 104 the offender had persuaded his girlfriend to carry on to an aircraft a bag, in which (unknown to her) he had placed an explosive device. The bomb was discovered before the aircraft took off, and he was convicted of attempting to place on an aircraft a device likely to destroy or damage the aircraft, contrary to the Criminal Attempts Act 1981 and the Aviation Security Act 1982. Upholding the sentence of 45 years' imprisonment, Lord Lane CJ, stated (at p. 105):

> Put briefly, this was about as foul and as horrible a crime as could possibly be imagined. It is no thanks to this applicant that his plot did not succeed in destroying 360 or 370 lives in the effort to promote one side of a political dispute by terrorism.
>
> In the judgment of this court the sentence of 45 years' imprisonment was not a day too long.

Both *Turner* and *Hindawi* were appeals in individual cases. During the 1980s the major developments came through guideline judgments, in which the Court of Appeal, usually with the Lord Chief Justice presiding, used the judgment in a particular case as a vehicle for laying down general guidance for dealing with offences of a certain kind. During the 1990s this approach has continued, bolstered by the use of judgments in Attorney-General's reference cases to give guidance. In the paragraphs that follow, special attention will be given to judgments of these two types.

22.1.1 ATTEMPTED MURDER

The penalty for murder is mandatory: life imprisonment. An offender who is convicted of attempted murder faces a maximum sentence of life imprisonment, but generally that sentence is reserved for offenders who are thought unstable and dangerous (see further **Chapter 23**). The range of sentences for attempted murder may be said to reflect the effective range for murder itself. Thus in *R* v *Al-Banna* (1984) 6 Cr App R (S) 426 the Court of Appeal upheld sentences of 35 and 30 years' imprisonment on men who had attempted to assassinate the Israeli ambassador in London, wounding him severely in the process. The court took the view that minimum recommended terms of 35 and 30 years for murder would have been appropriate if the victim had died. At the other end of the scale, sentences in the 10-12 year range have been approved for attempted murders arising out of 'domestic' quarrels (*R* v *Haynes* (1983) 5 Cr App R (S) 58; *R* v *Green* (1986) 8 Cr App R (S) 246; *R* v *Bedford* (1992) 14 Cr App R (S) 336).

22.1.2 ROBBERY

The judgment in *R* v *Turner* (1975) 61 Cr App R 67 remains the principal authority for serious armed robberies. However, the legal elements in robbery (theft, use or threat of violence) may be satisfied by a wide range of conduct, and for a push combined with the snatch of a purse the sentence will clearly be at the bottom of the scale. Whilst *Turner* sets the tariff at 15–18 years for armed robberies of banks, security vehicles and so on, much of the attention in recent years has focused on the sentencing of robberies outside the so-called 'first division'.

In *Attorney-General's Reference (No. 2 of 1989) (Major)* (1989) 11 Cr App R (S) 481 the offender had acted as lookout at a betting-shop robbery in which a gun had been used to injure the manager's leg and some £200 was taken. The offender had been unaware that the gun was loaded and played a secondary role in the offence, but the Court of Appeal nevertheless increased the sentence from three to seven years. In *Attorney-General's Reference (No. 9 of 1989) (Lacey)* (1990) 12 Cr App R (S) 7 the offender had smashed protective glass and threatened a sub-postmistress with a baseball bat, escaping with a small amount of money. The Court of Appeal increased the sentence from 30 months to five years. In *Attorney-General's References (Nos. 3, 4, 8, 9, 10, 11 and 16 of 1990)* (1990) 12 Cr App R (S) 479 the court seemed to establish a guideline range of four to seven years for cases of the following type:

> The small shop or off-licence often provides a valuable service to the local community. The shop is likely to have considerable sums of money upon the premises or

> upon the person of the proprietor. The premises are not likely to be able to afford the sort of protection in the shape of modern electronic devices which banks or building societies are able to install to protect their premises. Consequently . . . it is necessary for courts to make it clear that when this type of offender is apprehended he will be able to be subject to condign punishment.

In *Attorney-General's References (Nos. 5 and 6 of 1991)* (1992) 14 Cr App R (S) 425, two offenders who stole £10,000 from the safe at a service station, threatening the attendants with a loaded shotgun, had their sentences increased to seven and six years for the robbery (with 12 months consecutive for the shotgun offence).

22.1.3 RAPE

The Lord Chief Justice handed down a guideline judgment on sentencing for rape in *R v Billam* [1986] 1 WLR 349. The judgment begins with a discussion of the severe emotional and psychological trauma suffered by many victims of rape, and then moves to an examination of the sentencing statistics. Lord Lane concluded that rape was being under-sentenced in proportion to other crimes, and therefore set out guidelines designed to remedy that imbalance. Life imprisonment might be appropriate for mentally disturbed rapists, and a sentence of 15 years might be appropriate for an offender who has carried out a campaign of rapes. Beneath that:

> For rape committed by an adult without any aggravating or mitigating features, a figure of five years should be taken as the starting-point in a contested case. Where a rape is committed by two or more men acting together, or by a man who has broken into or otherwise gained access to a place where the victim is living, or by a person who is in a position of responsibility towards the victim, or by a person who abducts the victim and holds her captive, the starting-point should be eight years. ([1986] 1 WLR 349 at p. 351.)

The court then went on to list some of the possible aggravating factors and mitigating factors, which courts should take into account when assessing a particular case in relation to the guidelines (at p. 351):

> The crime should in any event be treated as aggravated by any of the following factors: (1) violence is used over and above the force necessary to commit the rape; (2) a weapon is used to frighten or wound the victim; (3) the rape is repeated; (4) the rape has been carefully planned; (5) the defendant has previous convictions for rape or other serious offences of a violent or sexual kind; (6) the victim is subject to further sexual indignities or perversions; (7) the victim is either very old or very young; (8) the effect upon the victim, whether physical or mental, is of special seriousness. Where any one or more of these aggravating features are present, the sentence should be substantially higher than the figure suggested as the starting-point.
>
> The extra distress which giving evidence can cause to a victim means that a plea of guilty, perhaps more so than in other cases, should normally result in some reduction from what would otherwise be the appropriate sentence. The amount of such reduction will of course depend on all the circumstances, including the likelihood of a finding of not guilty had the matter been contested.

Another important feature of the *Billam* judgment on rape is its clear statement of two factors which judges should *not* take into account when determining sentence:

> The fact that the victim may be considered to have exposed herself to danger by acting imprudently (as for instance by accepting a lift in a car from a stranger) is not a mitigating factor; and the victim's previous sexual experience is equally irrelevant.

The judgement also states that 'The starting-point for attempted rape should normally be less than for the completed offence, especially if it is desisted at a comparatively early stage'.

Subsequently, the guidelines have been developed in other decisions. In *Attorney-General's Reference (No. 7 of 1989)* (1990) 12 Cr App R (S) 1, the offender had been convicted of raping his former fiancée and had been sentenced to two years. The Court of Appeal increased the sentence to four-and-a-half years, for two main reasons. First, the mere fact that the parties had previously lived together and had regular sexual intercourse did not license the man to have intercourse with the woman after cohabitation had ceased, although 'it is a factor to which some weight can be given'. Second, there had not been a guilty plea, and therefore no reduction of sentence was due on that account. In *R* v *W* (1992) 14 Cr App R (S) 256 Lord Taylor of Gosforth CJ said that 'it should not be thought that a different and lower scale of sentencing attaches automatically to rape by a husband', and upheld a sentence of five years in a case with aggravating features and no plea of guilty. In two subsequent cases of rape of a cohabitant followed by forgiveness on the part of the victim, the Court of Appeal reduced the sentences (to five years in *R* v *Hutchinson* (1993) 15 Cr App R (S) 134, and to six years in a case with various aggravating features, *R* v *Hind* (1993) 15 Cr App R (S) 114), holding that the forgiveness meant that the trauma suffered by the victim was less than normal.

There is evidence that, even before the *Billam* judgment, sentences for rape were becoming longer. A Home Office study which compared rapes in 1973 and 1985 concluded that, although there were some increases in the seriousness of rape (in terms of the presence of aggravating factors), the overall change in sentencing levels between 1973 and 1985 was 'overwhelmingly attributable to a policy of severer sentencing' (Charles Lloyd and Roy Walmsley, *Rape Offences and Sentencing* (Home Office Research Study No. 105) (London: HMSO, 1989), p. 40). The effect of *Billam* was to endorse and accentuate that policy. Some evidence of its effects may be found in David Moxon, *Sentencing Practice in the Crown Court* (Home Office Research Study No. 103) (London: HMSO, 1988), based on analysis of the facts and sentences in some 2,000 cases heard in 1986–7. The six commonly sentenced offences with the longest average prison terms were as follows (p. 21):

	Average sentence (months)
Rape	62
Robbery	45
GBH (s. 18)	44
Drugs (supply)	22
Burglary (dwelling)	19
Fraud	14

These are 'net' figures, in the sense that they are the average sentences imposed after taking account of mitigating and aggravating factors, and they should not be confused with 'starting-points' for sentencing.

22.1.4 OTHER SERIOUS SEXUAL OFFENCES

Probably the oldest sentencing guideline case, *R* v *Willis* [1975] 1 WLR 292, gives some general guidance on the aggravating and mitigating features of buggery without the victim's consent. The most recent tendency has been to use similar starting points to those indicated by the *Billam* judgment on rape. Thus in *R* v *Mendez* (1991) 13 Cr App R (S) 94 the Court of Appeal upheld a sentence of five years, commenting that 'forcible buggery of a woman is equivalent to rape but worse than normal vaginal rape. . . . There is no mitigation here of a guilty plea. Indeed . . . one might well regard this as an aggravated rather than a standard rape'.

On incest the Court of Appeal laid down guidelines in *Attorney-General's Reference (No. 1 of 1989)* [1989] 1 WLR 1117. The judgment contains elaborate guidelines for the different forms of the offence, listing several aggravating and mitigating factors. A term of around six years was suggested where the girl is under 13 years; terms in the range from three to five years where the girl is aged 13 to 15; and terms of up to three years where the girl is aged at least 16. As with the *Billam* guidelines, a plea of guilty would reduce the sentence.

22.1.5 DRUG OFFENCES

The first major guideline judgment by Lord Lane CJ was *R* v *Aramah* (1982) 4 Cr App R (S) 407 on drugs. The judgment sets out sentencing levels for the importation, supply or possession of drugs in the various classes. An example of the style of the judgment is provided by the following extract, amended in the light of *R* v *Bilinski* (1987) 9 Cr App R (S) 360:

> I turn to the importation of heroin, morphine and so on. Large scale importation, that is where the street value of the consignment is in the order of £100,000 or more, sentences of [ten] years and upwards are appropriate. There will be cases where the values are of the order of £1 million or more, in which cases the offence should be visited by sentences of [14 years and upwards]. It will seldom be that an importer of any appreciable amount of the drug will deserve less than four years.
>
> This, however, is one area in which it is particularly important that offenders should be encouraged to give information to the police, and a confession of guilt, coupled with considerable assistance to the police, can properly be marked by a substantial reduction in what would otherwise be the proper sentence.
>
> . . . Importation of cannabis: importation of very small amounts for personal use can be dealt with as if it were simple possession. . . . Otherwise importation of amounts up to about 20 kilogrammes of herbal cannabis, or the equivalent in cannabis resin or cannabis oil, will, save in the most exceptional cases, attract sentences of between 18 months and three years, with the lowest ranges reserved for pleas of guilty in cases where there has been small profit to the offender. The good character of the courier (as he usually is) is of less importance than the good character of the defendant in other cases. The reason for this is, it is well known that the large-scale operator looks for couriers of good character and for people of a sort which is likely to exercise the sympathy of the court if they are detected and arrested. Consequently one will frequently find students and sick and elderly people are used as couriers. . . . There are few, if any, occasions when anything other than an immediate custodial sentence is proper in this type of importation.

The basis of the sentencing guidelines was changed more firmly from 'street value' to weight by the Court of Appeal in *R* v *Aroyewumi* [1994] Crim LR 695 (sometimes referred to as *Arunguren*). The intention of Lord Taylor CJ was to make the change without significantly altering effective sentence lengths. He held that sentences for the importation of 500 grammes of heroin or cocaine should be around ten years, and for 5 kilogrammes around 14 years. Other examples are also included in the judgment, which goes on to make the important point that not all drugs are of 100% purity. An allowance must therefore be made in the sentence where the drugs are of a lesser purity. The Lord Chief Justice laid down guidelines for the sentencing of 'ecstasy' cases in *R* v *Warren and Beeley* (1969) 1 Cr App R (S) 233, relating principally to the number of tablets involved in the importation or dealing.

22.1.6 SERIOUS DRIVING OFFENCES CAUSING DEATH

Guidelines for the former offence of causing death by reckless driving were laid down in *R* v *Boswell* [1984] 1 WLR 1047. In 1991 the offence of causing death by reckless driving was replaced by the offence of causing death by dangerous driving, a somewhat wider statutory formula. In 1993 the maximum penalty for causing death by dangerous driving was increased from five to ten years, and in *Attorney-General's References (Nos. 14 and 24 of 1993)* [1994] Crim LR 305 the Court of Appeal revised the *Boswell* guidelines upwards, so that they now read:

> The situation where there are no aggravating features present is that, so far as sentencing is concerned, a non-custodial penalty may well be appropriate, but where aggravating features, or an aggravating feature is present then a custodial sentence is generally necessary. At present, as already indicated, the statistics seem to show that the general maximum term is about 12 to 18 months as imposed by the courts.

> It is not easy to see why this should be so. Drivers who for example indulge in racing on the highways and/or driving with reckless disregard for the safety of others after taking alcohol, should understand that in bad cases they will lose their liberty for [upwards of five years]. It will seldom be that a community service order, or a suspended sentence will be appropriate in a serious case. By the same token that type of driver should be removed from the road by a long period of disqualification.

In 1993 the maximum penalty for the offence of causing death by careless driving while affected by alcohol, introduced in 1991, was also doubled to ten years. It is not clear whether this is the lesser offence of the two, and whether any case in which the driving was dangerous would be charged as causing death by dangerous driving. Prosecutors, seeing the same maxima, might select the easier offence on the facts of each case. The decision in *Attorney-General's References (Nos. 14 and 24 of 1993)* affords little guidance, since the offences there were committed at a time when the maximum stood at five years.

One apparent anomaly is that the offence of causing death by aggravated vehicle taking remains subject to a maximum sentence of five years (although this offence has fairly low culpability requirements). In *R* v *Ore* [1994] Crim LR 304 the Court of Appeal upheld sentences of four years' detention in a young offender institution imposed on young men of 20, on facts that were close to the worst conceivable type of case. Earlier, in the case of *R* v *Bird* (1993) 14 Cr App R (S) 343 the Lord Chief Justice laid down sentencing guidelines for this offence under the Aggravated Vehicle-Taking Act 1992. The most important circumstance is the fact that the vehicle was driven dangerously, since that bears on the culpability of the driver. In assessing that, the driving should be assessed according to 'how bad it was and for how long'. Presumably some of the factors stated in the guideline judgment on reckless driving in *R* v *Boswell* (above) are relevant. In this context, however, Lord Taylor acknowledged that 'the incidence and severity of any injury or damage caused were to some extent a matter of chance', and were thus only 'to a lesser extent' aggravating. This may be compared with *R* v *Krawec* (1984) 6 Cr App R (S) 367 on careless driving (sentence on degree of deviation from proper standard, not unforeseen results) and with *R* v *Steel* (1993) 14 Cr App R (S) 218 on reckless driving (gravity of unforeseen consequences relevant to sentence).

22.1.7 SERIOUS WOUNDINGS

Serious woundings in which an intent to kill can be proved may well result in conviction for attempted murder and will be sentenced accordingly. Sentences for wounding with intent to cause grievous bodily harm, and other forms of the offence under the Offences against the Person Act 1861, s. 18, slot into the tariff just below attempted murder. In *R* v *Sullivan* (1987) 9 Cr App R (S) 196 the Court of Appeal upheld a sentence of 15 years for luring a man out of a house and then shooting him in both legs. This case, aggravated by the use of a firearm, is among the most serious. The normal range seems to be from six to ten years for stabbings and for attacks with blunt instruments. For example, the beating of an elderly man with a hammer was held to justify nine years in *Attorney-General's Reference (No. 13 of 1992)* (1992) 14 Cr App R (S) 756. Offences of 'glassing', in which a beer glass is used to wound the face, have tended to attract sentences in the three- to five-year range.

22.1.8 THEFT IN BREACH OF TRUST

In the wake of several cases where uncertainty about the correct sentencing level for thefts in breach of trust had become apparent, Lord Lane CJ delivered a guideline judgment in *R* v *Barrick* (1985) 7 Cr App R (S) 142. Pointing out that most of these offenders will be of good previous character, Lord Lane stated that:

> In general a term of immediate imprisonment is inevitable, save in very exceptional circumstances or where the amount of money obtained is small. Despite the great punishment that offenders of this sort bring upon themselves, the court should nevertheless pass a sufficiently substantial term of imprisonment to mark publicly the gravity of the offence. The sum involved is obviously not the only factor to be considered, but it may in many cases provide a useful guide. Where the amounts

> involved cannot be described as small but are less than £10,000 or thereabouts, terms of imprisonment ranging from the very short up to about 18 months are appropriate. . . . Cases involving sums of between about £10,000 and £50,000 will merit a term of about two to three years' imprisonment. Where greater sums are involved, for example those over £100,000, then a term of three and a half years to four and a half years would be justified. . . . In any case where a plea of guilty is entered however the court should give the appropriate discount.

Lord Lane went on to list some of the aggravating and mitigating factors in this type of case. Many lesser forms of theft in breach of trust, committed by sales assistants and cashiers, might be dealt with summarily (but cf. *R* v *McCormick*, discussed at **21.5.2.1**). The Magistrates' Association Sentencing Guidelines (1993 version) indicate an 'entry point' of a community penalty for these offences, and list four factors that might reduce seriousness: impulsive action, newly employed junior, single item, small amount.

22.1.9 BURGLARY OF A DWELLING

Burglary of a dwelling still carries a maximum of 14 years, while the maximum for other forms of burglary was reduced to ten years by the Criminal Justice Act 1991. Some four-fifths of burglaries in a dwelling tried at the Crown Court result in custody, and there is much recent authority to the effect that a single burglary without aggravating features may justify a sentence of around 18 months' imprisonment on an adult. Thus in *R* v *James* (1991) 12 Cr App R (S) 624 the Court of Appeal held that a man who broke into an unoccupied house and stole a video recorder, admitting his guilt fully when arrested, should be sentenced to 18 months' imprisonment. The man had a long record of burglaries. (See also *R* v *Harvey* (1990) 12 Cr App R (S) 165 and *R* v *Tams* (1990) 12 Cr App R (S) 591.)

The decision in *R* v *Mussell* (1990) 12 Cr App R (S) 607 laid down general guidance for the sentencing of dwellinghouse burglaries. Lord Lane CJ held that the general level of sentences should reflect the anxiety and distress to householders commonly caused by the offence. He emphasised the aggravating effect of premeditation and planning, and also any ransacking or fouling of the house during the burglary. Particularly important was his concluding remark: that burglary of a dwelling is not always so serious that only a custodial sentence can be justified. 'An example would be that of a sneak thief walking past an open door, who puts his hand inside the door and steals a £5 note or some food from the kitchen table.' Indeed, some burglaries of dwellings are properly tried in magistrates' courts.

22.1.10 THEFT FROM A SHOP

In his survey of *Sentencing Practice in the Crown Court* (Home Office Research Study No. 103) (London: HMSO, 1988), Moxon found that 30% of persons sentenced in the Crown Court for theft from a shop received unsuspended custody. Many of these will involve offenders with previous convictions. We have already seen that since the 1991 Act some relatively minor property offences have been held to be so serious that only custody can be justified (see *R* v *Keogh* discussed in **21.5.2**). However, the majority of offences of shop theft will be sentenced in magistrates' courts, where the Sentencing Guidelines indicate that the 'entry point' for this offence should be a fine, the guideline fine being £270. Factors that may render the offence more serious include: offence committed on bail, adult involving children, high value, organised team, planned, previous convictions and failures to respond (if relevant).

22.2 Counsel and the Tariff

It will be evident that this chapter has discussed in outline only a small number of offences for which sentence may be passed. Within the context of the course, however, this should be sufficient to give a general idea of the sentencing tariff. How should counsel ascertain the 'going rate' for a particular offence? The following checklist may be helpful:

(a) Is there a guideline judgment for this offence? (This may be found in an ordinary appeal judgment or an Attorney-General's reference case.)

(b) If not, do the decisions collated and classified in Dr Thomas's loose-leaf encyclopaedia, *Current Sentencing Practice*, disclose a pattern or a clear range of sentences?

(c) How do those decisions relate to the actual sentencing practice of the courts for this crime? Court of Appeal cases are often said to be untypical, and it is important to find out whether the going rate in practice is significantly lower than the appellate decisions suggest. One way of doing this is to consult the latest volume of *Criminal Statistics*, although it must be remembered that the sentencing statistics give only 'net' figures, reflecting sentences arrived at after taking account of any aggravating or mitigating factors in each case. The importance of this factor may be seen in the cases of burglary in a dwelling cited in **22.1.9** above: 18 months' imprisonment for a single burglary might be approved for an adult offender with a long record, but it is most unlikely to be approved for a younger offender with few or no previous convictions.

(d) If the case is in a magistrates' court, consult the latest version of the Magistrates' Association Sentencing Guidelines (now, the 1993 revision). It is, however, worth checking whether the guidelines are respected in the particular court, since they have not been adopted in some areas.

22.3 The 1996 White Paper on Sentencing

The tariff will be altered in significant ways if the Government's proposals in its White Paper, *Protecting the Public*, (London: HMSO, Cm 3190), are implemented. We have already seen that the courts would be called upon to reduce the length of the sentences announced in court if the proposed move to greater 'honesty in sentencing' takes place (see **21.6.4**). There are also three further proposals for mandatory sentences for certain repeat offenders. In brief, the Government proposes:

(a) a mandatory sentence of life imprisonment for a second serious violent or sexual offence: the court would set the appropriate tariff term, but the sentence would enable the Parole Board to keep such an offender in prison if he was still considered dangerous (see further **Chapter 23**);

(b) a mandatory minimum sentence of seven years' imprisonment for a third conviction for class A drug dealing: the court would be required to impose this sentence unless there were 'genuinely exceptional circumstances', and the minimum term would be seven years under the new system (i.e. the equivalent of about ten years under the present system of early release);

(c) a mandatory minimum sentence of three years' imprisonment for a third conviction of burglary in a dwelling: the court would be required to impose this sentence unless there were 'genuinely exceptional circumstances', and the minimum term would be three years under the new system (i.e. the equivalent of over four years under the present system of early release). The major difference in the burglary proposal is that all three qualifying convictions would have to take place after the implementation of the statute, thereby delaying its effect for some years.

These proposals have been criticised by the Lord Chief Justice and others. Among the concerns are: that mandatory sentences may force judges to pass unjust sentences in certain cases; that 'genuinely exceptional' would have to be construed fairly tightly; that an offence such as burglary may be little more than a walk-in theft (see **22.1.9** above); and that the proposals appear to preclude any discount for pleading guilty (see **20.3.1**), which will result in more trials and longer delays. It remains to be seen whether, and in what form, the proposals are carried forward.

TWENTY-THREE

DANGEROUSNESS AND MENTAL DISORDER

23.1 Introduction

This is an enormous area which it is only possible to skate over in the course of one chapter. There are several good texts and research studies dealing with different aspects of the subject, which will certainly need to be read if counsel's practice is to take in, for example, considerable work with Mental Health Review Tribunals. It is also an area with which most members of the Bar will have some acquaintance, but one which will only be a commonplace for few. Mentally disordered offenders and offenders considered dangerous by the courts are only rarely encountered in criminal practice. (A good simple guide to the Mental Health Act 1983 is given in Gostin, L. and Rassaby, E., *Guide to the Mental Health Act 1983* (London: MIND, 1984).) Both medical diagnoses and legal provisions, as well as the problems with the system are covered in Bluglass, R. and Bowden, P., A *Textbook of Forensic Psychiatry* (London: Livingstone, 1990). Facilities for mentally disordered offenders are discussed in Gostin, L., *Secure Provision* (London: Tavistock, 1985). The main findings of the Floud report on dangerousness and a summary of the research evidence are in Floud, J. and Young, W., *Dangerousness and Criminal Justice* (London: Heinemann, 1981). The workings of Mental Health Tribunals and the legal criteria involved are meticulously argued and documented in Peay, J., *Tribunals on Trial* (Oxford: OUP, 1989).)

This is the paradox. The rhetoric of dangerousness is very prevalent in sentencing decisions, and the volume of academic literature and of policy decisions concerning dangerousness is considerable. However, the numbers of people given disposals reflecting dangerousness or mental disorder specifically are extremely small. There are several specialist sentences, but compared to the non-custodial alternatives previously discussed and compared to imprisonment, the numbers are minute. The rule must be that if you are likely to have to deal with someone for whom the words 'mental disorder' or 'dangerousness' are likely to crop up, it is important to look up the relevant powers of the court beforehand. They are complicated, and even if you are guided to the right sentence by medical and pre-sentence reports when you arrive at court, you still need to know what they are talking about.

In a study of mitigation in the late 1970s, the counsel interviewed found cases involving mentally disordered defendants problematic (Shapland, J., *Between Conviction and Sentence* (London: Routledge & Kegan Paul, 1981)). Part of the problem was that the perspective of defence counsel might need to be slightly different. In mitigation you are promoting the best interests of your client according to the instructions you are given. You may feel that your client's wishes are not always the best thing to get him or her the non-custodial sentence he or she desires. But providing you are not misleading the court you must follow them. With a mentally disordered client, it can be very difficult — you will feel that you need to do what will be in his or her best interests. But this may not entirely be as per instructions. Essentially there is no obvious fixed answer to this. Your twin duties remain, but it is specially important to listen to your client and to explain the options to him or her. Not all mentally disordered clients are incapable — if they have been found guilty, they must by definition be responsible for their actions. So they must be considered as being able to take some responsibility in considering what mitigation to put forward. It is now good psychiatric practice to include clients as far as possible in decisions affecting them. Decisions on mitigation are clearly important ones. But involving disordered people will take more time, which needs to be allowed for. It may be helpful to seek advice from the probation service, since they are likely to have more experience than counsel with certain kinds of disorder.

23.1.1 THE RELATION BETWEEN MENTAL DISORDER AND DANGEROUSNESS

It is very important to realise that there is no necessary connection between mental disorder and dangerousness. Violent offenders, terrorists and so forth, are clearly dangerous, but may well not be mentally disordered at all. Equally, most of the offences committed by the mentally disordered are property offences and such defendants should not be considered any more dangerous than any other offender committing the same kinds of offence. Though there may be a connection between the disorder and the commission of offences, there may well not be. For less serious offenders, the legislation on mentally disordered offenders has primarily been influenced by humanitarian considerations of the need to ensure treatment for such offenders.

At the most serious end of the spectrum of offences, however, the legislation has clearly been influenced by the problem of the continuing dangerousness of offenders who are mentally disordered. The protection of the public is seen as the priority, although treatment for the offender is also important, both to reduce the likelihood of re-offending and for humanitarian reasons.

It is important, therefore, to distinguish those sentencing provisions primarily intended to deal with the dangerous from those primarily intended for the mentally disordered. The new proposals in the 1996 White Paper (see **15.7**) are clearly intended for dangerous and persistent offenders, but not specifically for mentally disordered offenders.

23.2 Dangerousness

There are several provisions specifically designed to deal with those considered dangerous by the courts, but they vary in the extent to which the defendants given these sentences might be mentally disordered. The major provisions are:

(a) determinate prison sentences which are longer than those commensurate with the seriousness of the offence, under CJA 1991, ss. 1(2)(b) and 2(2)(b) (no need to show any evidence of mental disorder) — see **23.2.3**;

(b) a sentence of life imprisonment (only available for offences which carry life as their maximum sentence), for which the courts normally require some evidence of mental disorder (though no specific disorder need be diagnosed) — see **23.6.2(f)**;

(c) a restriction order under the Mental Health Act 1983, for which the offender must be diagnosed as mentally disordered and falling within one of the four categories of mental disorder defined in s. 1 of the Act — see **23.6.2(d)**.

We shall deal first with the problems of defining and measuring dangerousness, before turning to the CJA 1991 provisions for those who are not mentally disordered.

23.2.1 THE DIFFICULTY OF DEFINING 'DANGEROUSNESS'

There has been considerable and unceasing controversy about dangerousness, with the most vexed questions centering on the problem of definition.

The statutes have taken one of two approaches. Some have set out elaborate rules relating to previous convictions and the current offence in order to try to specify the kinds of defendants who would be eligible for what is usually considerable extra punishment. But these elaborate schemes have tended to pick up the persistent nuisance or property offender, rather than the violent offender at whom they were aimed, because violent offenders are only rarely reconvicted for violence on several occasions within a relatively short time span. The 1996 White Paper proposals do not, however, specify any time period for previous convictions to attract the 'automatic' life sentence.

The other approach is the 'everybody knows' approach: that you cannot define dangerousness but you can recognise it when you see it. It is sad that the 1990 White Paper and the CJA 1991 adopt this approach (see **Chapter 21**). The White Paper advocates that dangerous and serious offenders should be given long sentences out of the range of the normal offences of the type (though still within the statutory maximum). The requirement on judges to remain within a range specified by 'just deserts' and the tariff will be lessened, though reasons will clearly be required. The difficulty with the 'everybody knows' approach is that it leaves almost total discretion to the judiciary and the medical profession on necessarily imprecise grounds. There is thus some potential for abuse, and difficulty in formulating guidelines so that counsel, probation officers and the public can understand what is happening.

The White Paper states that:

> The Government proposes to take this approach (of the Court of Appeal) further by giving the Crown Court power to give custodial sentences longer than would be justified by the seriousness of the offence to persistent violent and sexual offenders, if this is necessary to protect the public from serious harm. There are a small number of offenders who become progressively more dangerous and who are a real risk to public safety. Some will be mentally disordered and can be detained under mental health legislation. For those convicted of the most serious crimes, a sentence of life imprisonment may be justified. The proposed restrictions on the use of custody in the White Paper will not apply to the most serious crimes which are tried only in the Crown Court. Some offenders will be convicted of less serious offences but the Crown Court will recognise that they are a serious risk to the public. In these circumstances the Government considers that an exception should be made to the principle that the length of the individual sentence should be justified by the seriousness of the offence. The Crown Court would be able to give a longer sentence within the maximum penalty for the offences for which the offender has been convicted. . . . The Court would, of course have to state in open court why it was giving a longer sentence and it would be open to the defendant to appeal against his sentence.

A similar approach is currently used in the restriction order where all that is required is to show that it is necessary in order to protect the public from serious harm, the nature of such harm being left undefined.

Note, by the way, the problems of this approach in dealing with the dangerous. The difficulty with all determinate sentencing (the foundation of a 'just deserts' approach) in relation to the dangerous is that it does not deal with those you do not want to release at the end of their sentence. In essence, it is the prospect of release that always causes concern, rather than the problem of detention at the time of sentencing (where the concern is usually from the human rights angle). It is not possible by definition to solve the problem of release at the time of sentence. This is the reason given for adopting an indeterminate sentencing approach in the 1996 White Paper — though requiring a mandatory life sentence for any second conviction for a serious violent/sexual offence seems a drastic remedy.

23.2.2 THE FLOUD REPORT

The major review of this subject in this country remains the Floud report (Floud, J., 'Dangerousness and Criminal Justice' (1984) *British Journal of Criminology*, pp. 213–18). The report weighed up all these difficulties. It fastened on the unchanging and most problematic area of dealing with the dangerous: the difficulty of definition and of prediction. Floud separated the idea of risk from the idea of danger. A risk can be measured: it is the basis of actuarial prediction (and of the cost of our insurance policies). But danger incorporates as well the weighting that people put on different kinds of risk. We tend to ignore the risk of driving or walking along the road. We are much more fearful of the much smaller risks of nuclear power, and of being injured or killed by a dangerous offender.

As Floud states:

> The English sentencing system does not provide explicitly for 'dangerous' offenders. The statutes contain no reference to them. There is mention of 'dangerous' driving and 'dangerous' drugs but the word 'dangerous' is nowhere used to define *persons* for sentencing purposes. It is not that the courts do not recognise the difference between 'ordinary' and 'dangerous' offenders, for in practice they do. But in marked contrast to the position in most other countries, our arrangements for protecting the public from legally responsible serious offenders who present a continuing risk are almost wholly discretionary and *ad hoc* in character. . . .
>
> The concept of the 'dangerous offender' is to be found at three points in the English system of criminal justice. It comes closest to legal recognition through judicial practice in the use of the life-sentence for those few non-homicidal offences for which it is available as the maximum penalty; and to administrative definition in the arrangements for classifying prisoners for security purposes. But even in these circumscribed contexts, it is imprecise. Not surprisingly, it is still more so when ordinary, determinate sentences are used for protective purposes, whether they be sentences outside the normal range for a handful of abnormal crimes whose perpetrators are explicitly judged to be dangerous, or sentences within the normal range but more or less covertly longer than they would have been had the court not perceived the need to provide the public with extra protection.
>
> In short, the concept of dangerousness in English criminal justice is prevalent but elusive. It is not used consistently or with any precision and the nature of the risk to which it refers is never clearly defined. . . .
>
> The practical difficulties and ethical dilemmas of protective sentencing are mutually reinforcing. ... We reached a conclusion which is not surprising, in so far as it amounts to saying that, since it is impossible to be sure how people will behave in the future, if only because of the working of chance, any attempt to apply precautions selectively against some persons for the sake of others is bound to be more or less wide of the mark. What is surprising — and very alarming — is to discover just how wide of the mark it turns out to be, whenever it is possible to put predictive judgments to the test by following the post-release careers of 'dangerous' offenders. Statisticians have calculated the probabilities: so many judgments of *dangerous* falsified by the offender's subsequent behaviour (that is to say, by his failure to cause further grave harm) and so many judgments of *safe* falsified by the further serious offences he commits. Not surprisingly, it tends to be the critics of protective sentencing who worry about the former and members of the general public who worry about the latter. But the former figure, the proportion of falsified judgments of *dangerous*, even at its lowest, is so uncomfortably high that no-one engaged in making predictive judgments in the administration of justice can fail to be impressed — or, more likely, depressed. As matters now stand, parole boards and similar bodies, to say nothing of courts, are, on average, at best as likely to be wrong as right in thinking that the offenders they decide to detain as dangerous will actually do further serious harm if left at large. Whatever be the prospects of improvement — and it must be admitted that, though they exist, they are not rosy and are forever constrained by a large factor of chance, it is likely that at least two persons are detained for every one person who is prevented from doing serious harm. This is to say that each offender in protective custody probably suffers, in addition to the usual

hardships of imprisonment, at least a 50% risk of being unnecessarily detained. On what grounds are we justified in doing him this grave harm — for grave harm it undoubtedly is, on any reckoning?

23.2.3 CRIMINAL JUSTICE ACT 1991 PROVISIONS RELATING TO DANGEROUSNESS

Under CJA 1991, s. 1(2)(b), for a violent or sexual offence, a court may pass a custodial sentence if it is of the opinion that 'only such a sentence would be adequate to protect the public from serious harm' from the offender. Under s. 2(2)(b), again only for a violent or sexual offence, the court may pass a custodial sentence 'for such longer term (not exceeding the maximum) as in the opinion of the court is necessary to protect the public from serious harm from the offender'. Both of these powers permit courts to pass sentences which are longer (or more severe) than normal on the grounds of public protection, i.e., that the offender is considered potentially dangerous.

Both 'violent offence' and 'sexual offence' are defined in s. 31(1) of the Act:

> *'violent offence' means an offence which leads, or is intended or likely to lead, to a person's death or to physical injury to a person, and includes an offence which is required to be charged as arson (whether or not it would otherwise fall within this definition).*

Note here that there is no specific list of offences and so any offence which either causes injury or is likely to lead to injury may qualify. This might, for example, include dangerous driving.

> *'sexual offence' means an offence under the Sexual Offences Act 1956, the Indecency with Children Act 1960, the Sexual Offences Act 1967, section 54 of the Criminal Law Act 1977 or the Protection of Children Act 1978, other than—*
> *(a) an offence under section 12 or 13 of the Sexual Offences Act 1956 which would not be an offence but for section 2 of the Sexual Offences Act 1967;*
> *(b) an offence under section 30, 31 or 33 to 36 of the said Act of 1956; and*
> *(c) an offence under section 4 or 5 of the said Act of 1967.*

The definition of 'sexual offence' has been revised by sch. 9, para. 45 to the Criminal Justice and Public Order Act 1994 to now include burglary with intent to rape.

The other approach to defining dangerousness — producing a list of offences — has not been used here. It might be thought that attempts (for example, attempted rape) are not included as 'sexual offences', since they are not specifically mentioned. However, since attempted rape (and most other attempted sexual offences) are included in the penalty schedule of the Sexual Offences Act 1956, it has been held to be an offence 'under' that Act and so defendants charged with attempted rape are potentially under the ambit of these provisions of the CJA 1991 (*R* v *Robinson* [1993] 1 WLR 168).

'Serious harm' is defined in the CJA 1991, s. 31(3):

> *In this part, any reference, in relation to an offender convicted of a violent or sexual offence, to protecting the public from serious harm from him shall be construed as a reference to protecting members of the public from death or serious personal injury, whether physical or psychological, occasioned by further such offences committed by him.*

Before imposing a longer than normal sentence under s. 2(2)(b), the court should always give a warning to counsel (*R* v *Baverstock* [1993] 1 WLR 202). The court should also obtain and consider a pre-sentence report, and obtain and consider any information about the circumstances of the case.

There have been some early indications of the Court of Appeal's view of these cases. They fall into two types: ones where the court has been reviewing ordinary determinate sentences passed under s. 2(2)(a), but has considered them as justified under s. 2(2)(b); and a very few which were originally given longer sentences for public protection under s. 2(2)(b). They have given us indications of the court's view on the kinds of information seen as suitable for courts to consider when thinking of a longer than normal sentence, and of the kinds of offence in which such sentences have been used.

23.2.3.1 The information the court may consider for s. 2(2)(b) cases

If the offence is a 'violent' or a 'sexual' offence, then it has been held that it is the court's *mandatory* duty to consider whether a longer sentence is necessary to protect the public from serious harm (*R* v *Bowler* (1993) 15 Cr App R (S) 78). Counsel should, therefore, be prepared whenever a client is charged with such an offence.

How can the court see if serious harm might result, i.e., whether there is a predisposition to violence or sexual assault? There is no bar to the court considering previous convictions and a range of similar previous convictions (for violent or sexual offences) may be seen as such a predisposition. There does not have to be evidence that serious harm was actually caused in the past (*Bowler*).

Though most of the cases have related to physical injury ('serious personal injury'), the likelihood of future serious psychological injury being caused to members of the public would also be sufficient to found a longer sentence (*Bowler*). The potential serious harm need not be to the public in general or to average members of the public: those who are more vulnerable to this kind of psychological injury should also be considered if the defendant is likely to prey upon them (*Bowler*). The target of this future serious harm might even be just one particular person. *R* v *Nicholas* (1993) 15 Cr App R (S) 381 was a domestic violence case involving a charge of actual bodily harm and here it was said that the likelihood of serious harm to that victim in the future would be sufficient, though in the circumstances of that case it was held that there was little likelihood of a recurrence. The potential scope of the s. 2(2)(b) provision is hence wide.

All reports and all information available to the court will be considered and both pre-sentence reports and psychiatric reports have been seen as providing evidence in relation to the risk of reoffending. In *R* v *Oudkerk* (1995) 16 Cr App R (S) 172, the Court of Appeal stated that where the court contemplates the imposition of a longer than normal sentence under s. 2(2)(b), in addition to putting the defendant upon notice, it will be necessary for the sentencing court to resolve by a *Newton* hearing any important issue relevant to the application of the section (in that case, whether the defendant knew the victim and the assault was a 'lover's tiff', or whether he had attacked a stranger). The court should also have adequate information on the defendant's previous convictions. In *R* v *Fawcett* (1995) 16 Cr App R (S) 55, it was held that the court should obtain a medical report before passing a s. 2(2)(b) sentence if the danger was due to a medical or personality problem, in order to exclude the need to make a medical disposal.

23.2.3.2 The offences for which s. 2(2)(b) has been used

There has been a range of cases of indecent assault in which the Court of Appeal has approved the use of a s. 2(2)(b) sentence. In fact, David Thomas, in his commentary on *R* v *Lyons* [1994] Crim LR 145 considered this case of indecent assault as a 'classic case'. The offender admitted a relatively serious indecent assault on a woman on her own in a public place and had previous convictions for similar offences (thus indicating a predisposition). The pre-sentence report indicated some disorder, including a distorted attitude to women and a psychiatric report said the appellant was a great danger to women. The sentence of five years under s. 2(2)(b) was upheld. Although this case involved possible mental disorder (though not treatable or in need of treatment), other cases (for example, *R* v *Bowler* discussed in **23.2.3.1**) have involved no element of mental disorder. Quite often the previous convictions have been relatively minor offences (for example, *R* v *Apelt* (1993) 15 Cr App R (S) 420).

It must not be thought, however, that these provisions are reserved for indecent assault cases. Longer sentences have already been justified by the Court of Appeal for charges of unlawful wounding (*R* v *Coull* (1993) 15 Cr App R (S) 305), robbery (*R* v

Fowler (1993) 15 Cr App R (S) 456), s. 18 wounding (*R* v *Utip* (1993) 14 Cr App R (S) 746, *R* v *Clarke* (1993) 15 Cr App R (S) 102), and even for s. 47 plus threatening to kill (*R* v *Etchells* [1995] Crim LR 754). Sometimes, the sentence upheld under s. 2(2)(b) is only slightly longer than that which the court would see as appropriate to the seriousness of the instant offence in any case.

In *R* v *Mansell* (1994) 15 Cr App R (S) 771, the Lord Chief Justice, sitting in the Court of Appeal, held that, in determining the additional period that needed to be added on, in a s. 2(2)(b) case, the sentencer had to perform a balancing act.

> In theory, someone who was addicted to conduct which could cause serious harm to members of the public might need to be prevented from doing so for a very long time. In the ultimate case, an indeterminate sentence might be necessary where the harm was likely to be very serious and the predilection for indulging in such conduct looked likely to continue for an indefinite time. The sentencer in each individual case had to try to balance the need to protect the public on the one hand with the need to look at the totality of the sentence and see that it was not out of all proportion with the nature of the offending.

This suggests that the extent of the risk of re-offending has to be balanced against the seriousness (and hence the potential harm) of the instant offence and of any future offences. Similarly, in *R* v *Crow and Pennington* [1994] Crim LR 958, it was indicated that the sentence should bear a reasonable relationship to the offence for which it is imposed.

23.3 Basic Premises of the Criminal Justice System in Dealing with the Mentally Disordered

23.3.1 DIAGNOSING MENTAL DISORDER

The basic choice for any criminal justice system in dealing with the mentally disordered is between keeping the offender in the penal system and dealing with him or her in the same way as any other offender (which is seen by many as fair), and handing him or her over to the mental health professionals. For many years now, the system in England and Wales has taken the view that, in theory, an offender who has been found to be mentally disordered should receive special treatment which is relevant to his or her condition. A number of special sentences have been set up which have the effect of handing him or her over for medical treatment to the mental health services. The court does not retain any further stake. In practice, however, the position is very much more complicated. First he or she needs to be diagnosed as mentally disordered, not just according to the prevailing medical criteria, but, if he or she is to receive a specific sentence, according to the legal criteria laid down in the relevant Act.

23.3.2 THE LEGAL DEFINITIONS OF MENTAL DISORDERS

For most of the civil and criminal disposals in England and Wales, the legal definitions of the various forms of disorder are set out in the Mental Health Act 1983, s. 1. Four main groups of mental disorder are defined: mental illness, severe impairment, impairment, and psychopathic disorder. Very briefly, 'mental illness' includes those abnormalities considered to be illnesses, such as schizophrenia or manic depression, but it is not actually defined anywhere. 'Severe impairment' and 'impairment' are defects in intelligence, where 'severe impairment' means that the patient is incapable of living an independent life or of guarding himself against serious exploitation. 'Psychopathic disorder', the most controversial, means 'a persistent disorder or disability of mind (whether or not including significant impairment of intelligence) which results in abnormally aggressive or seriously irresponsible conduct on the part of the person concerned'. Note that, in the case of offenders, the addition of the behavioural part of the definition does not change anything — it was primarily included on humanitarian grounds in respect of civil patients.

There are two points to note from the presence of these legal definitions for diagnosis:

(a) If a person is not considered by a doctor to fall within the categories laid out in s. 1, then, however much that doctor or that court may think that that person is mentally disordered, he or she cannot be given any of the disposals which take their definition from s. 1.

(b) For all 'medical disposals', the courts are dependent upon one or more doctors (depending upon the sentence involved) stating that the person fits the legal category before any sentence can be imposed. In this way, one can see the doctor as the 'gateway' to medical disposals, just as the probation officer is the gateway to probation or supervision orders. Particularly in respect to mental illness, which is undefined, it is difficult for anyone, including lawyers, to challenge current medical opinion. This is exacerbated by the lack of recognised medical standards as regards the diagnosis and treatment of mental disorder, so that what happens in an individual case is difficult to match against any accepted standards of treatment practice.

The definitions above come from the Mental Health Act 1983, which governs the entry criteria for hospital orders and restriction orders — the only powers for compulsory detention in a mental hospital. Other definitions lie in other Acts. For example, the condition of mental treatment with a probation order comes under the CJA 1991. The court may make such a condition if it receives evidence from a medical practitioner and the court is satisfied that the offender's mental condition 'requires and is susceptible to treatment but is not such as to warrant his detention in pursuance of a hospital order' (sch. 1A). Here there are no specific legal diagnoses and no attempt to define the nature of the treatment or the disorder. It is therefore a potentially much wider measure, but of course requires the consent of the defendant (like all other conditions to probation orders). It will, therefore, not be suitable for all.

Other provisions which often are used to deal with the mentally disordered fall under other legislation and rules: the M'Naghten Rules, manslaughter by reason of diminished responsibility, being found unfit to plead. Each has its own legal definition of the types of disorder which the defendant must satisfy. For each, medical evidence is often called, but its weight varies with the different provisions. These are all relatively rare matters, certainly when beginning practice, and all will require further preparation using the considerable literature which has accumulated on them.

23.4 Detection of Disorder

23.4.1 READING THE CLUES

The need for detection of disorder was mentioned in **23.3.1** above, and must occur before any medical report can be requested. What will give a clue that such a report might be useful?

Any defendant will have been seen by the police and by his defence lawyer before he or she appears in court. If he or she seems to behave in a bizarre fashion, either while committing the crime or while talking to these people, someone may think to ask for a medical report to be prepared. Again, if the defendant mentions to the probation officer who is preparing a pre-sentence report or to his or her defence solicitor or counsel that he or she has previously had treatment for mental disorder, then someone may think to ask to have a medical report prepared. It is all a bit hit and miss though — and it is important for counsel to be watching out for such signs.

Shirley Salem has carried out a large study of remands for psychiatric assessment in magistrates' courts, and this provides a considerable amount of clarification as to what the courts thought they were doing when they asked for psychiatric reports. Remands served two functions for the court: to provide information on that defendant, and, in some cases, to arrange psychiatric treatment. Courts did not normally expect a recommendation for treatment to be the result: only 25% of defendants in the sample were thought possibly to require a hospital order and an additional 11% a probation order with condition of psychiatric treatment.

In general, courts were responding to requests from courtroom participants (primarily defence legal representatives, but also police and probation officers — 44%) rather than taking the initiative themselves (21%). Note that this implies a need for representation in such cases.

23.4.2 PSYCHIATRIC MODELS

The people who were remanded fell into two groups: those thought to have serious mental disorder and those for whom the court thought that the offence and the possible sentence was serious enough to require agreement with any defence/probation officer request for a report. So, in these latter cases, the process focused on those more at risk of a custodial sentence.

However, doctors, courts and probation officers appeared to be working on different models of who is disordered and should receive treatment. This causes fundamental problems for the service provided for mentally disordered offenders.

The medical model (which the psychiatrist making the report will normally adopt, i.e. the gateway for treatment facilities) implies that the courts should identify defendants who are seriously disordered according to the current medical views of treatable disorder (i.e. psychotic or organic disorders and some emotive disorders). However, the courts also felt that medical intervention was required when defendants were incapable of surviving independently in the community due to past or present disorder. This includes people with chronic conditions (which would not be seen as 'treatable') or those with personality disorders (including psychopaths).

In addition, probation officers tended to be working on a psychotherapeutic model (not surprising, since this is still the currently fashionable model in training). This would include patients with personality disorders and alcohol/drug related disorders, who might benefit from out-patient or day-patient facilities.

So courts are to some extent limiting remands to available services and the views of those who administer them, but also registering protest. Clearly, doctors, courts and probation officers do not entirely agree on who should benefit from 'medical disposals'. It is a recipe for continuing disagreement, as has been shown in the pronouncements of the Court of Appeal. Other work also indicates that all parties are far more likely to think of psychiatric explanations for conduct and order psychiatric reports on women defendants than men.

23.4.3 MEDICAL REPORTS AND THE NEW POWERS

Most reports are requested after conviction. This will usually require an adjournment, which may be in custody. Medical reports on bail, which will enable the doctor to see how the patient will adjust to the specific treatment regimen in his or her institution, will, however, be unlikely to be welcomed in the case of serious offences. This dilemma was particularly prevalent before the Mental Health Act 1983, which introduced three new possibilities which should always be borne in mind by counsel. Recent figures by the Department of Health indicate that they are being under-utilised, possibly because they are not widely known.

These provisions are not described in detail here, nor those for the disposals for the mentally disordered, since they are well set out in *Archbold* and other texts. Counsel should refresh their memories on the specific requirements whenever they think it likely that there may be a need to use such provisions, since each differs significantly, and since the conditions are relatively complex. The scope of the provisions is briefly:

(a) The ability to remand to hospital (under the Mental Health Act 1983, s. 35) for a report on the accused's mental condition (Crown Court and magistrates' court). This requires the evidence of one doctor and a place already organised, so does not help with the original diagnosis, but does allow the client and medical team to work together for a period in the relevant institution before sentence. Much better than a remand in custody, if a hospital order is being contemplated.

(b) The power to remand to hospital for treatment (s. 36). Primarily a humanitarian measure for those clearly disordered and in need of treatment but charged with very serious offences, prior to trial. Crown Court only, two doctors required. Extremely limited use so far (e.g. 32 cases in 1985).

(c) The power for the court to request of the regional health authority whether a place is available (s. 39). It does not, however, require the authority to produce places. Again used very rarely (the Home Office and Department of Health are trying to make it more useful).

23.4.4 THE REQUIREMENTS OF THE CRIMINAL JUSTICE ACT 1991

The CJA 1991 contains new provisions for requesting medical reports where the 'offender is or appears to be mentally disordered' (s. 4). If the court is obtaining a pre-sentence report then, for such offenders, the court should also obtain and consider a medical report before passing a custodial sentence. However, if the court is of the opinion that it is unnecessary to obtain a medical report, it does not have to obtain one.

Before passing a custodial sentence on an offender who is or who appears to be mentally disordered, the court should consider any information which relates to his or her mental condition (whether in a medical report, a pre-sentence report *or otherwise)* and should consider the likely effects of such a sentence on the offender's mental condition and on his or her ability to have treatment for that condition. *R* v *Fawcett* (1995) 16 Cr App R (S) 55 indicates that the court should have a medical report before passing a sentence using s. 2(2)(b), if the danger posed by the defendant could be due to his or her medical condition or personality problem, in order to exclude the need for a medical disposal (such as a hospital order).

The purpose behind the provisions in the Act is clearly to encourage courts to obtain medical reports in most cases where the offender is mentally disordered. In the last few years, several London magistrates' courts have had the facility of obtaining an immediate medical report through a duty psychiatrist attending the court and this is now spreading throughout the country. The probation officer preparing the pre-sentence report will often suggest that a medical report be prepared, but defence counsel must also bear those provisions in mind and request an adjournment for such a report where necessary. If the client is in danger of a custodial sentence, it is quite clear that such a report should be prepared, given that the court should consider the effect of the sentence on his or her mental condition and the possibility of obtaining treatment. It is necessary to consult the probation officer, etc. locally before preparing any mitigation, in order to be aware of the local facilities for remands for medical reports.

23.5 Powers of the Courts in Relation to Mentally Disordered Defendants

23.5.1 BEFORE SENTENCE

(a) The police may use their powers under s. 136 of the Mental Health Act 1983 to remove someone who is disordered, etc. in a public place to a place of safety.

(b) The police or CPS may decide not to prosecute because voluntary treatment is to be undertaken by the defendant. Always think of telling the prosecution if this is the case.

(c) Compulsory admission under the civil provisions of the Mental Health Act 1983 and dropping of prosecution: in an emergency (s. 4) for 72 hours, for assessment (s. 2) for up to 28 days, or for treatment (s. 3) for initially six months. Definitions of disorder as in s. 1.

(d) Use of the Criminal Procedure (Insanity) Act 1964, s. 4 (whether the defendant is unfit to plead). Only 30–40 cases per year, though new legislation has improved the results for the defendant and may make the use of this provision more likely.

(e) Under s. 37 of the Mental Health Act 1983, the magistrates' court may make a hospital order without proceeding to conviction if the defendant is suffering from mental illness or severe impairment (rare).

(f) Use of the diminished responsibility defence in charges of murder, which has largely replaced the insanity defence (again because of the consequences, but also because the scope of the definition of mental disorder under diminished responsibility is wider than the largely cognitive disorders permitted for insanity).

(g) A few cases taken under the M'Naghten rules pleading insanity.

23.5.2 AT SENTENCE

(a) Probation order with condition of mental treatment under the CJA 1991. The definition of disorder is quite wide, but it only applies to 'treatment', though this may be inpatient, outpatient, or under the care of a named doctor. It requires the offender's consent and has the disadvantages that:

  (i) the offender may subsequently not go for treatment (there is no compulsory element);

  (ii) there may be problems of liaison between medical and probation personnel. It may be helpful to ensure the roles of each are thought about at the time of the reports.

(b) Probation order without condition, suspended sentence, etc. There are no statistics on the use of these non-specific measures for the mentally disordered, but it is likely that they are much more numerous than specific 'medical disposals'.

(c) Hospital orders under the Mental Health Act 1983. Compulsory treatment, initially for six months, but extendable. Can be discharged by the doctor responsible for the patient (Responsible Medical Officer), by the health authority, or by the patient applying to a Mental Health Review Tribunal. This is not a secure order and the conditions of detention can be varied by the hospital.

(d) Restriction orders — where the public needs to be protected from grave harm only. Crown Court only. Patient may be released through application to a Mental Health Review Tribunal, or the Home Secretary may release patients conditionally or absolutely. Only the Home Secretary may change the conditions of detention. The order is for compulsory detention under secure conditions.

Restriction orders have been dealt with by the Court of Appeal in *R* v *Birch* (1989) 11 Cr App R (S) 202. This stated that the court should go through the following questions in order in dealing with cases of mental disorder:

  (i) Is a period of compulsory detention apposite?

  (ii) If so, arc the conditions for a hospital order satisfied?

(iii) If so, should the person be given a hospital order, or be sent to prison?

(iv) If it is decided he or she should receive a hospital order, are the conditions for making a restriction order satisfied (protecting the public from serious harm)?

(v) If they are, should he or she be given a restriction order, or a life sentence, or a determinate prison sentence?

(vi) If a restriction order, should it be one for an unlimited period (favoured in *R* v *Gardiner* [1967] 1 WLR 464) and commended again in *Birch)* or one for a fixed period?

The court was held not to be bound by any medical evidence that the person is not dangerous in reaching its decision. It was also confirmed that protecting the public from serious *harm* in the provisions for making a restriction order meant serious *harm* and not serious *risk*. In other words, a person who committed frequent offences but none of these involved danger to others should not receive a restriction order. *Birch* reiterates that prison may be used for those who are dangerous even though they are also mentally disordered, but states that a hospital disposal is to be preferred. Prison should really only be given if no hospital place is available, or if there is an element of culpability which requires punishment and hospital is felt to be really inappropriate.

(e) However, placement in a Special Hospital is not something decided by the courts, but by the Secretary of State for Health. The courts may request placement in a Special Hospital, but cannot demand it. There is a great shortage of places, because of the difficulty of obtaining places in ordinary hospitals for patients released from Special Hospitals.

(f) Life imprisonment. The conditions for imposing life imprisonment have been set out in *R* v *Hodgson* (1967) 52 Cr App R 113 (judgment of Mackenna J) and *R* v *Wilkinson* (1983) 5 Cr App R (S) 105 (judgment of Lord Lane CJ). In *Hodgson* it was stated that:

> When the following conditions are satisfied, a sentence of life imprisonment is in our opinion justified: (1) where the offence or offences are in themselves grave enough to require a very long sentence; (2) where it appears from the nature of the offences or from the defendant's history that he is a person of unstable character likely to commit such offences in the future; and (3) where if the offences are committed the consequences to others may be specially injurious, as in the case of sexual offences or crimes of violence.

Wilkinson showed that:

> It seems that the sentence of life imprisonment, other than for an offence where the sentence is obligatory, is really appropriate and must only be passed in the most exceptional circumstances. With a few exceptions it is reserved for offenders who for one reason or another cannot be dealt with under the provisions of the Mental Health Act, yet who are in a mental state which makes them dangerous to the life or limb of members of the public. It is sometimes impossible to say when that danger will subside, and therefore an indeterminate sentence is required, so that the prisoner's progress may be monitored by those who have him under their supervision in prison, and so that he will be kept in custody only so long as public safety may be jeopardised by his being let loose at large.

However, in *Wilkinson*, it was also shown that just being a bad burglar or robber was insufficient — there needed to be the required mental element as well. The need for an element of mental disorder has been confirmed post the Criminal Justice Act 1991 in *R* v *Spear* (1995) 16 Cr App R (S) 242. This restriction on the use of the life sentence is welcome, but still the definition of disorder and dangerousness in such imprecise terms permits its use in a wide variety of circumstances, as Floud described above (see **23.2.2** above).

(g) Determinate prison sentences. Many disordered and most dangerous offenders almost certainly receive ordinary prison sentences. For the disordered, this may occur because no one has diagnosed their condition. It may occur because they do not fit the current medical ideas of the treatable, or the legal definition in the Acts. In a few instances, it may be under the provisions of s. 1(2)(b) though this is not intended for the disordered. More probably, it may occur because the facilities do not exist in their locality to permit their optimum treatment. One study of the South East prison population found that 31% of sentenced prisoners would benefit from psychiatric attention. The problem for both sentencers and counsel in dealing with the sentencing of mentally disordered offenders is a lack of suitable facilities. One clue as to why this might have happened may lie in the comment of the House of Commons Social Services Committee, which is still valid today:

Any fool can close a long-stay hospital: it takes more time and trouble to do it properly and compassionately. The Minister must ensure that mental illness or mental handicap provision is not reduced without demonstrably adequate alternative services being provided beforehand both for those discharged from hospital and for those who would otherwise seek admission.

(h) The 1996 White Paper (*Protecting the Public* (London: HMSO, Cm 3190)) indicates that the Government is now considering a new hybrid sentence, part hospital order, part prison sentence, in which any offender who is found to be untreatable in hospital, or who responds to treatment, is transfered to prison until he or she has served the length of time represented by his or her prison sentence.

TWENTY-FOUR

YOUNG OFFENDERS

24.1 Introduction

In this chapter we will be concerned with the sentencing of two distinct age-groups, which can be grouped together as young offenders but which in legal terms constitute the two separate categories of 'juveniles' and 'young adults' (the category of juveniles may be further separated into 'children' (aged 10-13 inclusive) and 'young persons' (aged 14–17 inclusive)).

Until 1992, juveniles were those aged under 17, and they were dealt with in juvenile courts. A major change under the Criminal Justice Act 1991 was to extend this age-group to those under 18. Since the lowest age at which someone may be brought before a criminal court is 10, this category consists of young boys and girls aged 10-17 inclusive. These boys and girls are dealt with in what are now called 'youth courts', which are specially constituted magistrates' courts with special powers (some of which are discussed below). Young adults are those aged 18 to 20 inclusive: they are dealt with in the ordinary adult courts, but the range of powers available to those courts is different for this age group.

24.2 Juveniles

24.2.1 JUVENILES AND THE WELFARE PRINCIPLE

The last three decades have seen conflicts of approach to the problem of dealing with juveniles who offend. The legal principle has remained throughout that of welfare: a court 'shall have regard to the welfare of the child or young person' (CYPA 1933, s. 44(1)).

The Children and Young Persons Act 1969 was designed to revolutionise the approach to young offenders in at least three main ways — first, by diverting many of them away from the courts altogether; second, by giving considerable discretion to social workers in cases where the court made a 'care order'; and third, by initiating the containment and treatment of these children in trouble in the community rather than in institutions.

During the 1970s considerable dissatisfaction with the Act was voiced, even though the Act had not been fully implemented, and the magistracy in particular campaigned for greater powers to deal with the 'tougher' young offenders. The 1980s saw the grant of more powers to the juvenile courts by the CJA 1982, but also an initiative towards the development of 'intermediate treatment' schemes as substitutes for custody. Thus, although the courts have their greater powers, the decade saw a fall in the numbers of juveniles sentenced to custody, from 7,900 in 1981 to 1,500 in 1991 (*Criminal Statistics 1991*), although the numbers have increased with the inclusion of 17-year-olds in this category.

24.2.2 DIVERTING JUVENILES FROM COURT

One of the policies behind the 1969 Act was to encourage the police and other agencies to deal with young offenders without bringing them before the court. The most common approach was to issue a formal caution to a juvenile offender: a youngster who was prepared to admit the offence would be required to attend a police station and would be cautioned by a senior officer in uniform. The Home Office circular to the police urges them to caution all juvenile first offenders unless there is a strong reason against, and goes on to state that 'a second or subsequent caution would only be precluded where the offence is so serious as to require prosecution' (see Home Office Circular 59/1990). As a result, the cautioning rate has risen for male juveniles from 55% in 1984 to 76% in 1991, and for female juveniles from 79% in 1984 to 90% in 1991. However, the inclusion of 17-year-olds has lowered the cautioning rates for under-18s to 69% (males) and 87% (females) in 1993. Home Office circular 18/1994 reverses the policy on second and subsequent cautions, confining them to exceptional cases. This is despite the fact that over 80% of offenders cautioned are not convicted of an offence within two years.

There remain considerable variations between police force areas in the proportions of juveniles cautioned, variations which are not explained by the different 'mix' of offences in those areas, and it remains to be seen whether the increasing involvement of the CPS will improve consistency.

24.2.3 THE FRAMEWORK OF THE CRIMINAL JUSTICE ACT 1991

The implementation of the Criminal Justice Act 1991 did not alter the reliance on cautioning as the primary response to juvenile offenders, but it made significant changes to the powers for dealing with those juveniles who are brought to court. The five key principles are: (i) that the welfare principle in s. 44 of the 1933 Act remains in place; (ii) that juvenile courts are re-named 'youth courts' to reflect the fact that they now deal with 17-year-olds as well as younger juveniles; (iii) that courts have more flexible powers when dealing with offenders aged 16 or 17, to be exercised according to the needs and maturity of the individual offender; (iv) that when dealing with younger offenders, aged 10-15, there is greater emphasis on parental responsibility; and (v) that the parents must (save in exceptional circumstances) attend court when a child under 16 is being dealt with.

Within those five general principles, the framework of the 1991 Act applies in youth courts in much the same way as in the adult courts. For the least serious forms of offending the court should consider a fine, discharge or bind-over. On the next level up, where the offence is serious enough to warrant it (s. 6(1)), the court should consider a community sentence, having full regard to the welfare of the offender. And in the relatively few cases of great seriousness, the custody threshold in s. 1 will be fulfilled.

The powers on these three levels of seriousness will be explained in the following paragraphs. It must be noted, however, that somewhat different powers are available for juveniles of different ages, even beneath the eighteenth birthday, which is the maximum age for youth courts.

24.2.4 DISCHARGES, BIND-OVERS AND FINES

The power to order an absolute or conditional discharge is the same as that for adult offenders (see **18.2** and **18.3**). But there are significant differences in respect of bind-overs and fines.

24.2.4.1 Binding over

A court has the same power to bind over a juvenile to keep the peace and be of good behaviour. The important difference in the youth court is the power to bind over the juvenile's parents. By s. 58 of the 1991 Act, the court has a duty to consider binding over the parents of a juvenile offender aged 10-15 inclusive, and a duty to give reasons in open court if it does not think it desirable to do so. The form of the bind-over is 'to order the parent or guardian to enter into a recognisance to take proper care of him and exercise proper control over him'. The sum may be no more than £1,000, and the maximum period is three years or until the juvenile's eighteenth birthday, whichever is the shorter. Where a youth court is dealing with an offender aged 16 or 17, it has the power to bind the parents over but no duties.

24.2.4.2 Fines

Where the juvenile is aged 10-15 inclusive, the parents must be ordered to pay the fine unless this would be unreasonable or they cannot be found. If the parents are paying their means are taken into account. If the child is paying, her or his means are taken into account. Where the juvenile is aged 16–17 inclusive, the parents may be ordered to pay: there are different rules where the juvenile is in the care of the local authority (s. 57), interpreted in *Bedfordshire CC* v *DPP* [1995] Crim LR 962.

24.2.4.3 Compensation orders

The same general principles apply in respect of compensation orders, which a court must consider making in every case involving injury, loss or damage (see **18.6**). The amount of the compensation must take account of the means of the person ordered to pay. Parents must pay if the child is under 16, and may be ordered to pay if the offender is aged 16 or 17.

24.2.5 COMMUNITY SENTENCES

Before a court passes a community sentence, it must satisfy the threshold test in s. 6(1), that the offence (or the combination of the offence and one other offence associated with it) is serious enough to warrant a community sentence. If this test is satisfied, the court is then governed by s. 6(2): the order or orders made must be both proportionate to the seriousness of the offence(s) and the most suitable for the offender (see **19.4** for discussion). In view of the welfare principle which applies in the youth court, the latter requirement is especially important.

The court's powers differ according to the age of the juvenile. If the offender is aged 10-15 inclusive, there are only two community orders available to the court: the attendance centre order and the supervision order. However, for offenders aged 16 or 17, sometimes referred to as 'near-adults', no fewer than six forms of community orders may be available.

24.2.5.1 Attendance centre orders

There are over 100 junior attendance centres in England and Wales, their aim being to deprive young offenders of a few hours' leisure time at weekends (usually Saturday afternoons) and to involve them in various constructive activities and physical exercise during their attendance. The minimum number of hours which a court may order is 12 hours except where the juvenile is under 14, and the court is of the opinion that 12 hours would be excessive. The maximum number of hours which a court may order is 24 hours where the juvenile is under 16 and 36 hours where the young offender is 16 but under 21 (CJA 1982, s. 17, amended by CJA 1991, s. 67).

The original idea behind attendance centres was that they would provide a 'short, sharp shock' to young offenders who were sent there, but it is doubtful whether this is now uppermost in the minds of those who run the centres, and juvenile courts seemed to use attendance centre orders in different ways and for varying types of offender (Gelsthorpe, L. and Tutt, N., 'The Attendance Centre Order' [1986] Crim LR 146).

24.2.5.2 Supervision orders

These are similar to the probation order, but they differ in certain ways. In particular, the supervision order does not require the consent of the juvenile unless certain additional requirements are made, and the supervision is usually carried out by the local social services department rather than by the probation service.

The order may run for up to three years, and the CJA 1982 empowered the juvenile court to impose various requirements as part of an order (CYPA 1969, s. 7(7) and s. 12

(as amended by CJA 1982)). Requirements to refrain from certain specified activities may also be imposed, but courts have rarely done so. The power to impose supervised activity requirements has been used more widely: the court specifies the nature of the activity programme in which the juvenile must participate (from among those activities offered by the local authority), and also specifies the duration of the requirement, which may be up to 90 days.

Perhaps the most important of the requirements which may be added to a supervision order is the requirement of intermediate treatment (IT). The idea behind IT is that constructive and challenging programmes in the community can be devised for offenders who are regarded as 'tough' or 'difficult' and who might otherwise be sent into custody. The significant decline in the use of custody for juveniles during the 1980s was attributed to the new initiative to develop intermediate treatment in the early part of the decade, with over 110 schemes available. The IT programmes are run by the local social services departments, but magistrates have also been involved in the direction of the schemes.

The legal requirements of the supervision order are unchanged by the 1991 Act, except that the order becomes available for 17-year-olds for the first time in consequence of the extended jurisdiction of the youth court. Before the court makes a supervision order with additional requirements, it must obtain and consider a pre-sentence report. Breach of a supervision order has the same consequences as breach of other community orders (see **19.10**).

24.2.5.3 Probation orders

We now move from the only two community orders available for offenders aged ten to 15 inclusive, the attendance centre order and the supervision order, to the other four orders available for those aged 16 and 17. The 1991 Act introduces probation orders into the youth court for the first time. The legal requirements are the same as for adults (see **19.5**). A court should use a probation order where it is of the opinion that this is more suitable for the offender than a supervision order. The difference lies in the additional requirements which may be inserted into each order, and in the different supervising agencies (the probation service for probation, and local authorities for the supervision order). Probation orders might be more appropriate for 16- and 17-year-olds who are thought to be relatively mature. The court must obtain and consider a pre-sentence report before making a probation order with additional requirements.

24.2.5.4 Community service orders

These have been available for 16-year-olds for some years. The only significant change in the 1991 Act is that the maximum number of hours for 16- and 17-year-olds in the youth court is now the same as for adults, i.e. 240 hours. For further discussion, see **19.6**.

24.2.5.5 Combination orders

This new form of order is available for offenders aged 16 and 17 on the same principles as adult offenders (see **19.7**). The court must obtain and consider a pre-sentence report, and must be satisfied, as always, that the restrictions on liberty are commensurate with the seriousness of the offence(s). This is regarded as the most restrictive order short of custody.

24.2.5.6 Curfew orders

This new form of order, in those areas where it is available, may be used for offenders aged 16 and 17 on the same principles as adult offenders (see **19.8**). A pre-sentence report is not mandatory, and this order may be added to other orders so long as the whole community sentence remains commensurate with the seriousness of the offence(s).

24.2.5.7 Community sentences for juveniles

To summarise, the youth court has a choice of two community orders for offenders under 16 (attendance centre, supervision), and a choice among all six orders when dealing with those aged 16 and 17. The powers for these 'near-adults' are similar to those of magistrates' courts when dealing with offenders aged 18 to 20, and the aim is to give courts greater flexibility to make orders which are suitable to the degree of maturity of the particular juvenile. The breach powers in respect of all community orders are the same as for adults (see **19.10**).

24.2.6 CUSTODIAL MEASURES FOR JUVENILES

It will be apparent that the emphasis in dealing with young offenders is, first, diversion from the courts altogether and, second, treatment in the community where possible. The considerable decline in the use of custody has already been described, but the numbers are now increasing for two reasons. First, 17-year-olds are now within the jurisdiction of the youth court: they tend to have longer criminal records. Secondly, the government has legislated for 'secure training orders' for persistent younger offenders.

A juvenile who is found guilty of murder must, by law, be sentenced to detention during Her Majesty's pleasure. Then there are three other forms of custody.

24.2.6.1 Detention in a young offender institution

The main custodial sentence for juveniles is detention in a young offender institution (CJA 1982, ss. 1A and 1B, as amended by CJA 1988). Courts are, of course, limited by the maximum sentence for the offence itself, but they are also limited by the age of the young offender: those under 15 cannot be sentenced to detention at all. For any juvenile, the sentence of detention must be not less than two months and not more than two years (s. 63 of the CJA 1991, as amended).

Before a court imposes a custodial sentence, it must overcome the threshold test in s. 1(2) of the 1991 Act. Length of the detention, within the limits just mentioned, is governed by s. 2(2). All the discussion of these sections in **Chapters 20** and **21**, including the discussion of previous convictions and aggravating and mitigating factors, is equally applicable here. One powerful mitigating factor is the age of the offender: this will often have the effect of bringing below the custody threshold an offence which, in an adult, would have been above that threshold.

24.2.6.2 Detention under s. 53(2) of the CYPA 1933

There is an extra power available to the courts when dealing with particularly serious offences by juveniles. It not only enables the court to exceed the limits on 'detention in a young offender institution', just described, but is also available from the age of ten upwards (Criminal Justice and Public Order Act 1994, s. 16). However, this power is only available to the Crown Court, and then only when the juvenile has been tried and convicted in the Crown Court (rather than committed for sentence by a youth court).

Section 53(2) of the CYPA 1933 empowers the Crown Court to order that a juvenile who has been convicted of an offence carrying a maximum of 14 years' imprisonment or more shall be detained for a specified number of years (within the statutory maximum for the offence) in a place approved by the Secretary of State. Although it is rarely necessary for courts to use this power, it gave rise to difficulties in several cases, and in 1986 the Lord Chief Justice gave a guideline judgment on the use of this power in *R* v *Fairhurst* (1986) 8 Cr App R (S) 346. However, much of that guideline judgment has now been overtaken, and it is not safe to rely on it.

It was widely anticipated that one consequence of extending the jurisdiction of youth courts to cover 17-year-olds would be a greater resort to s. 53(2). In fact the legislature has facilitated greater resort to s. 53(2) by extending the categories of offence that fall within it. Although all offences with a statutory maximum of 14 years qualify, statutes have now altered the boundaries somewhat. The reduction in the maximum penalty for non-residential burglary from 14 to ten years takes that offence outside the scope of s. 53(2) (see *R* v *Nagar* (1993) 15 Cr App R (S) 273); on the other hand, s. 64 of the 1991 Act (as amended) brings indecent assault on a woman by an offender aged 10-17 within the scope of s. 53(2) even though its statutory maximum remains at ten years, and s. 67(2) of the CJA 1993 also brings in the offences of causing death by dangerous driving and causing death by careless driving while under the influence of drink or drugs by an offender aged 14-17. However, the kindred offence of causing death by aggravated vehicle taking remains outside s. 53(2) (*R* v *Ore* [1994] Crim LR 304).

In determining the length of s. 53(2) detention, the court will be bound by s. 2(2)(a) of the 1991 Act to ensure that the term is commensurate with the seriousness of the offence, unless there is a crime of violence or sexual offence which leads to the imposition of a longer 'public protection' sentence under s. 2(2)(b). As a matter of procedure, a court which intends to invoke the s. 53(2) power must state clearly that this is the section under which a sentence is imposed. Thus in *R* v *Egdell* [1994] Crim LR 137 the trial judge had imposed six years' detention in a young offender institution, without mentioning s. 53(2), and the Court of Appeal held that this was an unlawful sentence. The maximum for detention in a young offender institution was then one year (now raised to two years), and so the sentence had to take effect as a sentence of one year's detention (see also *R* v *Venison* [1994] Crim LR 298). The Court of Appeal emphasised that it is the duty of prosecuting counsel to point out errors or omissions of this kind.

Section 53(2) also provides for the sentence of detention for life in appropriate cases, where the offence itself carries a life maximum. One example is *R* v *Bell* (1989) 11 Cr App R (S) 472. Before passing such a sentence the court must satisfy the requirements in s. 2(2)(b) and s. 3 of the 1991 Act.

24.2.6.3 Secure training orders

Sentences of detention under s. 53(2) are available for juveniles of all ages from 10-17, whereas the minimum age for detention in a young offender institution is 15. These restrictions gave rise to considerable public debate and the Criminal Justice and Public Order Act 1994 will introduce a new form of custodial order for juveniles aged 12, 13 and 14, called the secure training order (STO). By s. 1 of the 1994 Act, the duration of an STO may be between six months and two years, half to be served in a secure training centre and half to be served under supervision in the community. The sentence may be imposed by a youth court, notwithstanding that such courts are otherwise limited to sentences involving no more than six months' deprivation of liberty.

The conditions of making an STO are set out in s. 1(5):

(a) the offender must have been at least 12 years old when the offence was committed;

(b) he or she must have been convicted of three or more imprisonable offences; and

(c) the offender, either on this or a previous occasion, must have either been found to be in breach of a supervision order or been convicted of an imprisonable offence committed whilst subject to a supervision order.

Thus, although condition (c) requires the offender to have previously received a supervision order, there is no requirement that the other previous offences should have attracted any particular sentence (i.e., a discharge would suffice), so long as the offences carry a maximum penalty of imprisonment for an adult. However, an STO may not be imposed unless the offence is so serious that only a custodial sentence can be justified for it, since ss. 1 to 4 of the 1991 Act are applicable. Offenders who are so young might expect to benefit from considerable mitigation on account of their age.

The remaining sections in part I of the 1994 Act provide for the supervision of offenders subject to an STO, and then provide for the management of secure training centres. Section 1 is unlikely to be brought into force until these centres have been constructed, and at the time of writing it is unimplemented.

24.3 Young Adults

24.3.1 DEALING WITH YOUNG ADULT OFFENDERS

Offenders aged 18 to 20 are dealt with in the ordinary adult courts but under somewhat different sentencing provisions. The policy in dealing with young adult offenders is not expressly one of 'welfare', as with juveniles, but there remains the strong view that special measures are necessary to deal with young adults in the community rather than in custody and, when it is thought necessary to impose custody, to segregate young adults from older offenders. These policies show awareness that many young people cease offending in their lower twenties, and that as little as possible should be done which tends to confirm them as offenders and to classify them with more hardened, older offenders. Otherwise, sentences might have the effect of reinforcing criminal habits rather than allowing them to be broken.

The framework of the 1991 Act applies to young adults no less than to adults and to juveniles. The powers in respect of discharges, fines and compensation orders are exactly the same as for adults. If the court regards the offence as serious enough to warrant a community sentence, then it is bound by s. 6(2) to make orders which are both commensurate with the seriousness of the offence(s) and most suitable for the offender. The choice of community orders is slightly wider for young adults than for adults, since there are five possibilities: probation, community service, combination order, curfew order (where available), and an attendance centre order. The requirements for the attendance centre order are the same as when dealing with offenders aged 16 and 17 (see **24.2.5.1** above), but there are senior attendance centres for those aged 18 to 20. A court may only make an attendance centre order on a young adult if there is a senior centre in the locality.

24.3.2 CUSTODY FOR YOUNG ADULTS

Restrictions on the use of custody for this age group have been in force since the CJA 1982. Where custody is imposed, detention for offenders aged under 21 is in a 'young offender institution'. There the Prison Department endeavours to hold juvenile boys separately from older boys serving longer terms, but the institutions for females have insufficient numbers for any such separation. Young offender institutions have to deal mostly with boys and young men who have considerable criminal records. The aim is that:

> the regimes should build on existing experience in youth custody and detention centres, coordinating and developing for all offenders positive regime activities designed to promote self-discipline and a sense of responsibility. The personal development of the offender will be achieved through purposeful activity and positive relationships. (Home Office Circular 40/1988, 'Regimes in Young Offender Institutions'.)

The provisions in ss. 1 and 2 of the CJA 1991 apply to regulate the imposition of custodial sentences on young adults, as on offenders of all other ages. The leading case on s. 1(2)(a) is *R* v *Cox* (see **21.5.2**), a case of a young adult. A review of the decisions in **21.5.2** revealed no clear criteria, but offenders in this age-group can expect some mitigation on account of youth. There is no suspended sentence for offenders under 21.

Statistics on the use of sentences for young adults convicted of indictable offences appear in **Figure 24.1**, although it should be borne in mind that until 1992 the category of young adult referred to all offenders aged 17 to 20 inclusive, whereas since 1993 it refers only to those aged 18 to 20.

Figure 24.1 Percentage of persons aged 18 and under 21 sentenced for indictable offences by sex and type of sentence or order

England and Wales

Percentage of total persons sentenced

Sex and year	Total number of persons sentenced	Absolute or conditional discharge	Fine	Probation order	Community service order	Attendance centre order	Combination order	Young Offender Institution[1]	Imprisonment: Fully suspended	Imprisonment: Un-suspended	Otherwise dealt with	Total Immediate custody	Total community sentences
Males													
1984	100	8	44	10	14	2	*	21	*	*	1	21	46
1985	100	8	42	11	14	2	*	22	*	*	1	22	26
1986	100	9	41	11	14	2	*	22	*	*	1	22	27
1987	100	9	41	12	14	2	*	22	*	*	1	22	27
1988	100	9	42	12	14	1	*	21	*	*	1	21	27
1989	100	11	43	12	13	1	*	17	*	*	2	17	27
1990	100	13	42	13	14	2	*	15	*	*	2	15	28
1991	100	15	37	13	15	2	*	16	*	*	2	16	30
1992[2]	100	17	35	13	15	2	0	15	*	*	2	15	30
1993[2]	100	17	34	12	14	1	3	17	*	*	2	17	30
1994	100	16	31	13	14	1	4	19	*	*	2	19	32
Females													
1984	100	23	44	22	5	0	*	6	*	*	1	6	27
1985	100	22	43	22	5	—	*	6	*	*	1	6	27
1986	100	24	40	23	6	—	*	6	*	*	1	6	29
1987	100	27	38	23	5	—	*	6	*	*	1	6	28
1988	100	27	37	23	6	0	*	5	*	*	1	5	29
1989	100	31	36	22	5	—	*	4	*	*	2	4	27
1990	100	34	33	21	6	—	*	3	*	*	2	3	27
1991	100	38	28	21	7	0	*	3	*	*	2	3	28
1992[2]	100	40	29	19	7	0	0	3	*	*	2	3	26
1993[2]	100	37	31	17	7	0	2	5	*	*	2	5	25
1994	100	36	27	20	7	0	2	5	*	*	2	5	29

(1) Includes borstal training (abolished May 1983), detention centre orders and youth custody (both abolished October 1988).
(2) Improvements in the data collection methods used by the Metropolitan Police District have led to an increase in the number recorded as sentenced of about 2% in 1993 and 1% in 1992 for indictable offences.

Figure 24.2 Sentencing table by age

AGE	10	11	12	13	14	15	16	17	18	19	20	21+
DISCHARGE (ABSOLUTE/CONDITIONAL)	✓	✓	✓	✓	✓	✓	✓	✓	✓	✓	✓	✓
BIND-OVER[(1)]	MAX. £250				MAX. £1,000				✓	✓	✓	✓
COMPENSATION ORDER[(2)]	✓	✓	✓	✓	✓	✓	✓	✓	✓	✓	✓	✓
FINE[(2)]	MAX. £250				MAX. £1,000				✓	✓	✓	✓
ATTENDANCE CENTRE ORDER[(2)(3)]	MIN. 12 Hrs — MAX. 24 Hrs.						MAX. 36 Hrs.					×
SUPERVISION ORDER	✓	✓	✓	✓	✓	✓	✓	✓	×	×	×	×
PROBATION ORDER	×	×	×	×	×	×	✓	✓	✓	✓	✓	✓
COMMUNITY SERVICE ORDER	×	×	×	×	×	×	✓	✓	✓	✓	✓	✓
CURFEW ORDER	×	×	×	×	×	×	✓	✓	✓	✓	✓	✓
COMBINATION ORDER	×	×	×	×	×	×	✓	✓	✓	✓	✓	✓
DETENTION IN A YOUNG OFFENDER INSTITUTION	×	×	×	×	×	MIN. 2M MAX. 2 Yrs.			MIN. 21 DAYS			×
S. 53 DETENTION	✓	✓	✓	✓	✓	✓	✓	✓	×	×	×	×
DETENTION DURING H.M. PLEASURE	✓	✓	✓	✓	✓	✓	✓	✓	×	×	×	×
IMPRISONMENT	×	×	×	×	×	×	×	×	×	×	×	✓
SUSPENDED SENTENCE OF IMPRISONMENT	×	×	×	×	×	×	×	×	×	×	×	✓

(1) The Table refers only to binding over the offender. If the offender is under 16, the court *must* bind over the parents or give reasons; if the offender is aged 16 or 17, the court may bind over the parents.

(2) The Table refers only to compensation orders and fines imposed on offenders. If the offender is under 16, the court *must* order the parents to pay, using the adult scale; if the offender is aged 16 or 17, the court may order the parents to pay.

(3) The minimum number of hours is 12, except where the juvenile is aged under 14, and the court is of the opinion that 12 hours would be excessive. See **24.2.5.1**.

TWENTY-FIVE

TUTORIAL QUESTIONS FOR SENTENCING

The tutorial questions found over the next few pages are designed to encourage and promote discussion on the different areas of the law involved. Students should thoroughly prepare the questions for each individual tutorial as it arises and come ready to discuss the policies behind sentencing, conditions and requirements that must be fulfilled before any particular sentence can be imposed, and the likely sentence on the facts of each individual case, if possible. It should be remembered that each question is merely a starting point.

Tutorial 1 Community Sentences, Financial Penalties and other Non-Custodial Sentences

1. (a) David is aged 19. He is employed as a painter and decorator earning £130 per week net. He is charged with one offence of theft. It is alleged that on 1 October 1996 he stole various items valued at £85 from a parked car. He has the following previous convictions:

    (i) On 20 December 1995 at Greenacre magistrates' court he received a conditional discharge for two years for an offence of theft of car tyres.

    (ii) On 2 September 1996 at the Whiteacre magistrates' court he was placed on probation for two years for an offence of burglary.

David appears at the Blackacre magistrates' court and pleads guilty to the charge of theft. The pre-sentence report indicates that a financial penalty will be appropriate. What courses are open to the magistrates? What action can the court take relating to the conditional discharge or probation order?

(b) Edward aged 21 appears at the Barchester Crown Court and is convicted of theft. He is sentenced to 180 hours' community service. He completes 50 hours and then fails to attend on the next four occasions when required to do so. He is summonsed to appear before the Blackacre magistrates' court and is found to be in breach of the community service order. What options are open to the magistrates in dealing with Edward?

(c) Edwina appears at Whiteacre magistrates' court and pleads guilty to an offence of assault occasioning actual bodily harm contrary to the Offences against the Person Act 1861, s. 47. She is subject to a community service order of 80 hours imposed by another magistrates' court. What action can be taken in respect of the community service order?

2. Ben, aged 32, pleaded guilty in the Brentvale Crown Court to causing death by dangerous driving. He was driving his car within the speed limit at about 8 p.m. last November. He approached traffic lights which were showing red against him, drove

across them and collided with a motor cyclist who was killed. He had drunk a pint-and-a-half of lager at about 6 p.m. but it was not suggested that he was driving whilst unfit through drink.

Ben claims that he had failed to see the lights for some inexplicable reason and it was accepted by the prosecution that there was no evidence of bad driving before he had reached the traffic lights.

Ben is employed as a surveyor and earns £28,000 per annum. He has one previous driving conviction for careless driving two years, earlier, when he was fined £200 and his licence was endorsed with 4 penalty points.

You appear on his behalf. His pre-sentence report is not of great assistance. What factors would you ask the judge to take into account when considering the appropriate sentence?

What sentence would you suggest to the judge?

Would your answer be any different if Ben had been over the excess alcohol limit?

3. Jimmy, aged 22, pleaded guilty to four counts of burglary at Romchester Crown Court. He was concerned in four dwelling-house burglaries in which various items of personal property were stolen. He admitted that he had acted as a lookout while other accomplices entered the houses.

He has two previous findings of guilt as a juvenile for theft for which he was conditionally discharged on each occasion and one for burglary when an adult for which he was placed on probation for two years.

He is a self-employed window-cleaner and earns £250 per week take-home pay.

You appear on his behalf. His pre-sentence report confirms that he will consent to a community service order for which he is suitable. What factors would you ask the judge to take into account when considering the appropriate sentence?

What sentence would you suggest to the judge?

Would your answer be any different if Jimmy had been responsible for cleaning the windows of the houses concerned?

Multiple-choice Questions (Tutorial 1)

1. Under the Criminal Justice Act 1991 a court may make a probation order if it is of the opinion that the supervision of the offender by a probation officer is desirable in the interests of:

[A] Securing the rehabilitation of the offender.
[B] Protecting the public from harm from the offender.
[C] Preventing the commission of further offences by the offender.
[D] Any of the above.

2. Johnny, aged 19, appears before the Narrowview Magistrates' Court charged with three offences of theft (triable either way). He pleads guilty and asks for 20 other offences of theft to be taken into consideration. Which one of the following is a correct statement of the law?

The magistrates:

[A] Must obtain a pre-sentence report before sentence.
[B] Must obtain, but need not consider, a pre-sentence report before sentence.
[C] Must obtain and consider a pre-sentence report and may only impose a sentence recommended by that report.
[D] Must obtain and consider a pre-sentence report unless they take the view that one is unnecessary.

Tutorial 2 Custodial Sentences

1. Edward (aged 19) and Frank (aged 16) both plead guilty at Casterbridge Crown Court to robbery. Prosecuting counsel, in summarising the facts of the offence, states that Edward and Frank stopped the victim (a Mr Brown) as he was walking along the street late at night. Edward held a knife to Mr Brown's throat while Frank searched Mr Brown's pockets, and took a wallet containing £100. They both then ran away. Defence counsel, in mitigation, denies that either of his clients had a knife or any other weapon, although he concedes that they threatened to 'beat Mr Brown's face in' if he struggled. The antecedents of the offenders disclose that Edward has two previous court appearances, one in March 1994 for taking a car without the owner's consent (conditionally discharged for one year) and the other in June 1995 for shoplifting (ordered to perform 80 hours' community service). Frank has not been in trouble before. A pre-sentence report on Frank indicates that he would respond to a supervision order. In passing sentence the judge says:

> What I find most disturbing about this case is the use of a weapon. I listened most carefully to what learned Defence counsel had to say on the matter of the knife, but I read the statement of Mr Brown before I came into court, and I am quite satisfied that a knife was used to threaten him. Reluctant as I am to deprive young men of their liberty, I would be failing in my duty to the public if I did not pass a sentence which will serve as a warning to others that this kind of conduct will not be tolerated. You, Edward, had the knife and you will be detained in a young offender institution for three years. In your case, Frank, I thought about making a supervision order. In some ways it is an attractive alternative to a custodial sentence, but I have to deal with you in a way which will be a deterrent and an example to others. I take into account your age and your not having committed any offences in the past, but even so the shortest sentence I can pass is one of 27 months' detention in a young offender institution.

Advise Edward and Frank whether they have any grounds for appealing against sentence. How long are they likely to spend in custody?

2. On 21 November 1996 Rachel is convicted at Greenacre Crown Court of four offences of theft from shops. The offences took place on the same day and the total value of goods taken was £200. She has the following previous convictions.

Date	*Court*	*Offence*	*Sentence*
28 Feb 91	Magistrates' Court	Theft	Probation 2 years
5 April 93	Crown Court	Theft	Community Service 120 hrs
7 June 95	Crown Court	Criminal Deception	9 months' imprisonment suspended for 2 years

She was divorced in 1990 and is now 38 years old. Her two children aged 8 and 12 reside with her. Since her divorce she has suffered from bouts of depression. She has recently obtained employment as a nursing auxiliary and has formed a steady relationship with a man she hopes to marry. Her children are properly cared for and are doing well at school. According to her pre-sentence report she completed successfully and enjoyed the work she was required to do under the order for community service, and it is likely she would 'respond positively to some form of supervision'. What factors will the judge take into account in determining the appropriate sentence to be passed on Rachel?

3. Michael and Norman appear at Borough Green Crown Court jointly charged with theft of property valued at £1,600 from their employer. Both plead guilty. Michael is 35. He has three previous convictions for offences of dishonesty and is subject to a combination order imposed at the Doomchester Crown Court for handling stolen goods. When arrested he admitted the offence and gave the police information which led to the stolen property being recovered. Norman is 25. He has one previous conviction for common assault for which he received, and is now in breach of, a conditional discharge.

What sentence will the court consider in respect of both Michael and Norman and what factors will be taken into account in determining the appropriate sentence?

Multiple-choice Questions (Tutorial 2)

1. Spendthrift, aged 45, appears at the Rentacourt Crown Court on an indictment containing 45 counts of conspiracy to defraud, theft and false accounting. He pleads guilty to 15 counts and the remaining counts are left on the court file marked 'not to be proceeded with without leave of this court or of the Court of Appeal'. As a result, there has been considerable saving in time and cost of a lengthy and burdensome trial. In mitigation, you cite a recent Court of Appeal decision which indicates by way of general guidance that a certain proportion would be an appropriate discount from the sentence which would otherwise be imposed on a contested trial. What is that proportion?

[A] One-half.
[B] One-third.
[C] One-sixth.
[D] One-tenth.

2. Robin, aged 19, appears at the Dimview Crown Court where he pleads guilty to two counts of residential burglary. He asks for 12 other offences of residential burglary to be taken into consideration upon sentence. When sentencing, which of the following should the judge consider when deciding whether or not the case is serious enough to reach the 'custody threshold':

[A] That one count and one 't.i.c.' are so serious that only a custodial sentence would be justified.
[B] That one count and two 't.i.c.' offences are so serious that only a custodial sentence would be justified.
[C] That the two counts and one 't.i.c.' are so serious that only a custodial sentence would be justified.
[D] That the two counts and all the 't.i.c.' offences are so serious that only a custodial sentence would be justified.

Tutorial 3 Young Offenders

1. Barney is aged 17. He appears at Doomchester Youth Court charged with an offence of robbery (a handbag snatch committed at night) which he admits. His only previous court appearance was nine months ago when he was conditionally discharged for 12 months for an offence of theft. A pre-sentence report reveals that Barney's parents are unable to exercise any effective control over him, and that he has now left school with little prospect of obtaining employment. He will consent to any of the community orders. What factors will the magistrates take into account in deciding the appropriate sentence, and what options are open to them in passing sentence?

Would your answer be any different if Barney appeared in the Crown Court?

2. Scott, aged 15, has pleaded guilty at Brixgreen Youth Court to assaulting a PC occasioning him actual bodily harm contrary to OAP Act 1861, s. 47. The facts were

that when the officer stopped him in the street under the 'stop and search' provisions of PACE he picked up a piece of wood and struck the officer on the arm. Scott says that the officer made racist remarks and was just 'hassling me because I am black'. His pre-sentence report discloses that he has had a history of truancy and violence at school. His parents complain that he refuses to go to church with them and that he stays out until the early hours of the morning. He has one previous finding of guilt when aged 13 for criminal damage, i.e. spraying graffiti on underground trains, for which he was made the subject of an attendance centre order.

What factors will the court take into account in determining the appropriate sentence to be imposed on Scott?

What would be the position if the prosecutor does not accept that the officer made racist remarks?

Would your answer be any different if Scott were aged 14? aged 17?

3. Marcina, aged 15, appears at the Toxtown Youth Court with two others, aged 15 and 16, charged with robbery. They attacked a 14-year-old girl at a bus stop and forced her to hand over £4.50. They are found guilty, and the evidence given indicates that Marcina played a minor role in the offence. She has no previous finding of guilt, but the pre-sentence report discloses that she was sexually abused by her stepfather some six months prior to the offence and lives in an area of high delinquency.

What options are open to the court in dealing with Marcina?

Would your answer be any different if the victim had been an elderly woman?

Multiple-choice Questions (Tutorial 3)

1. Harry, aged 17, appeared at the Camberden Youth Court on a charge of unlawful wounding contrary to s. 20 of the Offences Against the Person Act 1861. The maximum custodial sentence for the offence is five years. Harry pleaded guilty to the charge and the justices committed him to the Crown Court for sentence under s. 37 of the Magistrates' Courts Act 1980. What is the maximum custodial sentence which may be imposed on Harry by the Crown Court?

[A] six months.
[B] 12 months.
[C] 24 months.
[D] five years.

2. Oliver, aged 12, appears in the Newburgh Crown Court jointly charged with Ted, aged 13, and Charlie, aged 14, on an indictment containing three counts of burglary of dwelling houses (the maximum sentence for each offence being 14 years' imprisonment in the case of an adult). Oliver was 11 years of age at the time of the commission of the offences. Oliver, Ted and Charlie are convicted of all three offences. Oliver is also subject to a supervision order for two previous findings of guilt for burglary.

Which one of the following sentences will the judge **not** be empowered to impose on Oliver?

[A] A secure training order.
[B] A supervision order.
[C] An attendance centre order.
[D] A sentence of long-term detention under s. 53(2) of the Children and Young Persons Act 1933.

APPENDIX

Answers to Exercises for Chapter 9

(1)

INDICTMENT No.________

The Crown Court at Bluebridge

The Queen v MICHAEL MASTERS

MICHAEL MASTERS is charged as follows

Statement of Offence

ATTEMPTED THEFT contrary to Section 1(1) of the Criminal Attempts Act 1981.

Particulars of Offence

MICHAEL MASTERS on the 14th day of February 1996 attempted to steal a wallet belonging to Mary Martin.

Date:________________ An officer of the Crown Court________________

(2) Provided that the prosecution evidence upon which the transfer took place discloses a case to answer on a count of attempted theft, that count could stand. You could of course add a count of receiving.

(3)

INDICTMENT No.________

The Crown Court at Newton

The Queen v NOREEN NAYLOR

NOREEN NAYLOR is charged as follows

Statement of Offence

POSSESSING A CONTROLLED DRUG contrary to Section 5(2) of the Misuse of Drugs Act 1971.

Particulars of Offence

NOREEN NAYLOR, on the 15th day of March 1996, had in her possession a controlled drug, namely cocaine.

Date:________________ An officer of the Crown Court________________

(4) The defence should apply to have the indictment quashed, since it is bad for duplicity.

(5) The offences of burglary and going equipped should be included in one indictment. They are founded on the same facts. It is arguable whether the robbery should be charged on a separate indictment. It is *not* founded on the same facts. Does it form part of a series of offences of the same or similar character? All are offences of dishonesty. But they are committed two months apart. The venue of the alleged offences, and other material factors, would be taken into account in deciding whether the robbery should be separated.

(6) The presence of a co-defendant would not in itself settle the matter. The factors outlined in the previous answer would still have to be examined.

(7) Richard's counsel would no doubt wish to apply to sever the charges which Robert faces alone. The two are still likely be tried jointly on the robbery charge, however prejudicial Robert's interview is for Richard. The judge will have to remind the jury that what one defendant says in interview is not evidence against the co-defendant.

(8)

INDICTMENT No.__________

The Crown Court at Blackbridge

The Queen v SIMON SCHOFIELD

SIMON SCHOFIELD is charged as follows

COUNT ONE

Statement of Offence

BURGLARY contrary to Section 9(1)(b) of the Theft Act 1968.

Particulars of Offence

SIMON SCHOFIELD on the 19th day of June 1996, having entered as a trespasser a building known as 108 High Road, Blackbridge, stole therein six necklaces and four bracelets.

COUNT TWO

Statement of Offence

HANDLING stolen goods, contrary to section 22(1) of the Theft Act 1968.

Particulars of Offence

SIMON SCHOFIELD, on the 19th day of June 1996, dishonestly received certain stolen goods, namely a necklace and four bracelets belonging to Stanley Sutton, knowing or believing the same to be stolen goods.

Date:__________ An officer of the Crown Court____________________

Note: On the given facts, the prosecution would no doubt say that either Simon was the burglar or he received the goods from the burglar. Since burglary is the more serious charge, it comes first.

INDEX